WORDS WE DON'T USE

[much anymore]

Dr Diarmaid Ó Muirithe is a distinguished historical lexicographer, whose book *The Words We Use* was chosen by William Trevor as one of his Books of the Year in *The Guardian*, and described by him as 'a delight from start to finish'. Dr Ó Muirithe, a graduate of both Trinity College Dublin and UCD, is the recipient of the degree of DLittCelt from the National University of Ireland.

WORDS WE DON'T USE

[much anymore]

DIARMAID Ó MUIRITHE ~

Gill & Macmillan

Gill & Macmillan
Hume Avenue, Park West, Dublin 12
with associated companies throughout the world
www.gillmacmillanbooks.ie

© Diarmaid Ó Muirithe 2011, 2012
First published in hard cover 2011
First published in this format 2012
978 07171 5446 3

Index compiled by Cover to Cover
Typography design by Make Communication
Print origination by Carrigboy Typesetting Services
Printed by ScandBook AB, Sweden

The paper used in this book comes from the wood pulp of managed
forests. For every tree felled, at least one tree is planted, thereby renewing
natural resources.

A CIP catalogue record for this book is available from the British Library.

5 4 3 2 1

CONTENTS

INTRODUCTION

An *Irish Times* reader suggested to me that I should write a book about words which are either on the brink of extinction or have already been deemed obsolete by the great dictionaries. Here it is. It could have been ten times this length: what I have salvaged are words which for one reason or another I happen to like and whose fate I regret.

The older readers of this book may raise an eyebrow at some of my choices. But, they may well exclaim, this or that word is still in use in Ballinafad or Tuam or Clonakilty or wherever, and in this they may be right. What I had in mind in choosing these words is that they have been deemed either obsolete or under sentence of death by reputable dictionaries. For example I raised an eyebrow or two myself when I read that *swank* was on the way out everywhere; when I asked two fourteen-year-old boys in a Munster town what *swank* meant, I was answered with shy smiles and told that it was a crude word. It took this innocent a minute or two to realise that they had confused the word with another, which *is* crude.

The words I have chosen are, in a sense, a *momento mori* for old-timers such as myself; they will probably have gone from common speech forever after our days have ended.

I have included, needless to say, many words which were lost to the language centuries ago. They are here simply because I like them.

My thanks to the editors of *The Irish Times* and *The Oldie* who published my treatment of some of the words discussed here.

There's no more to be said except to ask you to do what St Augustine once said about a better book: *tolle lege*, take up and read, or as another Augustine, my favourite Viennese waiter, Augustin 'Herr Gustl' Klampfer, exhorts when he puts a delicious meal in front of English-speakers, 'Do please you now to enjoying this, *bitte*.'

DÓM

THE WORDS

A

✦ ABEAR

This ancient word's disappearance from literary English is a mystery. It hasn't been recorded since it appeared in the *Ancren Riwle* about 1230, but Joseph Wright's correspondents told him that it was widely diffused throughout the dialects of England when he was working on his great *English Dialect Dictionary* (EDD) towards the end of the nineteenth century. It means to endure, tolerate, and is usually found with the word *can* and a negative. Recent researchers suggest that the word, which has adorned English since it appeared as *áberan*, to endure, suffer, in Old English, is almost on the verge of extinction everywhere now. Tennyson, for example, has 'I couldn't abear to see it,' in his 1860 Lincolnshire dialect poem about the Old Farmer, but I'm told that one could search far and wide in that county today and not hear the word. Joseph Wright has 'I hate smoke-reeked tea, I cannot abear it,' and 'They cannot abear her; they rantanned her out at last,' from the same county. Dickens in his *Sketches* (1836/7) has 'The young lady denied having formed any such engagements at all—she couldn't abear the men, they were such deceivers.' I see that the word has disappeared from the dialects of East Anglia, Cornwall, Berkshire and Gloucestershire; a recent survey found that in Devonshire Madox Brown's sentence in his 1870 *Dwale Bluth*, 'I can't abear the daps o' thee,' was not understood by any of the hundred people asked what it meant. The word has been recorded in Donegal, and in Fermanagh by the classical music composer Joan Trimble. She suggested to me that it was probably imported by Ulster workers who did seasonal work in the north of England, since the word is not found in Scotland. I note that *The Concise Ulster Dictionary* (CUD) has not recorded this word of honourable antiquity, first used in literature by King Ælfred about 885 A.D.

✦ ABED

What has happened to this old word, which means in bed, confined to bed by sickness, old age, etc.? Not a trace of it will you find now in my own county of Wexford, but I remember my grandmother using the word; and Bill Blake, an old sea-dog from Kilmore Quay, referred to a young neighbour as being a lazy bastard who spent the mornings abed. I heard the word in Glenmore, Co. Kilkenny, as well as in St Mullins in Co. Carlow, that beautiful historic spot on the banks of the river Barrow. The word was once widely diffused throughout the midland and southern counties of England, but regrettably, education, if that's what it is, and other influences such as television and the print media, have driven the old word almost to extinction in Warwickshire, where Shakespeare grew up. 'You have not been a bed then?' (from abed) wrote the great man in the third act of *Othello*. In the third act of *Romeo and Juliet* he has 'I would have been a bed an hour ago.'

The *Oxford English Dictionary* gives a translation of St Luke's Gospel of *c.*1000 as being the source of the word's earliest appearance in English literature. It was written there as *on bedde*. 'Some wolde mouche hir mete alone Ligging a-bedde,' sang Chaucer in *Troilus and Criseyde* around 1374. The word also occurs in *Piers Plowman*. It wasn't written as one word in the medieval period; perhaps Pepys was the first to write it as one word, in a diary entry of 1660: 'Our wench very lame; abed these two days.' *Abed* is made up of the Old English *on* plus *bed*. Oxford says that it is considered 'somewhat archaic'. They will soon be describing it as 'obsolete'.

✦ ABRICOCK

I met old Phil Wall in Carne, in the Barony of Forth, Co. Wexford, in the summer of 1970. He had an amazing dialect of English, and was well aware of it. He was ninety years old at the time, and appeared to be highly pleased that I made a note of his words. He took me to task, I remember, for hesitating to write down the word *abricock* in my notebook. 'You think that's just an old man getting the word apricot arse backwards, don't you?' he said. 'Well, let me tell you that it was my mother's word, and that the people of Somerset have it as well. I knew many of them long ago when I was a young chap working summers in their orchards.'

Somerset people do, indeed, have it, as I was to find out; perhaps I should write 'they did', because recently a reader from that county wrote to tell me that the variant is now almost obsolete there, remembered only by the very oldest of farmers and market gardeners. The word was also recorded in Cheshire in the nineteenth century, but appears to have died out there since.

Any good dictionary will give you the etymology of *apricot*; but consider this from W. Turner's *Names of Herbes*, published in 1548. 'Malus armeniaca is called in Greeke *Melea* armeniace, in highe duche Land ein *amarel baume*, in the dioses of Colon *kardumelker baume* . . . and some englishe men cal the fruite an *Abricok*.'

Oxford gives a full etymology. Originally from Portuguese *albricoque* or Spanish *albaricoque*, but subsequently assimilated to the cognate French *abricot* (*t* mute). Cf. also Italian *albercocca*, *albicocca*, Old Spanish *albarcoque*, from Spanish Arabic *al-borcoque*, probably from Latin *præcoquum*, variant of *præcox*, plural *præcocia*, 'early-ripe, ripe in summer', an epithet and, in later writers, appellation of this fruit, originally called *prunum* or *malum Armeniacum*. Thus Palladius (*c*.350): '*armenia vel præcoqua*.' The change in English from *abr-* to *apr-* was perhaps due to false etymology; Minsheu (1617) explained the name, quasi, '*in aprico coctus*', ripened in a sunny place: cf. the spelling *abricoct*. Indeed, or in Phil Wall's case, *abricock*.

✦ ACCOST

This word has gone through many shades of meaning from the naughty one in Shakespeare's *Twelfth Night*—'Accost is, front her, boorde her, woo her, assayle her'—to the innocuous 'to make up and speak to', no longer, as far as I am aware used in ordinary speech; to the one meaning to assault with intent to cause bodily harm, to the one now used only in police courts meaning 'to solicit for an improper purpose', as the police-speak goes.

Accost is what the raikers and fly-boys did in the old broadside ballads. 'I thereby accosted this maiden.' He meant simply that he met her, either by accident or design. And having accosted her, his next ploy was to get her into a tavern. A striking line in a nineteenth-century broadside ballad, published in Cork by Haly, reads, 'And we fell to drinking Beamish's porter, To coax her motions in high display.' Those nineteenth-century Irish raikers know a long time before the thought struck Mr Nash that candy is dandy, but liquor is quicker.

Accost, meaning to approach with the intention of harming a person, has been deemed obsolete by lexicographers in Britain; I haven't heard it in common speech in Ireland for many years.

These *accosts*, obsolete and still standing, started life in the English navy as *acoast* or *accoast*. This was a borrowing from the French *accoster*, from Old French *acoster*, from Late Latin *accostare*, to be side by side, from ac = ad, 'to', with *costa*, which means 'rib', and in Late Latin, 'side'. In 1611 Cotgrave's French–English dictionary has 'Accoster: To accoast, or joyne side to side; to approach, or draw neere unto.' While still connected with coast it remained accoast, but since the idea of 'to address' came to the fore, it has been pronounced and written accost.

We don't 'accost' people on the street any more when we mean to meet them or give them greeting. Women do, of course, sometimes accost men with a certain intent, and the only time I heard this meaning of accost was in a courthouse in Cork, when a Garda in evidence said that a young lady was previously found guilty of accosting a man. The judge wasn't too sure of what he meant. 'Did she assault the man?' he asked. 'Is that what you mean by accost?' 'No,' said the Garda, 'she approached a man with the intention of soliciting for immoral purposes.'

So, *accost* lives, but as it is now confined to a specific misdemeanour in law, it may be considered to be on a life support machine.

✦ ADAMITE

According to Mr Ogden Nash the very first words uttered by a human being were 'Madam, I'm Adam.'

Adam, in Hebrew *adám*, man, has given us many English words. The phrase *the old Adam* is used when people speak of man's corrupt nature. *Adam* is a metonym for water. Around 1700 Thomas Brown has 'Your claret's too hot. Sirrah, drawer, go bring a cup of cold Adam from the next purling stream.' *Adam's Ale* was mentioned in Matthew Prior's *Wandering Pilgrim* before 1721: 'A Rechabite poor Will must live / And drink of Adam's Ale.' *Adam's Apple*, the projection formed in the neck by the anterior extremity of the thyroid cartilage of the larynx, was referred to as *Adami Pomum* in a 1720 book on surgery. *Adamist* is an imitator of Adam as a gardener. John Taylor in a tract of 1630 wrote of 'fruit trees so pleasing and ravishing to the sense that he calls it *Paradise*, in which he plays the part of a true Adamist, continually roiling and tilling'. And Adam has also given us *Adamite*, which in modern times would be called a nudist.

The word was brought to my attention by a report I saw on German television about a court case in southern California. About fifty men and women were charged with public indecency by cavorting in the nude on a beach, and their leader offered the defence that they belonged to a religious sect called *Adamites* which today, as was the case 400 years ago, was persecuted for appearing in public in the nude. Addison referred to these Adamites in 1713 in the *Guardian*, and in the two centuries previous to his the phrase 'as naked as an Adamite' was common. One orthodox Christian railed in 1565 against the number of sects that had mushroomed in London: 'So many Adamites, so many Zwenckfeldians, so many hundreds of Anabaptists and libertines.'

Adamites seem to have disappeared until resurrected by the Californians the other day. The judge was lenient. He dismissed the charge with a caution as to future behaviour, having congratulated their leader on his ingenious, if implausible, defence.

✦ AGO, AGONE

Two words these that have not survived in the living language in the senses 'gone, since'. The people of the Barony of Forth in Co. Wexford had *ee-go*; Poole's glossary of the Dialect of Forth and Bargy, collected by the farmer Jacob Poole towards the end of the eighteenth century, published by the Dorsetshire poet William Barnes in the nineteenth, and re-edited by this author and T.P. Dolan in the twentieth, has 'Hea's ee-go' for 'He's gone.'

Ago was recorded in this sense in Devonshire by the EDD's field workers: 'Awl the tatties be ago, missis: there idden wan a-layved.' *Ago* was recorded in Middle English. 'For now is clene a-go / My name of trouthe in love for ever-mo!' wrote Chaucer in *Troilus and Criseyde* around 1374. He repeated the word in *The Legend of Good Women*: 'And thus ar Tisbe and Piramus ago' (i.e. dead); and in *The Book of the Duchesse*, or *The Dethe of Blaunche*, he has 'My lady bright / Which I have loved with al my might / Is fro me deed, and is a-goon.'

Agone, meaning 'ago, since', was common in Ireland in Samuel Lover's day. He has 'We started three days agon,' in his *Legends and Stories of Ireland*, written between 1831 and 1834. Poole, mentioned above, also has the word. In southern and south-western England, the sense survived until recently. Wright has 'He went to Africa some time agone,' from Cornwall; and 'Twas ever so long agone,' from Somerset. 'Such phrases are quite familiar to all West-country folk,' a correspondent told him. But that was long agone, and it wouldn't be true today, I'm told.

Shakespeare used *agone*. In *Twelfth Night*, Act V, he has 'Oh, he's drunk, Sir Toby, an hour agone.' In *Two Gentlemen of Verona*, Act III, we find 'For long agone I have forgot to court.' John Gower wrote 'A while agon' in *Confessio Amantis* (*Tale of the Coffers*) in 1390; and Chaucer has 'Nat longe agon is' in *The Canterbury Tales*.

Both *ago* and *agone* in the senses mentioned are from Old English *ágán*, past participle of *ágán*, to pass away, according to Wright.

✦ ALFRATCH

This is a word my friend Risteard B. Breatnach, the distinguished linguist, often heard in the 1940s in west Waterford, but I'm sorry to say that it seems to have died since then. I have mentioned the word many times to members of the younger generation since I came to live among them in Waterford about nine years ago, but none of the school children and very few of their parents and grandparents knew the word. The word was also common in my father's part of west Cork, that part comprising the baronies of Muscraí and Uíbh Laoghaire, say from Cúil Aodh to Gúagán Barra, when I was young; but when I enquired recently in a school in that part of the world, not one 'scholar', as they term school children there, had ever heard the word.

Spelled *alfraits* in Irish, it means a scoundrel, a rascal, according to Ó Dónaill's dictionary. Dinneen goes a little further, adding 'a scold, a barge, a man with rude manners at table, a peevish child' to the definition of the word. Dinneen noticed that the word's termination, *aits*, was like the English *atch*, and came to the conclusion that *alfraits* was simply the English *old fratch*. He knew, of course, that *fratch* was an English dialect word for a rude, quarrelsome person, and that it was common in Yorkshire and in other northern counties south to Derbyshire. Nobody ever contradicted Dinneen, nor should they.

Now that I come to think of it, the only time I ever heard the word *fratch* was in a stable in south Co. Wexford in the 1970s. A Yorkshireman had come to look at a young horse fancied to make a good showjumper. He started the negotiations after jumping some poles with his intended purchase, by insulting him in the time-honoured ritual of such dealing, telling his owner that his animal was nothing but a miserable, useless fratch. Half an hour later he forked out 30,000 jimmy o'goblins for him.

✦ AMPLUSH

I have heard this word in places as far apart as Donegal and east Cork, and sometimes as *amplish*. The Irish is *aimpléis*, defined by Dinneen as trouble, difficulty, intricacy; he also gave the adjective *aimpléiseach*, troublesome, difficult, intricate, and *aimpléiseacht*, noun, state of being difficult or troublesome, etc.

I first heard the word in Donegal from a sheepman called Paddy Joe Gill who came from Glenties direction. He was explaining to a friend of his that he bumped into a man who owed him money at a fair, but that he didn't want to embarrass the fellow, as he was involved in making a deal with some Six County buyers: 'I didn't expect to see him, so I was at a bit of an amplish,' he said.

The word is in literature. William Carleton from Tyrone has it in *The Battle of the Factions*: 'He was driven at last to such an amplush that he had no other shift for employment.' Samuel Lover in *Legends and Stories of Ireland* has 'There was no such thing as getting him at an amplush.' In the same book, set in Connacht, he has 'He'd have amplushed me long ago.' John Boyce in *Shandy Maguire*, set in the north, has '. . . prayin' to us this minit . . . to help ye in the amplish that yer in'.

About thirty years ago I was sent the word by people in mid-Tipperary, east Cork, Clare and Limerick when I was preparing a book on Irish words and phrases that have found their way into the English of Ireland. To have given the head-word as a word of Irish origin was, I now feel, not correct, because in fact it represents *non-plus*.

✦ ARLES

This word is found under various disguises in Ireland, Scotland and the northern counties of England to Lancashire and Lincolnshire. In Ulster they had *airles* and *earles*; in Connacht and Leinster *earls*; in Cumberland *yearls*; in the North Country and in Lancashire *yearles*; in west Yorkshire *arless*. We have the word in Irish too as *éarlais*. It means money paid on striking a bargain in pledge of future fulfilment, especially that given to a servant when hired; earnest money.

Jamieson's Scots dictionary of the early nineteenth century explains the matter further: 'A piece of money put into the hands of a seller . . . as a pledge that he shall not strike a bargain with another, while he retains the arles in his hand.' Robert Burns in 1786 wrote, 'An' name the arles an' the fee / In legal mode an' form.' Scott in *Redgauntlet* (1819) has 'He had refused the devil's arles (for such was the offer of meat and drink).'

The Ballymena Observer of 1892 says that 'In hiring a servant, for buying a cow, load of hay &c., you give a shilling or half-a-crown as "earls" to make the bargain sure.' Willie O'Kane of Dungannon, in his engaging book *You Don't Say*, has 'He paid five pounds of earls at the auction.' I myself heard two men discussing the trustworthiness of a west Corkman who was looking for a job as a farm labourer. One man counselled, 'I wouldn't trusht him an inch. Don't give him any éarlais anyway. You might never see the hoor again.'

There was a verb *to arle*: to bind by payment of money, to give earnest-money as a 'clincher' to a bargain, to engage for service, to secure. From Perthshire a correspondent of the EDD heard this at a hiring fair: 'Are ye feed lassie?'—'Yes, I was erled an hour ago.'

Then there were the compounds *arles-penny* and *arles-shilling*. 'Your proffer o' luve's an airle-penny, / My Tocher's the bargain ye wad buy,' sang Burns in *My Tocher's the Jewel* in 1794. (*Tocher* is a marriage portion, a bride's dowry, from Scottish Gaelic *tochar*.)

Blount's *Law Dictionary* of 1691 defined *arles* as '*Argentum Dei* . . . Money given in earnest of a bargain.' In *Hali Meidenhad*, an alliterative homily of *c.* 1230, there is this: 'þis ure lauerd giueð ham as on erles of þe eche mede þat schal cume þereafter.'

Oxford says that *arles* is 'apparently from Old French *erle, *arle: from Latin *arrhula diminutive of *arrha*. Cf. also Old French *erres, arres*, modern *arrhes*: from Latin *arrha*. Historically a plural, but sometimes used as singular; the formal singular *arle* is hardly in use.' [* denotes an unattested form.]

Indeed the word in the plural is hardly in use any more. How times change!

✦ ARSE-VERSE

Pádraig Mac Gréine, or Paddy Greene, or Master Greene of Ballinalee, Co. Longford, never got back to me about the above word which I heard from an English Gypsy while on holiday in Yorkshire. I had wondered whether the word had reached the cant of the Irish Travellers, many of whom wander across the Irish Sea from time to time and frequent the camps of the Gypsies. Master Greene was the ideal man to ask, as he knew more about the language of the itinerant people than any living person; but he died before he could tell me what he knew of *arse-verse* in Ireland. He had a good innings; he was 106 when he went to what some Munster Travellers call their *Honey Spike*, their lucky burial ground. Both Miley Connors and Annie Wall, two Travellers of Wexford background, could tell me that they had heard of the *arse-verse*, a verse said before the owners occupied a new caravan, to protect it from fire, but that the custom had died out before their time. Miley, quite rightly, said that the custom was English in origin.

In England the very use of a verse on a farmhouse wall points to its originally being the property of the settled community. Gypsies don't write verse. The word may be found in some of the dialect dictionaries of both southern Scotland and northern England, but the Scots say that the custom originated in England. *Notes and Queries* II of 1888 mentions it, and says that in Yorkshire it is thought of as 'a spell on a house to avert fire of witchcraft'. It was a word used by settled country people; the gypsies, as superstitious as they come, thought the saying of an arse-verse a good idea; it could do no harm at any rate.

How old the custom is I have failed to find out. Nathan Bailey's *An Universal Etymological English Dictionary* of 1721 has it, defining it as 'a spell written on a house to prevent it from burning'. The *arse* part of the word has nothing to do with the old word for the fundament. It's from Latin *ars-*, past participle stem of *ardere*, to burn. Compare, if you will, French *arson*, arson, wilful burning.

The latest surveys have found no trace of the word in living speech anywhere.

✦ ARVAL

The custom of giving a bite to eat to mourners after a funeral is widespread all over the world, though not all countries have a special name for the repast as the people of southern Scotland, southern Yorkshire, Lancashire, Cumberland and Westmoreland have, or had. The word had disappeared from the lexicon of most of Yorkshire and all of southern Scotland by about 1900.

Captain Grose had the word from the North Country in 1790; around the end of the nineteenth century a correspondent wrote from north Yorkshire to the English Dialect Society: '. . . usually for an hour preceding midday the hospitalities of the day proceed, and after all have partaken of a solid meal, and before the coffin is lifted for removal to the churchyard, cake or biscuits, and wine are handed out by two females whose office is specially designated by the term "arval servers".'

By this time the custom had died out in many parts of Yorkshire. In Harland and Wilkinson's *Folk-Lore* (1867), there is this from Lancashire which shows that the bite and sup came after the burial: 'After the rites at the grave, the company adjourned to a public house, where they were presented with a cake and ale, called an arval.'

Arval led to compounds such as *arval bread*, and *arval cake*. 'Every person invited to a funeral receives a small loaf at the door of the deceased; they were expected to eat them at home in religious remembrance of their deceased neighbour,' says an account from Westmoreland. A north Yorkshire account spoke of 'averill bread: funeral loaves, spiced with cinnamon, nutmeg, sugar, and raisins'.

The custom came with the Vikings. The Old Norse word *erfi-öl* meant a wake, funeral feast, a word composed of *erfi*, a funeral feast, and *öl*, an 'ale', banquet, feast. The Danish is *arve-öl*.

Both the ancient custom, and the ancient word for it, are, alas, now gone forever.

Schade, sehr schade! as they say where I have now pitched my tent.

✦ ASHET

This is another good word threatened with oblivion for reasons nobody can understand. The *Dictionary of the Scots Language* (hereafter DSL) defines it as 'an oval flat plate or dish, generally large, in which a joint or other food is served'.

The *Gallovian Encyclopedia*, published in 1824, describes the ashet as 'the king of the trencher tribe. Some time ago they were made of pewter ... and stood on the loftiest shelf [of the dresser] like so many shields.'

The DSL states that the word is not in Standard English or in English dialect. Well, it is in the speech of the descendants of the Scots planters of Ulster. C.I. Macafee's *Concise Ulster Dictionary* has it. The late Dr Michael Adams, academic publisher, once gave me the word; he remembered it from his young days in Fermanagh. The late composer and musicologist Joan Trimble sent me a card once from Enniskillen, reminding me of 'the Ulster Scots word *ashet*'.

Oxford points out that *ashet* appears in a catalogue of furniture printed in 1552. As to its present status, it appears that it may still be heard in the kitchens of some of the great houses of Scotland, but not elsewhere. Perhaps the reason it is is danger is that the ashet is too big for the ordinary kitchen or diningroom nowadays.

Considering the historical links between Scotland and France, it may come as no surprise to learn that the Scots borrowed *ashet* from French *assiette*, a plate, a word which has its origin in the Latin *assidere*, to sit beside.

✦ ASK

When I was a child my mother taught school opposite the farmhouse of an old lady named Margaret Whitty. Just before Christmas my father got a lift out from town in a friendly policeman's car to collect a turkey from Margaret, his own car being under a tarpaulin in a garage, due to Mr de Valera's decision that teaching school did not warrant a car to get to work; my mother had to cycle the nine miles to her school in all kinds of weather. We were allowed to play around the Whitty farm, but were warned to keep away from the well, not, mind you, because of the fear of falling in and being drowned, but because old Maggie frightened the life out of us by telling us of the monstrous *ask* who lived in the well, and who climbed up to spit poison at any person who approached its lair in the depths, to immobilise them so as to suck them down, never to be seen again. We gave Miss Whitty's well a wide berth, I assure you.

Years later I heard the word in Co. Carlow, upriver from where we lived; I was also able to trace the word to Co. Kildare and to north Co. Dublin. The *ask* is a newt or lizard and the word was once to be found in Scotland and in many dialects of England. Recently I conducted a very unscientific survey about this creature, which fascinated Mr Wodehouse's creation, Gussie Fink-Nottle, and another quare hawk, Mr Ken Livingstone, the London politician. I wrote to a number of rural schools in Counties Kildare, Carlow, Wexford, Wicklow, north Dublin and Waterford; none of the pupils knew the word *ask* or its variant *esk*, although they were all familiar with the 'poisonous' water lizard who infested wells. Joseph Wright's great *English Dialect Dictionary*, quoting a Scottish source, says that 'It seems to be a general idea among the vulgar, that what we call the ask is the asp of Scripture. This has probably contributed to the received opinion of the newt being venomous.'

Randle Cotgrave's French–English dictionary of 1611 has '*Tassot*, a newt or ask.' John Florio's Italian–English lexicon of 1611 has '*Magrasio*, an eft, an nute, an aske.'

Middle English has *arske* and *aske*. A *Metrical Homily* of 1323 has 'Snakes and nederes thar he fand, And gret blac tades . . . And arskes and other wormes felle.' The great Scot Henryson, whose *The Testament of Cresseid* and *Seven Fables* were so ably translated by Heaney recently, has, in a poem from around 1450, 'Cum with me in hy, Edderis, askis, and wormis meit for to be.' Old English has *áðexe*, lizard. You may compare the German *Eidechse* or *Echse*, lizard.

✦ AUNT

I was taken aback when an old Dublinman who lived near my son in Kimmage referred to a youngish female politician who snubbed him, he felt, when he requested that she do him a favour connected with fixing the roof of his house, as a bloody, useless aunt.

This *aunt*, he subsequently told me, meant a whore; he seemed surprised that I had never heard of the word. I was familiar with Shakespeare's *aunt*, an old woman, a gossip; this evidently was not what my friend had in mind. Neither was he thinking of elderly, practical women who show benevolence to acquaintances, be they young or old.

Aunt is used by Shakespeare in my friend's sense in *A Winter's Tale*, Act IV. The word was very much in evidence in seventeenth-century literature. Middleton has it in his *Michaelmas Terme* of 1607: 'She demanded of me whether I was your worships aunt or no. Out, out, out!' In a 1663 tract called *Parson's World*, there is this: 'Yes, and follow her, like one of my aunts of the suburbs.' In 1678 Dryden in *The Kind Keeper, or Mr Liberham*, a comedy, has 'The easiest Fool I ever knew, next my Naunt of Fairies in the Alchymist.'

And then, after Dryden, silence.

I searched the dialect dictionaries, and found only one bawdy aunt, in Lincolnshire. How did it reach Dublin's fair city? I wish I had the answer to that one.

✦ AVA

Once upon a time you would hear this word used in parts of Ulster in place of 'at all'. The last person I heard using it was the late Ginette Waddell, the actress, relative of the great classical scholar Helen Waddell, and Rutherford Mayne, the dramatist. Not long before he died last year, David Hammond, balladeer and film-maker, told me that the word was all but extinct in Co. Antrim, that great stronghold of Ulster Scots.

Because of its Scots origin I had thought that it never existed in the South, but my friend Mrs Rae McIntyre, an inspired teacher who achieved fame by getting her pupils in Ballyrashane Primary School near Coleraine to compile a book called *Some Handlin'* before the Department of Education decided that Ballyrashane no longer needed a school, tells me that although *ava* is not heard any more around Ballyrashane, she remembers her mother using the word over the border in Co. Leitrim. I enquired about the word's health from some Leitrim friends of mine, and was told that alas the word has by now disappeared from the speech of young and old.

'A dinna ken, ava. A'll hae nane o' that ava,' was recorded in Antrim by W.H. Patterson in his glossary of Antrim and Down words, which he sent to the English Dialect Society, and which found their way into Wright's EDD. 'I've aften wonder'd . . . what way poor bodies liv'd ava,' Burns mused in *Twa Dogs*, written in 1786. The Gallowayman S.R. Crockett nailed his colours to the mast in his engaging *The Raiders* (1894) by stating that 'There's no a Dutchman i' the pack That's ony guid ava man.' The word was exported to the northern counties of England as well as to Ulster. 'I could see naething ava,' wrote Richardson in his *Borderer's Table-book*, written in Northumberland in 1846.

If the useful little adverb is used no more by the descendants of the Ulster planters as well as by the drinking men in the pubs of Ayrshire and Northumberland, I for one, mourn its passing into oblivion.

B ～

✦ BAIN-MARIE

I came across this word written as *Bang-Marie* in *Passing English of the Victorian Era*, a book by J. Reddy Ware, no date given, but certainly late nineteenth century.

Mr Ware glosses his word, which he acknowledges to be a product of folk etymology, as 'The Kitchen'. He rightly corrects *Bang-Marie* to *Bain-Marie*, 'the small saucepan within another saucepan of boiling water', but then says that 'the word got its name from an operation devised by a French cook named Marie.' Oh yeah?

Oxford gives only two citations. The first is from Kitchiner's *Cook's Oracle* of 1822: 'Bain-Marie is a flat vessel containing boiling water; you put all your stewpans into the water, and keep that water always very hot, but it must not boil.' The second is from Andrew Ure's *A Dictionary of Arts, Manufactures and Mines*, 1875: 'Bain-marie, a vessel of water in which saucepans, etc. are placed to warm food, or to prepare it, and used in some pharmaceutical preparations.'

I recently asked ten ladies about this word. Only one, a cook who had been trained in Ballymaloe, Co. Cork, knew what it meant. Small blame to her, she had no idea where the word originated. Far from being called from a French cook named Marie, as the Victorian Mr Ware said, it is from French all right, but adapted from Latin *balneum Mariæ* (fourteenth century), literally 'the bath of Mary', so called, the French lexicographer Littré thinks, from the gentleness of this method of heating.

✦ BAKED MEAT

Hubert Butler, God look to him, used to write to me occasionally from his home in Bennetsbridge, Co. Kilkenny, about words. I recently came across a note I got from him about *baked meat*, what most people everywhere call *roast meat*. He knew I was interested in the English of Forth and Bargy, the old Anglo-Norman enclave of south-east Wexford, and wanted to know if I had heard the term there, or in south Co. Kilkenny, where I taught school at the time. He pointed out that the compound was recorded only in Lincolnshire by the monumental EDD. I replied that I heard it in both places but that it was being replaced by the younger generation by *roast meat*.

Forty years on, *baked meat* has been deleted from the Irish culinary lexicon, as far as I can tell. A pity, this, if only because it was Shakespeare's term. He has 'Look to the baked meats, good Angelica; Spare not for cost,' in *Romeo and Juliet*, Act IV; and 'The funeral baked meats / Did coldly furnish forth the marriage tables,' in *Hamlet*, Act I.

✦ BAKER'S DAUGHTER, THE

Indulge me for a moment while I tell you a story I heard when I was a very small boy. It concerned a bird that then as now fascinates me, Minerva's bird, the owl. This is how I remember the story:

Our Saviour passed by a bakery one day. [I thought at the time that this must have been my friend Jack Dunphy's daddy's bakery on Charleton Hill, but I was told gently that it wasn't.] Anyway, He smelled the lovely aroma of freshly baked bread and entering the bakery said that he was very hungry and would appreciate a little loaf if they could afford it. He explained that he had no money and could wait until they baked him just a little cake, seeing that the oven was hot, and obviously ready for the next batch to be baked. The baker's wife took pity on him and put a piece of dough she had got ready into the oven; but when the woman's daughter, a really nasty girl, and as mean as they come, saw this, she snatched the little cake from the oven and cut a tiny piece from it. This she put back in the oven, laughing at Our Saviour and telling him to come back when he could afford to buy a loaf. But to her consternation the little piece of dough began to swell and swell, and soon was so big that the oven couldn't contain it. The baker's daughter began to cry out something like 'Heough, heough!' which is like the cry of an owl when he senses danger. She began to curse and swear at Our Lord, and it was then that he transformed her into an owl. She flew around the bakery screaming 'Heough heough!' until her mother, a good woman, begged Him to turn her back into a girl again. He did so. The mother then gave him the huge cake, but he told her that he only wanted a little bit of it, and that she should give the rest to the poor.

And now you know, if you hadn't already known, where that mysterious line in *Hamlet*, Act IV, Scene V, came from: 'They say the owl is a baker's daughter.' I like to think that a small boy in Stratford-upon-Avon long ago must have heard the story as well.

✦ BAKSHEESH

This, according to Oxford, is an Oriental term for a gratuity, a present of money, a 'tip'. It is also slang for a bribe, which Oxford, strangely, failed to mention. The engaging book *Passing English of the Victorian Age*, by J. Reddy Ware and published in London sometime around 1870 (no publication date is given), is not so coy. Ware claims that the word is Arabic in origin and that, as the title of the book suggests, it is either passing from use or has already passed into oblivion. Not quite true. It may have had its day elsewhere, but it is common currency among the Del Boy Trotters of London to this day.

It first appeared in literature in 1625, in Samuel Purchas's *Pilgrimes*. Writing of an Arab lady, our author describes her as a woman 'Who would prostitute her selfe to any man Bacsheese (as they say in the Arabicke tonque) that is gratis freely'. In 1775 Richard Chandler, in his *Travels in Asia Minor*, refers to 'A demand of bac-shish, a reward or present; which term, from its frequent use, was already become very familiar to us'. By this time the word had entered London's slang or cant.

We find the word turning up in 'respectable' literature until the end of the ninetenth century; the last citation in Oxford is from the very decorous *The Times*, of 1876: 'Fresh baksheesh to the unworthy minions of the harem.'

The word may have entered English from Arabic, but it has its origin in Persian *bakhshísh*, a present, from *bakhshí-dan*, to give; it is however now used in Arabic, Turkish, and Urdu. And, as I said, in the rich argot of Peckham.

✦ BALOUR

This Irish English word which has different shades of meaning is from the Irish *baileabhair*, sometimes *ball* or *bail odhar*, given in a phrase by Dinneen's dictionary, 'rinne sé *baileabhair mhór de féin*', he got into a great fix. He says it is a Connacht term, and indeed I heard the phrase 'he made a balour of himself' and glossed 'he made a ballocks of himself' by a Galway friend, earthier than Fr Dinneen.

I have 'You are an awful balour, glossed as an unmethodical bungler,' from Dr Patrick Henchy from Corofin, Co. Clare, writing in the *North Munster Antiquarian Journal* xvii in 1975. William Carleton in *The Midnight Mass* has 'the girsha is makin' a bauliore of herself.'

Fr Leo Morahan or Leon Ó Morachán of Louisburgh, Co. Mayo, also gave me the word. In his parish journal *An Choineall*, he glossed it as 'a sorry plight, a state of frustration or helplessness'. Using the Irish head word he asks us to 'note the proper usage: you are in a bail odhar or this bail odhar is on you'.

Jack Devereux, a Kilmore Quay, Co. Wexford fisherman, who gave me in his time enough old words to fill a small glossary, told me in 1970 that a *balyore* meant uproar, confusion. Kilkenny's Michael Banim in his novel *The Croppy* had 'there's no use balourin' this way', and he kindly glossed the word for his readers as 'making a noise'. I found this beauty in a manuscript in the Department of Irish Folklore in University College Dublin, sent in by a teacher from Kilkenny in the 1930s: 'You'd hear him balourin in the Domhan Toir' [The Eastern World, a mythical place far, far away].

My spies tell me that this useful word is almost gone from the world now, and if they are right, this is to be regretted.

✦ BANDOG

I have often wondered how this word came to south Wexford. It is known in Scotland, Northumberland, Essex, Somerset and Devon; but as far as I'm aware has never been recorded in this country outside Wexford. It means a watchdog, and I heard it used by Phil Wall from Lady's Island, near Carnsore, in 1970.

It is an old word. *Molosus* was glossed as 'a band-dogge' in a tract of 1425. *Mastin* was glossed in Cotgrave's French–English dictionary of 1611 as 'a mastive or bandog'. Skinner in 1671 had 'Bandog, ban & dog, q.d. *canis vinctus*'. Later glossaries gave the word as well. Robertson in 1693 had 'a band-dog, *canis catenatus*'. And Ash in 1795 had 'Bandog, a large dog'.

The old literary men knew the word. Thomas Tusser in *Husbandrie* (1580) had 'Make bandog thy scoutwatch, to bark at a theefe.' In the same book he has 'Thy bandog, that serveth for divers mishaps, Forget not to give him thy bones and thy scraps.' Thomas Dekker in *The Gentle Craft* (1600) used an interesting phrase: 'O master, is it you that speak bandog and Bedlam this morning?' By that he meant that his master was speaking ferociously and madly. Spenser had 'We han great bandogs will tear their skin,' in *The Shepheardes Calender* in 1579; and Shakespeare, in *Henry VI, Part 2*, Act I, Scene IV, had 'The time when screech-owls cry and ban-dogs howl.'

The bandogs kept howling in Scots and English literature until the twentieth century, and then fell strangely silent. Walter Scott in *Waverley* had 'The keeper entered, leading his bandog.' In *Westward Ho!* (1865) Charles Kingsley, a Devonman, wrote of 'trying to effect an entrance without being eaten by a bandog'.

I am informed by some English and Scottish academics that *bandog* is now obsolete except in a part of Northumberland. I need hardly tell you that it went to the grave with old Phil Wall from Lady's Island when he died a few years over ninety in the early 1970s. According to Oxford the word is from *band*, a fastening, plus *dog*. This type of dog, it says, was kept tied or chained up, either to guard a house, or on account of its ferocity.

✦ BANE

Old Maurice Fraher was talking about rats in his little house in Abbeyside, Dungarvan. He had a plague of them in his garden, he told me, and had just bought a very effective remedy: he was going to *bane* the hoors, he said, in other words he was going to poison them.

Bane, noun, that which causes ruin, or is pernicious to well-being; the agent or instrument of ruin or woe, is common enough, but as a noun meaning poison, it is very rarely used nowadays, though it has been in literature since 1386, when Trevisa had it in his translation of Bartholomeus de Glanvilla's *De Proprietatibus Rerum*: 'Henbane is mannis bane.' As for Maurice's verb, I haven't seen it in print since Shakespeare used it in *The Merchant of Venice*: 'What if any house is troubled with a rat, / And I be pleased to give ten thousand ducats / To have it baned.'

Baned once meant ruined, destroyed, injured, hurt, a meaning now obsolete. Oxford's first citation is from 1568 and its last one is from 1639, in Thomas Fuller's *The Histoire of the Holy Warre*: 'The voyage of these two kings . . . baned with mutual discord and emulation.'

Bane is Common Teutonic. The Old English is *bana* = the Old Frisian bona, Old Saxon, Old High German *bano*, Middle High German *bane, ban*, Old Norse *bani*, Swedish, Danish *bane*, 'death, murder'.

✦ **BANG OF THE LATCH**

A well-known Irish jurist once told me about this phrase, which he heard from a north Wexfordman living in Co. Wicklow. This man, whose name was Paddy Cullen, was a thorough gentleman, a great host and ranconteur, and was an expert at tying flies. This expertise is what our jurist friend came to tap. He intended to spend the weekend fishing the Nore near Inisteague, and he said that after trying the stretch allotted to him week after week, year after year, he always came home without as much as a nibble at his flies, while salmon seemed to leap out of the river into the kishes of other anglers. After a great night in Paddy's company in the latter's house near Kilquade, he pocketed some flies, and decided it was time to hit the road. He was offered a *deoch an dorais*, a drink for the road, or *the bang of the latch*, which he accepted because he was walking to stay with another jurist who lived nearby, Cearbhall Ó Dálaigh, shortly afterwards to be appointed President of Ireland.

I told him when we met the following day that I had heard the little metaphor in south Wexford, where it meant both 'one for the road' and the last animal born in a litter.

The latch which one finds on old-fashioned doors is defined by Oxford as 'a fastening for a door or gate, so contrived as to admit of its being opened from the outside. It now usually consists of a small bar which falls or slides into a catch, and is lifted or drawn by means of a thumb-lever, string, etc. passed through the door.' I mention it only in case you've been living on the other side of the moon, or you're a foreign guest learning our kind of English. The word is around since Wyclif translated the *Song of Solomon* in 1485: 'The lach of my dore I openede to my lemman.' And many other lemmans, you may be sure: 'King Solomon and King David lived merry merry lives / With many many concubines and many many wives. / And when old age came on them with its many many qualms, / King Solomon wrote the *Proverbs*, and King David wrote the *Psalms*.'

Probably from the old verb *latch*, to grasp, catch, lay hold of, from Old English *læcc(e)an* (Northumbrian *læcca*) weak verb; not found in the other Teutonic languages.

I think Wyclif would have liked Paddy Cullen's phrase. Just as I do.

✦ **BANT**

Glancing through a journal in a doctor's waiting room lately I came on an interesting verb, new to me, and coined after a man who was surely born before his time. The verb was *to bant*, and it means to diet.

It was named for William Banting of London, who became the laughing stock of that great city in 1864. William had written a booklet which would probably have made him a fortune in our day. He was so fat that he found himself unable to bend and tie his boot laces and he had to resort to walking backwards down the stairs to ease the pain in his legs. And so he thought and thought and thought about eating different kinds of food as a means of losing a lot of his 28 stone, a novel thought at the time, believe it or not.

Mr Banting was an undertaker, and he claimed that this gave him a certain authority in the field. He lost about four stone and cut about a foot and a half off the circumference of his belly by eating meat and cutting out almost everything else. The medical men of his day protested and made fun of him, telling him that he was a menace to society. He was ostracised by the populace, who gave the language two new expressions, *to bant*, meaning to diet, and *banting*, dieting.

William ignored them. He went on banting himself and slimmed down to a trim 15 stone. He died in 1878 at the age of 81.

✦ BANVIL & HUSTLE

Mr Joe Drislane wrote to me about the word *hustle*, which he heard in Donegal instead of the Irish *meitheal*, a band of reapers, gathered to help the neighbours with the harvest, etc. *Hustle* is the Northamptonshire word for a crowd; apart from that it is not mentioned in the EDD. The Donegal hustle is defined by Michael Traynor in *The English Dialect of Donegal* (1953) as 'a gathering of many to a job'. He quotes the glossary assembled by H.C. Hart, pioneer lexicographer of the Donegal dialect, who published his valuable word collection in 1880. Hart had glossed the word hustle as 'a gathering of workers', and had added in explanation, 'We had a *hustle* and rid the avenue of weeds.'

Mr D. is married to a Donegal woman, and she also gave him the word *banvil* for a gathering of men engaged in similar work. Traynor also has this word but spelled it *banville*: 'a band of reapers or turfcutters'. He says that the word is found only in Donegal but mentions the word *banyel*, a bundle, a crowd of people, found in Aberdeen. He might have added that it is found in variant spellings in many other places in Scotland.

There can be little doubt that in *banyel* we have the same word as *banvil/banville* if in a slightly different form. The DSL has the word, glossed as 'a bundle; a crowd of reapers'. The association of 'bundle' with 'crowd' is shown in a reference to a 'banyel o' bairns'. *Banyel* is also spelled *bangyal*, a verb defined as 'to crowd, to move in a confused crowd'. The DSL also gives the verbal noun *bangyalan*, 'the act of crowding'.

As to origin the DSL says that it is probably from the French *ballon*, a small pack, a fardel, a word found in Randle Cotgrave's dictionary of 1611, but there seems to be contact, it says, with the Scots noun *bang*, a crowd.

Modern methods of farming have all but done away with Mr Drislane's old words. Perhaps they are still in use among good neighbours who help each other saving the turf; how long more they will survive is anybody's guess.

✦ BARM

There has long been a happy relationship between Dublin city and Liverpool. Many years ago an old lady who lived in Ringsend used to send me words that were common to both her village and the great city beyond the water; one of these was *barm*, described by Wright's dictionary as a Lancashire word, and found nowhere else. Well, Margaret Hennessy knew the word, and furthermore, she knew where it came from. 'Some of us Ringsend people knew Liverpool as well as we knew the middle of Dublin,' she told me.

Barm meant a woman's lap in Ringsend. (Wright's EDD has 'the bosom or lap'.) Mrs Hennessy also knew the word *barm-cloth* for an apron. That venerable scholarly journal *Notes and Queries*, still going strong, has this in its 1861 edition: 'Barm-cloth is the covering for the barm (bosom or lap), as neck-cloth is the covering for the neck.' *Barmskin* was the leather apron worn by Lancashire blacksmiths and farriers, but my correspondent wasn't aware of this word.

Both *barm* and *barm-cloth* are very old. Chaucer has 'And kist þaim oft apon his barm.' 'A barme, *gremium*', the *Catholicon Anglicum*, an English–Latin word book, explained in 1483. Almost a century before that we find the word in the *York Plays*: 'Hyde thy hande in thy barme.'

Barm-cloth, too, is as old as Chaucer. In the *Canterbury Tales* we come across 'A barmecloothe eek as whyt as morne milk'. The word is defined in the *Catholicon Anglicum* as *corium gremiale*, and in 1677 by Coles, who wrote his definitions for the common man, as 'apron'. We can go back beyond the Middle English period for the word's origin, to the Anglo-Saxons. We find *bearm* in a Gospel of John, and they also had *bearmclað*.

I am reluctant to say definitely that these ancient imported words did not survive Mrs Hennessy, who died in 1968, but Ringsend has changed a lot since then; I doubt somehow that the young women of the old village have retained them. I hope I'm wrong.

✦ BASK, HASK

This adjective was used of the weather in the Ards Peninsula, Co. Down, and in Scotland and Cumbria. It probably came to Co. Down from Scotland, where it is used to describe a very dry day. The Scots lexicographer Jamieson described a bask day as 'a day distinguished by drought, accompanied with a withering wind, destructive to vegetation'. The Galloway writer S.R. Crockett in his 1893 story *The Stickit Minister* referred to 'a bask blowy day in the end of March'.

The adjective is also used of fruit: sharp, bitter, rough to the taste. Jamieson has it from Roxburghshire in Scotland; and from Bangor, Co. Down, I was sent the phrase 'She's as bitter as a bask apple.' 'Pride and covetise and ipocrise . . . ben bask or bittir synnes,' warned Wyclif around 1380.

The word certainly travelled far from its Germanic roots. Norwegian linguist Ivar Aasen gave us the dialect adjective *bask*, proud. Widegren gave us *bask* and *barsk*, from Swedish. *Bask* and *barsk*, bitter, severe, were also reported to the EDD from the dialect of Bremen in northern Germany, while Holstein gave up *basch*, sharp, bitter. The German linguist Heinrich Berghaus suggested that the ultimate origin of proliferation was the Low German *basch*, *bask*, *barsk*, rough, hard to the taste. The Low German also gave German *barsch*, and the East Frisian *barsk*, rough, severe, according to that distinguished wordsman J. ten Doornkaat Koolman.

I have been asked if this word is related to *hask*, a word in general dialectal use in Ireland, Scotland and England, and which means 1. Of the weather, dry, parching; piercingly cold. 2. Rough to the touch, stiff, unyielding; hard, brittle, difficult to work. 3. Bitter, sour, tart. Hence *hasky*, bitter; figuratively, ill-natured, severe. 4. verb. To emit a short, dry cough; to clear the throat.

No. This is a northern by-form of Middle English *harsk*, which gave *harsh*. *Harsk* is a northern word, found from *c.* 1300, and it agrees in form (but hardly in sense) with Old Swedish *harsk*, Swedish *härsk*,

Danish *harsk*, rank, rancid, rusty (as bacon), not recorded in Old Norse; also in form and sense with Middle Low German and modern German *harsch*, harsh, rough. As a general English word, *harsh* (*harrish*) is not found before the sixteenth century.

✦ BEHOLDING

Last year I stopped my car on the road to Dungarvan, Co. Waterford, to help a woman whose own car had broken down. As I'm one of those who wouldn't know a carburettor from a sump, I offered to bring her to a garage in town. That evening there was a ring on my doorbell, and I answered it to find my passenger just about to take off in her mended car. She had left a bag of potatoes on my doorstep, and as I protested she waved me away, saying, 'I'm beholden to you.'

What a lovely old saying this is. Nowadays all we hear is some vulgar Americanism such as 'I owe ye wan,' or the like. *Beholden* is defined by Collins' dictionary as an adjective meaning indebted; obliged; under a moral obligation. It is from Old English *behealden*, past participle of *behealdan*, to behold; and thus related to Old High German *bihaltan* and Dutch *behauden*.

None of the great dictionaries consider the word in any danger, but it appears from some surveys conducted recently that the young especially have started to abandon it. The EDD has it from south Wexford. Hall's *Landlord Abroad* has 'I had no mind to let my daughter be behaulden to you.' A contemporary, and far better writer than Mrs Hall, Thomas Hardy from Dorset has 'I don't like my children going and making themselves beholden to strange kin,' in *Tess of the d'Urbervilles*. The first dictionary to cite the word was Jehan Palsgrave's *Lesclarcissement de la langue françoise* of 1530, which has 'I am beholden to you all the dayes of my lyfe, *je suis tenu a vous tous les jours de ma vie.*'

And what about the *beholding*? Not a printer's error, I assure you, and not a gentrification of *beholden* either. Once upon a time it may have started life as a corruption of *beholden*, but some great writers have given it respectability. This is George Eliot in *Adam Bede* (1859): 'As thoughtless as if you was beholding to nobody.' And in *Pericles*, Shakespeare has Simonides saying to Pericles, 'I am beholding to you for your sweet music last night.'

George Eliot was a Staffordshire lady, and *Adam Bede* was set there. I suppose she also knew the lovely word *beholdingness*, also recorded in west Somerset. Sweet music in a word.

✦ BEING

This is a noun once widely heard in Scotland, Ireland, Yorkshire, Lancashire, East Anglia and Sussex, and, according to recent surveys, as rare nowadays in most places as is the corncrake. It means, first of all, livelihood, existence, condition, maintenance. 'He has a good being.' 'He has nae bein' ava' [no visible means of support at all] was recorded in Fife. Tom McCuaig from Rathlin Island, with whom I worked once in the 1970s in the RTÉ newsroom, gave me this, not from the island but from old-timers on the north Antrim coast: 'There never was much of a being in the fishin'.' The EDD quotes J.C. Egerton's *Sussex Folk and Sussex Ways*: 'Why there, sir, it wasn't a livin', it was only a bein'.'

There is a second meaning, also in danger of being lost forever: a house, home, dwelling place. Dickens has it in *David Copperfield*: 'With the roses a covering our Bein'.' Cozens-Hardy also has the word in his *Broad Norfolk* (1893). I have not come across this meaning anywhere in Ireland.

Being, meaning any wretched or unfortunate person, is still to be heard in the speech of country people in many places. I've heard the likes of 'She's an unfortunate being' in many places in the south-east and in Antrim and Donegal. Dr Johnson was thinking about pitiful creatures when he referred to Oxford University wits in the *Rambler* (No. 114, 1751): 'A species of beings only heard of at the university.'

Then there is the conjunction *being*, once in general dialect use. Its meaning is since, seeing that, if; also used with conjunctions *as* or *that*. I've heard this *being* in many places in Ireland; I grew up with it in Wexford. I heard this recently there: 'Being as he have nothing to do but sit on his arse all day, you'd think he'd put a lick of paint on the house.' Seamus Ford the actor once reminded of me of its existence, as did that great Dublin woman the late Maureen Carter, chief make-up artist in RTÉ television, who became a very good friend of mine. She had a fund of Dublin speech and was immensely proud of her dialect. One night I barged into her make-up studio to get made up for my news-reading chore. Maureen thought she had locked the door, but hadn't, and Ursula Andress, in her pulchritudinous pelt, had to scurry to find a towel to cover her beautiful body. Maureen consoled her. 'Ah, Jaysus, child, never mind him. He's harmless, being as he's a Wexfordman.'

From Norfolk the EDD recorded, 'I couldn't meet you yesterday, being I was ill in bed.' Sweetman's *Wincanton Glossary* from Somerset (1885) has it.

Capt. Grose recorded 'Being it is so' in Devon back in 1790; and Charles Kingsley has 'But being that he is your cousin' in *Westward Ho!* (1885).

So, this usage has a distinguished pedigree, and we must give pride of place to Master Shakespeare. In *Henry IV, Part 2*, Act II, Scene I, he wrote, 'You loiter here too long, being you are to take soldiers up in counties as you go.'

✦ BENEDICITE

This lovely old word survived in English from the Middle Ages until the middle of the nineteenth century. It had many senses during this long period, the earliest being a blessing asked at table, first seen in *Ancren Riwle*, a treatise on the rules and duties of monastic life, in about 1225. The last use of the word in literature was in the Victorian novelist Mrs Catherine Gore's story *Fascination*, published in 1842. 'We may repent,' she wrote, 'having laughed at the benedicite last night at supper.'

Benedicite was also used as a pious interjection meaning 'God bless you.' As such Langland has it in *Piers Plowman* in 1377: 'He bygan Benedicite with a bolke [a belch].' Shakespeare has the word as well in *Measure For Measure*, Act II, Scene III: 'Grace go with you, Benedicite.'

Geoffrey Chaucer used the word as an interjection expressing astonishment, as we might say 'God bless us!' or 'Good gracious!' In *Troylus* he has 'What, liveth not thy lady? benedicite.'

As an invocation of a blessing on oneself or others it continued to be used until the nineteenth century, especially in Scotland, where Scott, in *Marmion*, has 'One eyed the swelling sail with many a benedicite.'

A special sense, as old as 1300, was a prayer to be delivered from evil, although the author of *Guy of Warwick* (1314) turned this on its head when he wrote, 'Gav hym swiche benedicite, that he brak his neck ato.'

The lovely word is from Latin *benedicere*, 'to praise, commend', later 'to bless, wish well to', from *bene*, well + *dicere*, to say, to speak. In early use it was often shortened to *bendicite* and *benst*. In one of the *Townley Mysteries* (*c.* 1450) we find 'Benste, benste, be us emang.' Amen to that.

✦ BEVERAGE

Written *baiverage* in Ulster, and now considered obsolete everywhere, this means a fine, either in money, drink or kisses, demanded of anybody on being seen out and about in new clothes. To comply with this ordinance was *to pay beverage*.

Oxford does not have this meaning of the word, but I wonder could it possibly be related to the common word for an alcoholic or other drink, which is from Middle English from Old French *bevrage, buverage* (modern French *breuvage*), a common Romanic formation, in the special medieval sense of a 'draught' which has been brewed, and must be drunk; the bitter or sorrowful sequel of any conduct, as found in the romance *Coer de Lion c.* 1325: 'A sorye beverage ther was browen.'

Nathan Bailey has the meaning in his *An Universal Etymological Dictionary* of 1721: 'To pay beverage, to give a treat upon the first wearing of a new suit of cloaths etc.' Dr Johnson had this in his great dictionary of 1755: 'A treat on first coming into a prison.'

John Jamieson, in his *Etymological Dictionary of the Scottish Language* (1808) has 'She gat the beverage o' his braw new coat.' MacTaggart's *Gallovian Encyclopedia* of 1824 has 'When a young girl gets any piece of new dress, she slyly shows it to her Joe, who gives her a kiss, which is taking the beverage of the article in question.' W.H. Patterson's glossary of Antrim and Down words, compiled around 1880, has 'When a young woman appears wearing something new for the first time, she gives her acquaintances the "baiverage of it," this is a kiss.'

It was alive and well in Scotland down to the twentieth century; the last citation in the DSL is from Galloway in 1901, in R. De Bruce Trotter's *Galloway Gossip, or the Southern Albanich of 80 Years ago*: 'C'wa in oot o' sicht till A kiss ye! A maun hae the beverige o' thae new claes!'

✦ BEYOND

I wonder how many meanings of this word, also found variously as *beyant, beyon* and *byun*, survive.

Take the adverb meaning yonder, outside. The anonymous *Paddiana* (1848) has 'Where's the mistress?—Beyant with Mrs Ryan.' Jane Barlow in *Irish Idylls* (1892) has 'Sure there's a letter for her they gave me down beyant.' In *Lisconnel* (1895) she has 'There was a fair down beyant.' This wasn't confined to Ireland. F.K. Robinson, one of the pioneers of dialect lexicography in the nineteenth century, in *The Song of Solomon in the North Yorkshire Dialect* (1860) gave us 'When hah sud find thee boyont, hah wad kiss thee.'

Then there is the preposition *beyond*, which I used to hear in my home place in Co. Wexford, used like this: 'That's beyond fair', used when a schoolboy was asked to mediate in a deal being made about the price of marbles.

There was also the phrase *to get or go beyond*, to get the better of, obtain mastery over; to overreach in a bargain. In Wicklow once I heard a man say of a local football team which was renewing rivalry with another club that had beaten them easily previously, 'They got beyond us before but it won't happen this time.' I found this in Porson's *Quaint Words*, published in 1875: 'My woman is very bad, sir; and the doctor can't get beyond it no how.'

Another phrase comes to mind, *to put beyond oneself*, to render conceited. This has been found in Ireland. Samuel Lover in *Legends and Stories of Ireland* has 'A little thravellin' puts us beyond ourselves sometimes.' This phrase, whenever I've heard it, was always used in a sarcastic manner. In Co. Donegal one day, a young woman was described by a not-so-friendly neighbour as someone 'who was put beyond herself when she married an aeroplane dhriver'.

In Lincolnshire and east Yorkshire, beyond means behind. The EDD has this from east Yorkshire: 'Wiv his gun riddy raised, he stayed boyont the car,' meaning behind the car.

Well, at least the phrase *beyond the beyonds* is still in use in Ireland to signify that something is outrageous, incredible; and also to describe an out-of-the-way place. The *Ballymena Observer* of 1882 had this: 'Beyont the beyons, wheer the aul meer foaled the fiddler: an answer to an inquisitive question.'

✦ BINT

A Dublin lady named Jane Hartley, who asks me not to divulge her address, sent me an interesting word which she is sure is pejorative. She was having a post-theatre drink with a friend in a Dublin hotel and quite enjoying tearing the guts out of what she thought a dreadful play, when two gentlemen who were sitting at a nearby table started getting over-friendly. They were slightly the worse for wear, and she and her friend ignored them. That really annoyed them. She then, she says, made the mistake of asking them to mind their own business, so one of them got up and approached their table, offering to buy them a drink and inviting them to come sit at their table. When she declined, your man returned to the other lout, saying that they were nothing but two stuck-up bints.

'I'm rather shy about asking you what a *bint* means, and what its origin is, fearing that it may be an obscenity. The tone of voice in which the two gurriers used the word leads me to believe that it certainly was not meant to be a compliment.'

I have never heard the word in my life, but a friend of mine, a Dubliner, tells me that it is common around Kimmage, where he comes from. He could offer no clue as to the word's origin.

Oxford has it, and I found it in Richard Wall's *An Irish Literary Dictionary and Glossary.* He told me that Roddy Doyle has the word in *The Van*: 'They were a right pair of bints, your women at the jack's door.'

It is one of those words which were imported by Dublin soldiers who fought in British regiments in the Middle East. There is nothing pejorative about the word in its language of origin. *Bint* in Arabic simply means a girl.

✦ BLADE

When I was young in Co. Wexford *blade* was used as a deprecatory term for a woman. It has long gone from schoolboys' speech, local teachers tell me. A blade would tell your parents, or worse still the Guards, if they suspected you of robbing orchards, for example. The word was once used extensively across the water in Cheshire and in Pembrokeshire, but there, as in some of the northern counties of Ireland, Antrim and Tyrone, for example, the word carried extra weight. Carleton had a character called 'Mary the Blade', a term applied to forward young woman. *The Ballymena Observer,* edited by W.J. Knowles in 1892, and a wonderful treasury of Co. Antrim speech, used the word to describe what was known in Counties Wexford and Kilkenny as a *bawshuk*, from Irish *báirseach*, a brawler, a shrew, according to Fr Dinneen.

I suppose the word originated in *blade*, the thin cutting part of an edged tool or weapon, a word common in Middle English and first seen in literature in Brunne's *Chronicles of England* in 1330. But a figurative use of this does not appear in literature in relation to women. A blade was always a man, a gallant, a free-and-easy fellow, generally familiarly laudatory, sometimes good-naturedly contemptuous. The original sense is difficult to seize: Bailey, in 1730, says, 'a bravo, an Hector; also a spruce fellow, a beau'; Johnson says 'a brisk man, either fierce or gay, called so in contempt'. No, I think our *blade* originally had something to do with the sharpness of a báirseach's tongue or with a forward woman's pushy, contemptuous demeanour.

The word is Common Teutonic: the Old English is *blæd*, neut., (pl. *blado*, *bladu*), Old Frisian *bled*, Old Saxon *blad*, Old Norse *blað*, Middle Dutch *blat*, Dutch *blad*, Low German *blad*, Old High German and Middle High German *blat*, modern German *blatt*. These words originally mean the blades of leaves or vegetables.

✦ BLEAZE

The only time I've ever heard this old word was back in the time the miniskirts hit the discos and the streets. Near Campile, Co. Wexford, an old woman looked at her granddaughter who was readying herself to go to a dance on a summer's night. As the youngster was heading for the door, having heard the noise of an approaching car, the old woman said, 'Put your overcoat on, for the love of God. That skirt is so short you'll get a could in the bleaze in no time, and your mother will blame me for not looking after you.' Her solicitude brought a laugh from the young woman, who skipped away, leaving me to enquire what a *bleaze* was.

It means the bladder. I have reason to believe that it is no longer used in south Wexford. So teacher friends of mine tell me, at any rate. Another old word gone. Where it came from I don't know, but I managed to run it down in Pembrokeshire, and anybody who knows the history of south Wexford will tell you that there is a connection between the two places which goes back a long time—over 800 years in fact.

A friend in the University of Exeter, an institution which is known for its work in the field of dialect studies, tells me that *bleaze*, sometimes spelled *bleeze*, is not to be found any more in Pembrokeshire. It turned up in Edward Laws's valuable study, *The History of Little England beyond Wales* in 1888, but only one correspondent from Pembrokeshire recorded it for the English Dialect Society. Not a trace of it since then, I'm afraid. There it meant a bladder of any kind; children kicked around a *bleaze* when they couldn't afford a football. How remiss of me not to have enquired if the same was true of south Wexford children in the old days. Too late now.

As to its ultimate origin, it represents the Old English blǽse, a bladder. Compare the Middle High German *bläse*, and Old High German *bláse*.

✦ BLEB

This is a good word long gone out of fashion in most places in Scotland, Ireland and the northern half of England from the Border south to

Lincolnshire. It means a blister; and also a bubble, and a drop of liquid. I've heard a Donegal woman describing blisters caused by nettles as *blebs*; and an old Wicklowman, John Vines from Kilpedder, now gone from us, once asked me to pour another bleb of water into his whiskey.

Stephanus Skinner in his 1671 dictionary glossed *bleb* as *vesica*. John Ash in his 1795 dictionary glossed the word as 'a blister' and remarked that the word was not much used. Nathan Bailey in his 1721 *Etymological Dictionary* gave 'Bleb: a blister, a blain; also a bubble or bladder in the water'. Captain Grose recorded the word in Co. Antrim in 1790. Marshall, the great agriculturalist, recorded the word in Yorkshire in his *Rural Economy* in 1788, and from the same county John Nicholson in *The Folk Speech of East Yorkshire* (1889) recorded, 'Mah stickin had all ruckt up i mi beeat [boot] an raised a bleb o' mi heel.' And poor John Clare, the Northamptonshire poet, had 'The spider's lace is wet with pinhead blebs of dew.'

Hence *blebby*, covered with blisters, a Yorkshire word; and the verb *bleb*, to bubble, to cover with drops of liquid; to rise in blisters. John Clare had the verb in a poem in *The Village Minstrel* in 1821: 'And bleb the withering hay with pearly gem,' and in another poem he had 'Black-eyed bean-flower blebbed with dew.'

According to Oxford *bleb* is apparently like *blob* and *blubber*, from the action of making a bubble with the lips. In relation to *blob*, *bleb* expresses a smaller swelling; cf. *top*, *tip*, etc.

With this modern craze for conformity, sponsored by various departments of education in both Britain and Ireland, and by the newspapers, television and radio, and by the advertising copywriters, lovely words like *bleb* are falling into disuse.

It is left to the likes of me to record these old dying or dead words. As Chaucer put it, '. . . wel I woot that folk han here-beforn / . . . ropen, and lad away the corn; And I am come after, glenynge here and here, / An am ful glad if I may fynde an ere / Of any goodly word that they han left.'

✦ **BOUN**

All the old-timers I heard in north Wexford singing that lovely old song *The Streams of Bunclody* said, 'I am boun for America my fortune to try.' They probably meant *bound*, I thought, until the English medievalist Alan Bliss pointed out to me in UCD one day over a cup of coffee that yes, they meant *bound*, from which it is derived, but that *boun* had a separate life of its own. We find 'Shippes . . . on the shyre water, all boune on the brode see' in *The Destruction of Troy* (*c.* 1400). 'Quhidder are they boun?' asks Gavin Douglas in his great Scots poem, *Eneados*, written around 1513. The form has survived in Scotland and in England's northern shires. From west Yorkshire a contributor to the EDD pointed to the subtle linguistic snobbery in the speech of his district: '"Whear's tuh barn tul?" "Am bown hoam." *Bown* is the least refined form, and is generally employed by the factory girls.'

Boun also means ready, prepared. I've heard 'I'm boun now, if you are,' in Glasgow. In Jamieson's *Popular Ballads* (1806) there is the line 'When bells were rung and mass was sung, And a' men boun to meat'; and long before those ballads were composed, Langland's *Piers Plowman* had 'And bed hem alle ben bowne . . . To wenden with hem to Weste mynstre.'

I once heard an old Donegal man say of his daughter who had gone to her bedroom to prepare herself for a dance that she might be all night *bounin herself*. Scott has this in *Waverley*: 'We will all bowne ourselves for the banquet.' This verb, to prepare, make ready; to get ready, to dress, is also old. Peter Levins' *Manipulus Vocabulorum* of 1570 has 'to boune, *parare, accingere*'. The *Destruction of Troy*, written 170 years earlier, has 'I wold boune me to batell.' The verb is a derivative of *boun*, past participial adjective, above, which has its origin in Old Norse *búinn*, prepared, past participle of *búa*, to get ready.

It's good to know from recent surveys that there's a spark of life in the old word still.

✦ BOWSSENING

We sat in a hotel in Penrith, Cornwall, looking out on a golden beach. My companion was a son of mine, mentioned in the Dedication of this book, who worked there as a psychiatrist, and he turned to me and said, 'I suppose you know the word *bowssening*.' I professed ignorance. 'Oh, the older people know the word here, and I wasn't long in the job here when I was told that it was an old treatment for madness, and that an Irishman was responsible for it.' 'Pre-Freudian hocus pocus?' I asked, knowing that there have been all sorts of charms against madness recorded in Cornwall, and he replied that the method called *bowssening* has been attributed to an Irish eighth-century hermit called Fillian who lived in a cave not far from where we sat. He was a bit of a night owl and he sat in his cave at night, reading by the light of a glow which his left hand gave off. As a result of his study, he came to the conclusion that bowssening madmen was the best way to cure them. *Bowssening* is from the Cornish *beuzi*, to immerse, drown, according to Oxford, a later form of *bedhy*, *bidhy*, or *budhy*, Breton *beuzi*, Welsh *boddi*, to drown. So, our proto-psychiatrist just had his patients trussed up and half-drowned in a well time and time again, and then placed in a corner of his cell until morning, where many of them were found to be cured of their ailment. I wonder were Mr Cheney and his CIA friends following his example at Guantánamo?

Well, this barbaric treatment has long been abandoned in Cornwall, but it was still practised in the middle of the nineteenth century. In James Pettigrew's *Superstitions Connected With Medicine and Surgery*, published in 1844, and recommended to me by my late friend the bibliophile Séamas Ó Saothraí of Greystones, we are told this: 'Casting mad people into the sea, or immersing them in water until they are well-nigh drowned, have been recommended by high medical authorities as a means of cure.'

The word lives in the folk memory and in the phrase you'll hear in some Cornish public houses. An old fisherman I struck up a conversation with kindly bought me a whiskey and, handing me a jug of water, said, 'Here, man, pour yer own water; I might bowsen it on ye.'

✦ BOX HARRY

I've heard this verbal phrase only once in my life, from a taxi driver in Dublin at the time of a threatened strike. He expected that the strike would last quite a bit, and when I asked him what he was going to do if an all-out walk-out was called he replied, 'I'll have to box harry, I suppose. What can I do?' By that he meant that he'd have to rough it, and do the best he could.

The phrase undoubtedly came from England. The EDD has it from Yorkshire, Lancashire, Cheshire, Derby, Lincolnshire, Northamptonshire, Warwickshire, East Anglia, Shropshire and Hampshire—quite a spread. It defines it as 'to go without food; to make a poor or coarse meal; to rough it, to take things as they are'. From Lancashire a correspondent told the EDD's editor, Joseph Wright, himself the son of a poor man who had boxed harry all the days of his life, 'I had no money, I could get nothing to eat, so I had to box harry till I reached Liverpool.' That invaluable scholarly journal *Notes and Queries*, 8th Series iii, 1883, defined the term as slang used by commercial travellers, implying dinner and tea at one meal.

Hence *boxharry-week*, the blank week between pay-weeks when the workmen lived on credit or starved. This compound is from east Lancashire.

The big question is, what's the origin of this striking verbal phrase? Albert Barrère and G.C. Leyland, in their *Dictionary of Slang, Jargon and Cant*, first published in 1888–90 and reprinted in 1897, suggest that 'to box harry probably means to box or fight the devil'. Harry, Old Harry, and Lord Harry are indeed common names for the devil in Scotland, Lancashire, Yorkshire and Norfolk. I'll accept Joseph Wright's assurance that it would be well to compare the French phrase *Il tire le diable par la queue*, which he found in the *Dictionnaire de l'Academie* 1786 edition, s.v. *queue*, he says; and tells us that the French phrase was once in common use in reference to one who was hard up.

In these hard times, I wonder would there be a place once more in our lexicon for boxing harry? I think so, alas.

✦ BRACHAN

I don't think those dishes much lauded in nineteenth-century books— the likes of *sowans* and *brose* and *boxty*—would appeal much to me. *Boxty*, a dish made from grated potatoes and cooked in a perforated tin box—hence its name—I have tried and found indigestible. *Brose* is simply Scottish and northern England porridge: oatmeal mixed with boiling water or milk; it is simply a modern Scots form of Middle English *browes*, a word found in *Promptorium Parvulorum Sive Clericorum*, an English–Latin glossary of *c.* 1440, and it comes from Old French *broez*, broth. The dish reminds me of the thin gruel served for breakfast in boarding schools in my time, and before my time in the nineteenth century, in workhouses. *Sowans* are the inner husks of oats, winnowed and threshed, which were fermented in salt water, then drained, and the mess served up as a porridge. Paddy the Cope wrote of eating the stuff in the bothies of Scotland when he was a child. Dreadful stuff, he told me.

The word takes its name from *Samhain*, the great pagan feast which was superseded by All Souls. This was a popular dish about that time of year. Did they regard it as penitential, I wonder?

Brachan, Irish *brachán*, is a different kettle of stirabout. Many years ago I sat alongside that wonderful cook Theodora Fitzgibbon on a trip to New York, and she gave me a recipe for the dish, which she had from a woman who lived near Churchill, Co. Donegal. When I got home, I tried it out. It is very good indeed, a great warmer in cold weather. To my surprise, my children loved the dish too. It is Scottish in origin, and here's how you make it:

Cut six large leeks into chunks an inch long. Leave the green part on. Heat 4 cups of milk, or 2 pints, with a heaped tablespoon of butter, and when boiling add 2 tablespoons of flake oatmeal. Add the chopped leeks, and season with salt and pepper. Put the lid on and simmer for 45 minutes. Add a tablespoon of chopped parsley, and boil again for a few minutes.

According to Theodora we have St Patrick to thank for *brachán*. 'St Patrick attended a dying woman, who said she had seen a herb in the air, and would die unless she ate it. St Patrick said to her, "What is the herb like?" "Like rushes," she said. Patrick blessed the rushes so that they became leeks. The woman ate it, and was well at once.'

I thought of Theodora as I last shopped in a Donegal Gaeltacht supermarket, a few years ago. A woman I knew was loading packets of soup mixture into her basket, and I asked her if she ever made *brachán*. 'Pauper's food,' she snapped derisively. 'They don't even know here any more what brachán is.' A pity, if that's the case.

✦ BRASSERS, BRASS NAILS, RIGGERS & ROSSIES

As I was going through Dublin city at the hour of twelve in the night, sitting in the back of a taxi, who should my Nigerian driver point to but a couple of enticingly clad ladies boulevarding down by the canal. 'A lot of brassers out tonight,' said my man, displaying a knowledge of Dublin slang far greater than mine. I had to ask him were the ladies he referred to ladies of the night, and he said that I must either be a native of Dublin 4 or else a culchie not to know what a *brasser* was. Here was a man who had definitely integrated into the community of rale Dubliners, out Crumlin way. He also gave me the word *brass nails*. I have no idea what the origin of these words is, except that they are in English slang and that the modern collections I found them in offered no etymology.

Many years later I thought of asking my friend Richard Wall, a Dubliner who was professor of English at the University of Calgary in

Canada. He has passed away since, when in the prime of his life. He told me that he was finishing a dictionary of words found in Irish literature, and he kindly gave me the following information.

Lee Dunne, he said, had the word in *Goodbye to the Hill*, published in 1986: 'The way fellas talk, you'd think it was impossible to get a bit unless you went with a brasser.' He told me that Hugh Leonard had the word in *Home before Night* (1986): 'Do you remember at the end of Stagecoach, where the Marshall turns a blind eye and lets the Ringo Kid and the town brasser go free?' I expected that Brendan Behan would have used *brasser*, and sure enough he did. In his play *The Hostage* (1958) Meg conflates *brasser* and *prostitute* when she calls one of the other girls a *brasstitute*. And in *Richard's Cork Leg* 'two Dublin brassers in working gear' appear. *The Brassers* is a name proposed for a band at the end of *The Commitments*, the novel by Roddy Doyle, later made into a very good film.

Riggers were, according to my taxi man and Richard Wall, old prostitutes that had seen better days. Richard Wall gave me this from Kevin C. Kearns' *Dublin Pub Life and Lore*, published in Colorado in 1997: 'If they were a bit advanced [in age] they were called riggers; they were cheap prostitutes.'

Rossie, sometimes spelled *rossy* and *rawsie*, were not prostitutes, as my taxi driver said they were, but brazen young women. James Joyce in *Ulysses* had 'If they could run like rossies she could sit, so she said . . .' Joyce also used the term in *Finnegans Wake* as rosy. John Banville has the term in *The Book of Evidence* (1989): 'I was surrounded suddenly by a gang of tinker girls, what my mother would have called *big rawsies*.'

The word, I think, was from the Irish *rásach*, defined by Fr Dinneen as 'a rambling woman, a gypsy, a jilt, al. *rásaí*. cf. Dublin *rossie*'. An Irish influence in working-class Dublin? you might ask. Indeed yes. There was a thriving Irish-speaking community in Dublin's Liberties in the 1800s, and many Irish words and phrases have survived there to this day.

✦ BRAWSE

A friend of mine who worked as a medical practitioner in Lancashire used to send me some interesting words, not heard in Ireland, but which had Irish ancestry. One of these was *brawse*. Oxford doesn't have it, which shows that it is now either obsolete or unworthy of consideration, but the *English Dialect Dictionary* says that it is confined to Lancashire.

It quotes two sources, John Davies' *The Races of Lancashire, as indicated by the local names and the dialect of the county* (London 1856), and Samuel Bamford's *The Dialect of South Lancashire, or Tim Bobbin's Tummus and Meary: with his rhymes and an enlarged glossary of words and phrases, chiefly used by the rural population of the manufacturing districts of south Lancashire* (London, 1850). The word is defined as 'brambles, furze', and a compound is also given, *braws-land*, defined as 'light moss land which will produce straw without grain', also attributed to Bamford.

I first came across *brawse* in an account of the plight of the Lancashire mill-children in the days when the great William Cobbett, newly elected Member for Oldham, was doing his utmost for them in a largely unheeding House of Commons. The account stated that the poor and their children had more to contend with than hunger and inhuman working hours and conditions; cold was sending many of them to an early grave. Whatever spare time they had they collected *brawse* for their fires, furze, brambles and assorted bushes from the hedgerows.

Brawse, according to the Scots lexicographer Macbain, is perhaps from Scottish Gaelic or Irish *preas*, a bush, briar. My own guess would be that it is from the Irish *breas*, glossed by Dinneen as 'a thicket, a bush'. The same word, really.

✦ BRENDICE

My old tutor at Dublin University, the Celticist Gordon Quin, brought me to his rooms to raise a *brendice* to celebrate my passing some exam or other. It is a pity that this old word has passed from general use. Oxford, which describes it as either obsolete or rare, defines it as a cup in which a person's health is drunk, a bumper, and it quotes John Dryden's *Amboyna* (1673): 'I go fill a Brendice to my Noble Captain's Health.'

The word's origin is the Italian *brindisi, brindesi*, 'a drinking of health to one', according to John Florio's charming Italian–English dictionary, *A Worlde of Wordes*, published in 1598, which he re-wrote in 1611 under the title *Queen Anna's New World of Wordes*, for the edification of James I's Danish queen, his patron, pupil and, some gossips said, his special friend, as a euphemism of the period went.

The Italian word was, according to Diez, perverted (by popular etymology) from German *bring dir's*, i.e. *ich bringe dir's zu*; whence also French *brinde*. So says Oxford.

C ～

✦ **CAFFLING**

Noel Costello, Night Editor of *The Irish Times*, sent me this word which he heard a cousin, Mary Coughlan, use in Tallow, Co. Waterford. He asked her what she meant by *caffling* and she glossed it as harmless messing, or trick-acting. She also gave cousin Noel the word *caffler* for one who indulges in such activity.

My friend the late Richard Wall, in his great book *Irish Literary Dictionary and Glossary*, defines *caffler* as 'a contemptible, cheeky little fellow'. *Cafflin' Johnny* is a play by Louis D'Alton, first produced in 1958. It became widely known through being produced by amateur dramatic societies all over the country.

Professor Wall wasn't sure where the word came from, and guessed that it was either from the Irish *cafaire*, a prater, or from *cavalier*. Terry Dolan in *A Dictionary of Hiberno-English* sees *caffler* as a disagreeable, cheeky, quarrelsome little fellow. He found the word in Cork and in Co. Meath. He sees the origin in English dialectal *cavil*, to split hairs, to jest and so on, from the French *caviller*.

He follows Oxford's line, which says that *caffle* is from *cavil*, to argue, to prevaricate, from Old French *caviller*, to mock, jest, rail, from Latin *cavillari*, but Oxford adds the meaning given in Randle Cotgrave's *A French and English Dictionary*, published in London in 1611, 'to cauill, wrangle, reason crossely, speake ouer thwartly'. That shade of meaning is, I think, Seán O'Faoláin's in *Midsummer Madness*: 'Are you going to be stopped by some city caffler?'

So, there are many shades of meaning, depending on where you come across the word. I asked an old school friend of mine in New Ross recently what he meant by a caffler. He said that a caffler was an argumentative person. 'A cheeky young prankster?' I asked. 'Absolutely not,' was the answer I got. D.H. Lawrence would have agreed with him.

In one of his *Love Poems* he has 'To think I should ha'e to haffle an' caffle / Wi'a woman an' pay o'er the price.' I asked a woman, a contemporary of mine who lives in the village of Rosbercon, just across the river from New Ross, what a caffler was, and she had a slightly different meaning: 'A trickster,' she said, 'a bit of a boyo but relatively harmless.' I probed further. 'In what age group would you place a caffler?' 'You were a bit of a caffler at sixteen, and I'd say you still have a bit of the caffler in you,' she courteously replied.

✦ CAITIFF

This word has a long history in English literature, and outside literature in the speech of the people. The latest surveys of English dialects have shown that the word is obsolete, not even found in its last stronghold in Yorkshire, where it survived until a few years ago, defined as 'a cripple, one who is deformed and helpless'.

It didn't deserve its fate. The Yorkshire meaning of the word is but one of many recorded throughout its history. Originally it meant a captive, a prisoner, and thus it first appeared in Brunne's *Chronicles of England* in 1330, and is seen no more with this meaning after 1603, when a polemicist called Cross wrote, 'As catiues and slaues bend the will to such inhumane cruelty.'

The word was also used to express commiseration: a wretched, miserable person, a poor wretch, one in a pitious state. One of the *Metrical Homilies* of *c.* 1325 has 'Hou sal it far of us kaytefes, That in sin and foli lyes.' 'To sorwe was she ful ententyf, That woful recchelees caitiff (*la dolereuse, la chetife*),' wrote Chaucer in *The Romaunt of the Rose*. 'Alas, poor caitiff,' sang Shakespeare in *Othello*, Act IV. Samuel Butler's *Hudibras* of 1678 has 'I pity'd the sad Punishment / The wretched Caitiff underwent.' After that we find no trace of this particular meaning in literature.

Caitiff was also used to express contempt: a base, mean villain. 'The wickedst caitiff on the ground' is a description used by Shakespeare in *Measure for Measure*, Act V. The last time this meaning got an outing was in Edward Freeman's *The History of the Norman Conquest* in 1867: 'Two caitiffs whose names are handed down to infamy.'

Caitiff was also an adjective with a variety of meanings. Wyclif mentioned his caitiff pupil in 1382. 'Full sade and caytif was she eek,' wrote Chaucer in a doleful mood in *The Romaunt of the Rose*. The adjective meaning base, vile, contemptible, had a long innings, from the *Cursor Mundi* of *c*. 1300: 'Ded es caitiue iudas nu', to Tennyson's *Enid* of 1859: 'bandit earls and caitiff knights' and Browning's *Baloustion's Adventure* of 1871: 'This or other caitiff quality'.

The word is from Old French *caitif*, captive, weak, miserable. Why the good word died out is a mystery to me. These things happen.

✦ CALLER

This good Ulster word, once sent to me by the Fermanagh musicologist Joan Trimble, seems to be falling rapidly into disuse. My friend Tomás Mac Gabhann once told me that it was one of his mother's words, but that he himself had only heard it once or twice in his native Co. Monaghan, and then only from old people. I see that it is recorded by the splendid *Concise Ulster Dictionary*. It means, of fish or vegetables, fresh, in proper season, newly-caught or gathered.

It used to be very common in Scotland and in some dialects of England. Walter Scott in *The Antiquary* (1816) has 'There's fish, nae doubt,—that's sea-trout and caller haddocks.' In Northumberland, according to a correspondent of Joseph Wright, editor of the EDD, it was very common as a street-cry: 'Here's yer caller harrin!'

Used of water and air it means fresh, invigorating. Robert Burns in *The Holy Fair* (1785) wrote, 'I walked forth to view the corn / An' snuff the caller air.' 'I think the air is callerer and fresher than anywhere else in the country,' wrote Scott in *Redgauntlet* (1824). Stevenson in *Catriona* (1892) has a character who complains, 'I do better with caller air.' And in *The Weir of Hermiston* (1896) he has 'And dry your bonny hair in the caller wind o' the muirs.'

The Scots have the phrase *as caller as a kail-blade*, as refreshing and cool as possible; and *as caller as a trout*, used of persons in good health; rosy, plump. Scott in *The Heart of Midlothian* has 'The dew, and the night-wind, they are just like a caller kail-blade laid on my brow.'

As you might expect the Scots had a verb *caller*, to freshen, cool, refresh. Scott again, this time in *Rob Roy* (1817): 'A night amang the heather to caller our bloods.'

The word is an old one. It is found in one of the *Legends of the Saints* from around 1400: 'In þe kirkyard was ladane ethiope & yet his fesche is caloure Inucht & als fres.' Gavin Douglas also had the word in *Eneados* (1513): 'The callour air'.

The word, according to the DSL, is from Old Scots *callour, calour, caller*, (1) of fish, flesh, etc., fresh, showing no signs of flabbiness or staleness; from ante 1400; (2) of air, water, etc.: fresh and cool, from about 1513. It is apparently a variant of Middle English *calver, calvur, calwar*, fresh (applied to salmon). For the dropping of *v*, cf. Scots *siller*, English *silver*.

✦ CALLET

I wonder why this good word fell out of favour. It was employed by many fine writers in both England and Scotland before it seems to have died the death suddenly after Walter Scott used it in *The Monastery* in 1820: 'Thou foolish callet, art thou confederate with this vagabond?' *Callet* means a prostitute, a lewd woman; a drab, dirty woman; also, a scold, virago, constant fault-finder; a quarrelsome woman.

I can find no trace of the word before 1500, when it turns up in a tract called *Cocke Lorelles Bote*, which was edited by the Percy Society in 1843: 'Yf he call her calat, she calleth hym knave agayne.' In 1532 Thomas More, who could give as good as he took when it came to invective, wrote in his *Confutacyon of Tyndales Answere*, 'Frere Luther and Cate calate his nunne, lye luskyng together in lechery.'

Holland's translation of Livy, done in 1600, has 'Any unhonest woman or wanton callot [*impudica*].'

And of course the word was no stranger to Shakespeare. In *Othello*, Act IV, Scene II, he has 'A Beggar in his drink Could not have laid such terms upon his Callet,' and in *The Winter's Tale*, Act II, Scene III, he has 'A callat of boundless tongue, who late hath beat her husband And now bayts me'; and in 1785 Burns in his *Jolly Beggars* gives us 'I'm as happy with my wallet, my bottle and my callet,' and in the same work, 'Here's our ragged brats and callets.'

The old dictionaries did not neglect the word. Cotgrave, in his 1611 French–English dictonary, defines it as '*Paillarde*, a strumpet'. Before him Jehan Palsgrave in 1530 gave us 'I rampe, I play the callet, *je ramponne*'. And Nathan Bailey's dictionary of 1731 has '*Calot*, a Drab'.

I was delighted to hear that this good word in all its shades of meaning is still to be heard in some places in Yorkshire. Long may it live there.

As to origin, nobody seems to know for sure, and I have come across some strange guesses in my time. Robert Nares in his 1822 glossary of strange words, edited in 1888 by Halliwell and Wright, says that it was from the name of a prostitute, Kitty Callet. Oxford, cagey as ever, and rightly so, has this: 'Many have suggested its identity with French *caillette* "foole, ninnie, noddie, naturall" (Cotgrave), diminutive of *caille*, quail (esteemed a silly bird); but this does not quite answer phonetically, does not quite suit the sense, and was in French applied to men as readily as to women. Others have thought of French *calotte*, a kind of small bonnet or cap covering only the top of the head, but no evidence appears connecting this especially with a "callet". The Gaelic and Irish *caille* girl has also been suggested.'

For what it's worth, this last etymology is the only one that would satisfy me.

✦ CANARIES

All literate people will know that *canary* was, in Shakespeare's time, a light, sweet wine from the Canary Islands, sometimes called *canary sack*. In *The Merry Wives of Windsor* he has 'I will to my honest knight, Falstaff, and drink canary with him.' He used it in the plural as well in *Henry IV, Part 2*, Scene II: 'But i' faith you have drunk too much canaries.'

A canary had another meaning: a lively Spanish dance, the idea of which is said to have been derived from the people of the Canary Islands. In early use it was often plural, as it was in Nashe's *Pierce Penilesse* of 1592: 'As gingerly as if she were dancing the Canaries.' Shakespeare in *All's Well That Ends Well* has 'I have seen a medicine / That's able to breathe life into a stone, / Quicken a rock and make you dance Canary / With sprightly fire and motion.' He also has this in *Love's Labour's Lost*, Act III, Scene I: 'To jig off a tune at the tongue's end, canary to it with your feet, humour it with turning up your eyelids.' In 1606 Thomas Dekker in *The Seven Deadly Sins of London* has 'They would make all the Hogges-heads that use to come to the house, to daunce the Cannaries till they reel'd again.' The wretched Puritans, it is said, killed the dance off, just as the priests of the last century in Ireland tried to kill the completely innocuous mumming in Co. Wexford.

What are we to make of Mistress Quickly's canaries in *The Merry Wives of Windsor*: 'You have brought her into such a canaries as 'tis wonderful'? It is generally accepted that this is one of the good lady's corruptions and supposed to mean 'quandary': a perplexity or predicament, a worry. When I overheard a young one in Dungarvan declining the offer of a young man to buy her a drink, saying that it was late already and that her mother would have canaries, Mrs Quickly's canaries came to mind.

✦ CANDLES

Here are a few candle compounds, for want of a better term, which you may not have come across. Small blame to you if you haven't; they all disappeared from the language many years ago.

The first is *candle case*. This was a receptacle for candle ends. Shakespeare has it in *The Taming of the Shrew*, Act III, Scene II: 'Petruchio is coming in a new hat and an old jerkin, a pair of old breeches thrice turned, a pair of boots that have been candle cases, one buckled, one laced.'

Candle-ends used in drinking a toast to a mistress: the early nineteenth century lexicographer Robert Nares observed, 'A piece of romantic extravagance long practised by amorous gallants. It may perhaps be asked why *drinking off candle-ends* for flap-dragons [q.v.] should be esteemed as an agreeable qualification. The answer is, that as a feat of gallantry, to swallow a candle's end formed a more formidable and disagreeable flap-dragon than any other substance and therefore afforded a stronger testimony of zeal for the lady to whose health it was drunk.' See Beaumont and Fletcher's *Monsieur Thomas*, Act II, Scene II: 'Carouse her health in cans / And candles' ends.' And you may remember the exchange between Jack Falstaff and Doll Tearsheet in *Henry IV, Part 2*, Act II, Scene IV: 'Doll: Why doth the prince love him so then?' 'Falstaff: Because he eats conger and fennel, and drinks off candles'-ends for flap-dragons.'

A *candle-holder* was an idle spectator. There was a Scottish saying, 'You will neither dance nor hold the candle,' i.e. neither be a participant nor an onlooker. In *Romeo and Juliet*, Act I, Scene IV, you'll find 'I'll be a candle-holder and look on.'

Candle-mine. This was a mine or inexhaustible source of fat or tallow. It's in *Henry IV, Part 2*, Act II, Scene IV, and the Prince refers of course to Falstaff: 'You whoreson candle-mine you.'

Finally, *candle-waster*. This was a bookworm, a person who sits up late at night, working, burning the midnight oil. Ben Jonson used the term in *Cynthia's Revels*, Act III, Scene II: 'Spoiled by a whoreson bookworm, a candle-waster'. Shakespeare has this in *Much Ado About*

Nothing: 'If such a one will smile and stroke his beard, / Bid sorrow wag, cry "hem!" when he should groan, / Patch grief with proverbs, / Make misfortune drunk with candle-wasters.' What he meant was, drown grief with the wise sayings of bookworms. Some have suggested that *candle-waster* means 'reveller' in the passage. Take your pick.

✦ CANGLE

This is a verb that has travelled to Ulster—and here I mean the historic province, not just Northern Ireland—from either Scotland or England, two places which sent planters to the north after the wars of O'Neill and O'Donnell ended in failure. It means to quarrel, wrangle, haggle; to cavil.

I first heard the word from the late Tomás Mac Gabhann from Co. Monaghan and later from both Benedict Kiely the writer from Co. Tyrone, and David Hammond the musician from Co. Antrim.

Paddy O'Brien, one of Dublin's most famous barmen, who ruled the roost in McDaid's pub in Harry Street, off Dublin's Grafton Street, used the word in a *sotto voce* conversation he had with me one day. I was having a quiet pint on my own having been rebuffed by a truculent Patrick Kavanagh, who refused to sign a copy of his *Collected Pruse* for me, telling me to f . . . off, even though I had just sent a glass of whiskey over to him to soften his mood. O'Brien told me that Kavanagh was cangling all day over the price of drink, complaining that the barman was making a fortune on the quiet by overcharging innocents like himself. He asked me to leave the book, and said that he would get Kavanagh to sign it at a more propitious time. I did so, and a few days later, O'Brien had got the poet to sign his *Pruse*, and then promptly barred him, not for the first time, for being obnoxious to his customers.

In the mid-seventeenth century, Dickson, a Scottish pamphleteer, warned his fellow-countrymen that they were spending too much time *cangling* with the Papists, a verbal noun meaning altercation, quarrelling; it's also as a past participial adjective meaning wrangling, quarrelsome. I suppose that *cangle*, noun and verb, a tangle, to entangle, found in Northamptonshire, Derbyshire and Oxfordshire, is related. From Northamptonshire a correspondent sent the EDD's editor the sentence 'My thrid be so kangled I can't wind it nowhows.'

The word, I feel sure, had its origin in Scandinavia. Compare the Norwegian *kjangle*, to dispute, argue.

✦ CANTANKEROUS

I have been asked many times about this word. It appears that many Irish people think that the word, defined by Oxford as 'showing an ill-natured disposition; ill-conditioned and quarrelsome, perverse, cross-gained', is a word found only on the Emerald Isle. This is not so. It is found wherever English is spoken, but according to recent surveys it is in decline in urban areas and may be in danger of being deemed obsolete in many places soon.

Certainly an Irish writer, Oliver Goldsmith, was the first to use the word, described by Oxford as colloquial, in his 1772 *She Stoops to Conquer*: 'There's not a more bitter cantanckerous road in all christendom.' Sheridan, too, used the word in *The Rivals* in 1776: 'I hope, Mr. Faulkland . . . you won't be so cantanckerous.' In 1865 Livingstone the explorer wrote in *Zambesi* about 'A crusty old bachelor or . . . a cantankerous husband.'

It was said by Captain Grose, the late eighteenth-century lexicographer, who spells it *contankerous*, to be a Wiltshire word. This spelling, in the opinion of the Oxford dictionary, gives some support to the conjecture that the word was formed on Middle English *contak*, *conteke*, contention, quarrelling, *contekour*, *conteckour*, one who raises strife, whence **conteckerous*, **contakerous* would be a possible derivative, like traitorous, which might subsequently be corrupted under influence of words like *cankerous*, *rancorous*. Its oddly appropriate sound, and perhaps some association with these words, have given it general colloquial currency.

Hence *cantankerously* and *cantankerousness* were added to the lexicon. Oxford added these examples from the nineteenth century: in 1868 A.K.H. Boyd in *Lessons of Middle Age* had 'One impracticable, stupid, wrongheaded, and cantankerously foolish person of the twelve'. In 1876 the prolific and, by some accounts, the cantankerous Mrs Henry Wood, in *Orville College*, remarked, 'You have behaved cantankerously to him.' A.R. Hope in *Boy's Own Paper* 10 September 1881 wrote, 'The roller had crushed the cantankerousness right out of him.' And in 1886 *The Christian Life* of 2 January told its godly readers that 'A member has been expelled for general cantankerousness.'

At a London literary lunch some few years ago, Auberon Waugh told me that his father, the novelist Evelyn, with whom he was never on the best of terms, was 'a cantankerous old bastard'. A case of the kettle calling the pot black, some would say.

◆ **CAP & CAUP**

This is an old-fashioned wooden cup or bowl, sometimes with two ears or handles, used in Scotland and Ireland until the beginning of the twentieth century. In Scotland it was known as *caup*.

The cap or caup was used for many purposes, such as doling out milk to workers in the fields during the harvest. It was also used in public houses. I suppose that those who say that the two handles meant that the utensil was used to help two people drink at the same time know what they are talking about. The late Professor Gordon Quin, who taught me at Trinity, had the word from his father, a cooper in Guinness's brewery, and said that the *cap* was a big wooden drinking cup, and that the two lugs were useful in lifting it when full of 'the devil's brew', as Rev. Paisley once referred to it.

The word is found in all the Ulster glossaries of the nineteenth century, and *The Ballymena Observer* of 1892 has it as well. Macafee's *The Concise Ulster Dictionary* also has it, as *cap* and *caup*, and glossed as 'a small wooden bowl, often left floating in the churn, for skimming the milk'. The dictionary also has *capper*, a person who makes wooden bowls; and the very interesting *caup pig* and *cappy pig*, a piglet brought up by hand and fed out of a cap.

The word has been used by many Scots writers. Burns has it in *Holy Fair* (1785): 'Drink gaed round in cogs and coups.' Scott has it in *Nigel* (1822): 'It is a pity but he could keep caup and can frae his head.'

The Scots had some good compounds as well, such as *cap-ambry*, a press for holding caps and other wooden vessels, and *cap-ale*, defined as 'a kind of ale drunk by the middle classes'. *To kiss caps* meant to drink out of the same vessel. Burns in *Five Carlins* (1789) has 'And monie a friend that kiss'd his caup / Is now a frammit wight [a strange, unrelated person].' John Jamieson's early nineteenth-century dictionary has 'I wadna kiss caps wi sic a fellow.' There is also the phrase *to drink cap out*, to leave nothing in the vessel. Walter Scott has this in *Rob Roy* (1817): 'Drink clean cap out, like Sir Hildebrand.' A minor Scots poet, Pickens, quoted by Jamieson, wrote in 1813, 'We may swig at clean-cap-out / Till sight and siller fail us.'

This forgotten Scots and Ulster word is from Old Northumbrian *copp* and Old Norse *koppr*, a cup, small bowl.

✦ CARL(E

This word is found in Scots, in the English of the northern shires, and also in Co. Wexford until very recent times. It meant a countryman; also an ignorant lout. James Kelly, in his *A Complete Collection of Scottish Proverbs, Explained and Made Intelligible to the English Reader* (London 1721, and often reprinted since then), has this piece of Scots savvy: 'Kiss a carle and clap a carle, And that's the waay to tine [lose] a carle. Knock a carle and ding a carle, And that's the way to win a carle.' The proverb is still known in Scotland. Indeed, a literate follower of Glasgow Rangers, and there are some of these extant, believe it or not, told me that Sir Alex Ferguson has based his extraordinarily successful management of his teams over the years on the homely wisdom contained in this proverb.

'O welcome most kindly, the blythe carle said,' sang Rymer Rab frae Ayr in *Kellyburn*, in 1786. In more recent times the EDD's editor was sent many examples of the use of *carle* from northern England. I am reliably informed that to call a man a carl in a council meeting in some of the border areas is tantamount to an invitation to step outside.

In Wexford, old Phil Wall from Carne in the Barony of Forth said to me back in 1970, 'For an educated man, that priest behaves at times like a carle.' A few miles further west, in Kilmore, Barony of Bargy, Liz Jeffries told me, 'My mother would call an ignorant bosthoon of a man a carl.' Indeed *bosthoon*, from Irish *bastún*, from Anglo-French *baston*, a cudgel, a lump of a stick, is a very good definition of *carl(e*.

The Anglo-Normans, as we all know, pitched their tents in this part of Wexford and stayed there, but carl(e, whether it came into the language with the arrival of the settlers from Pembrokeshire or later from other parts, or whether it predates their coming, we'll probably never know. What we do know is that the word is Scandinavian in origin, from the Old Norse *karl*, man, male, free man. It was also used in an abusive sense; *fret carl*, for example, meant 'fart carl', a vagabond, etc.

✦ CARLING

This good word is found in Ulster, in Scotland, and in Northern England. It means an old cantankerous woman, a witch. W.H. Patterson has it in his glossary of Antrim and Down words sent to the English Dialect Society in 1880, and subsequently incorporated in the EDD by its editor, Joseph Wright.

I first heard the word some time in the 1960s from a Donegal sheepman, Paddy Joe Gill, who hailed from Glenties direction. He came into my father-in-law's house one day, and appeared distressed. He had been attacked by a dog owned by a friend of his, and he blamed this man's wife. 'That aul' bitch of a carlin he married set the bloody dog on me,' he explained. I next heard the word from an old lady on a plane to Rome. She employed it to describe one of the superannuated stewardesses they employed during the years of the Celtic Tiger; this person had told her that she should have asked for the glass of water she requested to wash down her medication earlier, when drinks were being served. The old lady did get her glass of water, but only when she complained to the captain, who had left the cockpit to speak to somebody he knew. She was an Ulsterwoman, to judge from her accent. No daws, those Ulsterwomen.

The word *carlin(g* undoubtedly came to Ulster by way of Scotland. James Kelly has it in his *A Complete Collection of Scottish Proverbs*, first published in 1721: '"Crooked carlin," quoth the cripple to his wife.' Robert Burns, in his *Epistle to R. Graham*, has 'Shaking hands wi' wabster loons, / And kissing barefit carlins.'

The word is from Old Norse *kerling*, a woman, almost always an old woman, according to the great Icelandic lexicographer Vigfusson. I'm glad it has survived, although recent research shows that its use is in decline in many areas.

✦ CARNAPTIOUS

Michael Cleary from Ballyhaunis, Co. Mayo, contacted me about the word *carnaptious*, which he heard used by a friend in Co. Antrim. It means irritable, touchy, bad-tempered, always finding fault. Michael had never heard it before; indeed, it seems not to have penetrated south of the border. It is not as widely known in Ulster as it was when I first heard it in the 1960s.

It came to Ulster from Scotland, where it is also found as *curnaptious*. *Car/cur* is an intensifying prefix, and *nap* is from *knap* in the sense to bite, snap, related to Dutch and Low German knappen, to break with a sharp crack. The ending *-tious* is used as in loan words from Latin.

The word is listed in the *Concise Ulster Dictionary*. W.H. Patterson has it in his 1880 glossary of Down and Antrim words; so has the *Ballymena Observer* of 1892, and Simmons's glossary of south Donegal words, compiled in 1890. Interestingly the EDD only has one citation from Scotland, and that from Galloway, which has had a long association with Ulster. I've heard *carnaptious* myself in Antrim, Down, Fermanagh and Donegal. The DSL has the word without the *car/cur* prefix from some of the northern counties of England close to the Scottish border. 'He's a (k)naptious little man.'

Oxford has four listings, two of them from Ulster. This is one, from W.G. Lyttle's *Readings by Robin*, published in 1878: 'He's a cross carnapshus wee brat, so he is.' A good word it is, no matter how you spell it.

✦ CARP

This word, in the sense to talk, to chatter incessantly, has been recorded in Scotland, in northern England and in Ulster. It is an old word; Chaucer employed it in *The Canterbury Tales*: 'In felawschip wel coude she laughe and carpe.' But *carp* was in English long before Chaucer's time. Oxford's first citation is from *c.* 1240, from *The Wohunge of Ure Lauerd*, edited by the Early English Texts Society: 'Carpe toward ihesu and seie þise wordes.' About 1300 the northern text *Cursor Mundi* has 'Als þai come narre þe castelle, to-geder carpand.' In Middle Scots, Barbour used the word in *Legends of the Saints* (*c.* 1380). Peter Levins, in *Manipulus Vocabulorum*, a dictionary of English and Latin words (1570, republished by the Camden Society in 1867), has 'To carpe, talke, *colloqui, confabulari.*' It would seem that both in English and Scots the word simply meant to speak, converse, talk, discourse; later the sense to chatter incessantly, thus annoying one's neighbours, was introduced; also the vituperative sense, to talk querulously, censoriously, or captiously; to find fault, cavil, the current sense, was introduced.

I was surprised to find that the DSL has no mention of the word being used in our time, but the late Nora O'Donnell, who lived at the foot of Errigal in Donegal, knew the word as having come from Scotland. She complained to me, 'I couldn't sleep on the bus with the young one sitting alongside me carping away on her mobile phone.' One of my Yorkshire correspondents said this about a football manager: 'He was better carping to the press than actually getting his team to play better,' and he explained that he was *not* using the word in its present vituperative sense, a sense, by the way, as old as Langland, who wrote in *Piers Plowman* (1377), 'Abasshed to blame yow or to greve, And carpen noght as they carpe now, Ne calle yow dumbe houndes.'

The word also meant to sing. 'It most probably denotes that modulated recitation, with which the minstrel was wont to accompany the tomes of his harp.' This is from *Lochmaben Harper* in *The Minstrelsy of the Scottish Border*, edited by Scott in 1803: 'Then aye he harped, and aye he carped Till a' the Lordlings footed the floor.'

At any rate, the word is from Middle English *carpe*, to speak, talk, according to Stratmann, from Old Norse *karp*, boasting. The Icelandic has *karpa*, to boast. But the vituperative sense appears to be derived from, or influenced by, Latin *carpere*, to pluck, figuratively to slander, calumniate.

✦ CASSON

This word, generally found in the plural in days gone by, was sent to me by Peadar Ó Casaide from Monaghan and by Joan Trimble, renowned musicologist from Fermanagh. It may be safely assumed that it is now obsolete everywhere. The EDD recorded it in Northumberland, Yorkshire, Derbyshire, Lincolnshire and Leicestershire, but makes no mention of Ireland. Variants given in Wright's great dictionary are *casing, casin, cazon, cazzan* and *cazzon*.

Casson was defined by my correspondents as dried cow dung used in the bad times for fuel. My father, who came from west Cork, told me that *bualtrach* (cow dung), when dried, was used for the same purpose. John Nicholson in his 1889 book *The Folk Speech of East Yorkshire* explained 'Sometimes used with clay intermixed, for fuel. The cassan was formed either by casting the soft dung against a wall, from which it could easily be detached when dry; or it was spread, two or three inches thick, on a piece of level ground, and cut into squares, oblongs, diamonds, or other shapes. When dry it was stacked or stowed away ready for use. A fire made with cassans and chalk stones burnt well and long, giving off great heat, little smoke, and a pleasant perfume.'

Worlidge in his *Dictionarium Rusticum* of 1681 has 'Casings, cow-dung dryed and used for fewel, as it is in many places where fewel is scarce'. Stephanus Skinner, a Lincolnshireman, in his etymological dictionary of English, written in Latin in 1671 and subsequently used without attribution, of course, by many lexicographers, had this to say: '*Stercus siccum jumentorum quod pauperes agri Lincolniensis ad usum focorum colligunt.*' [The dry dung of domestic beasts which the poor of the county of Lincolnshire gather to use on their hearths.] A less learned

Lincolnshireman sent this to the EDD: 'I was that dry for a sup o' gin, 'at if I seed ony o' th' top o' a casson, I should hev sup'd it.'

The EDD also gives the phrases *as dry as a casson*, very dry indeed; and *a primrose in a casson*, a proverb answering to 'a jewel of gold in a swine's snout'.

As to etymology, Oxford says that the word is a northern dialect word for *casing*, a word with the same meaning, but it does not say where either word came from. The EDD (and I think we should give its editor Joseph Wright credit here) asks us to compare Swedish dialect *ko-kase*, cow droppings, mentioned by Rietz in his *Svenskt Dialekt Lexikon* in 1867.

✦ CERTES

The only man I ever heard use the word *certes*, certainly, was my friend and colleague Augustine Martin of University College, Dublin. He used it in jest, as when he would say, 'Certes you'll have a drink, old cock,' or the like. We both were of the opinion that the word was obsolete for centuries, but recent research has shown that it has not long gone from common speech, and that in the form *My certies*! it still clings to life in places in Scotland and northern England. I see that Scott used 'By my certie,' in *The Antiquary* in 1816, and that the Etterick Shepherd, James Hogg, Scott's friend, has, 'My certy! he wasna lang in turning,' in one of his *Tales*, published in 1838.

'For, certes, these are people of the island,' wrote Shakespeare in *The Tempest*, Act III; and long before his time Chaucer had 'ffor certes lord ther is noon of vs alle, That she ne hath been a duchesse or a queene', in *The Knight's Tale* around 1386.

Certes is the Old French *certes*, 'a well-known Ballinamore word', I heard Gus Martin telling a Japanese professor one day. I think your man believed him.

✦ CHANGE

The word *change* had various dialectal uses in Ireland, Scotland and England, most if not all of them by now redundant. Take the noun meaning custom, the practice of buying from a certain shop. A person might have said, 'I always gave them my change,' I always bought from them.

There was also *change* meaning a shirt, or undergarments in general. The EDD gave a sad little example from the bad old days of the poorhouses; this is from Somerset: 'An old woman who had got her "leave out" from the Union came to ask in all seriousness if "you wid be so kind, mum, as to give me a change that I could put away in there, 'cause I would like to be a-buried respectable like.'"

In Scotland a small inn or an ale-house was called a *change*, sometimes a *change-house*; and a tavern keeper was called a *change keeper*. Burns in *Holy Fair* wrote, 'Now, butt an' ben, the change-house fills, / Wi' yill-caup commentators.' Galt, a later Ayrshire writer, in *The Provost* (1822) had 'Mrs Fenton kept a small change-house not of the best repute.' In *The Heart of Midlothian* Scott has a character 'puffing tobacco reek as if he were in a change-house'. Stevenson, too, in *Catriona* (1892) has a character who 'got some supper in a change house'.

There is also the verb which means to exchange, trade. 'Turn round and change a blow with me,' wrote James Hogg, the Etterick Shepherd from Selkirkshire, in a poem.

To change also meant to substitute, exchange, as fairies were believed to do with children, and not only in Ireland. The EDD reported from Lincolnshire, 'When a child, usually good-tempered, becomes suddenly irritable without any obvious reason, it is common to remark, "Bless the bairn, he must have been changed."' Hence, of course, changeling, a child supposed to have been changed by the fairies. A correspondent from England's North Country reported to the EDD's editor, Joseph Wright, 'The fairies have been represented as famous for stealing the most beautiful and witty children, and leaving in their places either prodigiously ugly and stupid, or mischievously inclined.'

Used of milk or meat, the verb meant to turn sour or to cause decomposition. It was commonly thought that thunder and lightning caused this.

Of fruit and grain, to change meant to pass out of the green state and assume its final colouring. It also meant to be a little intoxicated. And in the Co. Wexford of my long-lost youth *to have lost his or her change* was said of a person who was defective mentally.

From Anglo-French *chaunge*, or Old French *change*, from Late Latin *cambium*, exchange, from *cambire*, to change.

✦ CHAUNTER

Many years ago as I was sauntering down London's Regent Street I saw an old man selling broadside ballads. He had a satchel draped over his shoulder and across his chest he had a sign which read, 'Buy my songs.

They will make you smile.' I bought a few songs, one, I remember, a satire on Margaret Thatcher. I suggested to him that Regent Street mightn't be the best place in London to sell ballads, and that the Irish pubs might be a better bet, but he replied that he could sell more songs where he was standing in one morning than he would in pubs in a week. 'The Irish, mate,' he whispered, 'won't buy anything from a chaunter if it isn't about people dyin' of 'unger or being shot or somefing.' It was the first time I heard of these *chaunters*, broadside ballad sellers and singers.

The Slang Dictionary, published in London in 1874, has an account of the old chaunters, a word I can't find in the dictionaries. I assume the word is a variant of *chanters*. The book's anonymous author tells us that these ballad singers and sellers provided him with a rich vein of secret words. He gave us the following interesting and, he assures us, genuine letter from a chaunter to a gentleman who took an interest in both his songs and his welfare. He alludes in his letter to Thomas Drory and to Sarah Chesham, two notorious murderers. I have given the meaning of the cant words in parenthesis.

Dear Friend: Excuse the liberty, since I last saw you i have not earned a thick un [*sovereign*] we have such a Dowry of Parny [*a lot of rain*] that is completely stumped [*bankrupt*] Drory the Bossman's [*Drory the farmer's*] Patter [*trial*], therefore I am broke up and not having another friend but you i wish to know if you could lend me the price of a gross of Tops, Dies, or Croaks [*dying speeches*], which is seven shillings, of the above mentioned worthy and Sarah Chesham the Essex Burick [*woman*] for the poisoning job, they are both to be topped [*hanged*] at Springfield Sturaban [*prison*] on Tuesday next. I hope you will oblige me if you can, for it will be the means of putting a James [*sovereign*] in my Clye [*pocket*]. I will call at your Curser [*house*] on Sunday Evening, for I want a Speel on the Drum [*a spin on the coach—that is, to be off to the country*]. Hoping you and the Family are All Square [*all right*]. I remain your obedient servant . . .

I think I may have spoken to the very last of London's chaunters that day in Regent Street.

✦ CHEVAUX DE FRISE

An interesting compound this in its own right, but what settled it forever in my mind was it application to a human face by an old Wexfordman I met in a pub many years ago. He was referring to a well-known television personality of the time; he couldn't think of his name, but called him the man with 'the *shiver de freeze* face', which he explained to me as craggy and bony. Not long afterwards my mother told me that she had heard the expression near Campile, in the south-east of the county, where she taught school.

Cheval de frise, plural *chevaux*, is glossed by Oxford as a defensive appliance of war, employed chiefly to check cavalry charges and stop breaches. A citation from 1708 explains their use: 'Chevaux de Frise are large Joists, or pieces of Timber, Ten or Twelve Foot in length, with Six Sides into which are driven a great Number of wooden Pins aboue Six Foot long, crossing one another, and having their Ends armed with Iron-Points.'

The compound means, literally, 'horse of Friesland', because it was first employed by the Frieslanders in their struggles for freedom during the latter half of the seventeenth century; cf. the Dutch name *Vriesse ruyters* (Frisian horsemen). In the seventeenth century *Horse de Freeze* occurs in English accounts.

The Frisians had no cavalry in the seventeenth century, but this idea was their brainchild to upset the French horse. It was so called in scorn by the French, but they learned not to laugh at the Friesland horse fairly quickly when their own cavalry were cut to pieces by the appliance.

I enquired recently of my friends and helpers, the schoolmasters, if the term was still used in south Wexford. Alas, no. Gone forever, like many's the old word.

The question remains: how did the term reach Wexford in the first place? Through the smuggling trade with the Lowlands in days gone by, possibly. You may remember P.J. McCall's rollicking song: 'Dunmore we quitted / Michaelmas gone by, / Cowhides and wool and live cargo; / Twenty young wild geese / Ready fledged to fly, / Sailing for the Lowlands low . . . / Sean Paor's the skipper / From the church of Crook, / Piery keeps log for his father, / Crew all from Bannow, Fethard and the Hook, / Sailing for the Lowlands low . . . / Pray holy Brendan, Turk nor Algerine, / Dutchman nor Saxon may sink us / We'll bring Genever, / Sack and Rheinish wine / Safely from the Lowlands low . . .'

Yes, I think they brought *chevaux de frise* as well, no matter how they spelled it.

✦ CLABBER

'I'm livin' in Drumlister, / An' I'm getting very oul' / I have to wear an Indian bag / To save me from the coul' / The diel a man in this townlan' / Wos clainer raired nor me, / But I'm livin' in Drumlister / In clabber to the knee.'

Rev. William Forbes Marshall's poem is a wistful, funny piece about the vicissitudes of love and marriage. He was a Tyroneman who died in 1959 having spent a long life collecting the words and phrases of his native dialect. He would have known that *clabber* is from the Irish or Scottish Gaelic *clábar*, mud, muck, and that the word was once common all over the country. P.L. Henry has the word from a north Roscommon dialect; I've heard the word used recently in south Tipperary. A north Co. Dublin man once complained to me about his son: 'It's hard to keep the house clean and the way he walks in with his boots all clauber.' Séamas Ó Saothraí, scholar and bibliophile from Co. Westmeath, who died in his eighties two years ago, told me that in his native place the word for muck was *tlauber*. Eamon Mac an Fhailigh recorded the word in the same county: 'Mud, mire-tlauber'.

The word is still used in Counties Wexford and Carlow, but it appears to be in decline everywhere, like so many good dialect words. I'm told that that's the case even in rural Ulster, where once it was known and used everywhere. The *Ballymena Observer* of 1892 has the compound *road-clabber*, as has Simmons in his glossary from south Donegal, compiled around the same time; while W.H. Patterson in his glossary of Antrim and Down words (1880) has 'They clodded clabber at me.' Derryman Seamus Heaney used it in his poem *Death of a Naturalist*: 'Or in the sucking clabber I would splash / Delightedly and dam the flowing drain.'

The word was also found in Scotland. It is used in some places in Galloway to this day.

As far as I know it has appeared in England only in the north, in Cumbria.

It deserved its popularity. I recently asked my grandson James, aged seven, to remove the clabber from his shoes after we had explored the nearby woods, so as not to risk his mother's annoyance when he left a trail of it all over the house, and he volunteered that he thought clabber a good word. 'I love the squelchy sound of it,' he said. So do I, James, so do I. And I hate to hear that it is being abandoned.

✦ CLAP

I once heard this rather unusual word from a Co. Wicklow sheep-farmer. Let me explain first of all that all dogs seem to hate me; the minute one sees me it generally bares its teeth and shows that I am not welcome in its presence. I am told that they sense fear in me, and that this sets them against me. At any rate, John Roberts, a kindly man who gave me grazing for a hunter in summer on his upland farm, had a dog who, from the minute he laid eyes on me, decided that I was public enemy number one. 'Why don't you try clapping him, instead of growling back at him!' said John. 'Clap him on the head and you'll convince him that you're his pal.'

My son, who spoke Wicklow English better than I did, told me that what Mr Roberts meant by to clap was to pat, stroke, fondle, something I was not prepared to do.

I have never come across this word anywhere else in Ireland, but it is native to Scotland, the northern shires of England, and Lincolnshire, where on emerging from the safety of my car I was growled at by an ancient terrier, an animal I was also told to clap by its amused owner. 'Clap her and she'll not bite,' he said. The Scots scholar Jamieson, who did more than most to encourage the use of Scots in the post-Burns era, has this in his *Popular Ballads* of 1806, a book many times reprinted: 'He neither kist her when he cam, Nor clappit her when he gaed.' The EDD has the word from a man who found himself in the same predicament as I was in Lincolnshire, but it seems that he was a bit braver than me. He complained to a farmer, 'That dog o' yours weeant let ma clap him.'

Hence we find the verbal noun *clapping*, patting, caressing. The word was in Scots in 1600, when Montgomerie's *Sonnets* were edited and published by Cranstoun: 'A loving dog wes of his maister fane . . . His courteous maister clappit him again.'

The word is of Norse origin. See the Danish *klappe*, the Swedish *klappa*, to pat, caress, and the Old Norse *klappe*, to pat, stroke gently.

✦ CLUNTER

Ever since the late Liam de Paor brought this word to my notice I liked it, because of its sound. We both thought of it as onomatopoeic, and when we read the EDD's paragraph on it we were surprised to find that we were probably wrong. It gives as its definition 'To make a noise with the feet in walking; to tread heavily.' Liam had the word from Co. Louth; Peadar Ó Casaide sent me the word from Monaghan. The word is also found in England's northern shires, Cumbria, Northumberland, Westmoreland, Yorkshire and Lancashire, and as far south as Derbyshire, where they also have *clunterer* for a heavy-footed person, and *clunterers* for wooden-soled shoes or clogs.

There is a noun *clunter* meaning noise, clatter; confusion. The EDD has this from Derbyshire: 'I'll make a clunter agen the window wi some gravel.' I wonder what he was up to. A Lancashire novel, *David Grieve* (1892) by a gentleman named Ward, supplied the EDD's editor, Joseph Wright, with the word. A character in the story, obviously a little the worse for wear, related that he gave his foot 'a bit of a clunter again a stone'.

As I say, I am reluctant to abandon the notion that this good word is onomatopoeic, but at the same time we must respect the opinion of a lexicographer as eminent as Jan Koolman, who wrote a Frisian dictionary in 1879, and insisted that it was from the East Frisian *kluntern*, to walk clumsily and noisily. Perhaps *kluntern* itself is onomatopoeic. It sounds like it at any rate.

✦ COB

Many years ago in my home town a school child was the victim of shocking bullying, and ended up in hospital. The police were called and in the ensuing court case the perpetrators got away with a severe talking-to from the beak; a firm purpose of amendment and an apology was enough to allow the two thugs, boys of fourteen, I might add, to walk free. They came from good families, you see, and that was enough to keep them out of the hell-holes of Letterfrack or Artane.

A man who was a champion welterweight boxer in his time was discussing the case with a friend as I passed by, and I heard him remark that if he had his way there would be no need for a court case at all; what he would like to see happening was that the head of the school the boys attended, on being told of the event, would order the two thugs to let down their britches and they would then have their backsides cobbed until they couldn't walk.

I have wondered since is Co. Wexford the only place in Ireland where this verb was used? The EDD has it from there away back in 1867, in

Patrick Kennedy's *The Banks of the Boro*: 'How do they cob an offender? They draw the trousers very tight around the thick part of the thigh, and then slap the swelled muscles with all their force.'

The verb was common in parts of Scotland, in northern and central England, in the Isle of Wight, Kent and Cornwall. In a Cornish court a woman was fined and bound to the peace for cobbing her husband over the head with a broom. Scott, in *Waverley*, has 'The porter shall have thee to his lodge, and cob thee with thine own wooden sword.'

In Roxburghshire, according to an EDD correspondent, *cobbing* was 'a particular mode practised among shepherds. At clipping time . . . certain regulations are made, upon the breach of any one of which the offender is to be cobbed. He is laid on his belly on the ground, and one is appointed to beat him on the backside while he repeats a certain rhyme; at the end of which the culprit is released, after he has whistled.'

Whistled? Yes, indeed. In other parts of England *cobbing* meant to pull the hair or ears of a fellow-schoolboy, and getting the unfortunate victim to whistle while he was being tormented was part of the 'fun'. This was recorded in Shropshire: 'The penalty consists of having the hair pulled whilst the offender whistles, counts ten and touches wood.'

Cob is from Middle English. The *Destruction of Troy* from *c.* 1400 has 'Thre thousand full þro þrang into batell . . . And cobbyt full kantly.'

✦ COISCÉIM CHOILIGH—COCK'S STRIDE

We use both of these terms, the first where Irish is still spoken or where it has recently lost the battle with English; its English equivalent is common in many rural areas especially in Munster, and Dinneen tells that 'a cock's step is the increase of the day's length on New Year's Day'. A recent enquiry revealed that the expression is almost obsolete everywhere. It doesn't take long for dialect words to die.

Oxford seems to have got rid of the expression in its new edition, but Sir James Murray has it in his 1893 edition of the great dictionary: 'the length of the step of a cock, as the measure of a very short distance or space'.

I recently asked some Wicklow, Wexford and Waterford schoolchildren what the above expressions meant to them, and to my disbelief not one of them ever heard of them. There is no more to be said, except that they have been deprived of a charming conceit, centuries old in both our languages.

I love Nicholas Breton's mention of it in his 1626 *Fantasticks*:

It is now February and the Sun has gotten up a cocke-stride of his climbing, the vallies now are painted white, and the brooks are full of water. The frog goes to seek out the paddocke, the gardiner falls to sorting out his seeds, and the husbandman falls afresh to scowring of his ploughshare. The taverns and the inns seldome lack guests, and the ostler knows how to gain by his hay; the hunting horse is at the heels of the hound, while the ambling nagge carrieth the physitian and his footcloth; the blood of youth begins to spring and the honour of Art is gotten by exercise. The trees a little begin to bud and the sap begins to rise up out of the root; physick now hath work among weake bodies and the apothecaries' drugs are very gainfull; there is hope for a better time not farre off . . .

This charming writer also uses another country expression that deserves to live. *Cock-shut* is one of his words for twilight, the roosting time of fowls. It is still in use in East Anglia. Shakespeare used it too; Nicholas Breton must have known him. In *Richard III*, Act III, Shakespeare has 'Thomas the Earl of Surrey and himself / Much about cock-shut time . . . Went through the army.'

Heaven be praised, another of Nicholas Breton's expressive words still survives in Thomas Hardy's country and in Somerset and Devon. It is *cock-light*, daybreak. But it also means twilight. As one Devon farmer told the EDD, 'so called as being a very suitable time for shooting woodcocks, so plentiful on the moors'.

Nicholas Breton is featured in many anthologies. His work is still worth reading, soothing and gentle and wise.

✦ COLLYWESTON

This is found in Lancashire, Cheshire, Staffordshire, Northamptonshire, Lincolnshire, Warwickshire and Shropshire among them, and in Wexford as well as west of the Shannon.

First of all it means 'nonsense'. Wexfordman Patrick Kennedy has it in *The Banks of the Boro*, written in 1867: ' "Oh, that's all collywest," says I. "What is the good of being an ordained clergyman, if you have not the power of doing something for an unlucky disciple like myself?"' *Notes and Queries*, Sixth Series II, 1880, recorded it in the west of Ireland; it doesn't say where: 'Don't be talking collywest.'

As an adverb it means in an opposite direction. It is also used as an adjective meaning contrary, contradictory. 'When a man is altogether unsuccessful in his schemes, he says that everything goes colly-west with him,' wrote a Lancashire man, John Davies, in *The Races of Lancashire, as indicated by the local names and the dialect of the county*, published in the *Transactions of the Philological Society* in 1856. From Chester this landed on the desk of the editor of the EDD in a crowded little room in Oxford: 'Am I right for such and such a place?' 'Nao, it's collyweston.'

This strange word may also mean out of square; askew, awry; also as an adjective, crooked, not straight or level. *Notes and Queries*, Series 6, II, 1880, has, from Hertfordshire, 'A bricklayer or carpenter having planned his work "out of the square" was said to have it all collywest. To a comrade whose dress was untidy the remark would be, "You're all collywest today."

Where did the word originate? Well, the oldest citation in the Oxford dictionary is from W. Harrison's *Description of England* (1587): 'The Morisco gowns, the Barbarian sleeves, the mandilion worne to Collie weston ward, and the short French breches, make such a comelie vesture.' So it's not very old.

Its origin lies in the village of Collyweston in Northamptonshire, once famous for a slate used in roofing. Every student of architecture with an eye for colour and form should admire those mellow, lichened roofs of Collywestons seen far from Northamptonshire; the lovely roof of Nuffield College, Oxford, for example, is of Collyweston stone slates.

A distinguished English architect told me that the *collywests* cited above came from the fact that Collyweston, being a poor place in the old days, and surviving on its slate quarries, sold their best slates, and retained the rest for roofing their own *bothán*s of houses with slates of various sizes, which gave them a quaint, anything but symmetrical appearance.

✦ COLT

Just in case you don't know what a colt is, let me quote Oxford for you: 'The young of the horse, or of animals of the horse kind. In Scripture applied also to the young of the camel. The sense "young ass" is now perhaps only dialectal. While the young of the horse is still with the dam it is usually called a *foal*; afterwards the young horse is a *colt* to the age of 4, or in the case of a thoroughbred, 5 years, while the young mare is a *filly*.'

But *colt* also has various dialectal uses in Scotland, Ireland and England. Let's take compounds first. *Colt's ale* or *colt's beer* is, or was, an allowance of ale made to the blacksmith when a young horse is first shod. John Lynch, the Kilcoole, Co. Wicklow, farrier, remembered the term being used when he was an apprentice; also used in Scotland, in Northern England, and in England's south-west, especially in Somerset and Devon, where a farmer was quoted in a provincial Agricultural Report of 1884: 'I could not bring the colt's ale with me, but I will send it.'

Colt's ale was also a fine or 'footing' paid by a young man entering on new employment to those already in it. He usually paid the fine in money, not ale, but the money was spent on drink afterwards. In East Anglia this fine was called *shoeing the colt*. A correspondent told the EDD that 'this is said of a new man engaged in the harvest field. He is caught and the sole of his shoes is tapped with a stone. He is then expected to treat his mates.'

In Devon and in south Wexford, a *colt's tail* is what is called in other places *a mare's tail*, a cloud with bushy appearance like a ragged fringe, which portends rain.

Colt, in Scots as *cowt*, is still used in both Scotland and Ulster as a term of contempt, used of a man. 'Frae my sight, ye filthy ragged cowt,' bellowed Black the Lanarkshire novelist in *The Falls of Clyde* in 1806, a book often quoted in the EDD. The CUD has recorded *cowt*.

A colt, used of a woman, implied skittishness in parts of Ulster. In Somerset it implied lewdness if applied to females. Hence *colting*, romping, hoydenish, loose, apt to play the hobby-horse, as they say in that lovely, lush part of England.

When a Wexford young one speaks of a young fellow as a bit *coltish*, she means that he is a little too interested in *the tally-ho*, as they call sex in the Model County.

✦ CORDOVAN, CORDWAIN

Once upon a time, and a long time ago it was, I was given a present of a wallet for my birthday. It was, I remember being told, a cordovan wallet, and to be sure not to lose it. I have it to this day. It is related to another, older word for soft leather, *cordwain*, deemed by Oxford to be archaic.

Cordovan/Cordwain is often referred to nowadays as *Morocco leather*. It is named from Cordova, a town in Spain which became famous for the quality of its leather goods in the Middle Ages. The English word may have entered the language directly from Spanish *cordován* (now *cordobán*), or *cordováno*, of Cordova; or it may have come through Old French *cordouan*. The leather used in the Spanish town was goat skin.

Cordwain was favoured by many of the old writers, the great Chaucer among them. In the *Canterbury Tales, Sire Thopas*, he has 'His here, his berde, was like safroun, / That to his girdle raught adoun, / His shoon of cordewane.' John Fletcher, the Jacobite playwright, in *The Faithfull Shepheardesse* opted for the newer word: '[He] Puts on his lusty green, with gaudy hook, / And hanging scrip of finest cordevan.' John referred to the word again in *The Loyal Subject* written in 1618: 'You musk-cat, Cordevan-skin!' he thundered. Two hundred years later, in 1828 Walter Scott in *The Fair Maid of Perth* mentions a man of fashion whose 'walking boots were of cordovan leather'. And the Great Snob himself, Thackeray, in *Vanity Fair*, introduced us to a lady who 'removed the cordovan leather from the grand piano'. I mean, what else would one cover the grand joanna with!

Cordovan served other purposes as well. Boswell was a visitor at a clinic off London's Strand which was run by a chap named Ainsworth. Mr Ainsworth had a profitable sideline: he sold French letters 'of the softest, thinnest cordovan' to his clients. If Mr Boswell used them, they didn't seem to work, as he confides in his London Journal. Their use would have entailed another visit to Mr Ainsworth in his capacity as barber surgeon to the nobility.

✦ CORE & COMMON

The word *core* has been sent to me by many correspondents. All of them complained about the word, heard in childhood, being no longer used by the younger generation.

The original Irish is *comhar*, which means, according to Dinneen, co-operation, especially in tillage, mutually borrowed labour; alliance, reciprocity. Dr Patrick Henchy had this in a paper he gave to the *North Munster Antiquarian Journal*: 'They were working in comhar, helping each other in turn.' A Kerry correspondent to the Irish Folklore Commission back in the 1930s wrote, 'We always returned the core.'

P.W. Joyce in his seminal study *English As We Speak it in Ireland* has this: 'I send a man on core for a day to my neighbour; when next I want a man he will send me one for a day in return. So with horses. Two one-horse farmers who work their horses in pairs, borrowing alternately, are said to be *in core*. Very common in Munster.'

It was common as well in many Irish counties. A Wexford horse breeder I know described a neighbouring farmer as 'a man who wouldn't *core* very much with anybody'. A Laoisman, D. Ó Concubhair, writing in the learned journal *Éigse* in the 1940s, told his readers that 'all the Dunmore farmers *coor*'. He added, 'Where were you today?' 'I was *cooring*.' This verbal noun was also recorded in Kilkenny, Kildare, Wexford, Limerick and Clare. The Medieval Irish was *comar*, defined in the Royal Irish Academy's *Dictionary of the Irish Language* as 'co-tillage, ploughing partnership'.

And if a man helped his neighbour out he would not be in his common. *I'm in your common*, meaning I am obliged to you, was once a common expression from Donegal and Fermanagh to Wexford. *It was ill your common* was recorded by Michael Traynor in *The English Dialect of Donegal* in the mid-1950s. It meant 'it was ungrateful of you'. Another Ulsterman, John Boyce in *Mary Lee, or The Yank in Ireland*, wrote, 'We're obliged to ye . . . for sendin' us over what ye did in our hour of need, and ill it'd be our common to forget it.' And Seumus MacManus in *Bold Blades of Donegal* has 'It's ill our comin to say a hard word again' the sae.'

The origin of *common/comin* is the Irish *comaoin*, compliment, recompense. Compare the Irish phrase *b'olc an chomaoin ort é*—it would be a poor return to you [for your kindness].

Are these old words and phrases still used in Donegal? I very much doubt it.

✦ COURANT

I once heard this word in an unlikely place. In a tutorial I was giving, a young man from Donegal rambled in, twenty minutes late as usual, and I told him politely to saddle his ass and get out. When the class had finished I went back to my office to find him at my door. He apologised for his behaviour and told me that he deserved the *courant* I gave him.

Later I found the word in Michael Traynor's *The English Dialect of Donegal*: 'Courant: A hasty retreat, a quick send off. Of people going to a house where there are wicked dogs, one would say, "they are apt to get a merry courant."'

Seumus MacManus the Donegal novelist and short-story writer used the word a few times, and I heard it as *cúránt* in the Irish of Proinsias Ó Maonaigh of Gaoth Dobhair, teacher and fiddle master, and of a lovely lady who lived at the foot of Errigal mountain, Nora Patrick O'Donnell.

The word is also found in Scotland and in some English dialects from the North Country south to the Isle of Wight, Devon and Cornwall, where it has a variety of meanings including the Donegal one. It also means 1. A lively dance, and figuratively, a hasty walk, a hasty journey. 2. A revel, carouse, a spree; a social gathering, merry-making. 3. A great fuss about anything; a telling off, a scolding. I suppose my Donegal student had this in mind. It was what my friends Nora Patrick and Proinsias, better known as Francie Mooney, meant by the word at any rate. The EDD has this from Shropshire: 'A perty courant 'er's made of it.'

The word comes from the French *courante*, 'sort de danse', according to Littré's dictionary. The word came into Italian as *corranta*, according to John Florio's *Queen Anna's New World of Words, or Dictionarie of the Italian and English Tongues* of 1611.

You'll be glad to hear that my student learned his lesson, and graduated with a First.

✦ COWL

In a Vienna coffee house my companion, a Co. Louth-born engineer, long retired, watched the ultra-efficient municipal workers getting ready for the snow that was forecast. They parked their vehicles at the kerbside, and locked up their gear in a portable hut, ready to cowl away the snow, of which there was no sign yet in the clear, blue sky. *Cowl* was my friend's word, one which meant to rake together, to gather into a heap. 'We'd use it of muck, or leaves, or dung,' he said, 'but I'm told it is as dead as doornails now. A lot of the old words are dying, and more's the pity.' It was he who told me to put together a collection of old, dead or dying words which took my fancy.

It snowed in Vienna overnight, as was forecast, and the beautiful city was turned into a fairyland. The workers had cowled away the snow from the streets before dawn. I looked up the verb *cowl*, and found not a trace of it in Oxford. But there it was in Joe Wright's dialect dictionary, though no mention was made of its appearance in Ireland. It was in common use in northern England. An unnamed poet 'cowled auld legends into rhymes', in Westmoreland. A man was 'cowled' into an enterprise in Yorkshire. Farmyard dung was cowled into heaps everywhere. The *cowling* was done with a *cowler*, an iron rake. This word was also applied to a rake used to draw cinders from boilers in Northumberland and Yorkshire.

I have enquired of some Co. Louth teachers about *cowl*. Ne'er a sign of it, I'm sorry to say. Another good word gone. It's from French *cueillir*, to gather, reap, cull, according to Randle Cotgrave's *A Dictionarie of the French and English Tongues* of 1611.

✦ CRAPPIN

This word was known only in Scotland and in the north of Ireland, where it was also written *crapen*. It was a farmyard word, and it meant the stomach or crop of a bird; and I'm sorry to say that in Antrim and Down, where W.H. Patterson recorded it in 1880, it is on its last legs, if not completely obsolete. It was also figuratively used of people.

'The road was gayan lang, and Jock's crappin began to craw,' wrote Hogg the Selkirk poet and storyteller in *The Perils of Man* in 1822. 'So theatre nymph in borough town . . . Disclose the beauties o' her crappin,' sang another Scots poet, Nicholson, a Gallowayman, in 1814.

It is the same word as *crop*, the stomach, another word no longer in common use, and ultimately from Old English *cropp*, the stomach of a bird.

✦ CRASSUS

Many years ago I was bought a drink in the Dáil bar by Deputy John Wilson, a gentleman and a classical scholar who once taught in UCD, and whose daughter I once had the pleasure of teaching there. I remember him referring to a passing deputy as a *crassus*, which could be defined as an avaricious, unscrupulous scoundrel, and as it happened, time proved his assessment right. The other day I saw the word *crassus* in print in an article by an American journalist to describe a fallen real estate mogul, and noted the initial lower case *c*.

The gentleman who gave us this very useful word was the old Roman Marcus Licinius Crassus, who lived between, approximately, 115 and 50 BC. He, like the American gentleman, was a real estate agent, and went on to become an incompetent army general and a crooked politician. Crassus should have stayed in the real estate business because he was good at it: his means of getting to the pinnacle of his profession were, however, dubious in the extreme, if ingenious.

To boost business he formed his very own fire brigade. 'Always at the service of the people' was his motto, but his firemen were under orders not to appear at the scene of a fire until the house was consumed by flame, thus enabling your man to buy cheap and make an enormous profit. He kept great with the politicians, and they looked the other way when Crassus bought, for a nominal sum, property confiscated by Sulla. Not content, he went into the banking and the slavery business, and it was he who supported the slave revolt of Spartacus in 71 BC. He was now the richest man in Rome, and, of course, courted by the politicians.

He was elected consul with Pompey and afterwards the pair joined Caesar to form the First Triumvirate. Always a schemer, he encouraged the Cataline conspiracy. Then, alas for him, his ambition got the better of him. He made himself leader of a military expedition against the Parthians in Syria, and in one of the most inept campaigns in history his forces were wiped out by the Parthian archers in the battle of Carrhae. He was captured, and one account says that he was executed by having a bowl of molten silver poured down his throat.

I have always remembered John Wilson's description of his fellow politician as a crassus, but to give that devil his due, although he was indeed notoriously avaricious, and a thorough-going scoundrel, he wasn't even close to being in the same league as the old Roman fire-brigade chief.

✦ CRATCH

In my younger days I was often visited by single families of Travellers and made friends with most of them. I was particularly great with Annie Wall and her family when I lived in Co. Wicklow, and as she spoke Sheldru or Gammon, as she referred to it, to her daughter, I wrote down many words that had eluded even my friend Paddy Greene, or Pádraig Mac Gréine, the Ballinalee schoolmaster who published a seminal collection of Gammon and an account of Travellers' lives in 1935; he died only a few years ago aged 106.

Anyway, Annie Wall brought a small child, her granddaughter, with her one day. I brought them in for tay and cake as it was Christmas time, and the child, who was perhaps four or five, gave me a holy picture in leaflet form on Annie's instruction, and told me that she would like to go to school to learn how to read and write and to find out more about the Baby Jesus. 'Tell the nice man what you know about Him,' prompted a proud Annie. 'When he was born his mother put Him in a *cratch*, and the donkey kep Him warm with his breath,' said the child. Needless to say, I asked Annie what she meant by *cratch*, and I was told that it was a manger.

I phoned Master Green that evening, and sure enough he knew the word from a Kildare Traveller, to whom it meant a rack to hold hay in a stable, as well as being specifically applied to the stable at Bethlehem. It was not Sheldru, he said, but English dialectal. 'The old *tincéirí* brought the word here; they don't call themselves Travellers without reason,' he said. Master Green also explained the origin of the children's game *cat's cradle* to me. It is clearly a corruption of *cratch cradle*. You'll find a description of the game in the EDD. The same source will tell you that *cratch* in some English dialects means the tailboard of a cart or wagon, particularly one such as the West Cork dung cart, the *butt*. It is also applied to various wooden frames used in the household, in which provisions are stored.

Wyclif has the compound in his *Luke*, ii, 7, 1388: 'And sche bare hir first borun sonne and wlappide hym in clothis, and leide hym in a cratche.' Wyclif's and young Mary Wall's word comes from the Old French *creche*.

✦ CRIB & COG

In those far-off days when I was young certain boys and girls were known to *cog* in an examination out of necessity. I'm told that the word *crib* is now fashionable in many schools. This is an importation from Britain. *Cog* is old. This verb first appears in 1532, as 'Ruffians' terms' of dice-play; whence it passed into general use in various transferred senses. As in other cant terms, the origin has not been preserved; but the persistent notion is that of dishonest or fraudulent play, cheating.

Crib also belongs to the ruffians of England. It means to pilfer, purloin, steal; to appropriate furtively a small part of anything. It was undoubtedly originally thieves' slang, connected with the noun which means something 'cribbed' or taken without permission.

In the 1748 *Dyche Dictionary*, we first find 'Crib, to withhold, keep back, pinch, or thieve a part out of money given to lay out for necessaries'. The verb is also found in 1772 in Foote's *Nabob*: 'A brace of birds and a hare, that I cribbed this morning out of a basket of game'. The great William Cobbett has the verb in his 1825 classic *Rural Rides*: 'Bits of ground cribbed . . . at different times from the forest'. One of my favourite poets of the nineteenth century, the neglected William Praed, in his 1839 collection has 'Both of old were known to crib, And both were very apt to fib!'

It is thought that our meaning evolved from the name of a light basket or *crib*, often tightly woven, that thieves carried their stolen goods in. This light crib was a deliberate choice; the same type of basket was used by thousands of women shoppers, fishwives and traders of all kinds, and it was ideal to help confuse the servants of the law. In 1935 a Wexford court heard that 'a crib' was used by a woman in which she had, it was claimed, goods stolen from a shop, to wit, a loaf of bread and a pound of butter, according to the evidence of the arresting Garda Stúcána, as our guardians of the peace are irreverently known in parts of west Waterford. 'Six months, madam,' cribbed, cabined and confined in the Joy.

✦ CUDDY

The fish cod *Gadus morrhua*, which inhabits the North Atlantic and its connected seas, is a word whose etymology has been troubling historical linguists for many years. Origin uncertain, Oxford says. No connection with the modern zoological *Gadus* is tenable, it says. One suggestion, rightly discarded by the great dictionary, is that it is the same word as *cod*, a bag, as if 'bag-fish', from its appearance. Another discarded notion is that it is from the obsolete Flemish *kodde*, a club, cudgel, a theory of the linguist Wedgewood, comparing the analogy of Italian *mazzo*, beetle, club, mace; and also a cod-fish, according to John Florio, the Tudor lexicographer. The trouble with this theory is that the Flemings never called the fish *kodde* in the first place. Collins does not even guess as to the word's origin, and Webster says 'Middle English', and leaves it at that.

Oxford says that the word *cod* has no known relatives outside English. I would dispute that.

The American scholar William Sayers of Cornell University Library, Ithaca, New York, says in *Some Fishy Etymologies*, an article he published in the Danish journal *Nowele* in 2002, that cod is a back-formation from the north of England dialect word *cuddy*, a borrowing from the Scots Gaelic *cudainn*, the coalfish, *Merlangus* or *Pollachius carbonarius*, or *Gadus virens*, a species of cod. It got its name from the dark pigment which tinges its skin and soils the fingers like moist coal. It too is found in the Northern Seas. It has many local names, *black cod* among them. W.H. Patterson in his Antrim and Down glossary of the 1880s gives *cudden*; and where Scottish Gaelic is spoken, the young coalfish is called *cudaig* or *cudainn*.

Novelist Beryl Bainbridge told me of eating *cuddy and chips* in her youth in Lancashire but she said the cuddy was a haddock. This is a smaller species of cod. The Irish for haddock is *cadóg*.

Alexander Macbain the Scottish lexicographer suggested over a hundred years ago that the ultimate origin of cod might well be Gaelic. Nobody listened to him. Perhaps the great dictionaries, still groping in the dark about the word's origin, might consider doing so now.

✦ CUMMER

This good Scots word, also spelled *comer* and found in the form *kimmer*, has not, as far as I know, ever travelled outside Scotland. According to the EDD the word has not been recorded in England, and the *Concise Ulster Dictionary* makes no mention of it. *Cummer/kimmer* means a godmother. It also means a woman's female companion or intimate. It was often used contemptuously as well as in familiar address. 'But yet, despite the kittle kimmer', wrote Robert Burns in his *Epistle to J. Lapraik* in 1785. [*Kittle* here may mean 'kitten,' used contemptuously of human beings, according to the DSL.]

Interesting as these nouns are, the derived compounds are even more so. *Cummer-fealls* were an entertainment given on the recovery of a mother from having a baby. *Cummer-skolls* was an entertainment given to visitors on the occasion of a baby's birth. [Perhaps, Oxford conjectures, 'introduced through the visit of James VI to Denmark in 1589'.] Glossed by the DSL as 'a drink taken as evidence of the drinker's good wishes for the welfare of another person or other persons; a toast; also, the cup or glass from which the health is drunk'. *Skolls* is from Old Norse *skál*.

There was also the adjective *cummerlyke*, a woman; especially a young woman. 'Something sweet of Atholl cummers', wrote Hogg, Scott's protégé, in a poem; he had an eye for cummers of this kind, by all accounts. Nicholson, a Galloway writer of the mid-nineteenth century, had in one of his historic tales: 'This cummer, for all so young and rosie as she looks, has nae touch of natural flesh and blood.'

Cummer also meant a midwife. Jamieson the Scottish lexicographer of the early nineteenth century quoted a poet named Train: 'No kindly kimmer nigh there was / To mitigate her pain, / Nor ought to hap the bonie babe / Frae either wind or rain.'

And then there was *cummer* meaning a witch or hag. 'There's a fresh and full-grown hemlock, Annie Winnie—mony a cummer langsyne wad hae sought na better horse to flee over hill and how,' wrote Scott in *The Bride of Lammermoor* in 1819.

You might expect a verb *cummer/kimmer* and there was one: to meet for crack or gossip. 'Where bogles bide an' frightful worricows / That nightly kimmer in the lanely hows,' wrote the dialect poet Andrew Scott in 1808.

These words are from Old French *commère*, from Late Latin *commater*, from *com-*, together with + *mater* mother.

✦ CUPBOARD LOVE

I must have lived a very sheltered life, but when the term was mentioned to me by a friend in Dungarvan, Co. Waterford, where I reside for half the year, I thought she might have been referring to the sort of shenanigans attributed to that German tennis star who won Wimbledon at eighteen and who in later life had achieved notoriety as a latchico who indulged in sex with a waitress in a broom cupboard of a restaurant I certainly couldn't afford. I refer to Herr Boris Becker. My Dungarvan friend looked at me with pity in her eyes. 'Do you mean to tell me', she said, 'that you don't know what *cupboard love* really means?' So she kindly told me, alluding to a mutual acquaintance who was also partaking of dinner at the other end of the restaurant where we were.

He was sitting with his lady friend, his fourth in as many years, I was informed, and my companion predicted that it was she who would pay the bill, as usual. Oh, he would go through the motions of attempting to pay, but as my friend put it, he was a good man at putting his hand in his pocket, and leaving it there. Eventually, she would get fed up with him, realising that his was only *cupboard love*, a term afterwards explained by my friends at Oxford as love insincerely expressed or displayed for the sake of what one can get out of it.

Oxford refers us to *Poor Robin's Almanack* of 1757: 'A cupboard love is seldom true, / A love sincere is found in few; / But 'tis time in folks to marry, / When women woo, lest things miscarry.' There is an earlier reference in the *Roxburge Ballads* (1665): a dalliance was described as 'all for the love of cupboard', for a free meal, in other words.

And yes, our man went through the motions, as predicted, and she paid up.

◆ **CURTILAGE**

John Quinn, a distinguished Irish broadcaster now retired, sent me an unusual word which he heard a Co. Meath farmer use on the wireless. He referred to his land as his *curtilage*.

I had thought the word dead as doornails, and it probably is close to it. Only once before have I heard it, in Kilmore Quay, Co. Wexford, from Jack Devereux, an old fisherman. Jack was a man who read widely, and I assumed, probably wrongly in the light of the Meathman's use of the word, that he had picked up the word from some book or other. I see that *curtilage* is also widely used in the West Country of England, and it probably came to Ireland with the Anglo-Normans. Let me give you Oxford's definition: 'A small court, yard, garth, or piece of ground attached to a dwelling-house, and forming one enclosure with it, or so regarded by the law; the area attached to and containing a dwelling-house and its out-buildings. Now mostly a legal or formal term, but in popular use in the south-west, where it is pronounced, and often written, *courtledge*.'

The word is from Anglo French *curtilage*, from Old French *cortillage* or *courtillage*. We find the word in medieval Latin as *cortilagium* and *curtilagium*, from *cortil*, *courtil*, little court or yard. The suffix in the Anglo-French word is the Romanic *-age*, as in village, etc.

D ∽

✦ DAG

What a useful word this is. Relegated now in status to a dialect word in the dictionaries, it deserves better than to be forgotten in most places. It has a variety of meanings, of which the following are some.

1. Dew, dewdrops. This is a word I heard from the late Elizabeth Jeffries of Kilmore, Co. Wexford. Compare the Yorkshire verb *dag*, to droop or hang down, as curtains do when they hang unevenly. In Cornwall 'the trees are daggin with fruit' has been recorded. This is surely the same word as *dag*, a lock of clotted wool that hangs on the tail of a sheep, a word found in Kent and Wicklow, and the verbal noun *dagging*, a Wicklow sheepman's word for removing clots of dirty wool from a sheep. The late Séamas Ó Saothraí, whose book on the English of Westmeath I look forward to very much, told me that *dag* is used as a verb in Cloonagh townland, Co. Westmeath, his native place. He once heard a woman driving a pony and trap shouting this to a woman who had said something offensive to her: 'Yeh clotty oul' streel, c'm'ere till I dag ye.' This was an invitation to approach and have the loose, dirty bits hanging from her skirt removed with a scissors.

2. To sprinkle water with the hand, as is done when ironing. John Vines of Kilpedder, Co. Wicklow, had the word. After a frightening thunderstorm John admitted to dagging himself more than once with holy water during a sleepless night. 'To dag a garden is to water it,' wrote Captain Grose from Lancashire in 1790.

3. To trail in the dew, to bedraggle. The EDD has this from Shropshire: 'Molly, w'y dunna yo' 'oud yore petticoats up out o' the sludge; yo' bin daggin 'em 'afe way up yore legs.' From Cornwall, the EDD recorded, 'Her dress is daggin in the mud.' Hence we have *dagged-ass*, a slatternly woman, from Lancashire; *dag-tail* and *daggle-tail*, a slut, slattern, from the same county.

The EDD gives the source of all these words, quoting the Icelandic lexicographer Vigfusson, as the Old Norse *døgg*, dew.

✦ DARK

When I was young blind people were called *dark*. Probably because Irish speakers referred to them as being *dorcha*, I accepted that *dark* in this context was a translation from Irish. I now know better. True, Dinneen glosses *dorcha* as blind, but *dark* was a very popular adjective in English-speaking Ireland to describe blind people. Mr and Mrs S.C. Hall in *Ireland, Its Scenery and Character* (1842) have 'Look at the poor that can't look at you, my lady, for the dark man can't see if yer beauty is like yer sweet voice.'

'Tim was dark, and did not well know who was playing,' is a sentence from Crofton Croker's *Fairy Legends and Traditions of South Ireland* (1862). Towards the end of the century a correspondent sent a sentence he heard at a fair in Antrim to the EDD's editor at Oxford: 'Will you give something to a poor dark woman?'

J.M. Synge had this in *The Well of the Saints*: '. . . and it's more joy dark Martin gets from the lies we told of that hag is kneeling in the path than your man will get from you, day or night and he living by your side'. In the same work he has 'Why should he be vexed, and we after giving him great joy and pride, the time he was dark.' 'Dark men they call them,' wrote James Joyce in *Ulysses*.

Across the water, from the North Country south to Cheshire, Derbyshire and Leicestershire, and in the deep south, in Hampshire, Devon, Dorset and Cornwall, they also had *dark* for 'blind'. The following examples were sent to the EDD in answer to the queries of its editor:

From Lancashire: 'Help him o'er the road, poor lad, he's dark.' From Cheshire came 'Old Dobson had summit growin' over his eyes for ever so long, and now he's quite dark.' A Northamptonshire reader offered 'Almost dark, nearly blind; quite dark, stone blind. Very common.' A Leicestershire lady offered 'A's gon quoite daak o' th' off oy.' From Cornwall came 'Th' ould man es daark an' most totelin.' 'It's five years, sir, since I have been quite dark,' a man told Mayhew, who reported the saying in *London Labour and the London Poor* (1851).

Hence *darky*, a blind man; a beggar who pretends to be blind. Stagg in his *Miscellaneous Poems* of 1807 has the lines 'A darky glaum'd her by the hip / Still the blind man held his grip.' And Mayhew reported this: 'We called them as did the blind dodge, *darkies*.'

So you see why I don't agree with those who say that *dark*, blind, is a translation of Irish *dorcha*. At any rate, the term is now considered obsolete, and more's the pity.

✦ DEADMAN'S HAND

One night in an Abbeyside, Dungarvan, hostelry, where in a little room at the back the winter nights are shortened by participation in a friendly card school, a man emerged and sat beside me at the counter. He had just won a good pot in a poker game, his winning cards being what he called 'the deadman's hand'. I asked him what that was, and he replied, a pair of aces and a pair of eights. 'You bluffer,' I said to him, 'I wouldn't bet a shilling on a hand like that.' He was unable to tell me where the phrase originated, and I failed to find it until I came upon it in a book called *The Facts on File Library of Words and Phrase Origins* by the reliable Robert Hendrickson.

The strange card-playing term brought me back to the morning Seán Mac Réamoinn brought me in from Wicklow at an unearthly early hour to kick-start RTÉ's first morning radio programmes in Henry Street, above the GPO. We discussed card-playing terms used in Ireland for an hour, but *the deadman's hand* was not among them. It's not Irish, of course.

In 1876 James Butler Hickok, better known as Wild Bill Hickok, came to Deadwood, Dakota Territory, to stake a claim for gold. He had just got engaged. Deadwood was a notoriously lawless place, and Wild Bill, a gunslinger of high renown, was approached by the townspeople to take up the job of marshall. Persuaded by his wife-to-be, Wild Bill agreed. But a gang of bad elements in the place hired a gunman named Jack McCall to assassinate him, paying him $500 up front.

Hickok liked to play poker, and his enemies knew this. He played into their hands one night by sitting with his back to the saloon door. McCall approached him from the rear and shot him in the back of the head, the .45 bullet passing through his brain and through the arm of the man sitting opposite him.

Hickok's last hand, which he held in a death grip, was found to be a pair of aces and a pair of eights, known thereafter as *the deadman's hand*. The dealer had no time to deal the fifth card.

McCall was freed by a packed jury in a miners' court, but he was later arrested and found guilty in a federal court which ignored his plea of double jeopardy on the grounds that the miners' court had no jurisdiction. He was hanged.

So, there you are, Brian O'Connor.

✦ DHORKO

This is a word which has entered Irish English from Irish, and as far as I know is known only in Donegal. I always have difficulty with words which have been corrupted—there is no other word for it—in their movement from one language into another, and even native speakers of Irish such as Carleton and the Banim brothers from Kilkenny have made an unholy mess in the rendering of Irish words into an Irish English garb. At any rate *dhorko* is *dobhar chú* in Irish, literally 'water hound'.

A few years ago I made enquiries about the survival of the word in Co. Donegal, and the teachers who kindly did the work for me told me that in most cases, the children didn't know from Adam what was meant by the word. Even in the Gaeltacht areas, children thought it might mean a retriever or a water spaniel, but they had no idea of the legend of the animal, described by the Donegal lexicographer Henry Hart, from Fanad, as 'a fabled monster, the Phooka or lake-seal of Lough Gartan'. Another Donegalman, Seumus MacManus, in *The Leadin' Road to Donegal* has:

> If you ask me what is a Dhorko, I will tell you that a Dhorko is an amphibious animal shaped much like a greyhound, with this one material difference, that the snout of the Dhorko is prolonged, running with a straight hand, very hard, sharp-pointed horn, some two feet or more in length, with which weapon it is enabled to execute fearful vengeance on its foes. This Dhorko was at one time . . . common to all the lakes in Ireland; but at the present time, owing, I suppose to the hostile and intolerant spirit fostered towards him by unbelievers, is to be found only in the numerous lakes in the remote districts of Donegal . . .

It was true for the man who said that the electric light, then the radio, then television, killed a lot of things in rural Ireland: the feared and fabled Dhorko may be counted among them.

✦ DIGHT

I wonder how the word *dight*, spelled as *deight*, got to Co. Wexford, at least to the south-eastern corner of it. Poole's glossary has it, but I, personally, haven't come across it anywhere else in the county, or anywhere else in Ireland for that matter, although the CUD has recorded it.

The word is found in Scotland as *dicht*, and in the northern counties of England south to Derby and Lincolnshire, and in Sussex. As a verb it means to prepare, make fit for use; to tidy, clean, sweep, dust, etc. It is also used figuratively. The most frequent use is in the sense of tidying, setting in order, and so, cleaning. 'Them lassis 'll ha to dight up their waays o' gooin' on, noo the'r feyther's broht a wife hoame,' was a Lincolnshire example of the word's use sent to the EDD. Hence the verbal noun *dighting*: 'It was an auld stocking leg she performed the dighting process with,' is an example from Ayrshire. Sir Walter Scott, in *Old Mortality* (1816), has 'Morton underwent a rebuke for not "dighting his shune."' Robert Burns has 'Let me ryke up to dyght up that tear,' in *Jolly Beggars*.

It is also used ironically, often in the past participle *deet* or *deeted*. It means to dirty, to soil. 'Mother! aar Tom's deeted on t' floor,' was recorded in west Yorkshire. Hence *dichted*, foul, dirty, used figuratively. From Ayr this: 'He affected a very scunnersome kin' o' dichty water in his talk.'

The *dight* recorded in Wexford by Jacob Poole in the late eighteenth century was in the sentence 'ha deight ouse var gabble', which he explained as 'you have put us in talk'; you or I might say, 'you have cleared the decks for a good chat.'

Crocket's Galloway story *Cleg Kelly* (1896), interesting to lexicographers because of the late Scots dialect it contains, has the fightin' talk 'He could dicht the street wi' your brither.' Figuratively then, *to dight* meant to thrash, beat up, 'to wipe'. Service's Ayrshire story *Dr Duguid* (ed. 1887), also interesting for its late dialect content, has 'When I was quite sure they had ta'en their dicht, I gaed doon the road.' The CUD's *dight* is glossed as a wipe; it also has 'to dight up, to dress (yourself) up'.

The word is a very old one, from the Old English *dihtan*, to appoint, order.

✦ DILDER

Here is a word found in the Orkneys and in parts of Ulster. As far as I know it is not found in mainland Scotland, which makes its appearance in the English of Donegal and Antrim something of a mystery. It means to shake, jolt or jerk, and I've heard an old Falcarragh woman say of a young hooligan from the neighbourhood who had let down a friend who had been good to him, 'Many's the day she dildered that wastrel,' by which she meant to throw a baby up and down to amuse it.

An Antrim correspondent, Rab Sinclair, tells me that the verb is used of the jolting of a cart. In Orkney it is also used of the trembling of one's limbs caused by sickness, or age, or fear.

To dilder also means to waste time, to work carelessly, to dawdle. I've heard a west Donegal woman tell a child of hers who was pretending to do her school exercise, 'Stop dilderin' and finish whatever you're doing.'

The word is of Scandinavian origin. Compare the Norwegian *dildra*, to trot along; to shake.

✦ DISCOMBOBULATE

A correspondent sent me a section of a newspaper article about the novelist Cormac McCarthy's old Olivetti typewriter. The piece read, 'Hemingway stood before his to hammer out tales of men and bulls who were noble and brave and doomed. E.E. Cummings used his to innovate and discombobulate, and now Cormac McCarthy is ending a five-decade partnership that has corralled five million words by selling his. I'm sure it will sell well; there is always a market for such things.'

The word *discombobulate* is in the American lexicon, but as far as I know is not used in this part of the world. It means to upset, disconcert, disturb, and it suits Mr Cummings' poetry down to the ground. It seems to have come into being in print in the 1830s, and it is still used. In 1834 *The New York Sun* printed a variant of the word: 'May be some of you don't get discombobracated.' In 1838 J.C. Neal, in *Charcoal Sketches or Scenes in a Metropolis*, used another interesting variant: 'While you tear the one, you'll discombobberate the nerves of the other.' In 1839 *Spirit of the Times* had this: 'Finally, Richmond was obliged to trundle him, neck and heels, to the earth, to the utter discombobulation of his wig.' In 1943 *The Saturday Review of Literature* stated that 'President Roosevelt's sarcastic reply, when asked as to the wisdom of raising an army too large to be supplied from the home-front, in terms of "discombobulating the domestic economy" . . .'

Robert Frost used it as a noun in a letter written in 1964: 'I put my own discombobulation first to lead up unnoticeably to yours.'

The word has been given the stamp of approval by the great dictionaries, but nobody is sure of its origin. Most American dictionaries dismiss it as slang, and a coined word. Oxford speculates that it is probably a jocular alteration of 'discompose' or 'discomfit'.

✦ DOCTOR FELL

'I do not like thee, Doctor Fell!' used to be a sort of catchphrase when I was young. Girls would say it referring to a boy they disliked; a teacher might say it to a youngster who displeased him. I have been asked a few times about this mysterious doctor and about the jingle about him which runs, 'I do not like thee, Doctor Fell. / The reason why I cannot tell. / But this I know, and know full well, / I do not like thee, Doctor Fell.'

John Fell was an eccentric English divine who died in 1686. He taught at Oxford University, where he was thought by some to be quite dangerous if not completely bonkers, because he permitted his students to argue with him during his lectures, and to interrupt him whenever they felt like it, so long as the interruptions were not of a facetious nature. That they were often of a very serious nature indeed is shown by the great university's records, which describe many fist fights which took place during the debates that followed Dr Fell's lectures.

Fell must have been highly regarded in church circles because he was made Dean of Christ Church and Bishop of Oxford, although he seemed to enjoy arousing the passions of his students, and, according to university folklore, considered charging those many townspeople who sneaked in to his lectures an entrance fee. He realised that they only came in to see the fun and games that followed his lectures. The authorities considered this fee business a step too far, much to Dr Fell's annoyance.

Dr Fell became famous for the Fell Types he made for the Oxford University Press, and for the great building programme he persuaded his sometimes reluctant bosses to initiate. And yet his name is now used by a dwindling number of people when they speak of someone disliked for some unspecified reason. Bernard Farrell wrote a good play entitled *I Do Not Like Thee, Doctor Fell*.

Master Thomas Brown is responsible for Dr Fell's unjust fate. Brown was once Dr Fell's student at Christ Church. He was given to acting the maggot, and when he was about to be sent down he was saved by Fell, who gave him a chance. The authorities were convinced that Brown had learned nothing at his Latin lectures, and he was asked by a panel which was to decide his fate to translate an epigram of Martial's. He responded with the jingle which starts 'I do not like thee, Dr Fell.' It bears little resemblance to Martial's 33rd Epigram, but it amused Fell, and that was enough to save Master Brown's bacon. He was allowed to graduate, and he became well known as a translator.

The only translation he is now remembered for is the enigmatic jingle that named his Oxford benefactor.

✦ DOUSE

Douse meaning extinguish is still in use in parts of rural Ireland, and fast becoming obsolete in the neighbouring island, it seems. A friend of mine who teaches in Dorset told me recently that eight pupils out of a class of twenty did not know what 'douse the fire' means.

Oxford told me that 'all the senses of the word belong to the lower strata of the language'. It gives only three citations, one of them from America. It quotes Capt. Grose's 1785 *Dictionary of the Vulgar Tongue*: 'Dowse the glim = put out the candle'. In 1824 Washington Irving's *Tales of a Traveller* had '"Dowse the light"! roared the hoarse voice from the water.'

I turned to the EDD. It defined the word as 'to extinguish, put out a fire, light etc.' It has it from Ulster, recorded by W.H. Patterson in Antrim and Down in 1880. From western Scotland it had Grose's phrase 'douse the glim': 'Having clapped a red worsted extinguisher on his head he dowsed the glim and proceeded to bed.' I was interested to see that he had the word from Devon exactly as I heard it used by my grandmother in a west Cork bog: 'This rain will dowse the fires on the moor.'

Having dealt with three other senses of the word, 1. To strike, punch; 2. To strike (a sail); to lower or slacken suddenly or in haste; 3. To put off, doff; it has as 4 our sense of extinguish a light, fire. It concludes, 'Of obscure origin: known only from 16th century. In sense 1, perhaps related to Middle Dutch *dossen*, or early modern Dutch *doesen* to beat with force and noise; cf. also East Frisian *dossen* to beat, strike, punch, knock, and German dialectal *dusen*, *tusen*, *tausen*, etc. to beat, strike, butt. Senses 2 and 3 may be the same word; cf. 'to strike sail'; sense 4 is more doubtful, and may be distinct.'

So there we are. Not even the greatest dictionary of English knows for sure where this useful word originated. I can't help wondering whether it will survive in Ireland. Come to think of it, it must be about sixty years since I heard anybody say 'douse the light'.

✦ DRITE, FIRKEL, EVEN-DOWN

David Hammond, God rest him, was almost as passionate about words as he was about folk-song, and he had little time for those who spoke and wrote about Ullans as if it was a living language; he suspected me of being in their camp, I think. Occasionally he would phone me to ask about words he remembered from his youth and that are now dead or dying; he liked the word *firkel*, a term of abuse for a young hooligan, either fully-fledged or in the making. He was amused to hear that this is the same word as the German *Ferkel*, a young pig.

He gave me the verb *drite* from Antrim. *Cacare* is the Latin explanation in the *Catholicon Anglicum*, a Latin–English glossary from *c*.1483. Kelly's *Complete Collection of Scottish Proverbs* (1721) advised that one should answer them that say, 'Guess what I dreamed?' with 'You dreamed that you drite under you, and when you rose it was true.' Mr Kelly was an earthy Scot, and his verb is from the Old Norse *dríta*, defined demurely by Geir Zoëga in his *Old Icelandic Dictionary* as 'to ease oneself'.

David Hammond was one of those who believed that the local glossaries and dictionaries should be updated often and that local speech should be given pride of place in schools. He expressed his delight on hearing one of his mother's words, *even-down*, in a Belfast schoolyard. It had been termed obsolete by some scholars recently. Over the phone he gave me examples of how the word was used.

It means, both in Ulster and in Scotland, utterly, absolutely. 'That's an even-down good goal.' You might, too, he said, call a man an even-down bastard; and you should always tell the even-down truth, the plain, unalloyed version. He also knew of the third meaning, attested to in Jamieson's Scots dictionary: habitual, confirmed. In *Petticoat Tales*, written in 1823, a woman defends her man: 'I may hae said that Andrew likes a drap o' drink, but that's no just an even down drinker.'

David Hammond and I had a wee drap on occasion, and now, as I write this in the Frauenhuber café in Vienna, where both Mozart and Beethoven played for their suppers, I raise a glass to the memory of a fine musician in his own right, a great lover of words, and an even-down good man.

✦ DRUTHEEN

This is an Irish English corruption of the Irish noun *drúchtín*. It means light dew, and was so glossed for me by many people in Co. Mayo, who didn't know about the figurative meaning of the word in the south, of which more anon.

The word also means a slug, a snail without a shell, the greatest pest to be found in a suburban garden. But not so long ago at all, marriageable girls used to get up at the break of day on May Morning and go outside to see if the drutheens left any hint in their nocturnal movements as to the identity of a man they might marry; it was believed that they traced the man's initials on the dew. In parts of rural Co. Kilkenny it was the colour of the first drutheen a girl looked out for; a light-coloured slug hinted that a fair-haired man was for her, while a black or brown-bodied drutheen told its own story.

Crofton Croker, early folklorist, in his *Fairy Legends and Traditions of the South of Ireland*, collected in Munster between 1825 and 1828, had this to say: 'The young girls go looking for the drutheen to learn from it the name of their sweetheart.' He went on to explain that a drutheen was 'a small white slug or naked snail sought by young people on May Morning, which if placed on a slate covered in flour or fine dust, describes, it is believed, the initials of their sweethearts'.

There is the compound *Garra Druthteen*, a corruption of *Gearradh Drúchtín*. This compound was sent to me from Co. Mayo and it means 'soreness under the toes from walking on dewy grass barefooted'.

Drutheen, the slug, has taken on a new meaning entirely in west Waterford. Doting mothers washing their little sons refer to their small penises as drutheens. And I found out one night in The Marine, a popular pub outside Dungarvan on the Youghal road, that more than doting mothers used the word in a figurative sense. A strikingly good-looking young woman was being pestered by a townie who was the worse for wear. Finally she answered his drunken pleas to be allowed to see her home. She said, 'Would you please go away? I have no interest in you or in your miserable little drutheen, so leave me alone.' He got the message.

✦ DUB

I wonder if this little word is still alive in Tyrone, where in William Carleton's day in the mid-nineteenth century it meant a small pool of rain-water; a puddle; a small pond or pool of water. In his most famous work, *Traits and Stories of the Irish Peasantry* (1843), he had 'That was beside the dub beside the door,' which suggests a puddle. The word is also found in Scotland, England's North Country, Yorkshire and the Isle of Man. The EDD also recorded the word in Co. Down, where it meant a duck pond. In 1815 Scott in *Guy Mannering* wrote, 'They live . . . by the shore-side . . . with six as fine bairns as you would wish to see plash in a salt-water dub.'

Burns has it in a poem dedicated to a G. Hamilton, Esq.: 'O ye wha leave the springs of Calvin / For gumlie dubs of your ain delvin.' Hogg the Selkirkshire poet complained that 'the burn was grown a drumly dub'. Caine's novel *The Manxman* (1895), often quoted by the EDD for its dialect content, has 'Going to a turf pit, he dipped both his hands in the dub, and brought some water.' Hence *dubby*, abounding with small pools; *dub-skelper*, a bog-trotter, used contemptuously for a rambling fellow; and in praise of a horse that jumps well.

In a pub near Lifford, just across the Finn river, on the Donegal side of Strabane, I struck up a conversation with a man who was wetting his whistle before trying his luck on the river. It was a rainy day, and he said that he would take his chance on the dubs, by which he meant deep, still pools in the river.

There is still another *dub*. It is used in Cumbria when referring to the ocean, especially that stretch of it between England and America. 'He's a clane long way over the dub' meant to one Cumbrian man, he's over in America.

The word is old and was a favourite of the old Scots poets. The great Gavin Douglas had 'The streetis . . . full of fluschis, doubbis, myre and clay' in *Eneados*, written in 1315 and re-published many times since.

As to origin, ultimately it is Germanic. The DSL says 'Old Scots has *dub*, a small and stagnant pool, from 1456, a puddle, from ante 1500; Low German, West Frisian *dobbe*, a water-hole, a puddle.'

✦ DULL

This is an anglicised spelling of the Irish word *dol*, defined by the great Fr Dinneen as 'a loop; a running knot or noose; a gin or snare; a fishing net; a syringe; the line of threads between two turns in warping; used in English as: *put a dol in that cord* (Armagh); a wooden peg, a thole pin'. He gives some compounds: *dol gliomach*, a wicker-work lobster pot, a kind of crib in which lobster is preserved in the salt water; *dol eangaí*, a cast of a net.

When I cast my own net for the word *dull* many years ago, I got this definition from a Leitrim reader: 'a loop, a running noose, a snare for catching rabbits'. W.H. Patterson's glossary of Antrim and Down words of 1880 has 'a horsehair noose for catching trout; also applied to a noose in a rope or cord.' Another correspondent from Antrim told the EDD that '"put a dull on the rope" is frequently heard.'

I heard *dulling* from a sheepman at the bottom of Errigal mountain, a method of catching sheep stuck in a ravine by means of a noose. Michael Traynor in *The English Dialect of Donegal*, published in 1953 by the Royal Irish Academy, has the compound *dulling-boat*: 'one man stands on the shore holding the end of a net, while the boat on the sea moves about'. The Donegal novelist Seumus MacManus in *Bold Blades of Donegal* has 'It was lurch and lumber forward he did, like an Inver dulling-boat tacking in a gale of wind.' In the same book he has 'The thrill of steering a dulling boat round and round the rushing herring shoals'.

The days of the herring shoals and the dulling boats are long gone, alas, and so are the days of the word *dull*, in all its shades of meaning, so my spies tell me.

✦ DUM

In the old days hurling goalkeepers had to be incredibly courageous, as they could be challenged in ways that would not be tolerated nowadays under the new rules; I still look back in awe on the likes of Tony Reddan of Tipperary, who was as agile as a cat and as brave as a bullfighter, the best I have ever seen. I took pity on a few of them in my time, men who hadn't the likes of Mark Marnell of Kilkenny or Michael Maher or John Doyle, of Tipperary, or Johnny O'Connor of Waterford, or Nick O'Donnell or Bobby Rackard of Wexford to protect them for marauding forwards. Not so long ago I took pity on a goalkeeper I saw in a club match in a south-eastern county, who was given little protection by either his backs or the referee. I grant you that the poor man, like the Ancient Mariner, stoppeth one of three, but it wasn't entirely his fault, and I felt that one of his team's supporters who was standing by my side was unfair to him when he shouted, 'Look at him, rooted to the ground like a bloody dum.' I sensed that my companion would not just then have appreciated an inquiry as to the meaning and etymology of 'dum', but there were places where the word meant anything fixed in place, like the pillar of a gate, or the jamb of a door.

The word was once to be found in north County Dublin, and the dialect dictionaries say that it was once common both in the West Country and in Yorkshire, in the sense 'a lazy, incompetent person'.

As to origin, consider the Norwegian *dom*, judgement, capacity, wisdom. There is a Shetlandic and Orcadian *domless*, wanting in natural vigour, impotent, from the Norwegian source I mentioned + -*laus*, negative suffix. This, I think, is where our word originated.

✦ DUNSH

Also spelled *dunch* in places, this verb is getting scarce in England's North Country, in Warwickshire, Gloucestershire and East Anglia, where it once was in common use. It was also known in Monaghan and Fermanagh, Antrim and Down, and was still used in these counties until recently. It means to nudge, push, jog with the elbow; to knock against, jostle; to strike on; to head-butt; to knock, beat, thrash.

The CUD has it from Antrim; '"She dunshed against me"—very common,' a correspondent told the EDD. Joan Trimble remembered the word from Fermanagh, where it was a common excuse for a blotted exercise or untidy needlework: 'My sister dunshed me as I was writing, Miss.' Sir Walter Scott used the verb in *The Heart of Midlothian*: 'What gies her titles to dunch gentlemans about?' He uses it again later in the same text: 'Ye needna be dunshin that gate, John.'

To dunsh instead of 'to butt with the head' was common in Ulster. The great Ulster collections, Grose's, Patterson's, *The Ballymena Observer*, the EDD and the CUD recorded it. The verbal noun, *dunching*, was, I'm told, still used in the Glens of Antrim in 1970, as it was in 1790 when Captain Grose, on his travels to collect dialect words there, heard '"A dunching stirk"—a steer or young bull that begins to butt before he has got horns'. Hence W.H. Patterson's Antrim and Down '*duncher*, a hornless or moiled cow which has a habit of knocking people down with its head'. [*Moiled* is from Irish *maol*, bald, and by extension, hornless.]

Dunsh/dunch, a nudge, push, poke; a crash, bump, shock, was common as a noun, and has been used frequently by Scottish writers, including Stevenson in his 1886 *Kidnapped*: 'It [the ship] struck the reef with such a dunch as threw us all flat on the deck.' Somerset Maugham knew the word. He has this in 1930, in *Cakes & Ale*: 'Verbs that you only know the meaning of if you live in the right set (like "dunch").' Stevenson's hefty dunch reminds me of Tomás Mac Gabhann's Monaghan expression 'a good dunsh in the *magairlíní* was the softener he needed, and the softener he got', used of a footballer who got his retaliation in first on a dirty opponent.

Dunch, *dunsh* and *dunching* are old. The *Promptorium Parvulorum Sive Clericorum*, an important English–Latin glossary of *c.* 1449, has 'dunchyn, *tundo*'. But Oxford, always careful, says, 'Derivation unknown. Mätzner, in *Altenglische Sprachproben, nebst einem Wörterbuche* suggests connexion with Icelandic *dunka* to resound, give a hollow sound, Swedish *dunka*, Danish *dunke* to beat, knock, thump, throb; but these are modern forms, having no historical connexion with English.' A mystery it remains.

✦ DÚTHRACHT, TILLY

Dhuragh is a corruption of the Irish word *dúthracht*, and William Carleton from Tyrone explained it in a footnote in *The Battle of the Factions*: 'An additional portion of anything thrown in from a spirit of generosity, after the measure agreed to is given. When the miller, for instance, receives his toll, the country people usually throw in several handsful of meal as a Dhuragh.' I've heard the word used in this sense in west Donegal in my time. Fr Dinneen gives *dúthracht*, 'good will, best wishes, a kindness, a tip, a luck-penny, an extra given through friendship or favouritism'. *Dúthracht* also means devotion: *Le gean is dúthracht* means 'with love and devotion'. Think of that the next time you send the Loved One a card or a present.

Simmons's glossary of south Donegal English, published in the *Educational Gazette* in 1890 and used by Joseph Wright in the EDD, tells us that the word is used 'in a somewhat different sense in southern Ireland. When you pay great attention to a person, pet him, feed him with goodies, take care of him in every way, this is called *dooracht*.' P.W. Joyce's *English As We Speak It In Ireland* uses the original Irish headword *dúthracht* and defines it as 'Tender care and kindness shown to a person. The word in the sense of kindness is very old; for in the Brehon Law we read of land set aside by a father for his daughter through dúthracht.'

In places *dúthracht* means energy. 'He put dúthracht into it' was sent to the academic journal *Éigse* by Eamon Mac an Fhailigh from Co.

Westmeath, and I heard it with the meaning 'energy' from Dr Patrick Henchy, former director of both the National Library of Ireland and the Chester Beatty Gallery, who hailed from Corofin, Co. Clare.

In my part of the country the extra drop of milk the milkman doled out 'for the cat' was known as a *tilly*. Publicans were known to pour a *tilly* for favoured customers at Christmas or on New Year's Eve. This is the Irish *tuilleadh*, more, extra. James Joyce used the word *tilly* in Ulysses: 'She poured again a measureful and a tilly.' *Tilly* is the first poem in Joyce's *Pomes Penyeach*, published in 1927.

Eamon Mac Thomáis, in his charming *Janey Mack Me Shirt is Black*, published in Dublin in 1983, has the compound *tilly measure*, a small measuring can used by milkmen to pour a *tilly*: 'She never needed a bell as the pint, half-pint, and tilly measures rattled against the milk cans.'

I am assured by my collaborators the schoolteachers that both *dúthracht* and *tilly* are known now only by the older citizens. These good words are, it seems, soon to join the dialect dictionaries with the word *obsolete* appended to them.

✦ DWABLE

This word is found in a variety of spellings in Ireland and Scotland, *dwabil, dwaible, dwebble, dweeble,* and *dwyble* among them. As an adjective it means flexible, wielding, loose, shaky; weak, infirm, feeble.

Jamieson's great nineteenth-century Scots dictionary says, 'the limbs are said to be *dwable* when the knees bend under one, or the legs have not strength to support the body.' I heard this in a few pubs in Co. Donegal in my time. That good dialect poet Alexander Ross frae Aberdeen, in *Helenore*, written in 1768, had 'As water weak, and dweeble like a bent'. The Fife writer W.D. Latto, in his very popular *Tam Bodkin* (1864), has 'But noo I am douce, dowie, dweeble an' skair.'

Hence *dwaibly* or *dwibly*, feeble, shaky, tottering, infirm. 'She was a dwaibly body from the first,' is from Stevenson in *Weir of Hermiston*. 'She's a poor dwibly thing,' is from the *Ballymena Observer* of 1892. I'm told that the word is no longer used in Co. Antrim.

As a noun, the word means a weak, lanky overgrown person or child; anything long and flexible, with the notion of weakness. Jamieson had 'He's just a dwable o' a bairn,' from Lothian in his dictionary. I am reliably informed that this adjective is no longer in use.

And finally there is the verb meaning to walk with weak, faltering steps; to totter, to walk feebly. Still in use in Antrim and Donegal, I'm glad to say. I have often wondered if the word is related to the dialect noun *dwam*, a faint, a sudden feeling of faintness, a weak turn, a sudden fit of sickness; the verb *dwam* means to faint, fall ill. This Ulster and Scots word is related to Old English *dwolma*, confusion.

Pé scéal é, the DSL says that Old Scots has *dwabbling*, feeble, halting, which may be the same word. Apparently a late formation, based on the root meaning of stupefaction, giddiness, unsteadiness, in such words as *dwam*, q.v. above, + *-ble* suffix.

✦ DWAM

The word has a variety of spellings, of which *dwam* is perhaps the most common. It used to be commonly used in Scotland, Ireland and Northern England, as well as in Gloucestershire, Devon and Cornwall. It means a swoon, faint, sudden feeling of faintness, a sudden fit of illness. It is, the statisticians say, rapidly falling into disuse.

'He was but in a kind of dwam', wrote Scott in *The Antiquary* in 1816. The EDD gives the following examples of the word's use in Scotland: 'When a child is seized with some undefinable ailment it is common to say "It's just some dwaum"'; 'A man fell down intill a dwam; He lay an hour ere back he cam'; 'It's only a bit dwam; it will soon gang aff'. That last example is from the Etterick Shepherd, James Hogg, from Selkirkshire. The great dialect dictionary also gives a poetic example from Moir's *Mansie Wauch*, published in Edinburgh in 1828 and often pillaged by Joseph Wright for its dialect content: 'As if the heart of the world had been seized with a sudden dwalm.'

In Ireland, the word was recorded by all the usual suspects in the nineteenth century, Simmons in south Donegal, W.H. Patterson in Down and Antrim. It has lived. Correspondents of my own have sent me the noun, Seán Kilfeather from Co. Sligo; Patrick Gallagher from North Leitrim; David Hammond from Antrim; Tomás Mac Gabhann from Monaghan; Mary Reilly from north Louth. All those correspondents also sent me the adjective *dwamy*, inclined to faint; sickly, weak.

The verb *dwam* to swoon, faint; fall sick, is also found wherever the noun has been recorded. The EDD gives many examples. From Perthshire, 'He began to dwam in the end of the year, and soughed awa in the Spring.' Moir's *Mansie Wauch*, mentioned above, has 'We lifted the poor lad, who had now dwalmed away, upon our wife's handbarrow . . .'

Another good survival is in Scots literature since the time of Dunbar, who flourished around 1510. He has 'Sic deidlie dwawmes . . . Ane hundrithe tymes hes may hairt oirpast.' And I'm glad that the old word is still being used in Scots literature. Sheena Blackhall's *The Bonsai Grower* (Aberdeen 1998) has 'A wearisome warssle [watch] it wis . . . fur a hett-bluided lass tae pit by the rigg [backbone] o ilkie [every] nicht wi a shargeret [knackered] auld bodach fa snored and snochered [made snot] an dwaumed awa, aa the oors sud be keepit fur luvin.'

As to origin, the Old English has *dwolma*, confusion, chaos, abyss, Old High German *twalm*, Middle Dutch *dwelm*, stunning, stupefaction, giddiness, Old Saxon *dwalm*, delusion.

✦ DWINE

This word, I'm glad to say, is still to be found alive and well in parts of Counties Antrim, Down, Donegal, Tyrone and Fermanagh. It is also to be found in Scotland, in the northern shires of England, in East Anglia and Sussex, and in Lincolnshire and Shropshire. But the bad news is that it is falling into decline everywhere. It means to waste away, languish, pine, to decline in health from sickness, sorrow, etc; to dwindle.

The EDD collected these in Scotland: 'They dwined away, sweet Nell an' Tam, When Autumn bared the beechen tree,' wrote the forgettable poet Watt in his collection *Poetic Sketches* of 1880. 'I fear some will dwine and die,' wrote Christopher North in *Noctes Ambrosianae*, a valuable source of both dialect and folklore material. Any erratic behaviour in animals was considered a sign of impending doom from Donegal to Lincolnshire; from west Yorkshire a man wrote to Joseph Wright telling him that 'His horses and beas dwined away and deed, and nobody knew how.' I have heard 'Poor Sharkey dwined away in the wunther, and died as soon as the Spring came to the glen,' in the Rosses of Donegal.

Hence *dwining*, sickly, wasting away, commonly used when referring to plants, as Marshall recorded in his *Rural Economy*, written in south Yorkshire in 1796. Scott in *The Bride of Lammermoor* has 'Being up early and doun late . . . wi' his dwining daughter.' I heard an Antrim woman not long ago, saying that 'a pet lamb makes a dwining ewe'.

Dwiny is an adjective, meaning sickly, emaciated. 'Mothers lament over a dwiny child' ran a headline in an East Anglian newspaper. An English Midland mother, who didn't appove of her daughter's choice of boyfriend, was reported to have given this verdict on him: 'I don't say but what he might be a very nice gentleman, but I never seed such a dwiny pair o' legs.'

This useful verb, now described by the great dictionaries as dialectal and archaic, is from Old English *dwínan*, *dwán*, *dwinen*, an original Teutonic strong verb, represented by Old Norse *dvína*, Swedish *dvina*, Middle Dutch *dwînen*, early modern Dutch *dwijnen*, Dutch *verdwijnen*, to vanish, disappear, Middle Low German and Low German *dwînen*.

The verb *dwinge*, also found in Norfolk as *dwingle*, meaning to shrivel up and shrink, as an apple does if left in the sun too long, is from Middle Low German *dwengen*, to press, squeeze, according to Schiller-Lübben's *Mittelniederdeutsches Wörterbuch*, another example of great German historical linguistic scholarship of the nineteenth century. The modern German is *zwängen*.

E

✦ ELDIN(G

This is a word they have in Scotland and in all the northern shires of England for firing or fuel of any kind, turf, sticks, brushwood, etc. I heard it once from old Paddy the Cope in Dungloe, Co. Donegal, but he had spent many years in Scotland in his youth and undoubtedly brought the word back with him. I asked many people in the Rosses did they know the word, and not one of them did.

It's a good word, a bothy word, and it crops up many times in literature. 'Good elding for our winter fire' was one of Ramsey's prayers in *Tea Table Miscellany* in 1724. Scott in *Guy Mannering* has 'Ye'll be wanting elding now, or something to pit ower the winter.' 'Gunpowder is hasty eldin,' is a Scots proverb.

The following Bellman's Cry was recorded in Ripon in Yorkshire in the eighteenth century: it concerned a baker who paid the Bellman to proclaim all over town that 'This is to give notice that John Smith will yett t'ewin [heat the oven] te-neet, te-morn, an te-morn at neet, an' then nae mair til Tuesday week because there is nae mair eldin.'

It is now in decline everywhere but I am glad to hear that the word still lives in parts of Yorkshire and in the Lake District. It's been around for a long time, the earliest mention of it in literature being in the *Cursor Mundi* of *c.* 1300: 'Ysaac þe elding broght.'

The word is of Scandinavian origin. The Old Norse is *elding*, fuel, from *eldr*, fire. Ivor Aasen in his Norwegian dictionary has '*elding*, fuel'. The Danish is *ilding*.

✦ EMBOSS

I am not referring to the verb which means to carve or mould in relief; to cause figures to stand out, project, or protrude, and also, figuratively, the earliest and the prevailing modern sense. This *emboss* is as old as

Chaucer's *The Legend of Good Women* (ante 1385) which has 'Dido, Of gold the barris vp enbosede.' This was also the meaning employed by Shakespeare in *King Lear*, Act II, Scene IV: 'Thou art a boil, / A plague-sore, an embossed carbuncle / In my corrupted blood.'

No, the *emboss* I have in mind was clearly associated with the hunt in times long gone by, and means to press hard and exhaust. In 1590 Spenser in *The Fairie Queene* has 'Like dastard Curres that, having at a bay / The Saluage beast embost in weary chace, / Dare not adventure on the stubborne fray.' In 1601 Shakespeare in *All's Well That Ends Well*, Act III, Scene VI, has 'We have almost imbost him, you shall see his fall to night.' Shakespeare knew a thing or two about deer hunting, they say, and again in *Antony and Cleopatra*, Act IV, Scene XIII, he wrote, 'O he is more mad / Than Telemon for his shield; the boar of Thessaly / Was never so embossed.'

I have in my possession a most interesting book called *A Shakespeare Word Book, being a Glossary of Archaic Forms and Varied Usages of Words Employed by Shakespeare*. It was by John Foster, a well known historical linguist, and published in London in 1908 by Routledge. Foster says that the word's etymology is doubtful, but that 'it is supposed to be from French *bosse*, a bunch, because *bosses* or lumps of foam were thrown from the mouth of an animal when hard hunted'. He quotes the linguist Mahn's reminder about the Spanish *embocar*, to cast from the mouth. He also quotes from George Turberville's *The Noble Arte of Venerie or Hunting* (1575): 'When the hart is foaming at the mouth we say that he is embossed.'

Foster doesn't appear to believe that we can trust this etymology and he was right. Oxford itself is not too sure about its origin but is content to say that 'The verb is from Middle English *embose*, perhaps from *en-* + Old French *bos, bois* wood; the equivalent Old French *embuiser* occurs with sense of ambush.'

✦ EMULOUS

Although I've seen this word many times in literature, I don't believe I've ever heard it spoken. It means, first of all, ambitious, desirous of superiority. Shakespeare in *Troilus and Cressida* wrote, 'But in mine emulous honour let him die.' Edmund Burke in one of his *Letters on the Proposals for Peace with the Regicide Directory in France* (1796) has 'Emulous of the glory of the youthful hero'. In 1856 Emerson in *English Traits* wrote of 'Kingdoms emulous of free institutions'.

The word has other meanings. One is envious, jealous. Master Shakespeare knew this. In *Troilus and Cressida* he speaks of 'A good quarrel to draw emulous factions and bleed to death upon'. In the same play he writes, 'He is not emulous, as Achilles is.'

Again in *Troilus* Shakespeare uses the word, this time as an adjective meaning factious, contentious: 'Whose glorious deeds, but in the fields of late, / Made emulous missions 'mongst the gods themselves, / And drave great Mars to faction'.

Lastly there is the shade of meaning 'filled with emulation'. In 1851 Longfellow wrote in *The Golden Legend* about the great school of Salerno, where, it is claimed, Medicine was first studied: 'Where every emulous scholar hears . . . The rustling of another's laurels!' And in 1876 George Eliot, in *Daniel Deronda*, spoke of 'The stream of emulous admirers'.

Emulous is from the Latin *æmulus*.

✦ ETTLE

There was a time when one could say with confidence that this word *ettle* was thriving in Ireland, Scotland and the northern counties of England south to Lancashire. Now, alas, dialect words are treated with suspicion in the home and with disdain in schools, and children are warned by teachers not to use them in examinations. How long it will take for dialects to be replaced in Ireland by a kind of cosmopolitan English is a moot point. Two of our leading historians, John A. Murphy and Joe Lee of University College Cork, think that the dialects are dwindling at such a rate that the writing is already on the wall and that there may not be much time left.

What a pity it would be if *ettle* disappeared. As a verb it means to intend, propose. It is frequently used with *at*. In the far north, on Shetland, George Stewart in his charming *Fireside Tales* has 'Dis is no what I was ettlin to speak o.' Back home the *Ballymena Observer* has 'I ettled that yin [one] for me.' W.H. Patterson also has the word from Antrim and Down, and many years ago now, Drew Donaldson, a Belfast wordsman, asked me after an Irish language radio debate in which he and I took part if I ettled to come to visit Belfast soon.

'He's ready to ettle but never to do,' is a Lancashire saying. John Buchan in *John Burnet* (1898) has 'I dinna think he ettled it, for when he began I think he didna mean mair than to punish him for his words.'

An article called *Ulsterisms* published in *The Northern Whig* in 1901 has 'As the mornin' was lookin' to be saft, and I wasn't very throng, I ettled to get there early afore the hurry begun.' [*Hurry* means trouble. The 1978 rebellion was called 'the hurry' in the north.]

Ettle also means to essay, venture. Tobias Smollett uses the word in his play *The Reprisal* in 1757: 'He's a gowk, and a gauky, to ettle at diverting the poor lassy with the puppet-shew of her ain misfortune.' The word has survived thus far in Scots literature. In 1929 W.D. Cocker in the excellent *Scots Readings* (ed. T.W. Paterson) has 'Lassies noo-a-days a' want to dae something oot o' the or'nar. They ettle to dae a' things that men can dae.' And in J. Bridie's 1935 *Tragic Muse* in *Scottish One Act Plays* (ed. J.M. Reid) there is the line 'It's like ettling tae sleep on the big drum of a jazz orchestry.' Hence the verbal noun *ettling*, striving.

This good word is still alive in a few places in Ulster and Scotland. According to the DSL it's from Old Scots *ettle*, *ettill*, etc. = to intend, from *c.* 1400; = to direct one's course, from *c.* 1450; = to direct one's efforts, from 1581; = to aim, from *c.*1470. The verbal noun *etlyng* = intention, from 1375. The word's origin is Old Norse *ætla*, purpose, intend. The noun is a late formation from the verb.

✦ EVELYN'S WORDS

I have been re-reading John Evelyn and enjoying again the vivid picture of life he paints for us in his century, the seventeenth. He was a charmer in many respects, and had a wide range of interests. He was an acknowledged expert on mechanics, on the sewers of London, and on forestry; he had a passionate interest too in the welfare of his language.

Although he was not, as far as I remember, a member of the Royal Society's inquiry into the improvement of English, he did write to that body on occasion to point out that there was need for imported words when there was no equivalent to be found in English, an idea found offensive by many in the Society who seemed not to realise that their beautiful language was already a hybrid tongue. He wrote in his *Memoirs* that the language had already been 'corrupted' by 'Victories, plantations, staples of Commerce, pedantry of Schools, affectation of Travellers, translations, fancy and styles of Court, mincing of Citizens', but, he asked, who would disagree that the language gained immeasurably by the importation of *ennui*, *bizarre*, *concert*, *emotion*, and *naïveté*.

That last word appealed greatly to him, as he thought, rightly it seems from contemporary evidence, that the English were apt to confuse its counterpart *ingenuous* with *ingenious*.

Oxford gives him credit for introducing most of the above words, but gives Jeremy Taylor credit for introducing *emotion*, and says that Lord Herbert introduced *bizzare* in 1648, when he described a woman's attire as being 'as bizzare as her person'.

Our John could be a pain in the neck at times. He called a village a *dorp*, a vine-grower a *vigneron*, and in describing the Great Fire of London in 1666 he preferred *incendium* to the homely word *fire*. Writing about that Great Fire, he was the first to use in an English sentence the phrase *annus mirabilis*. And it was he who championed the use of *museum*, through Latin from Greek *mouseion*, a place sacred to the Muses, and we must be grateful to him for that.

He conditioned people into accepting more foreign words, and when the wandering Charles II returned from his travels and settled down in London with his fancy continental court, the people accepted the strange words they brought to England. Of course some tut-tutted over their introduction of *faux pas*, first used in literature by Wycherly in *The Plain Dealer* in 1676; but *chagrin, burlesque, ridicule, badinage, jocose, clique, manouevre* and *caprice* caused nobody but the odd pedant offence.

Few nowadays would disagree that these were useful and elegant additions to the English vocabulary, and let us give John Evelyn due thanks for first postulating that there was no affront to Englishness in borrowing from the unpopular French. Of course there may be something in the opinion that their quick acceptance by the people was due to a reaction against the Puritans' dislike of them.

✦ EVEN ASH-LEAF, OR EVEN-ASH

The first person to tell me about the *even ash-leaf*, sometimes called *even-ash*, and the pishogue or superstition attached to it was Paddy McCarthy, a farmer and carpenter from Drumkeen in Co. Limerick, who, sometime in the late 1950s, rented me a house. The most generous of men, he more than made up for taking a pittance in rent money by giving us free milk and free timber. He knew his timber, and had a particular fondness for the ash, possibly because hurleys were made from it. In the hedgerows surrounding his farm he used to cut down other saplings, bushes and *sceach*s surrounding little ash trees, to allow them space to grow without hindrance.

The superstition I allude to was not confined to Drumkeen. W.H. Patterson, in his late-nineteenth-century glossary of words from Antrim and Down, has this: 'Even-ash, an ash-leaf with an even number of leaflets, used in a kind of divination. The young girl who finds one repeats the words, "This even-ash I hold in my han," the first I meet is my true man." She then asks the first male person she meets on the road what his Christian name is, and this will be the name of her future husband.'

Liz Jeffries from Kilmore, Co. Wexford, had this rhyme: 'An even-ash and a four leaved clover, You're sure to see your lover before the day is over.'

The superstition was believed all over England as well, from Northumberland and Yorkshire to Shropshire, Wiltshire and Devon. One northern English contributor to Joseph Wright's great dialect dictionary wrote, 'Even-ash under the shoe will get you a sweetheart. It is placed in the left shoe.' Another person wrote, 'Even-ash is a lucky find, and is put into the bosom, or worn in the hat, or elsewhere, for luck.' But most of the emphasis was placed on divination. I like this rhyme from the North Country: 'The even ash-leaf in my left hand, The first man I meet shall be my husband; The even ash-leaf in my glove, the first I meet shall be my love; The even ash-leaf in my breast, the first man I meet's whom I love best; The even ash-leaf in my hand, The first I meet shall be my man; Even-ash, even-ash I pluck thee, This night my true love for to see.'

I'm sure the old superstition, and the term associated with it, are dead everywhere by now, and devout clergymen of all denominations have no more need to warn innocent youngsters of this pretty piece of paganism. 'Oh, yes, I heard a priest giving out hell about the even ash-leaf pishogue when I was a young one,' said Liz Jeffries to me. 'We just laughed at him, the oul' boldoon [tom-cat]. I used to go out in the summer evenings looking for the leaves, but divil the one did I ever find. Still, I got a nice man without them.'

| F ~

✦ FAIN

What a nice little word this is, and useful; unfortunately it is getting less and less common in its habitat, Ulster, Scotland and northern England south to East Anglia. It is an adjective meaning glad, happy, well pleased. Here's Walter Scott in *The Heart of Midlothian* back in 1818: 'If your honour's Grace would but accept a stane or twa, blithe and fain and proud it wad mak us.' 'Fair words make fools fain,' is a proverb from England's North Country; while the *Ulster Journal of Archaeology* has its brother: 'An east rain makes fools fain.' The CUD has that, but with an addendum which explains it, 'they think it's goin to fair but it rains the mair'. Swainson's *Weather Folk Lore* from 1873 has the word from Ulster as well.

Hence *fainly*, an adverb meaning gladly, eagerly, excitedly, and as an adjective meaning pleasant, welcome; also the noun *fainness*, gladness.

Fain also means desirous, eager. 'He's fairly fain of a drap o' whisky,' was an example I got from an Ayrshire friend. 'I'm fain to hear all the news,' was an example sent to me from Yorkshire.

Fain meaning fond, affectionate, in love, is common still in Ayrshire, where it was known to their greatest poet. He has 'Nae doubt but they were fain o' ither,' in *Twa Dogs*.

And lastly they use *fain* for gladly, willingly; fondly in northern England and in East Anglia. Friends who live in Norfolk sent me an invitation which read, 'We'd fain have you come and stay with us in the Summer.'

The adjective *fain* is from Middle English *fain(e, fayn(e, feyn(e,* etc., from either Old English *fægen,* or Old Norse *feginn,* glad, joyful.

✦ FAINAGUE

Here's a very good word I have heard in both Wexford and south Tipperary and yet the EDD has not recorded it here. It means, first of all, to revoke at cards, to renege. But the word has another meaning, one I heard from a man who came from the boglands near Thurles, from the chanteuse of Kilmore, Co. Wexford, Liz Jeffries, and from old Phil Wall of Carne.

No. The Tipperary man and the two Wexford people I mention thought of *fainague* as meaning to deceive by flattery, to achieve by improper means, to cheat, which is close enough in meaning to renege, I suppose. The Tipp man was talking about a business enterprise which went wrong. 'I knew men who let the year's turf go to the divil', he said, 'to take up jobs in that man's factory. He promised them the divil and all, and never paid them a red penny in the heel of the hunt, but fainagued.' An interesting note in the venerable *Notes and Queries*, Series I, 1854, reminded me of Mrs Jeffries' and Phil Wall's use of the word in cases of jilted lovers. A Cornishman wrote, 'Most frequently applied to cases where a man has shown appearances of courtship to a woman and then left her without any apparent reason.'

The EDD quotes a line from an old Cornish song: 'But a maiden came one day / And faineaged his heart away.' Cornwall also has the good present participial adjective *fainaiging*, as in 'a fainaging villain'; and the noun *fainaguer*, a cheat, a scoundrel.

The EDD suggests that for an origin of this useful and expressive word we should look at Old French *fornier*, 'nier, dénier', found in La Curne's *Dictionnaire Historique* (ed. 1882); from Latin *foris* + *negare*. And for the dialect form *-eague* (*-aigue*) we should compare *reneague* (*renege* in Shakespeare), to deny, revoke, and French *renier*.

✦ FAIRING

I was surprised to find that the dialect dictionaries, without exception, say that this old word is not found in Ireland outside Co. Antrim. I myself heard the word in New Ross, Co. Wexford, when I was a boy; I heard it too in Counties Kilkenny and Carlow. It meant a present brought from a fair. In my grandmother's time it also meant a present given at a fair to one's sweetheart; and by transference it meant a complimentary gift of any kind.

The fairs in question were not the kind at which cattle were bought or sold; we would call them *patterns*, fairs or festivals commemorating the feast-day of a saint. In the case of my home town, the feast or fair was held upstream on the Barrow, in the beautiful village of St Mullins, a sedate affair in my day, but up to about 1830 the scene of high jinks and tally-ho of all kinds, culminating in a famous faction fight between the men of St Mullins and the men from Brogue Lane in New Ross. According to my granny there was no animosity between the two groups; indeed, the opposite was the case. Matches were made at the fair, and no dowry was asked when a Carlow man wanted to wed a Ross girl.

England had her great fairs, of which St Bartholomew's was perhaps the most famous. In 1614 Ben Jonson's play *Bartholomew Fair* has in the Prologue 'The Maker . . . hopes, to night To giue you for a Fayring, true delight.' Pepys's *Diary* of 31 August has 'To Bartholomew Faire . . . Mr. Pickering bought them some fairings.' In 1786 Fanny Burney's *Diary* of 8 November has 'Presenting her one of my fairings', and in John Clare's *Shepherd's Calendar* of 1827 mention is made of a girl 'With kerchief full of fairings in her hand'. The custom was still to the good in 1883 when *Longman's Magazine* of April 1883 reported that 'The lasses get their "fairing" from the lads in gingerbread and nuts from the stalls.' Interestingly, gingerbread was the culinary treat given by the wives and girlfriends of the St Mullins women to their counterparts from Ross in the old days.

As I mentioned, the giving of fairings was not confined to pattern days. Shakespeare in *Love's Labour's Lost*, Act V, Scene II, has 'We shall be rich ere we depart, If fairings come thus plentifully in.' In 1668 Pepys confided to his *Diary*, 'I . . . did give her five guineas as a fairing.' He was speaking of his wife, who was regularly given a fairing of a flaking with a broom handle; this new present was conscience money, perhaps.

This lovely old word, now in danger of death if not already gone, is from Old French *feire* (modern French *foire*) = Spanish *fería*, Portuguese *feira*, Italian *fiera*: all from Latin *feria*, holiday. It was borrowed into Irish as *féirín*.

✦ FAMBLE

This old word is now obsolete, according to the best dictionaries, including the great Oxford.

The late Liam de Paor gave me the word from north Co. Louth. He heard it in a country kitchen where the woman of the house subjected her young, reluctant daughter to reciting an Irish poem for him, telling her to give it out without fambling or stumbling over the words. The word is still heard in north Co. Dublin, but if it is not obsolete in Ireland, it's close to it. It means to stammer, stutter; to mumble, to speak imperfectly.

I found the word in *Political, Religious & Love Poems from the 13th to the 15th centuries*, edited by the English Texts Society in 1866, and republished by them in 1903: 'His tonge shal stameren, oþer famelen.' This particular poem is thought to date from the 14th century. In 1611, Randle Cotgrave in his *A French and English Dictionary* has '*Beguayer*, to famble, fumble, maffle in the mouth'. Edward Phillips in his 1658 work, *The New World of Words*, edited and revised by J. Kersey in 1707, has 'Famble, to Faulter or Stammer in Speech'. Elisha Coles, in his 1679 work, *An English Dictionary explaining the difficult terms that are used in Divinity, Husbandry, Physick, Phylosophy, Law, Navigation, Mathematicks, and other Arts and Sciences*, has 'To famble in one's speech: *in sermone hesitare*'. The word is also noted by Nathan Bailey in *A New Universal Etymological Dictionary* of 1721, an important work because it contained words from the dialects of many English counties. *Famble* is also to be found in the 1886 *South-West Lincolnshire Glossary*: 'He fambles so in his talk; she seems to famble, as if she could not get her words out.'

The EDD says the word is from the Danish *famle*, to fumble, stammer. Its sister work, the Oxford dictionary, offers 'Of obscure origin; the word may originally have had the sense 'to grope, fumble'; cf. Swedish *famla*, Danish *famle* to grope, metathetic form of Old Norse *falma* (Icelandic *fálma*), cognate with Old English *folm*, hand.

✦ FANDANGLES, SHINGERLEENS

I was surprised to find that the dialect dictionaries have recorded *fandangles* in only a handful of counties in England, Cumbria in the north, and Somerset and Devon in the south-west. It also says the word is known in Ireland and in America. It means ornaments, trinkets; antics, capers, as in dancing about. It is thought by many authorities to be in danger of dying out.

I have heard this good word for gaudy ornaments many times. It was usually used by women of a certain age to disparage younger women: 'You never saw such a heejous dress, made even worse by her ladyship by the fandangles she wore as accessories, as she calls them. She looked like a Gypsy Queen, honest to God.' In Somerset the word meant high jinks, and a correspondent from the Orchard County sent the EDD the sentence 'The old mare is full of her fandangles this morning.'

Hence *fandanglement*, found in Cumbria, and meaning a whim; gewgaw. The EDD has 'He wadn't gie the vally of a brass farden for any o't new fandanglements.'

The only citation from Ireland in the EDD is from Jane Barlow's *Irish Idylls* of 1892, set in the west of the country. Jane gave us the meaning 'to hang about, trifle, waste time, to fool around'. The quotation reads, 'Over fond of keepin' the lads fandanglin' after her, to be makin' fools of them'.

Max Adeler in his 1876 story *Elbow Room*, set in New York, has the word; to him it meant nonsensical, outlandish. 'Don't fool with any of those fandangling ways women have of fixing their hair.'

The EDD says the word is an arbitrary formation. Perhaps it is suggested by *fangdangs*, meaning trinkets, trifles of personal adornment, according to the *Whitby Glossary* of 1876. The word *fandangs* is still used in Yorkshire.

In parts of Munster fandangles were called *singirlíní*, anglicised *shingerleens*. In P.W. Joyce's *English as we Speak it in Ireland*, *shingerleens* are defined thus: 'Small bits of finery; ornamental tags and ends-of-ribbons, bow knots, tassels etc. hanging on dress, curtains, furniture etc.' In Co. Limerick Mainchín Seoige, scholar and conservator of Limerick's heritage, told me that *shingerleens* were icicles. And Julia Crowley, who lived in Clohina, near Ré na nDoirí in the west Cork Gaeltacht, told me that *singirlíní* were the flowers of the fuschia.

✦ FARD

This good word went out of fashion in the nineteenth century. It was both a noun and a verb. The noun meant paint, especially white paint, used on the face. As a verb it meant to colour, embellish, paint. Hence *farded*, past participle, adjective, painted, embellished; *farding*, noun, painting, embellishment.

It seems that Palsgrave first used the noun in 1540 in his translation of Acolastus: 'A certain gay glosse or farde, such as women paynte them with'. In 1629 Zachary Boyd says in his *Last Battell of the Soule in Death*, 'Fard and foolish vaine fashions of apparell are but Bawds of allurement to vncleannesse.' Thanks mainly to puritanism it took a long time to convince the English that they should use *fard* as French women did. In 1667, however, John Evelyn wrote, 'I now observe that the women began to paint themselves, formerly a most ignominious thing and us'd only by prostitutes.' Tobias Smollett in his 1766 *Travels Through France and Italy* proclaimed that 'Rouge and fard are more peculiarly necessary in this Country.' In 1839 Thackeray, in his *Second Lecture on the Fine Arts*, admonished a painter, 'Why will he not stick to copying her majestical

countenance instead of daubing it with some fard of his own?'
Eventually French fashions won the hearts of the ladies, and pastel-
shaded fard became the height of fashion all over Europe.

The verb *fard*, to paint the face with fard to hide defects or improve
the complexion, was used figuratively by Walter Scott. In *Old Mortality*
he has 'Nor will my conscience permit me to fard or daub over the
causes of divine wrath.' The verb had popped up as early as 1450 in a
tract named *The Book of the Knight of la Tour-Landry*: 'A lady . . . that
folks said she popped and farded her'. The bigoted divine George
Gillespie used the verb to great effect in his *A Dispute Against the
English-Popish Ceremonies Obtruded Upon the Church of Scotland* in the
1630s: 'The . . . inveagling trinkets, wherewith the Romish Whoore doth
faird her self,' and, in another fire and brimstone sermon, 'Her comely
countenance is miscoloured with the farding lustre of the mother of
Harlotes.'

Gone now, as far as I know, this good word which came to us from
the French *fard*, from Old French *fart*, masculine, *farde*, feminine, of
obscure etymology, Oxford thinks; but it refers us to Old High German
gi-farwit, coloured, painted (fem. *givarida*, glossed *fucata*), past
participle of *farwjan*, to colour.

✦ FASH

Once upon a time, and not so long ago either, one could find the word
fash, as noun, verb and adjective, all over Scotland, Northern England as
far south as Warwickshire, and most of the historical province of Ulster.
My spies from the great dictionaries and from some of those
universities who show an interest in dialects tell me that *fash* is fast
heading into that limbo where it is deemed to be on the verge of
oblivion, the victim in this case to official discouragement of the use of
the vernacular in schools.

The verb *fash* is defined as to trouble, afflict; to inconvenience, vex,
annoy by importunity, to weary. It can also mean to trouble oneself,
bother. The EDD has a few quotations from Ulster. *The Ballymena
Observer* from 1892 has 'Daeny fash yoursel' and 'A canny be fashed.'
There is no doubt that the word came in the wake of the Ulster
Plantation. Sam Hanna Bell told me once that the word could still be
heard in the Ards Peninsula, but he added ominously, 'But for how
long?' Scott, in southern Scotland, was fond of the word. He has 'When

the countryside was na fashed wi' warrants and poindings', but the word was common from the Border Country right up to Shetland. Hence *fashed*, past participle, troubled in mind, weary. Sam Hanna Bell had it: 'I'm a wee bit fashed for the want of few good days.' And there are a few interesting phrases which have crossed the Sea of Moyle to us. 'Never fash your heid,' was heard in many places in Scotland and in Antrim. Davy Hammond from Belfast substituted 'arse' for 'heid' or 'head'. Scott had 'Never fash your beard, Mr Bide-the-Bent,' in *The Bride of Lammermoor*; and in Northumberland the phrase was 'Never fash your thumb.' Perhaps those two were polite substitutes for 'arse'.

As a noun the word was once common all over Scotland. It meant trouble, disturbance, care; labour, hardship, vexation. Burns used the word in his *Poet's Welcome*: 'An auld wife's tongue's a feckless matter To gie ane fash.' And the word as a noun is also found in most of the old glossaries of England's North Country.

The transitive verb *fash* was first seen in print in 1533, in Bellenden's *Livy*: 'The Veanis war sa faschit be continuall ambicioun and desire of honouris.' Cotgrave's French–English dictionary of 1611 gives the word as derived from Old French *fascher*, to annoy, weary.

✦ **FEAL**

This is a word sent to me from Co. Monaghan by the scholar Peadar Ó Casaide many years ago. I have also heard it from Co. Fermanagh, from musicologist Joan Trimble, and from Co. Louth, where it was defined by a correspondent, Mary Reilly, as a verb meaning to hide. A Meath teacher, John Gaughan, told me that he knew an old priest who used the word in a sermon, admonishing his flock not to feal their sins in confession. The word was first recorded in this country in the *Ulster Journal of Archaeology* in its 1852–62 volume, series 2.

Even at the beginning of the twentieth century when the great EDD was finally published there were signs that *feal* was almost obsolete. From Westmoreland it was reported that it was 'seldom heard but preserved in an old saying, "them that feals can find."' A Cumbrian correspondent assured the EDD's editor that 'rooks are so cunning that they can pick up the young growing potatoes with their bill, fly away with them to the moors, and feal them until they want them'.

There is no mention in the EDD of the word being used in Scotland, or in English counties south of Chester. Recent surveys have shown that the word is still used by older people in some places in Yorkshire, where the EDD recorded 'he felted the bag under a stone in the garden'; 'Gan and git felt'; and 'they felt it'. Yorkshire boys at play in a school yard were heard to say 'Feal your een' when their eyes were to be covered with their hands in games such as 'tig'.

The word is old. It is first recorded in *c.* 1325 in a *Metrical Homily*: 'In al thing es he nouht lele That Godes gift fra man will fele.' The same Homily has 'For his [Christ's] Godhed in fleis was felid Als hok in bait.' *Morte Arture* of *c.* 1400 has 'Thurghe that foreste I flede . . . ffor to fele me for ferde of tha foule thyngez.' Peter Levins's *Manipulus Vocabulorum*, a dictionary of English and Latin words (1570), has the word: 'To feale, *abscondere.*'

It is of Scandinavian origin. The Old Norse is *fela*, to hide.

✦ FEFNICUTE

I heard this word from the late Beryl Bainbridge, distinguished novelist and playwright, a few years ago, and this is how it came about. We both wrote columns for the London journal *The Oldie*, she a theatre review, and I a column on words, and as I had known her for many years I thought I might ask her to look at a radio play of mine RTÉ had produced, to see whether she thought it could be adapted for the stage. She invited me to visit her in her house in Camden, and having squeezed in to her livingroom past an enormous stuffed bison and a larger than life statue of St Joseph guarding the stairway, I presented her with a bottle of Jameson's Crested Ten. She whooped with delight and opened it immediately, saying that she needed an anaesthetic to roll around a tooth she was to have filled later in the day. We drank some Jameson, then went to a cosy pub, where we had lunch and more Jameson. We left three hours later, Beryl sharing a taxi with me. I dropped her off at her dentist's surgery, where a young man was doing locum for her usual dentist, an old friend of hers, who was on holidays.

Later that evening she rang me, calling the locum some choice names, including *fefnicute*. The fefnicute had refused to put a filling in her painful tooth, because, he said, she was under the weather.

She said that the word meant a miserable git, a mean, sneaking fellow. It was a Lancashire word she remembered from childhood.

It's in the dialect dictionaries, and found only in Lancashire, it seems. Not one of them could hazard a guess as to its origin. Some dictionaries said that the word was confined to describing cunning little children, but one source said that it was 'used to describe people of feeble moral and intellectual endowments'. There is also a verb meaning to fawn, play the hypocrite, or as we might say, act the sleeveen, according to one source.

I am glad now that I wrote down the word from the lips of a great-hearted woman and as they say in Belfast, an even-down good friend.

✦ FELL

The word means a skin, hide. You won't be surprised that it is not known in Ireland outside that dwindling community of Travellers who earn a living buying and selling horses and ponies. I met one of them recently outside Dungarvan, and he told me that the arse had fallen out of the market because of the banks' reluctance to lend money; you couldn't give children's ponies away since the market collapsed, he said, and as for middling-to-useless point-to-point horses, 'they are not worth the fell they stand up in'. My friend's word is as old as *Beowulf*.

Flesh and fell is a Scottish phrase. Walter Scott has 'The horse belongs to a person who will make your honour . . . most welcome to him, flesh and fell,' in *The Bride of Lammermoor* (1819). There is a line in his *Minstrelsy*: 'I wad hae had you flesh and fell.' Hence *fell-monger*, a dealer in hides; this is a west Yorkshire word, found in Banks' *Wakefield Words*, an important glossary from 1865. In Somerset they use *fell-wool* for the wool taken from sheep-skins in distinction to the 'fleece-wool' shorn from the living animal.

The flesh immediately under the outer skin is also called the fell. Jamieson the great nineteenth-century Scots lexicographer said that 'it more properly denotes the cuticle immediately above the flesh'. So, in a tract of 1549, *A Myrroure for Magistrates*, we find 'She haply with her nayles may claw hym to the fell.' Burns in *Ordination*, written in 1780, has 'See how she peels the skin an' fell, / As ane were peeling onions!'

Fell is found in an old proverb mentioned in a chronicle of 1548: 'If Shepe ronne wilfully emongest Wolves they shall lese ether Life or Fell.'

Origin? Oxford says that it's Common Teutonic: Old English *fel, fell* str. neut., Old Frisian *fel*, Old Saxon *fel*, Dutch *vel*, Old High German *fel*, modern German *Fell*, Old Norse (*ber-*) *fiall*; cognate with Latin *pellis*, skin. A derivative from the same root is *film*.

✦ FERE

A Cork lady of my acquaintance wrote to ask me where the word *fere*, in Ezra Pound's *The Ballad of the Goodly Fere*, originated.

Well, the word means friend, companion, and it is found in English as early as *c.* 975 in a translation of St Matthew.

The Scots were very fond of the word. Barbour's *The Bruce*, written about 1375, has 'Till hunt hym owt off the land, as he war a theyff, or theyffs fer.' Robert Burns famously has 'And there's a hand, my trusty fiere' in *Auld Lang Syne*. Scott has 'Well be ye met, my feres five' in his 1802 *Minstrelsy*. Christopher North, a neighbour of the good Sir Walter from Selkirk, in his delightful *Noctes Ambrosianae*, published a few years later, has this: 'There—my trusty fere—you have indeed clapped the saddle on the right horse.'

Langland, like Pound, uses the word in *Piers Plowman* in a religious context; he refers to 'Peter and hus fere Andreu'. *Fere* has survived. It is still in dialectal use in parts of the border counties of England, and in southern Scotland, and in the mid-twentieth century it was in the lexicon of English speakers who lived among the Cruacha Gorma—the Bluestack hills of Donegal. But it was sad to see recently in an academic linguistic survey that the word teeters on the brink of oblivion everywhere.

The Middle English was *fere*, the Old Northumbrian *fǽra*, which came, through Old English, from a Germanic form of pre-English, *gifôrjon-*, from *gi*, together, plus *fôrâ*, going, way. I was taught *The Ballad of the Goodly Fere* in primary school. How times have changed!

✦ FERLY

This adjective, once common in Ulster, Scotland and northern England south to Leicestershire, seems to be in danger of being marked in the dictionaries as obsolete. It means strange, wonderful, surprising. It is also used adverbially.

Scott in *Rob Roy* has 'Its nae mair ferlie to see a woman greet than to see a goose gang barefit.' In a Leicestershire glossary I came across 'He took it ferly = he was surprised at it.'

As a noun it means a wonder, a marvel; a curiosity, novelty, strange spectacle, used of inanimate things or events. 'Sic geat ferlies, sir, my Muse can do,' boasted the poet Ramsay in 1721. The Galloway writer S.R. Crockett, often quoted in the dialect dictionaries because of his rich tongue of Scots, has, in his most famous work, *The Men of the Moss Hags*, published in 1895, 'That had been a ferlie, even in a day of miracles.' The noun was also known in Ulster, and was recorded in W.H. Patterson's glossary in the 1880s. Brendan Adams, an Ulster lexicographer of our own days, gave me the word from Antrim in 1977; he warned that the word was only used by the elderly speakers where he heard it, near Ballymoney.

The word is also used of living things, and meant a strange sight; it was often used as a term of contempt. 'Ha! whar ye gaun, ye crowlin ferlie,' wrote Burns to a louse he saw in a lady's hair. W.H. Patterson heard, 'Ye farley ye,' in Antrim. Some time in the 1970s I heard a Donegalman describe a woman who wore an outlandish dress to Mass as 'a ferly and a half'.

But a *ferly* could also mean a slight peculiarity or eccentricity; a failing or foible. It wasn't considered right to dwell on these, and to do so was termed *to spy ferlies*. The *Ballymena Observer* of 1892 commented, 'Used in the sense of prying or trying to see what you have no right to see, as, "Are you spying farlies?"'

Finally *ferly* was used as a verb meaning to wonder, marvel; to be astounded at. 'An' ferlie at the folk in London' is a line from Rab Burns's *Twa Dogs*, written in 1786.

According to the DSL the origin of *ferly* is Middle English *ferly*, *ferli*; from Old Norse *ferligr*, monstrous, dreadful. Both the EDD and the OED say that the word is the same as Old English *fǽrlic*, sudden.

It is certainly very old. With the meaning strange, wonderful, it is in *Cursor Mundi* around 1300: 'He sal be of ful farli fame.' It is in Chaucer's *Reeve's Tale* around 1386: 'Wha herkned ever swilk a ferly thing?' What a pity it would be if after seven centuries it were allowed to die.

✦ FEY

This adjective, meaning fated to die, doomed, predestined to death or calamity, was once common all over Ulster, Scotland, and northern England. It also meant frenzied, mad. If you used the word nowadays most people would't know what you were talking about.

'"The gauger's fie," by which the common people express those violent spirits which they think a presage of death', wrote Walter Scott in *Guy Mannering*. Gregor's *Folk Lore* of 1888 says that it was believed in north-eastern Scotland that in washing if the soap did not rise on the clothes, there was a fey person's clothes in the tub; and that in the brewing of the ale for Christmas, if the wort boiled up in the middle of the pot there was a fey person's drink in the pot. Scary stuff.

The north of England people were just as superstitious. Oliver's collection of Northumberland songs and folklore says that 'the word *fey* was used to express the state of a person who was supposed to be dying, but who would rise from his bed and go about the house conversing with his friends, as if nothing ailed him. Persons also in health, whose eyes displayed unusual brightness, and who appeared to speak in a wild and mysterious manner when preparing for a perilous journey, were said to be *fey*, that is, doomed shortly to meet their death.'

Hence *fey-crop*, a crop more than unusually good. This was considered to foreshadow the farmer's death. *Feydom*, or *fidom*, was a presentiment or warning of death or disaster. The *Ballymena Observer* of 1892 said, 'If a person does anything unusual or contrary to his customary way of doing things, it will be said, "there's a fidom before him."' Jamieson in his early-nineteenth-century Scots dictionary reported that 'when a peevish man becomes remarkably good-humoured, or a covetous man becomes liberal, it is common to say "He's surely fey". Anything of this kind is called a "fey taikin," a presage of death.'

Fey was also a noun, the warning or predestination to death or calamity. I asked two correspondents of mine, one from Co. Antrim and the other from Ayrshire, if people believed in these matters still, and the answer I got didn't surprise me. Yes, here and there the old beliefs survived, I was told; it was just that people didn't talk about them any more.

Origin? Common Teutonic. Old Saxon *fêgi* (Modern Dutch *vêge*, Dutch *veeg*), Old High German *feigi* (Middle High German *veige* in the same sense, also timid, cowardly; modern German *feige*, cowardly). The Old English is *fæge*, which you'll find in *Beowulf*, fated to die, near to death; but compare the Old Norse *feigr*, mad, frantic, out of one's mind.

✦ FIENT

I first heard this word in the parish of Falcarragh, Co. Donegal, in the early 1960s. Two old sheepmen were renewing acquaintance in Doogan's pub. One said, 'Any news, John?' The other answered, 'Fient a haet,' which was later explained to me as, not a bit, the devil a bit.

I need hardly tell you that the word *fient* is Scots in origin. It is used as an exclamation or oath, generally with a negative sense; it means the devil, nothing, damn the bit, especially in phrases such as my sheepman's *fient a haet*, *fient ane*, not one, *fient ma care*, no matter, *fient nor*, *fient that*, would to the devil that . . . !

Robert Burns had this in *Twa Dogs* (1786): 'Tho' he was o' high degree, The fient a pride—nae pride had he.' In the same work Burns has 'Fient haet o' them ill-hearted fellows.' Walter Scott wrote in *Guy Mannering* (1815), 'Fear'd! fient a haet care I . . . be she witch or devil.' The DSL quotes the *Weekly Magazine* of 15 March 1781: 'A' beggars wha are stout an' stark, But hate the very name o' wark, Fient nor they lie without a sark.' Hogg, the Etterick Shepherd, has, in *The Brownie of Bodsbeck* (1818), 'I gat collied amang the mist, sae dark, that fient a spark I could see.'

I doubt if I would find the word *fient* in today's Donegal, but there seems to be no fear of the word in parts of Scotland. The DSL recorded this in Aberdeen in 1993: 'Fient a bit o ma piece did I gie im.' And the poet Sheena Blackhall, also an Aberdonian, has this in *The Singing Bird*, published in 2000: 'An fa can snib [put a check on] the door o Time wi feint a backwird teet [small sound, squeak] / At sonsie simmer's reamin [creamy] quaich [drinking cup] wi barley bree replete.'

In Scotland they also called An Fear Dubh *fiendin*, *fyandeen* and *finnin* as well as *fient*. The Old Norse is *fjándinn*, *fjándi*, the Old English *feond*, the devil, Modern English *fiend*.

✦ FIGAIREY

This old word, spelled in a variety of ways, *figary* and *fegary* being perhaps the most common, is still alive in Ireland, though I was recently told by the mother of a sixteen-year-old Wicklow schoolgirl that she was told by her teacher that she should avoid using the word, as it wasn't 'correct English'. A Yorkshire chef who works in a Dublin restaurant, and at whose invitation I dined for solving some Yorkshire word problems for him, told me that in a lot of schools around Bradford the Wicklow kid would nowadays be treated in a similar fashion. Dialect is still looked on with suspicion all over Britain.

The word is found, apart from Ireland and Yorkshire, in Scotland, Northamptonshire, Warwickshire where Shakespeare grew up, Shropshire, Oxfordshire, Berkshire, East Anglia and Cornwall. I was astounded to hear that it has been placed on the list of words thought to be in danger of not surviving past 2050 by some university dialect surveys.

It has been defined by Joseph Wright's EDD as 'a whim, freak; a frolic, antic, foolish action,' and figuratively as 'a wild excitable temper or humour; a tantrum.'

Wright's first citation is from Wexford, from old friend Patrick Kennedy's *Evenings in the Duffrey*, 1869. The Duffrey is on the outskirts of Enniscorthy, by the way: 'I wouldn't mind all your former figaries.' 'Let's have none of your fegaries, daughter,' warned a no-nonsense Northamptonshire mother. The word goes back to the time of Decker's *Fortunatus*, *c.* 1600: 'Your body is little mended by your fetching fegaries.' What was that rogue Shirley thinking of in his *Love-tricks*, *c.* 1625: 'I have a great desire to be taught some of your figaries.'

In Yorkshire, the word means an excitable temper. A correspondent of Wright wrote, 'Our mistress is past livin wi' at taims, she gat inta saik a figairy ower next to naut.' William Bottrell, in his *Traditions and Hearthside Stories of West Cornwall*, a fascinating book I picked up in a Truro bookshop last year for a song, has this: '. . . she got into her fagary with the poor woman she abused so.'

Figaries, in the plural, means finery, fanciful clothes, superfluous adornments. Near Shakespeare's birthplace Wright collected this: 'A bow under 'er chin, another atop av her bonit, an' a 'ankircher all th' colours o' the rainbow, with a big 'air broach stuck in it—she was in fine figaries, I can tell yer.' Hence *figariments*, fanciful attire, finery, superfluous adornments. A Shropshire woman, obviously a sensible person, wrote, 'I should like it made nate an plain—no figariments about it.'

The word is, Oxford says, probably from *vagary*, from the Latin *vagari* (Italian *vagare*), to wander. Which is no reason for ignorant teachers to 'correct' pupils who use the better word *figary*, given the 400-year-old benison of speakers from all over Britain and Ireland. Benison? Dear me, they would probably deem that 'incorrect' too.

✦ FLAP-DRAGONS

Have you ever, dear reader, swallowed a flap-dragon? No? Well, neither have I, nor am I ever likely to do so, having read Benjamin Disraeli's description of one in his *Curiosities of Literature* published in 1866: 'Such were flap-dragons, which were small combustible bodies fired at one end and floated in a glass of liquor, which an experienced toper swallowed unharmed, while still blazing.'

The Elizabethans and Jacobeans seemed to have been enamoured with this caper. Ben Jonson in *Cynthia's Revels* refers to them: 'From stabbing of armes, Flap-dragons . . . and all such swaggering Humors'. So does Thomas Dekker in *The Honest Whore*: 'Give me that flap-dragon. Ile not give thee a spoonefull.' In 1622 Fletcher's *Beggar's Bush* has 'I'le go afore and have the bon-fire made, My fire-works, and flap-dragons, and good back-rack.'

The raisin or other piece of fruit such as an almond or a plum eaten in this dangerous caper was also called a flap-dragon. In 1588 Shakespere in *Love's Labour's Lost* has 'Thou art easier swallowed then a flapdragon.' And his friend Philip Massinger in *Old Law* (1599) has 'I'd had . . . my two butter-teeth Thrust down my throat instead of a flap-dragon.'

In the course of time, the word came to mean something of no value. In his sparkling play *The Way of the World* (1700), Congreve has 'A flap-dragon for your service, Sir!'

Earlier, the word was used as term of abuse for a German or a Dutchman. In 1630 John Taylor, the Water Poet, has 'As bumsie as a fox'd flapdragon German'. And it entered the vocabulary of those of the gurrier persuasion. The *Dictionary of the Canting Crew* (1700) has '*Flap-dragon*, a Clap or Pox'. Captain Grose's *Dictionary of the Vulgar Tongue* (1785) also has the word.

Yes, there was a verb, found only once in literature, as far as I can see. Shakespeare employed it in *The Winter's Tale*, Act III, Scene III. It meant to engulf, to swallow at a gulp, as gallants in their revels swallowed flap-dragons to the health of their mistresses: 'To see how the Sea flap-dragon'd it [the Ship]'.

As to origin, nobody is sure. Oxford has a guess: 'The original sense may have been identical with a dialectal sense of *snapdragon*, viz. a figure of a dragon's head with snapping jaws, carried about by the mummers at Christmas; but of this there is no trace in our quotations.' I can do no better than that.

✦ FLISKMAHAIGO, FLISK

I heard the word *fliskmahaigo*, which I must say appealed to me, in the north-west of Donegal; but as it was used by a man who had spent the greater part of his life in Scotland, and because it is not listed in Macafee's *Concise Ulster Dictionary*, I can't say it belongs properly in the Ulster lexicon. It means a giddy, showy or frivolous woman, according to the DSL, which prefers it to the perhaps more common *fliskmahoy*, which means the same thing, and which the great Scots dictionary thinks was invented by Sir Walter Scott in 1816 for use in *The Antiquary*: 'That silly fliskmahoy, Jenny Rintherout, has taen the exies, and done naething but laugh and greet.' Scott also used the word in *St Ronan* in 1824: 'A very decent man, Thamas, and a douce credible house. Nane of your flisk-ma-hoys.'

Fliskmahaigo first appeared in print in 1821 in *The Edinburgh Magazine*: 'Buskit up wi' sae mony lang rairds o' dan dillie teehein an' fliskmahaigo chit-chat . . .' Nearer to our own day, in 1928, J. Carruthers, in his story *A Man Beset*, has 'Just a fliskmahaigo that had led your son astray.'

The first element is *flisk*, the second meaningless variants with possible influence from the placenames *Dalmahoy* in Midlothian and *Lesmahagow* in Lanarkshire, according to the DSL.

Flisk seems to be firmly rooted in Ulster. I have heard it many times in Donegal, where it means to whisk, move busily around the house; and of a horse, to prance about, to be restive: 'Thou never fetch't, an' fliskit,' wrote Burns about his *Auld Mare*. It is a noun as well and means a whisk, a brush. Nora O'Donnell from Dunlewey, at the foot of Errigal, had the word, which she defined as a brush made from *fraoch*, heather. This noun seems to be more common in England than in Scotland. It is found in many dialect dictionaries, including a Goucestershire glossary from 1851, which defines it as 'a brush to remove cobwebs'. Friends of mine who live in Cirencester tell me that the word is still in use. A Berkshire correspondent told the EDD, 'Made by carters from hair taken from a horse's tail, bound on a short handle. A vlisk is found in all stables, being used to vlisk flies off horses in hot weather.'

The DSL says that the word is from Old Scots *flisk*, to frolic. Mainly onomatopoeic, it says, with influence from *frisk*, *whisk*, etc.

✦ FLOURISH

The verb *flourish* is, well, flourishing everywhere English is spoken, but the noun *flourish*, with its variety of meanings including a blossom or mass of flowers on a fruit tree, is in danger of extinction. Indeed, according to the latest surveys carried out by some English universities, it is found in common use only in some northern dialects and in parts of Scotland.

Oxford, in relation to the meaning given above, gives some interesting citations. The first is from the charmingly named *Cockelbie Sow* (Proem, ante 1500): 'A fair flureiss fadit in a falty tre.' The 1548 *Complaynte of Scotlande* vi. 38 has 'The borial blastis . . . hed chaissit the fragrant flureise of euyrie frute tree far athourt the feildis.' In 1868 Atkinson's *Cleveland Glossary* gives 'Flourish, the blossom on fruit-trees'.

There are other dead flourishes listed by Oxford as well as the above floral one. Joshua Sylvester's translation of *Du Bartas* (1605) has 'Childe-great Women, or green Maydes that misse Their Termes appointed for their flourishes'. What a lovely term this is compared with the awful 'the curse'. If I may digress for a moment I was once nearly lynched at a seminar in an American university addressed by a lunatic feminist who blamed men for inventing this term. 'Nay, madam,' I protested, 'thrice nay! It was invented by a woman! Have you not heard of the line "'The Curse is come upon me,'cried The Lady of Shalott."'?'

There are many surviving flourishes, of course, for example in pen-manship a florid decoration such as one sees on Saturday night pub cheques, or in Tudor manuscripts; literary or rhetorical embellishments; in music, a florid passage; a florid style of composition; a decorative addition introduced by player or singer. There are others.

The noun is from the verb *flourish*, from Old French *floriss*—lengthened stem of *florir* (modern French *fleurir*) = Italian *fiorire*, from a vulgar Latin type **florire*, from Latin *flor-*, *flos*, flower.

✦ FOND

This word in the sense foolish, silly, daft, I have come across only once in Irish literature, in an early-eighteenth-century Christmas carol once sung in the parish of Kilmore, Co. Wexford: 'You show yourself fond, I declare.' This meaning was also known in Scotland, Northumberland, Durham and Cumbria; in Yorkshire and Lancashire, Lincolnshire and East Anglia, and in the south-west in Somerset.

A Yorkshire man explained to the EDD that 'fonder and fonder' meant more absurd than ever, 'fondest' the greatest fool of the lot. Another Yorkshireman offered this advice: 'Doant tawak so fond, pretha! The fondest fellah ah iver clapt me ees on—ah think fur shure it's fonder an fonder at he gets ivvry daay.'

Hence *fondish*, weak of intellect; *fondling* or *fondlin*, an idiot; *fondness*, foolishness, nonsense; *fondly*, a simpleton, an idiot, an imbecile.

I have heard 'as fond as a brush' near Lady's Island in south-east Wexford. The EDD records 'as fond as a besom' from Northumberland. In Cumbria they have a saying, 'as fond as the folks of Token'. Apparently the people of Brampton assert that the first coach that passed through Token was followed by a crowd of its inhabitants in order to see the big wheels catch the little ones. Another saying, from Lincolnshire, is 'as fond as the men of Belton, 'at hinged [hanged] a sheep for stealin a man'. John Baret describes foolish as 'fond, *stolidus*' in his 1580 four-language dictionary. The *Catholicon Anglicum*, an English–Latin wordbook of 1483, has 'Fonde, *astrosus*'.

Then there is the *fond* meaning foolishly affectionate, sentimental, 'spoony'. 'How many fond fools serve mad jealousy!' wrote Shakespeare in *The Comedy of Errors*, Act II, Scene I. Hence *fondsome*, loving, affectionate.

Fond, meaning simply affectionate, seems to be in no danger, but the other meanings given above seem to be in trouble, and there is nothing we can do about it, alas.

Oxford says that it is tempting to connect the noun with Swedish *fån(e*, Middle Danish *fåne* fool, modern Icelandic *fáni* swaggerer, vain person; but the history of the English word shows no trace of a long vowel, and the northern English forms have *o*, and not the *a* which in that dialect normally represents Old Norse *á*. Collins points to the fourteenth-century *fonned*, from *fonnen*, to be foolish, from *fonne*, a fool.

✦ FOUNDERED

It must be twenty years ago since I met a man from Derry city who had been in college with me. It was a bitterly cold January day and we decided to have a jar in Trinity's Buttery, because, as he put it, he was *foundered*, by which he meant frozen with the cold.

The word, which is rare nowadays, was once found all over Ireland in a variety of meanings. In the eastern part of Co. Wicklow to be foundered means to be full to the gills of drink, well on the way to being completely sozzled. In Wexford, Carlow, south Tipperary and Kilkenny the word means exhausted, prostrate with tiredness.

In the lexicon of the Irish Travellers *foundered* means lame, used only of horses. One of them, a man called Miley Connors, gave me a cure for a child's pony who was foundered with laminitis; his cure didn't work, by the way. This meaning was also sent to me by correspondents from

Monaghan, Cavan and Fermanagh. It was recorded by W.H. Patterson in his glossary of Antrim and Down words, sent to the English Dialect Society in 1880. Jonathan Swift once wrote of galloping a foundered horse up a causeway; he meant lame.

I'm not sure what old Geoffrey Chaucer meant when he wrote in the *Knight's Tale* that 'his hors for feet gan to turne and leep asyde and foundred as he leep'. Perhaps foundered here meant that he collapsed, as a building might. Caxton had this meaning in 1489 in *The Boke of Fayttes of Armes and of Chyvalrie*: 'The toure foundred and sanke doune in to the grounde.'

Foundered in all its meanings is from the Old French *fondrer*, to submerge, collapse. The word seems to be rare in Old French but is common in compounds such as *esfondrer* and *enfondrer*, words that have a variety of meanings such as to burst, smash; of a boat, to fill with water and sink; of a building, to collapse. The origin of the French words is Latin *fundus*, bottom.

✦ FRANK

This word for a pig sty is long obsolete and is not even included in the EDD, but the great Oxford dictionary has recorded it for posterity. I don't know what happened to it, but words come and go.

The word first appeared in about 1400 in *Morte Arthure*. It was recorded in the English–Latin glossary of *c.* 1440, *Promptorium Parvulorum Sive Clericorum*: 'Frank, kepynge of fowlys to make fatte, *saginarium*'. In 1562 W. Bullein's *Defence Against Sickness* said that 'The fatte Oxe, or vglie brauned Bore . . . can not come out from their frankes or staules.' In 1563 Becon's *Comparison of The Lord's Supper & Pope's Mass*, a scurrilous polemic, has 'I may speake nothyng of that most fatte francke of Whoremongers, Adulterers and suche other idle beastes.'

Shakespeare, the country-bred boy, knew the word. In *Henry IV, Part 2*, Act II, Scene III, he has 'Where sups he? Doth the old boar feed in the old frank?' He has 'He has franked up to fatting for his pains' in *Richard III*, Act I, Scene II.

The word is included in Bailey's *Household Dictionary* of 1736: 'The Frank should be in form something like a dog kennel, a little longer than the boar.' In 1823 Crabb's *Technological Dictionary* included the word. After that date the word disappears from the printed page, and to judge from its omission from the EDD, from the common speech as well.

We find the adjective *frank-fed*, meaning well-fed, in Holland's translation of Pliny in 1601: 'These guests of his fared so highly, that a man would haue said they had bin franke-fed.' And our own Stanyhurst in his 1583 *Æneis* has the nonce word *franky*, looking as if frank-fed: 'We view'd grasing heards of bigge franckye fat oxen.'

The word is from Old French *franc*, in the same sense of sty.

✦ FREEHEEN

It is all of fifteen years ago since a woman from Cashel wrote to me to give me an interesting word which, she said, had not long since died out in Tipperary. The word was *freeheen* and was the name given to the men who sold loads of turf from the county's central bogs, in the towns of Cashel and Thurles. These people arrived in town at the break of day, deposited their loads, and carefully rebuilt them in stacks of approximately half a ton. *Freeheen* was a slightly derogatory term, my correspondent said, just as *culchie* is today, and the local smart boys were careful not to use it to the turfmen's face, on account of their known skill with the ash plant.

Freeheen is from the Irish *fraoch*, heather. Let us not forget that Irish died out in that part of Tipperary from Thurles south to the Suir comparatively recently; the last native speaker, a man called Séamas Ó Maolchathaigh, or Mulcahy, died in the 1970s. He left a very interesting memoir behind him. The turf-sellers got their name not because they lived in the bog—they didn't—but because they bound the tops of their carefully constructed loads with decorative bands of heather. These, my informant told me, were the freeheens, *fraoichiní*, from which the turfmen took their name.

✦ FRIEND

Fifty years ago you'd hear the word friend, with the meaning 'a relation by blood or marriage', still in use in parts of this country, from Co. Antrim to Co. Cavan, and in Scotland from Caithness south to Galloway, and down the east coast from Edinburgh to the Border. It was used in England too, from the North Country south to Worcestershire and Cheshire.

The EDD heard this from a Co. Cavan correspondent: 'We are near friends, but we don't speak.' W.H. Patterson in his glossary of Antrim and Down words (1880) has 'They are far out friends of mine, but I niver seen them.' I am reminded of the West Cork Gaeltacht woman's dismissal of a neighbour's boast of being related to somebody important with 'Sea, leis, gaol mhadar' Úna le madar' Áine!' [Ah yes, the relationship of Úna's dog and Áine's dog]: a far-out relationship indeed. Prof. Proinséas Ní Chatháin gave me that one.

Across the Sea of Moyle James Kelly in his famous collection of Scottish proverbs, written in 1721 and often reprinted since, has 'Friends agree best at a distance,' and he explained that 'friends' here means 'relations'.

I have to thank an Ulsterwoman, Helen MacGowran, now living in Canterbury, New Zealand, for bringing the word to my attention.

The word is Norse in origin. The Old Norse is *frœndi*, but the word may have come directly from Norwegian *frende*, a kinsman, a relative, according to the great Norwegian lexicographer Ivor Aasen.

✦ FROLIC

When *frolic* came to the English language it came as an adjective meaning joyous, mirthful; later it came to mean sportive, full of merry pranks. John Bale, English divine, is credited with introducing the word in 1539 in his *Thre Lawes*: 'And make frowlyke chere, with hey how fryska jolye!' Master Bayle took the word from the Dutch *vrolijk*, from Old Saxon *frólic*, which gave Old High German *frólích* and modern German *fröhlich*; the first element is from Middle Dutch *vró* = Old High German *fró* and modern German *froh*, glad, joyous.

The verb *frolic*, to make merry, to play pranks, appeared in 1593, and the noun, meaning an outburst of fun, a prank, did not appear until 1638. Boy, did the old-timers know how to frolic! We are indebted to Thomas Woodcock for giving us a marvellous account of life in Oxford University in the late seventeenth century; what jolly frolics the staff got up to: 'Of Dr Thomas Goodwin, when ffelow of Catharine Hall, he was somewhat whimsycall, and in a frolic pist once in old Mr Lothian's pocket. This I suppose was before his trouble of conscience and conversion made him serious; he prayed with his hat on and sitting.'

I mention *frolic* because a recent survey has shown that the word is virtually on the brink of joining the *obsolete* category in both American and English dictionaries. Another lovely word has, it seems, fallen on hard times.

✦ FROTH AND LIME

Public house keepers can't get away these days with messing around with the drink they sell. They can't sell slops, for example; and the penalties are so high if they are caught watering the spirits that the exercise is simply not worth it. A retired barman once told me that his employer in the 1950s kept special bottles of watered down gin and vodka to be sold only to ladies, who were thought not to know the difference. He made a bad mistake one night in selling diluted gin to a demure young thing who happened to be a customs inspector. He lost his licence, and my informant consequently lost his job.

Tavern keepers have long been known for skulduggery. There is an interesting line in *The Merry Wives of Windsor*: 'Let me see thee froth and lime.' The allusion here is to the tapster's tricks of frothing beer and liming wine. A beer with no head on it was, and is, considered stale, and the frothing was done by the likes of Mistress Quickly by putting a little soap into the bottom of the barrel or soapy water into the customer's tankard. John Cotgrave's *Wits Interpreter; the English Parnassus* (1655) says that the trick could be thwarted if the customer watched his opportunity and rubbed the inside of the tankard with the skin of a red herring. I see, faix.

But why, you might ask, would tavern keepers stoop to putting lime in wine? Shakespeare mentioned the practice in *Henry IV, Part 1*, Act II, Scene IV: 'You Rogue, here's Lime in this Sack too.' Sir Richard Hawkins in *Observatons in his Voiage into the South Sea*, published in 1622, tells us why it was done: 'Since the Spanish Sacks haue beene common in our Tauernes, which (for conservation) is mingled with Lyme in its making, our Nation complaineth of Calenturas, of the Stone [etc.].' So it seems that the tavern keepers limed their wine to preserve it from destructive influences, and natural decay.

It may have happened in the Boar's Head in Eastcheap but surely not in the Mermaid Tavern in Cheapside immortalised by Keats, or in Dr Johnson's favourite, the Cheshire Cheese, near his home off Fleet Street. Whenever I'm in London I drop in there, and to the Cock Tavern, a short distance away, a place as old as the Mermaid, it is claimed.

I must confess that the power of nostalgia affects me greatly as far as pubs are concerned. It used to draw me back to Frank Swift's Toby Jug in Dublin, now sadly demolished to make way for a big commercial building, and still does to Peter's Pub opposite the old Mercer's

Hospital. I used to drink in both places during my short time studying at the College of Surgeons, a lifetime ago.

✦ FRUITION

The word *fruition* has suffered a fate worse than death in recent times. How often do we read nowadays about 'plans coming to fruition' because slipshod writers and politicians confuse the word with fruit and maturity. The word has nothing at all to do with fruit but comes from the Latin *fruor*, I enjoy, and means enjoyment. The meaning of ripeness, Oxford has found it necessary to proclaim *ex cathedra*, is not to be countenanced anywhere English is spoken.

Christopher Marlowe used the word correctly and beautifully: 'That perfect bliss and sole felicity, / The sweet fruition of an earthly crown.' And Charles Lamb mourned, like many's the man after him, of having been banished from the company of the 'blest Tobacco Boys': 'Where, ... by sour physician, Am debarred the full fruition / Of thy favours ...'

Ivor Brown, Scottish wordsman and editor of the London paper *The Observer* during the Second World War, made sure that none of his journalists misused *fruition*. 'We owe it to Marlowe', he pontificated, 'to save *fruition* from the hackneyed misuse to which modern ignorance and carelessness have brought it.'

✦ FRUMP

Many years ago I wrote about *frump* in *The Irish Times*, and shortly afterwards Benedict Kiely, a much travelled man, remarked to me in his namesake's hostelry in Donnybrook that once upon a time you would hear the various meanings of the word I gave all over Ireland, England and Scotland, and that all of them would be obsolete in this country at any rate in a few years' time. This, I felt, was too bleak an outlook, but recent enquiries on my part suggest that the word is indeed obsolete in all but one meaning, the still fairly common one of a shabby, carelessly dressed woman.

What happened to the meaning of *frump* I heard in Co. Kildare among the stable boys and their masters: a bad-tempered horse? In that lush county, and in neighbouring Carlow, *frump* was also an argumentative woman, a *bawshuck* (Irish *báirseach*), as they used to say in Wexford and Kilkenny. In Waterford recently I asked a few youngish women if they knew that *frump* meant a harridan, a scold; they had never heard of the word, which was common in this meaning in Scotland, northern and midland England, as well as in the southern counties of Somerset and Hampshire. Dickens had the word as an adjective in *Our Mutual Friend*. When he wrote, 'Don't fancy me a frumpy old married woman,' he didn't mean a woman slovenly in dress and habits, but a cantankerous old dame. The origin of both these meanings is probably the verb *frumple*, to wrinkle, once heard all over Ireland and now on the way out, it would seem; it in turn is from the Dutch *verrompelen*, with the same meaning. *Frumple's* first appearance in literature is in the 1398 translation of a medical tract by John de Trevisa. John told his readers that 'the fleshe in the buttocks is fromplyd and knotty'.

I think it can be safely assumed that another *frump*, which I heard in south-east Wexford from Liz Jeffries, Mike Flynn and other old people in Kilmore in the early 1970s, is now obsolete there. It was a verb meaning to jeer, mock, make fun of. It was once common in Scotland, in the northern and midland districts of England, and in the south-west, in the dialects of Devon, Dorset, Cornwall and Pembrokeshire, from which it may have reached Wexford through the age-old contacts of fishing fleets. This verb is possibly connected with *frumple*, some say. Beaumont and Fletcher have this *frump* as a noun in *The Scornful Lady*, first performed in the year of Shakespeare's death, 1616: 'Sweet lady, leave your frumps and be edified.' It is clear from the context that the lady was a scoffer, a mocker.

✦ FRUSH

Deemed obsolete everwhere by the great dictionaries, it was a good, useful word. It meant to crush, batter, bruise. The Scots were very fond of it and it was employed by many good writers. It is in English literature since around 1300, when we find it in the metrical romance *Kyng Alisaunder*. Around 1380 Wyclif had it in one of his sermons: 'Lest þei frushen her owne brest at þe hard stoone.' A hundred years later, Caxton used the word in *The Historie of Jason*: 'They frusshed his helme and made him a meruaillous wounde in his hede.' In 1588 Robert Greene in *Pandosto* observed that 'High Cedars are frushed with tempests, when lowe shrubs are not toucht with the wind.' And Shakespeare employed the word in *Troilus*: 'I like thy armour well! / I'll frush it, and unlock the rivets all, / But I'll be master of it.'

The verb was used chiefly in texts that told of martial deeds, but it made its way to the kitchen as an expression for to carve a chicken, and to dress a fish. It lived on until the end of the eighteenth century. A cookery book written for the upper classes by a snobbish old bags called W. King in 1708 has 'Persons of some Rank and Quality, say, Pray cut up that Goose: Help me to some of that Chicken . . . not considering how indiscreetly they talk, before Men of Art, whose proper Terms are, Break that Goose, frush that Chicken.'

The adjective *frush*, which stemmed from the verb, seems to have had a longer life. It meant brittle, fragile, liable to break. It was recorded by W.H. Patterson in his Antrim and Down glossary in 1880: '*Frush*, brittle, as applied to wood, &c.: said of flax when the "shoughs" separate easily from the fibre.' Enquiries I made recently in the North failed to come up with the word.

It may still be in use in some places in Scotland, since the DSL recorded the word in many works written in the first half of the twentieth century.

The word, which did not deserve to become obsolete, is from Old French *fruissier, froissier* from unattested popular Latin *frustiare*, to split in pieces, from Latin *frustum*, a fragment.

✦ FURNISHED AND BURNISHED

Miss Joan Hunter Dunn was, according to her admirer, John Betjeman, 'furnished and burnished by Aldershot sun' in the charming *A Subaltern's Love Song*. As you will know, Betjeman scarcely knew her, and his publisher, John Murray, feared that the lady would sue him over the poem, in which she supposedly got engaged to the poet in a Hillman car in the car park of a Surrey golf club. She didn't sue; indeed, she said in an interview with *The Sunday Times* newspaper many years later, 'I must say I was absolutely overwhelmed. It was such a marvellous break from the monotony of the war. It really was remarkable the way he imagined it all. Actually, all that about the subaltern, and the engagement is sheer fantasy, but my life was very like the poem.' Writing the same year to Peter Crookston, who conducted the interview, Betjeman recorded his memories of the twenty-five-year-old Joan Hunter Dunn:

> She wore a white coat and had a clean, clinical, motherly look, which excited hundreds of us. She had bright cheeks, clear sun-burned skin, darting brown eyes, a shock of dark curls and a happy smile. Her

figure was a dream of strength and beauty. When the bombs fell, she bound up our wounds unperturbed. When they didn't fall, which was most of the time, she raised our morales without ever lowering our morals. When I first saw her I said to my friends Osbert Lancaster and Reginald Ross-Williamson, 'I bet that girl is a doctor's daughter and comes from Aldershot.'

He was right. He wrote to the artist Roland Pym in 1943 that 'she was a girl to lean against for life and die adoring'. Betjeman's muse attended his funeral service at Westminster Abbey as Mrs J. Jackson and not a soul recognised her. She herself died in London in 2008.

'Furnished and burnished' have intrigued me since I first read the poem. Oxford defines *furnish*, verb as to accomplish, complete, fulfil, and also to decorate, embellish. The verb is from Old French *furniss*—lengthened stem of *furnir*, also *fornir*, *fournir*. (The modern French is *fournir*.)

What our poet's *burnish* does not mean is the more usual 'To make shining by friction; to furbish; to polish.' This *burnish* is from Old French *burniss-*, stem of *burnir*, variant of *brunir*.

Burnish is, in Betjeman's sense, a verb used only of the human frame, and means, according to the EDD, to grow lusty, strong. Our John liked his women just like that. Etymology unknown, Oxford says, and adds that East Anglian dialect uses *furnish* in the same sense, which makes me think that Betjeman picked up the phrase *furnished and burnished* in his beloved Norfolk.

G ∼

✦ GABARDINE

Mary MacCarthy from Limerick city tells me that in her mother's time, out in Caherconlish direction, a *gabardine*, sometimes spelled *gaberdine*, was a loose kind of smock worn by 'farmers' boys' or agricultural labourers. So it was too in my own county, Wexford.

Why, I have often wondered, was it considered in England to be a Jewish garment? You may remember the line in *The Merchant of Venice* 'You spit upon my Jewish garment.' Our own Miss Edgeworth, in *Harrington*, has 'Before his eyes we paraded an effigy of a Jew, dressed in a gabardine of rags and paper.' In 1820 Scott, in *Ivanhoe*, wrote, 'The very gaberdine I wear is borrowed from Reuben of Tadcaster.'

I asked some Jewish friends of mine about the Jewish connection and they are as much in the dark as I am. One suggested that as a gabardine was a garment of extremely poor quality, and consequently cheap, it was therefore favoured by very poor Jews. That seems perfectly plausible to me.

At any rate the earliest forms appear to be directly from Old French *gauvardine*, *galvardine*, *gallevardine*, perhaps a derivative of Middle High German *wallevart*, pilgrimage; the word passed into other Romance languages as Italian *gavardina*, Spanish *gabardina*, the latter of which has influenced the form of the English word.

✦ GABERLUNZIE

This good old Scots word has not, as far as I know, ever travelled to Ireland. The *Concise Ulster Dictionary* hasn't found it at any rate, and there are very few words that have escaped its net, which they rightly threw over the entire historic province, not just Northern Ireland. The word is defined in the EDD as 'a licensed beggar or mendicant; a Bluegown [one who wore the Queen's badge of accreditation as a licensed beggar];

a travelling beggar or tramp'. It gives variants: *gaberloonie* and *gaberlunyie*.

The word is first seen in print in 1508, in Pitcairn's *Criminal Trials of Scotland*: 'Andrew Crossar, Convicted of art and part of the Slaughter of Adam Turnbull of Chalmerlane-Newtoune, and Adam Turnbule, called Gabirlenzeis.' Sir Walter Scott has the word in *Waverley*: 'A species of emblazoning more befitting canters, gaberlunzies, and such like mendicants.' Whitehead, a later author, and a sadly neglected one, wrote in *Daft Davy* (1876), 'I have known as many as four ragged gaberlunzies in the barn at one time.' But by the end of the century a correspondent from Lothian reported to Joseph Wright, then editing the EDD, 'By some of the peasantry this term is still used, but confined to a Bluegown, or beggar who wears the Queen's Badge.'

I should point out that the *Concise Ulster Dictionary* has gaberloonie, and its variants *gaberloon*, *gabaloon*, *gamberlin*, *gamerlooney*, *gobberlooney*, defined as 1. a stupid, awkward fellow. 2. a gullible person. 3. a person who acts the fool. It associates it with the Scots *gaberloonie*, a professional beggar.

As to origin Oxford hasn't much to offer: 'Of unknown origin; *-lunzie* is traditional Scots spelling for *-lunyie*.'

✦ GAD

A man from Gurteen in Co. Sligo sent me the word *gad*, used, he tells me, in his part of the country in the expression 'as tough as a gad'.

The word is from the Irish *gad*, a withe. I remember my father referring to *gad sailí*, a sally withe, a flexible thin rod used for binding things together, and used in the making of a Kilmore Quay fisherman's lobster pot.

Gad appears several times in our Anglo-Irish literature. The late Richard Wall, by an Irish mile the most important of those whose specialism is Irish literary dictionaries and glossaries, gives these two quotations: 'Have you the gad and the suggain wid you?' is from *Tales and Sketches of the Irish Peasantry* by Tyroneman William Carleton, a man who could hould his own wid the besht of 'um in the Paddywhackery stakes. Lady Gregory did better. In one of her plays she has 'What is there but love can twist a man's life, as easily as sally rods are twisted for a gad.' The Breifny Antiquarian Society's Journal furnished me with this: 'Some old Cavan farmers never let out their cows to pasture on May Morning unless there was twisted on each cow's tail a gad of rown tree twigs. This ensured milk and butter against all malign influences for the ensuing season.' The word is also found in *Lisheen Races, Second Hand,* by Somerville and Ross.

Oxford has the word from the 1728 *Songs Costume* (Percy Soc.): 'Or if you'd be reckon'd tight Irish lads, Throw off your cravats and bands, and tie on your gads, And then you'll resemble your primitive dads.' In 1841 Mr and Mrs S.C. Hall's *Ireland, Its Scenery and Character* has '[They] at once twisted a gad round his neck and hung him from the next tree.' This Irish English *gad* is from the Irish *gad*, 'a band or rope made from twisted fibre or rough twigs'. The *a* in the word should be pronounced like the *o* in 'sod', not like the *a* in 'bad'.

Johnny O'Connor, the great Waterford hurler of the late forties and mid-fifties, gave me *Gad ort!*, a nasty imprecation from the west Waterford Gaeltacht; I myself have heard *Gad on ye!* from an old timer in Dungarvan—the *gad* in question being the hangman's noose. *Rince an ghaid*, the noose dance, was gallows humour—a man's dance at the end of the rope. Dinneen's great dictionary, a copy of which James Joyce had by his bedside, by the way, given to him by his friend and mine, Niall Sheridan, has many interesting compounds, including *gad mara*, sea tangle, corrupted by folk etymology to *cat mara* in Conamara; and *gad um ghainimh*, a rope around sand, a useless expedient.

The word has been in Irish since early medieval times. It's good to know that it survives in the English of Ireland as well as in modern Irish.

✦ GAD SEANG

A teacher from west Waterford wrote to me about a term still to be heard in the rich English of his area. He is not sure, he says, how to spell it, but he chances *gad seang*, which means 'a narrow or slander withe' in Irish. The reason he considers the term very strange is that it is used only in sentences such as *he got up on his gad seang to me*, he became slightly belligerent.

He hit the nail on the head in spelling it as he did. I mentioned this *gad seang*, which I also heard in both the Gaeltacht and Galltacht of west Waterford as *gad sanns*, more than fifteen years ago; I am glad it has survived, although it certainly is a quare one, its origin being far removed from slender withes or thin switches. The late Dick Walsh, better known in academic circles as Risteard B. Breatnach, distinguished scholar and author of two superb books on the Irish dialect of Ring and its surrounding districts, gave me both *gad seang* and *gad sanns* around 1972. He attributed them to Archbishop Sheehan of Melbourne, who published a glossary of Ring Irish under the title *Seana-Chaint na nDéise*, a work which was the starting point for Dick's study, called, confusingly I have always thought, *Seana-Chaint na nDéise II.* (When I first saw it, I thought it merely a second edition of Sheehan's book. That it isn't.) At any rate, *Gad seang* is not of Irish origin at all, my friend Dick explained, but a mishearing of the English asseveration *Zounds!* which was a softening of *By God's wounds!* So, the Irish *Dh'éirigh sé ar a ghad seang chugham* would have meant something like 'He started to use Zounds! or By God's wounds! when he addressed me.'

✦ GAMS

The golden era of gams was the era of Sam Goldwyn and his fellow moguls in Hollywood. Betty Grable and Jane Russell spring to mind. Gams, in case you are a person of tender years, are legs.

Kruger Kavanagh once appeared on a televison show with me. Kruger was the fabled owner of a guest house and pub in the Kerry Gaeltacht, and was known to the literati of Ireland as well as to the art world. He had, or so he said, been deported from America when he was caught smuggling booze for the Mafia during the Depression. He boasted of having been friendly with Caruso and the lovely soprano Amelita Galli-Curchi—so friendly with the latter that she crept into his bed in the Waldorf Astoria one night, and announced her arrival by saying, 'Shove over there you Kerry hoor and I'll sing "Killarney" for you. And I won't tell Kate.' He was also friendly, he said, with Al Capone, Bing Crosby and Frank Sinatra. Nobody believed him until the latter two arrived at his doorstep to pay their respects one summer and to talk of auld lang syne.

Well, Kruger never ceased to talk of the lovely gams he had seen and inspected in his time, and when two model girls who were approached and asked to participate on the Irish-language programme about the Miss World Contest cried off, Kruger was asked to come up from Kerry. He revelled in the proceedings, talking about what he called '*geamanna*', gaelicising the word. I asked him what he meant, and he answered, '*Annlaí; féach na h-annlaí atá fúithi.*' *Annlaí* were handles, legs not arms, as I thought they might be.

Gams and Kruger's *geamanna* were originally London cant from the eighteenth century. In 1781 George Parker *Life's Painter* has this in explanation: 'If a man has bow legs, he has queer gams, gams being cant for legs.' The same man has the compound *gam cases* for stockings. Ireland adopted the word very quickly and Patrick Kennedy has this in his *Banks of the Boro* in the year of the Fenian rising, 1867.

Damon Runyon's work was said to make *gams* permanent in American slang. The word, beloved of Harry the Horse, Hymie Banjo-Eyes and their acquaintances, has its origins in the Old Northern French *gambe*, which also gave English *jambe*, used in heraldry signifying a leg; in armoury, a metal leg-piece; and in architecture the side posts of a door. *Gambe* and *jamb* are related to the Late Latin *gamba*, a hoof, in later Vulgar Latin, a leg. But the words may ultimately be of Celtic origin; compare Irish *cam*, bent. Kruger would have savoured that.

The interview was, I find, later scrubbed by some RTÉ person, who needed the tape for another purpose.

✦ GARRET

Lucy Shaw, who hails from Waterford city, wrote to ask about a phrase her English mother used when referring to somebody who was not the full shilling: 'He, or she, hasn't furnished the garret.' Is this the same *garret* as that used for the room under the eaves in a dwelling house or barn, she asks.

Captain Grose's 1790 *Dictionary of the Vulgar Tongue* has this: 'Garret or Upper Story, the Head. His garret or upper story is empty or unfurnished; i.e. he has no brains, he is a fool.' A later collection, the *Lonsdale Glossary* of 1889, has 'To be wrang in yan's garrets, to be wanting in intellect, or suffering from temporary delirium'. I haven't heard the expression used in Ireland.

As for the word's origin, *garret*, the upstairs room, is from Old French *garite*, *guerite*, a watch-tower (modern French *guérite*, a watch-tower, sentry-box, refuge), connected with Old French *guarir*, *warir*, to preserve, guard, cure; ultimately from Teutonic *warjan*, to protect, guard against. *Garret* was first used in English literature in a tract called *Sir Beues* shortly after 1300.

Well, there's no fear of this *garret* becoming obsolete, but here's one which has disappeared many years ago, and never likely to make a comeback.

His other Garret was encapsulated in the now obsolete term *Garret Election*. No, this had nothing to do with the former Taoiseach. No, a Garret Election was a bawdy ceremony held in the borough of Garret, a hamlet of a few tumbledown cottages over which Wandsworth prison, in the vicinity of London, was subsequently built. The Garret 'election' took place to coincide with real elections to parliament in the early eighteenth century. The only qualification necessary to vote for the 'election' of two members of Parliament was to have open-air sex in or near Garret. A contemporary account tells us that 'the candidates are commonly fellows of low humour . . . As this brings a prodigious con-course of people to Wandsworth, the publicans of the place jointly contribute to the expenses, which is sometimes considerable.' Well, it seems that the ladies involved got a few bob for their efforts in putting Garret, and Wandsworth, on the map.

It has struck me that such elections might be an answer to the real problem of voter apathy in this country at present. Any takers, lads?

✦ GILFER

Thomas Greene, a Traveller I met in Dungarvan, asked me over a pint if I have ever heard the word *gilfer* in my travels. A gilfer, he said, is a foul-mouthed woman, given to destroying people's characters. Yes, I've heard the word in the south-east of Ireland from an old woman who lived close to where my mother taught school. The word is also found in various places in England, from the border country to Lancashire and East Anglia. This good word is also from the Norse word hoard. Their *gylfra* means, according to the great Icelandic scholar Vigfusson, an ogre, a she-wolf.

How fares *gilfer* nowadays? It has been described as become obsolete in recent surveys of English dialects, and as for Ireland, we may safely say that the word is no longer used anywhere.

✦ GLORY HOLE

An old friend, the chanteuse Seosaimhín Ní Bheaglaoich, contacted me about the term *glory hole*, now considered obsolete slang by many dictionaries. The term may be defined as a room, or indeed any receptacle, in which things are heaped together without any attempt at tidiness or order. The expression first saw print in 1845 in a book called *The Purgatory of Suicides* by the poet Thomas Cooper, in which he refers to 'a filthy stifling cell to which prisoners are brought from the jail on the day of trial, and which in the language of the degraded beings who usually occupy it, is called the glory hole'.

The expression quickly found its way into British nautical slang. It is the space between or below decks where the stewards sleep.

The word is undoubtedly related to the obsolete verb *glory*, to dirty; and consider this from the glossary *Purgatorium Parvulorum Sive Clericorum* of *c*. 1440: 'gloryyn, or wythe onclene thynge defoylen, *maculo, deturpo*'. Oxford sees a relation between this *glory* and the word *glar, glaur*, mud, slime, found in Scots, Ulster Scots and the English of Northern England. The Scots poet Henryson has the word in *The Wolf and the Lamb c*. 1450: 'That suld presume, with thy foul lippis vyle, to glar my drink, and this fair watter fyle.' Dunbar, another great Scot, in a poem written about 1500, wrote, 'He in a myre, up to the ene, Amang the glar did glyd.' Seamus Heaney, in his poem *Fosterling*, wrote: 'I can't remember not ever having known / The immanent hydraulics of a land / Of *glar* and *glit* and *dailigone*.'

But what is the ultimate origin of these three great poets' *glar*, and if my reasoning is right, of the *glory* in *glory hole*? The Old Norse *leir*, mud, would be my bet.

✦ GOLFING WORDS

A weekend golfer of my acquaintance contacted me to remind me of rounds we played together in a club on the east coast long ago, of which we both were members. The club had many old members who were once members of Her Majesty's forces, including a retired brigadier general and an admiral, I remember. The membership fee was small, and it wasn't until the old guard died and a new breed of business types replaced them that the fees became exorbitant and my weekend partner and I were forced to retire.

My friend reminded me in his letter of the atmosphere that persisted in the clubhouse when we graced the place. It had its oldest members sipping their pink gins, and enquiring gently about how we played; and we were forced to listen out of courtesy to accounts of their own exploits in courses in far-away places such as Singapore and Kuala Lumpur. They were straight out of a P.G. Wodehouse novel. My friend remembered the quaint terms they used when referring fondly to remembered shots played on exotic courses with clubs such as *mashies* and *cleeks* and *niblicks*. My friend's letter asked me to tell him something about these sticks, of which, I venture to say, few modern pros know anything.

Let's take the *mashie* first. My old golfing adversary thought that this was what is now known as an eight iron, but in this he is mistaken, I feel pretty sure. Forgan's *Golfer's Handbook*, published in 1881, refers to it, and it seems to me to have been more like the modern five iron: 'The Mashy is used for the same purpose as the Niblick proper, and only differs from it in its sole and face being straight instead of rounded.'

Some of the golfing bibles say that the club was named from some kind of masher used in their kitchens by Scottish housewives. Ah yes. When in doubt, compose. *Mashie* comes from the French word for a club, *massue*, itself from Vulgar Latin *matteuca*, from *mattea*.

Niblick is a mystery. R. Browning's *History of Golf*, published in 1955, is pretty vague about it: 'Even the niblicks were originally wooden clubs: the first iron-headed niblicks were excessively short in the blade.' 'It is an excellent choice when striking the ball from a cart-rut or from a heel-mark in sand,' said another expert. I thing we'd call the thing a *wedge*. None of the golfing histories I've consulted give the word's origin. Oxford says, 'origin unknown'.

I doubt if my fellow golfer Mr T. Woods knows that the long iron we play for safety off the tee was, since 1800 until fairly recently, called a *cleek*. Oxford says that the word is related to Southern English *cleech*, from Middle English *cleche*, to seize, grasp, lay hold of. I'll take their word for it.

✦ GOLLAUN

This word, sometimes spelled *galaun*, and *galan*, always seemed to me to be native to west Cork, where, until recently, Irish was the vernacular in many of its beautiful districts. I have never heard the word uttered by anybody other than those people, famously described by Conor Cruise O'Brien as being as remote and polite as the Chinese, but I hear that the words are known in other districts where Irish was spoken until recently: in south Kilkenny, south Tipperary and west Waterford, for example.

A *gollaun* is a standing stone, a menhir, a monolith, and is the Irish *gallán* in disguise.

Richard Wall describes one in *An Irish Literary Dictionary and Glossary*: 'Found singly, in alignments or circles, in over 400 locations in West Cork alone, *galláns* are a prominent feature of the Irish landscape, and appear to have been erected in the latter Bronze Age (*c.* 1500–750 BC). Many theories have been advanced to explain them: ritual or burial sites, solar or rural calendars, route or tribal boundary markers, but their precise function is as yet unclear.'

It surprised me to learn that Christopher Nolan knew the word. In *Under the Eye of the Clock* (1987) he has 'The teachers accompanied their pupils and drew their attention to the megalithic gallán or pillarstone, which marked the burial site.' Eric Cross also recorded the word in *The Tailor and Ansty*, straight from the heart of west Cork, near the beautiful lake of Gúagán Barra: 'He has a notion to dig up that big galaun that's on his land to see what's under it.'

The word is also used figuratively. I've heard Nicky Rackard the great Wexford full forward of the 1950s described by my uncle Tom, a west Cork man, as 'a great gallán of a man'. The east Kerry storyteller Eamon Kelly, in his book *English That for Me and Your Humble Servant* (1990) has 'He'll have only one tooth . . . standing up like a golaun stone in the middle of his lower jaw.'

I was in west Cork recently. I stopped to look at the Sullaun river at a place called Poll na Bró, the hole of the quern stone, not far from Baile Bhúirne. There was a gallán in a field nearby with a big black bull rubbing his rump against it. Not wanting to give my celebrated imitation of Luis Miguel Dominguin, I could not examine the monolith, but asked a strapping young fellow who was passing by on a bike with a basketful of schoolbooks on his carrrier if he knew anything about it. No, he didn't. 'What do you call the thing?' I asked. 'A shtone, *airiú*,' he replied. The word *galán* meant nothing to him. Ah, the blessings of education.

✦ GORSEYJACK

Liz Jeffries lived in Neamstown, near Kilmore, Co. Wexford, in the Anglo-Norman Barony of Bargy. She was a fine singer, with an immense repertoire of old songs; her other hobby was collecting words, many of which she sent me. One of favourite ones was *gorseyjack*, a word which I could not find in any dialect dictionary, but which is not, I believe, a remnant of the old dialect of Forth and Bargy. It must be a later word, that is, post 1800, and a native of Bargy, as I couldn't find it in the neighbouring districts. Bill Blake, an ancient mariner from Kilmore Quay, also had the word, as had another Bargyman, Mike Flynn, who lived in Kilmore village a few miles from the waterfront.

Old Mrs Jeffries' definition of *gorseyjack* amused me. 'A young pup,' she said, 'a young scamp who would pinch the like of me on the arse as he passed me by in a pub.'

I can only guess where the word originated. You may have guessed that it has a French ring to it; *garçon Jacques* came to my mind. Did French fishermen, once frequent visitors to Kilmore Quay, bring it with them? Who knows?

I enquired from the young people in Quigley's hospitable pub recently, where both Mrs Jeffries and a young Chris de Burgh (who lived in Bargy Castle not far away) regaled us with song occasionally, what a *gorseyjack* was. Not a soul could tell me.

✦ GRABBLE

In Ulster they have a good word for what a hungry baby does at its mother's breast: they grabble or clutch at the source of nourishment. The late Peadar Ó Casaide sent me this word from Co. Monaghan; he didn't say if it also meant what bould boys do to their girlfriends in the backs of cars, grabbling, not, of course, in search of nourishment. The late Tomás Mac Gabhann from Castleblayney confirmed to me that the boys of that musical town went in a lot for this activity in his youth. The late Davy Hammond had this saucy meaning of *grabble*, a verb heard all over Co. Antrim in his youth. But Rab Sinclair from the same county stressed that grabble also had the meaning to grab trout from river pools after tickling them with the hand.

The verb came, not from Scotland, but from the dialects of England, where it is found in Lancashire, Derbyshire, Northamptonshire, Berkshire, East Anglia, Hampshire, the Isle of Wight, Dorset and Devon—quite a spread. The word is also common in Wales. The word probably came to Ulster with English planters.

The EDD has Rab Sinclair's meaning from north-east Lancashire: 'to grabble for trout'. It also quotes Barnes's Glossary of 1863 from Dorset; and the indefatigable Captain Grose recorded the word from England's North Country back in 1790. It also records an example from Devon, where a complaint was made about young pups 'a grabbling of women's tetties'. A long way from Castleblaney the English *gasúr*s were also at this game. In Devon the word was also used of groping in the dark, an activity known in Irish as *dornásc*.

Another meaning, this one from Northamptonshire, was to work lazily. It was used of men working on the roads, or pretending to, 'grabbling about'. And there was the Welsh *grabbling*, defined by Joseph Wright in his EDD as 'the system of catching salmon by means of a hook'. He explains: 'There is a Welsh system called *grabbling*, that is heaving a large hook over, and as the fish spring, they catch them under the belly.' Wright also records that the Welsh farmers claimed a *grabbling fee*, for allowing people to walk through their fields on the way to the river pools.

Strangely, Wright does not give an etymology, but there can be no doubt that the word came to England from the Dutch *grabbelen*, an extended form of Middle Dutch *grabben*, which gave us *grab*.

✦ GRAFF, GRAFT

Graff or *graft* is found in Scots and is widely diffused through the dialects of England, from the North Country south to Warwickshire, Shropshire, Gloucestershire, Surrey, Sussex, Hampshire and Wiltshire, in a variety of spellings and meanings.

It means, first of all, a grave. Jamieson, in *Popular Ballads* (1806) has the line 'Ye'll mak my greaf baith and lang.' Walter Scott, in *Nigel* (1822) has 'But then there are dainty green graffs in St. Cuthbert's kirkyard.' Before his time the great Ayrshireman Robert Burns has 'Ev'n as he is, cauld in his graff,' in his *Epigram on a Henpecked Squire*. Hence they called a gravestone a *graff-stane*.

Then they had the word meaning a ditch, a cutting or channel in a bog, in Scotland and in many English dialects. Streatfield has the word in his absorbing *Lincolnshire and the Danes*, first published in 1884, a book whose title gives a clue as to the word's origin. In England's North Country a *graff* is also a type of hoe or scuffling implement, used in cleaning ditches. This reminds me very much of the modern Irish *grafán*, a hoe. Remove the diminutive suffix *án* and you have the same word. The Royal Irish Academy's *Dictionary of the Irish Language* gives no etymology of *grafán*, nor of the verbal noun *grafadh*, to hoe. In Shakespeare's country a *graff* is a shallow crescent-shaped implement used for the same purpose and also for cutting shallow drains. From this dialect word it is thought that the modern word *graft* for hard work, often wrongly termed slang in my view, came. The word *grafter*, as in 'he's a great grafter', is common in Irish English. A proud Dublin working man, whose daughter had just gone into the College of Surgeons to study medicine, said to me, 'She's a great little grafter. She'd work the whole bloody night long if you let her.'

So, where does this *graff*, *graft*, and the Irish *grafadh* and *grafán*, I suggest, come from? From Scandinavia. Compare the Danish *grøft*, a ditch, trench; so the Swedish dialect word, according to Reitz, from the Old Norse *gröftr*, a digging. I see that a few dictionaries tentatively suggest that we compare the Old English *græft*, a sculpture. Raamaash, as they used to say in south-east Wexford. Rubbish.

✦ GREAVE

I was sent the word greave, spelled *grieve* by its anonymous sender. He or she heard the word in Arklow, Co. Wicklow. I wonder how the word came to that pleasant little seaside town, where many's the schooner and yacht was built and launched in the old days from Tyrells' thriving shipyard. The word has been recorded in only two places, in Lancashire, and in the late eighteenth century by the Quaker farmer Jacob Poole in the Anglo-Norman Baronies of Forth and Bargy in Co. Wexford. It means a grove of trees.

I have never come across the word, but old Chaucer knew it. He has 'To maken him a gerland of the greves' in the *Canterbury Tales*. 'Greave or busshe, *boscaige*,' wrote Jehan Palsgrave in his 1530 *Lesclarcissement de la langue françoyse*. Spencer, in his *Fairie Queene* of 1596, has 'She fled into that covert greave.' The word has been recorded in Samuel Bamford's 1854 *The Dialect of South Lancashire . . . an enlarged glossary of those words and phrases chiefly used by the rural population of south Lancashire*. Bamford has 'The gryevs or greves in the ancient forest of Rossendale.' Bamford's was a seminal work, drawn upon by many subsequent scholars such as Skeat and Joseph Wright, editor of the EDD.

The word is still alive in Lancashire. At least it was remembered by the novelist Beryl Bainbridge, who gave me the word in The Coal Hole, an old literary pub on London's Strand, now destroyed by the din of pinball machines and juke boxes. Many of the guests at Richard Ingrams' annual *Oldie* luncheon at Simpson's-on-the-Strand gather there for a scoop or two of harder stuff before the champagne reception. Beryl told me that she had used many old Lancashire words in her novels but that she had been forced by her publisher to delete them on the grounds that they might confuse her readers. She appeared pretty annoyed about it.

Anyway, the origin of Beryl's word is the Old English *græfa*, a grove. I wonder does it still survive in Arklow?

✦ GRECIAN BEND

More than once I have been asked what the devil is this compound, found in the song *The Garden where the Praties grow*, so ably sung by McCormack, Frank Patterson and others, and murdered ever since McCormack's recording hit the shops by Ireland's public-house tenors. You'll remember the line 'She walked throughout the world, me boys, without the Grecian Bend.' It caused a lady from Co. Kildare to write to me telling me that having had to suffer her husband's celebrated imitation of McCormack on Saturday nights for the last thirty years, she was beginning to wonder if the Grecian Bend was caused by drink.

Eric Partridge in *The Macmillan Dictionary of Historical Slang* said that the posture was an affected walk used by many women between 1860 and 1890. He says that *The Daily Telegraph* used the phrase in the 1860s of the demure, stooped walk affected by society belles, and that it was anticipated by *The Etonian* as early as 1821. That journal used it of a scholarly stoop; this may be its origin. By 1874, however, *Grecian Bend* was used in milliners' slang for an exaggerated bustle. I have a feeling that the line in the song meant that the girleen in the pratie garden walked without the aid of any such dress improver.

The nineteenth century knew all sorts of affected walking habits. *The Alexandra Limp* was a walk affected by society ladies *c.* 1865–1880 as a compliment to the Princess of Wales, who was lame. Dublin ladies who belonged to a society unknown to Her Royal Highness often had recourse to *The Tout's Twist*. *Tout* was a word in cant use since the sixteenth century. It meant the buttocks.

The men had their own styles of walking while the women were limping and twisting. The fashionable young man of the mid-century affected the *Roman Fall*, an extraordinary walking style in which the head was thrown well forward while the small of the back was pulled well in. This was meant to impress the limpers but not the tout twisters. When the older swingers tried to impress the, shall we say, more spirited young society gals they frequently used the *Roo Roll*, considered a very sexy, lascivious saunter, in which the head was kept well back and the pelvis thrust out, while the hips were rolled. *Roo* was slang for a rake; from French *roué*.

Go on then, have fun. But mind th' oul' back.

H ~

✦ HAIVEREL

This good word, also spelled *haverel* and *havrel* in places, was once common in Ulster, and was recorded by W.H. Patterson in his glossary of Antrim and Down words in 1880. It means a stupid, half-witted person and also a talkative, garrulous man or woman. *The Ballymena Observer* of 1892 also recorded the word. I see that the word may be still alive in the North, because Macafee's *Concise Ulster Dictionary* has it with the following added meanings: a rough, awkward person, a slovenly woman, and a large, untidy heap.

The word is an importation from Scotland. Walter Scott was referring to talkative women when he wrote, 'It was only the New Inn, and the daft havrels, that they caa'd the Company, that she misliked,' in *St. Ronan* (1824). The DSL quotes many Scots writers who used the word down through the years. Scott's friend and biographer, John Lockhart, in *Reginald Dalton* (1823) wrote, 'You don't know what side your bread's buttered on, you havrel you, ye gowk!' Nearer to our own time, J.M. Barrie in *Julie Logan* (1932) has 'Neither good luck nor mischief, so far as I can discover, comes to the havrels of nowadays who think they have talked or walked with a Stranger.'

Robert Burns in *Halloween* uses the word as an adjective: 'Poor hav'rel Will fell aff the drift, An' wander' thro' the Bow-kail.'

There is also the verb. Another Ayrshireman, John Galt, in *The Provost* (1822) has 'Some ne'er-do-weel clerks ere seen gaffawing and haverelling with Jeanie.'

Our word seems to be from *haver*, *haiver*, a verb meaning to talk nonsense; to talk in a foolish, incoherent manner. 'He just havered on about it,' wrote Scott in *The Antiquary*. Hence *haverer*, a foolish talker, and *havering*, talking nonsense. The noun *haver* means chatter, nonsense. Rarely in singular, Scott has 'Dinna deave the gentleman w' your havers,' in *Redgauntlet*.

Hence the interjection *havers!*, nonsense, rubbish! found in many Scottish works such as Perthshire's Ian Maclaren's *Kate Carnegie and those Ministers* (1896): 'Havers, man, ye dinna mean tae say they pack beds and tables in boxes.'

And lastly, *haver* also means a piece of folly or nonsense. 'Fu' lang had he hirpled aboot her, / An' mony a haver had said,' wrote McNeill, a good dialect poet from Lothian in 1890.

As to origin, the SND has this to say: 'Not in Old Scots. Origin very doubtful. The word may be simply an imitation of quick or rambling speech . . . from obsolete English *hav(i)our*, Old French *avoir*, deportment, behaviour, in plural manners, extended to mean specifically foolish or trivial behaviour, fuss, "carry-on," and mainly restricted to talk. The verbal usage would then be derived from the noun.'

✦ HARMING

Helen Gladney, who comes from south Carlow, not far from the lovely village of St Mullins, sent me an expression which she often heard in her youth, relating to school bullies. 'Stop harming that girl or I'll tell your mother.' *Harming* did not mean doing physical damage, but means dwelling on a trifling fault or misfortune; harassing by mocking or imitating in speaking; mimicking. I haven't come across the word anyhere else in Ireland.

And its origin? The Norwegian dialect *herma*, to ape, to mimic, according to the great linguist Aasen, but there is an Old Norse *herma*, to mimic, especially in a bad sense, according to the Icelandic Vigfusson. And please, just because the Norwegians visited St Mullins on many occasions, don't jump to conclusions. The word was imported from Northern England, much later than their time. The sad news is that the usage is now almost certainly obsolete by the banks of the lordly Barrow.

✦ HASLETS & TRAYN ROSTE

I had tried the Scottish delicacy *haggis* many times and liked it. Indeed, I am partial to all kinds of puddings and sausages, including our own *ispíní*, which came our way with the Vikings: the Old Norse was *í-spen*, described as a kind of sausage filled with lard or suet; from *speni*, a teat. I must confess to liking the frankfurters sold on the sidewalks of New York, and the German and Austrian sausages and puddings I find absolutely delicious.

Many years ago a woman called Cathy Barrington from Lincolnshire wrote to me to sing the praises of a dish called *haslet*, which she described as thick puddings, and once a favourite Lincolnshire dish. She sent me her mother's recipe for haslet and they couldn't be simpler to prepare and cook. They are made from minced pork, sage and onions, and the mixture is baked in a pig's intestine. 'A good hog's harslet, a piece of meat I love!' wrote an unusually content Samuel Pepys in 1664.

Mrs Barrington's reason for writing to me was not to extol the wonders of this item of Lincolnshire cuisine, but to ask where the word came from.

Gawayne and the Green Knight, a romance of *c.* 1360, refers to these puddings or sausages as *haslettez*. They probably were French originally: *hastelet* was the Old French word for roast meat, a diminutive of *haste*, a spit, which gave its name to the meat cooked on it. The origin of this *haste* was the Latin *hasta*, a spear.

I replied to Mrs Barrington and asked her if *haslet* was still a popular dish where she lives. 'You must be joking,' she replied. 'Not fanciful, not international, not used by the chefs in posh restaurants, and therefore not really fit for consumption by the upwardly mobile classes.' In another twenty years, she said, even the word *haslet* would be lost to the language.

Just like the word *trayn roste*, mentioned in a fifteenth-century *Two Cookery Books*. A *trayne* (our modern *train*) was a dish consisting of dates, figs, raisins and almonds hung upon a long thread and covered with batter: 'Take dates and figges . . . and then take grete reysons and blanched almonds and pricke them throg with a nedel into the threde of mannys length . . . rost the treyne abought the fire in the spete; cast the batur on the treyne as he turneth abought the fire.'

That would still go down a treat and would make a lovely dessert to follow Mrs Barrington's Lincolnshire *haslet*.

✦ HEARTSOME

What a lovely homely word this is. It is many years since I heard anybody use it. It means merry, cheerful, lively; pleasant, genial, attractive. It was a Scots word, which translated to Ulster and to some of England's northern shires. I heard it from that delightful man James Vittie, who, as librarian in the Linenhall Library, Belfast, helped me with my research on many occasions. W.H. Patterson's glossary of Antrim and Down (1880) also has the word.

Scott, in praising the town of St Ronan, wrote, 'The honest auld town of St Ronan's, where blithe, decent folk had been heartsome enough for mony a day.' John Service of Ayrshire, in his spoof *The Life and Recollections of Dr Duiguid*, written in 1887, praised 'the heartsomest grave in the kirkyard'. But the word was usually reserved for praising the charms of women. 'She laughed a heartsome laugh,' wrote the Etterick Shepherd, James Hogg; and a lesser writer from the border country, John Mackay Wilson, wrote about 'the heartsome smile that arrayed her still'. His work, *Historical, Traditionary, and Imaginative Tales of the Border*, published in six volumes between 1835 and 1840, contains a valuable glossary.

Hence the Scots adverb *heartsomely*, cheerfully, merrily. 'To my frank neighbours heartsomelie I'll drink wi' hail good will,' wrote the Perthshire poet Alexander Nicol in his *Poems on Several Subjects, Both Comical and Serious*, which was a bestseller in 1766.

Alas and alack, the DSL has only two citations from the twentieth century, which tells its own sad story.

✦ HEFT

This word is confined, according to the EDD, to Scotland, Ireland and the midland and southern counties of England. It is a noun meaning weight, especially the weight of a thing as ascertained by weighing it in the hand. Ireland provides the first citation for Wright's dictionary, which is now over a hundred years old. It's from Jacob Poole's Glossary, which was collected towards the end of the eighteenth century in the Anglo-Norman baronies of Forth and Bargy and edited by William Barnes of Dorset in the middle of the nineteenth. T.P. Dolan and the present writer re-edited the manuscript in the 1970s. The citation reads, 'Th' heiftem o' pley vel all ing to lug,' which means 'The weight of the play fell into the hollow.' From south Somerset a correspondent sent this illustration to Wright: 'There's a good heft in this 'ere block.' 'How shall my prince and uncle now sustain so great a heft?' wrote Harington in *Ariosto* in 1591.

We also find the word glossed as 'the act of heaving, an effort, a heave, a lift'.

From Devon, Wright was sent 'It was a tremendous heft to raise the boat to the wall.' Shakespeare had this meaning in *A Winter's Tale*, Act II: 'He cracks his gorge, his sides, / With violent hefts.'

Hence the very common adjective *hefty*, heavy, weighty, ponderous, and the now rarish verb *heft*, which means to raise, lift. I heard 'It's too heavy to heft,' recently in west Waterford. *To heft* also means to weigh in the hand, to lift in order to judge the weight. Wright was sent this explanation from Hampshire: 'To heft the bee pots is to lift them in order to ascertain how much honey they may contain.' From east Devon came 'He took up a root or two here and there, and "hefted it" (that is to say poised it carefully to judge the weight, as one does a letter for the post.)'

One last *heft*: to throw, heave. I once heard old Paddy Ryan from Old Pallas, Co. Limerick, who broke the world record in hammer throwing in 1913 and won Olympic gold for the USA in 1920, tell the then Olympic champion, Harold Connolly, who came to visit him, that he had a day when he'd heft him and his hammer out of the stadium. Connolly enjoyed the night's crack.

Heft is a late derivative of *heave*; from Old English *hebban*; related to Old Norse *hefja* and Old Saxon *hebbian*.

✦ HEFT 2

This is a farmer's word, or used to be. The nature of farming has changed greatly in recent years, particularly of dairy farming, and I suppose I shouldn't have been surprised that a young west Waterford farmer, a particulary good one, I should add, never heard of this word *heft*, defined in the EDD as a verb meaning 'To confine or restrain nature; especially to let a cow's milk increase until the udder gets large and hard, as is done with milch cows taken to market'. This is an improper practice and causes the animal a lot of pain. It has, thankfully, been eliminated from farming since I heard it about half a century ago.

I heard this verb *heft* on one other occasion, and in a different context. A medical doctor and a very good friend of mine, Tom Gilroy, a Mayo man who practised in Newbawn, Co. Wexford, about ten miles from New Ross, was very interested in what he called 'alternative' words for different ailments, words used by the ordinary people in describing what was wrong with them. He was told one day by a farmer that he thought he was *hefted*, and this proved to be an accurate diagnosis: to be hefted meant that a patient's bladder was distended owing to a retention of urine, causing severe pain.

These words I refer to, both involved in the confining or restraining of nature, are Scandinavian in origin. Aasen in his great Norwegian dictionary has *hefta*, to bind, restrain.

✦ HEND

I wondered the other night when I found the verb *hend* among my notes how it came to be used in Counties Wexford and Waterford, and as far as I know, nowhere else in Ireland. I looked it up in Joseph Wright's EDD, and I was surprised not to find a trace of it anywhere. I then searched the great DSL which comprises electronic editions of the two major historical dictionaries of the Scots language: the twelve-volume *Dictionary of the Older Scottish Tongue* (DOST) and the ten-volume *Scottish National Dictionary* (SND), twenty-two volumes in all. And what did I find? Nothing. I tried the CUD as well. Same result.

I found the word in Oxford. It means to hold, catch, handle. It probably predates its use in English literature in the romance of *Coer de Lion*, written some time after 1300, in which we find 'They . . . toke the temple of Apolyn. They felde it down, and hende Mahoun.' Oxford also cites it from a poem of *c.* 1460, published in *Political, Religious & Love Poems*: 'That bondis of helle can me nat hende.' In 1596 Spenser used the verb in the *Fairie Queene* v. xi. 27: 'As if that it she would in peeces rend, Or reave out of the hand that did it hend.'

Oxford calls the verb obsolete, and it is probably obsolete by now in Carne, Co. Wexford, where I heard it in 1970, used by Phil Wall, who was then ninety, and in Dungarvan in 2000 by Maurice Fraher, then in his eighties. Phil Wall was speaking about hurling. He said that hurlers should pull on the ball on the ground and not hend it every time it came near them. Good advice. I never saw the great Wexford hurler of the 1950s, Ned Wheeler, hend the ball unless it fell into his hand. I send my regards to him, as I note the passing of the great Cork corner back of the 1940s, Din Joe Buckley, another great ground hurler who rarely hended the ball. In Dungarvan one night, Maurice Fraher asked me to hend his pint for him as he lit his pipe in a crowded bar.

So, did the Viking invaders leave this word in their south-eastern stronghold? Perhaps. Oxford says that it may be the same word as *hand*, either from Old English *gehendan*, or directly from the Old Norse *hende*, to catch with the hand. Swedish has *hände* and Danish *hende*. I think it sad that this venerable word is now probably extinct, killed off, like so many others, by baneful modern influences.

✦ HENTING & HONING

Friends who were contemplating a trip to the Isle of Skye phoned me to ask my advice about travelling there. I phoned a friend who lives on that lovely, romantic island off Scotland's western shores, and he said that it was a pity that they couldn't visit in the autumn when he could help him to *hent* his sheep on the hills behind his house—to drive them down from their summer pasture to graze nearer his farmstead.

Hent is an interesting verb and the dialect dictionaries usually describe it as an Orkney and Shetland word. But it has travelled, and I have heard it at Brocagh fair in Co. Donegal, used by a man from Glenties direction.

In Shetland and Orkney the word also means to gather up and stow away; to gather oneself up, to be off. The word is of Scandinavian origin. The Old Norse has *heimta*, to bring home, specifically to bring back the sheep from the hill before the snows set in. Norwegian has the dialect word *hemta*, also *heimta* and *henta*, to gather, take up, pluck, according to the great lexicographer Ivor Aasen.

Far from the Scottish isles, deep in Co. Tipperary, John Travers, a Dubliner born and bred, heard the word *honing*. 'She's always honing about something,' said a man in a Newport bar to his friend. Mr Travers wrote to me to ask if *honing* is from the Irish cry of lamentation, *ochón*.

Hone is common in Scotland. In *The Fair Maid of Perth* Sir Walter Scott has 'Thou wakest to hone and pine and moan.' It looks as if it travelled from Scotland to the USA with the reluctant immigrants of the sixteenth and seventeenth centuries, because we find it everywhere they settled, from Boston to Alabama. It has been welcomed into the rich English of Black America as well, and I once heard 'Why are you whinin' an' honin'?' from the lips of a black woman trying to calm her tired baby on a Philadelphia bus.

Not many people read the Uncle Remus stories any more, I suspect, but in one published in 1884, *Nights With Uncle Remus*, there is this: 'He does nat'ally hone for ter be los' in de woods some mo'.'

In answer to Mr Travers's question, the word is not Irish in origin. It is from the Norman French verb *hoigner*, perhaps from *hon*, a cry of discontent.

✦ HEPPEN

This adjective and adverb never travelled to Ireland as far as I know, and more's the pity. It means tidy, neat; respectable; handsome. It would serve us here as a word that is the antithesis of the native *streel*; it is elegant, and it has a lovely sound to it.

Captain Grose recorded the adjective from the North Country in 1791; Nathan Bailey has it in his dictionary in 1721. The editor of the EDD was sent 'All the stacks is thacked [thatched], an' the place looks real heppen noo,' from north Lincolnshire. A Yorkshire correspondent sent this: 'Bessy, his wife, was the heppenest woman you'd find i' ten toons.' *The Leeds Mercury*, in its Christmas supplement for 1890, had '"It's nice and heppen". This word is applied to linen and cotton to describe the evenness of the texture.'

Heppen also means handy, deft; clever at work. From one of Wright's Lincolnshire correspondents came this example: 'Bill is a heppen lad; he is wonderful heppen. He is a deal heppener than I was.' Most of the EDD's citations came from Lincolnshire and Yorkshire, a clear pointer towards the word's origin, for this is the country of the Danelaw. The Old Norse is *heppinn*, lucky, also dexterous; and *heppen* is the same word as the Norwegian dialectal *heppen*, lucky, fortunate.

And the bad news is that the word is dying out gradually across the Irish Sea.

✦ HEW

Unless you come from coastal areas of Devon or Cornwall it's unlikely that you'll have come across this word. It's a fisherman's word, used until recently by those who fished for pilchards in seine boats, and I made a note of it because of a fascination I have with words connected with the sea and with fishing in particular, be they weather words to describe various kinds of fogs and hazes, or taboo words which fishing people discard and substitute with made-up terms because they bring bad luck.

To hew means to make signals from the cliffs to the fishermen to let them know in what direction the pilchards are. An old Cornish account I read has this: 'The more general and successful method of enclosing fish is for the seine boats to receive their signals from a man called a *huer*, stationed on the top of the nearest cliff, who, from this vantage ground, can have a much clearer sight of the shoals. The *huer* has a furze bush or other signal in each hand, and by preconcerted movements can accurately guide the boats below.'

Hence *hewer*, the signal man, and *hewer-house*, a shed built on the very high cliffs to shelter him from the gales.

On one of my fairly frequent visits to Cornwall (as I mentioned previously, a son of mine had a medical practice there at the time), I expressed surprise that boats would not have up-to-date equipment to find the pilchards, and was told that not all the old seine boatmen were rich, and that the old method was as good as any. I doubt that, somehow, and there are some disturbing accounts of the hewers, schoolboys some of them, falling from the treacherous cliffs in bad weather.

The old ways die hard in Cornwall but the days of the *hewer* are now gone forever. So too, needless to say, is the need for the word *hewer*, which is from the French *huer*, 'crier' according to the lexicographer La Curne de Sainte-Palaye's *Dictionnaire historique de l'ancen langage françois*, published in 1882.

✦ HIND

Many years ago, in a Carlow town hotel, I heard a waitress call an obnoxious reveller a *hind*. She glossed it for me in very colourful language. As far as I remember she was a Wexfordwoman. What intrigued me later when I looked up the word is that it is found, according to the EDD, in only one district in England, East Anglia, and in Ayrshire in Scotland. In Cozen-Hardy's book *Broad Norfolk*, published in 1893, and of which I have a copy thanks to friends I have there, the word is used to describe a nasty character; it is found too in east Suffolk.

The late Billy Rackard, the Wexford hurler, told me that the word was common among old people who lived around the foot of the Blackstairs mountains; but outside of that part of the south-east, I have never come across it.

The word is related to *hind*, a farm labourer or ploughman; a menial farm servant; hence it was a term of disparagement in East Anglia and in Carlow/Wexford. 'Summon the hind in to perform his appointed duties in the barn,' wrote a rather pompous Ayrshire man, White, in *Jottings*, published in 1879. There wasn't much hope that the poor hind's family would get on well in life: his wages were generally pitifully small, and they had a saying in East Anglia, 'The hind ploughs as his father ploughed.'

There was, however, another stratum: there were hinds who were hired by the year and who were well treated by the standards of the day. Their only worry was they could be turfed out at the end of the year, and replaced by a younger man, at the farmer's whim. A Scottish correspondent of the EDD's editor explained that these hinds were 'farm labourers engaged by the year, their wages being so much in money, with house, firing milk, meal, and potatoes—all which things in kind go by "the benefit"'.

One can readily understand how the word *hind* was reduced from meaning an honest working man to an unprincipled hooligan; but originally the word was formed from Old English *hí(g)na*, genitive plural of *híwa*, *híga*, member of a family, a servant.

✦ HIRSEL

There is a Scots saying, quoted by the poet Ramsay in his *Proverbs* of 1737, 'Ae scabbed sheep will smit the hale hirsel,' which is the equivalent of saying that a bad apple will destroy a bagful. A hirsel is an old word for a flock of sheep, and it is, or was, used figuratively in their sermon by preachers. 'This was deny'd, it was affirm'd; The herds an' hissels were alarm'd; The rev'rend gray-beards rav'd an' storm'd,' wrote Ayrshire's Burns in *To W. Simpson* in 1785. 'We are His hirsel, He does us feed,' wrote a somewhat more pious Scot, Ellis of Roxburghshire, back in 1885.

Hirsel also means the gathering place or feeding ground of a man's flock. 'Like a poor lamb that has wandered from its ain native hirsel' is from Walter Scott's *Nigel*, published in 1822. Figuratively it means a gathering, a company; a large number of people or things; a quantity, a collection. This meaning is found to this day in Counties Antrim and Down. Davy Hammond the folksong expert sent *hirsel* to me from his native Co. Antrim: 'She has a hirsel of weans to feed.' I see that *The Ballymena Observer*, edited by W.J. Knowles in 1892, has the same phrase, and adds, 'a hirsel of clothes'. From Northumberland the editor of the EDD was sent, 'A great hirsel of wood.'

The DSL has the following etymology: 'Old Scots *hirsell*, a flock, from ante 1400; Middle English *hirsill* from 1366; Old Norse *hirzla*, *hirðsla*, safe-keeping, from *hirða*, to tend sheep.'

This word is not to be confused with another Scots *hirsel*, defined by the EDD as to move or slide with grazing or friction; to move in a creeping or trailing manner; to cause to push, slide or roll down, and exemplified by its use by both Scott and Stevenson. The former has 'He sat himself doun and hirselled himself doun into the glen,' in *Guy Mannering* (1815); while the latter in *Catriona* (1893) has 'There is many a father, sir, that would have hirselled you at once either to the altar or the field.'

The EDD invites us to compare Danish *ryste*, to shake, and Old Norse *hrysta*. This *hirsel* has also been recorded in Ulster by the CUD, but C.I.

Macafee's excellent dictionary thinks that the word is onomatopoeic. She may be right. She usually is. The DSL agrees with her.

✦ HIST

This is an interjection I once heard from a farrier, the late Jack Lynch, near Priestsnewtown, Kilcoole, in Co. Wicklow: 'Hist up, boy!' I wouldn't have paid much heed to it if I hadn't come across it in Wright's EDD: it is also found in Scotland, Cumberland, Lancashire, Lincolnshire, Berkshire, East Anglia and Kent, where it has Jack's meaning: a call to a horse being shod to lift up its leg.

A friend who lives in Norfolk has heard the interjection, as a call to a horse when it stumbles: 'Hist, boy!'

Oxford defines *hist* as a verb meaning 'to urge on, to incite', and points to the exclamation *hist*, 'a sound made to encourage a dog or other animal'. The DSL points to the Middle Dutch *hiss(ch)en*, to incite a dog. It may well cover Jack Lynch's meaning of the exclamation, and the Norfolk horsewoman's as well.

✦ HOAST

This word once had a safe habitation in Southern Irish English, in Northern Irish English, in Scots and in various dialects in England, from the Border to Nottinghamshire, Leicestershire, Northamptonshire and East Anglia. It was also written *host*, *hawst*, *hust*, *whust* in the English dialects. It means 1. A cough. 2. A hoarseness, huskiness; a cold on the chest or in the throat. 3. Figuratively, a thing or matter attended to with no difficulty.

The word is an old one. It is found in Old English as *hwósta* around 1000, and in *Cursor Mundi* around 1300: 'Als aand with host in brest is spred.' It survived in dialect, and some literary men used it. Scott has 'Mony a sair hoast was amang them,' in *The Antiquary*. *Hoast* meant a cough here. Streatfield, in his engaging book *Lincolnshire and the Danes*, published in 1884, gives the word as meaning 'a hoarseness'. A contributor to the EDD from west Yorkshire gave editor Wright the explanation 'Hoast is a very sore throat.'

The figurative meaning is explained by the Scottish lexicographer John Jamieson in his *Etymological Dictionary of the Scottish Language*, written in 1808 and revised between 1879 and 1882: 'It did na cost him a host, he made no hesitation about it.'

The word is also found as a verb meaning to cough. 'Have you heard her hosting?' asks J.M. Barrie in *Sentimental Tommie*, written in 1896. The verb also meant 'to belch up' in Ayrshire. Robert Burns has 'Some laird . . . may . . . host up some palaver,' in *Willie Chalmers*.

Hence we have the verbal noun *hoasting*, the act of coughing. 'Something gaed doon the wrong hass [var. of *hals*, throat, gullet], and sic a fit o' hoasting cam on,' wrote John Service from Ayrshire in *Notandums*, published in 1890, a very valuable repository of late Scots. And the adjective *hoast*, husky, was sent to Joseph Wright from many parts of the England midlands. 'He war that hoast he could scarce speak,' wrote a Nottinghamshire correspondent.

As for the origin of this long-neglected word, the Old English *hwósta* is not known to have survived in Middle English; and it may be said that our *hoast* was the cognate Old Norse *hóste*, a cough.

✦ HOISE

When, as schoolboys in New Ross, Co. Wexford, we watched coal being unloaded from the last of the old schooners, *de Wadden*, we paid no heed to the dockers shouting *Hyse her up*! because this local variant of *hoise* was heard all around us. *Hoise* was rarely used among working people, unless they had gone to school and were told not to use *hoise*, it not being 'good' English.

Hoise and its variant meant, of course, to lift up, and it is quite old. Found nowadays only in Scotland, Cumberland, Yorkshire and Lancashire in our neighbouring island, it is a noun as well as a verb. 'They gie her on a rape a hoise,' wrote Burns in *Ordination*. 'The little man gave him one hoise,' wrote Crofton Croker in his *Fairy Legends and Traditions of South Ireland*, of 1862. Patrick Kennedy the Wexford folklorist and writer used the noun in his most famous book, *The Banks of the Boro* (1867): 'Ay, and ourselves get a hoise, and maybe fall down on the top of Castleboro and be kilt.'

Kennedy had the noun *hoising*, used to describe the action of being lifted on the back of another child in school, the better to give the master an angle to administer a flogging on the backside. 'The result was a severe hoising,' he wrote in *Fireside Stories* (1870); and again, in *The Banks of the Boro*, he had 'Won't you call me to hold up John Dunne the next time he desarves a hoising?'

As a verb *hoise* is found in Scotland from the Border country to Orkney in the far north, as well as in southern Ireland. To those who would say that here we have merely a corruption of *hoist*, I would answer, tell that to Master Shakespeare, who, in *Henry IV, Part 1*, Act I, has 'We'll quickly hoise Duke Humphrey from his seat.'

Our New Ross *hyse* was given the blessing of lexicography by Jehan Palsgrave in his *Lesclarissement de la langue francoyse* in 1530: 'I hyse up the sail, as shypmen do, *Je haulce*.' Standard English *hoist* is a corruption of *hoise/hyse*, according to Oxford; and our Wexford word corresponds with Icelandic *hisa*, Norwegian and Swedish *hissa*, Danish *hisse*, Low German *hiesen*, *hissen*, whence German *hissen*, Dutch *hijschen*: 'het zeyl ophijsen, to hoise the sail', as Hendrik Hexham the Dutch lexicographer put it in his 1658 *Het groot Woorden-Boeck: gestelt in't Neder-duytsch, ende in't Engelsch*.

✦ HOOSHT

A few years ago I heard the word *hoosht* in a Dungarvan hostlery. Two old-timers were talking about banks, and one man, eighty-seven-year-old Maurice Fraher, who was born at the foot of the Comeragh Mountains, said that having thought about it long and hard he had come to the conclusion that it would be safer to keep his money in the hoosht by the bed. This was before the revelations about our bankers' nefarious capers came to light; what a wise man old Maurice proved to be. *Hoosht* is from the Irish *húiste*, a word known to my friend Risteard B. Breatnach, the UCD linguist who wrote two classic books, *The Irish of Ring* and *Seana-Chaint na nDéise II*, a study of words collected by Archbishop Sheehan but never published by him. *Hoosht/Húiste* is either from the English *hutch*, in the sense a chest or coffer in which things are stored, or directly from the French *huche*, 'a hutch or binne', according to Cotgrave's French–English dictionary of 1611.

Hutch is in English since 1303, when it appears as *hucche* in R. Brunne's *Handlyng Synne*: 'To ley hyt vp . . . Oþer yn cofre, oþer yn hucche.' Another early appearance is in *Promptorium Parvulorum Sive Clericorum* of about 1440: 'Hoche . . . *cista, archa*.' Both the French and English words are from the Medieval Latin *hutica*, defined in the eleventh century as 'cista, vulgo Hutica dicta'; but nobody is sure what the origin of that word is. Some refer it to the Old High German *huota*, care, keeping, or *hüten*, to watch, guard. The Middle English *hucche*, according to Oxford, 'ran together more or less with *whucche, whicche*, from Old English *hwicce* in same sense.'

I like both the Southern Irish English *hoosht* and its Irish parent *húiste*. The trouble is that, try as I might recently, I could find nobody in Dungarvan, An Rinn or An Seana Phobal who could bring either word to mind. Good words now gone forever from the speech of the people, I fear.

✦ HORBGORBLE

I wonder does this word still survive in Antrim. It was sent to me many years ago by a Glensman, but a few years ago I asked David Hammond how it fared and he said that it was thirty years since he came across it.

A friend of mine from Philadelphia asures me that the word is alive and well in that part of the world, where it came, we can safely assume, with the great Scottish Presbyterian exodus in the eighteenth century. My friend sent me a newspaper cutting from the time of Mr Al Gore's failed attempt to gain the presidency. You may remember that Gore spurned Bill Clinton's offer to give him a helping hand—some scruples he harboured about Bill's capering in the Oval Office with Miss Lewinsky was, it seems, the cause of his rejection of help. The writer of the piece, obviously a Democrat who wore his heart on his sleeve, complained of 'Gore horbgorbling around'. By this he meant mooching around in a feckless manner, to no purpose. Mr Gore paid dearly for his horbgorbling.

The late Ivor Brown, Scottish journalist and scholar, once wrote of the trial of a young Caithnessman for alleged sexual assault on a servant girl. It was a strange case. The charge was brought not by the girl but by her employer, who was, he insisted, *in loco parentis*. It became clear that there was no suggestion of rape, but there was a sexual misdemeanour of a gross type involved which should not be allowed in a Christian society to go unpunished, according to the lassie's employer, even though she was over the age of consent. The magistrates decided to hear her evidence. She said that her boyfriend was only horbgorbling when her employer arrived on the scene. The magistrates readily accepted her explanation; there was no need for her to amplify or explain what she meant. Her unco guid employer was told that he was a meddling auld fool and the case was dismissed.

✦ HOUGHER

Northumberland Words. A Glossary of Words used in the county of Northumberland, by R.O. Heslop, was one of the valuable works used by

Joseph Wright in compiling the EDD. The collection was published by the English Dialect Society between 1892 and 1894. I had fun recently sending words from the glossary to a man who was in primary school with me in New Ross in old God's time, and who has spent most of his life since then in Newcastle-upon-Tyne. My purpose was to find out if the more interesting of the words had since survived, and I was amused to find that *houghers* was still used by some of the members of the criminal classes there to denote members of the police force. Wright's great dictionary, by the way, declared the word obsolete in 1906.

Heslop's work defined *hougher* as 'the public whipper of criminals; the executioner of felons at Newcastle', and it relied on the *Gentlemen's Magazine* of 1794 for the following information: 'the hougher was appointed to be common executioner in hanging of felons, putting persons in the pillory, clearing the streets of swine, and to do and perform all the other matters belonging to the place and duty of the hougher'. Part of his duties was whipping hooligans at the cart-tail, leading round the inebriate in his 'drunkard's cloak', and following around the scolding woman in her 'branks', or iron bridle.

In the course of time the hougher became simply an inferior officer who informed police of the breaking of the Corporation's laws on dumping rubbish, after-hours drinking, illegal clubs and other such matters; and as that job became a thing of the past, the riff-raff of the town became the sole possessors of the word *hougher*.

Wright quotes Brand's *History of Newcastle* (1789) in explanation of the word. 'He is called hougher from the power he is said to have formerly in cutting the houghs or sinews of swine that were found infesting the streets of the town.' In 1827 he had a yearly salary of £4.6s.8d.

My friend tells me that the behaviour of certain elements on a Saturday night after football matches leads some people to wish that the Corporation would bring back both the cat and the hougher for a while to teach them a lesson they wouldn't easily forget. Perish the thought.

✦ HOVEL

A Traveller who dealt in horses and who belonged to one of the travelling clans of Co. Wexford, Miley Connors, gave me this word many years ago. It means a nosebag for a horse. I have enquired since of quite a few Travellers, but they did not know the word. Neither did the late

Master Paddy Greene, or Pádraig Mac Gréine of Ballinalee, Co. Longford, our most eminent commentator on the lives and language of our indigenous nomadic people.

Where Miley got the word I don't know; it may have come here courtesy of north of England farmers. It was recorded many times in Yorkshire as *hovel* and *huval*. In a nineteenth-century journal still pored over by dialect studies people, *The Barnsla Annual*, we find this in the 1852 edition: 'Bless me wot truuble yo hev we that noaze a yors, if I wor yo ide hev a huval for it.' Hence *hovel* or *huvil*, to enclose in a nosebag.

Hovel also meant a cover for the protection of a sore or cut finger. It was usually made of leather. If old Miley Connors knew this he never mentioned it to me. It has been recorded in Cumbria, Lancashire, Lincolnshire and Yorkshire. Marshall mentions it as being common in south Yorkshire in his *Rural Economy* of 1788.

I'm pretty sure that the *hovel* of the Wicklow farrier Jack Lynch is from the same source. What Jack called the *hovel* was the hood over the forge fire. This hood was mentioned in Holmes's *Armoury* of 1688 as 'The Hovel or Covel of the Hearth which ends in a Chimney to carry the Smoak away'.

This useful word, now obsolete or close to it, is, perhaps, a derivative of Old English *húfe*, a head covering, according to the *English Dialect Dictionary*; but others favour a connection with Middle High German *hobel*, covering, lid.

I/J ∼

✦ IMPUDENCE

The usual meaning of the noun impudence is, to use Oxford's definition, shameless effrontery; insolent disrespect, insolence; unabashed presumption. As Master Shakespeare wrote in *A Winter's Tale*, Act III, Scene II, 'I ne're heard yet, That any of these bolder Vices wanted less impudence to gaine-say what they did, Than to perform it first.'

I heard another meaning in Co. Limerick, back in the 1950s, and later from people who lived in Offaly and Laois: shamelessness; immodesty, indelicacy. This meaning is now obsolete according to Oxford, but only the other day I heard a Waterford woman describe a girl who wore a rather skimpy summer dress as an impudent hussy.

Chaucer had this meaning in the *Parson's Tale, c.* 1386 [Twigs of Pride]. 'There is . . . Arrogance . . . Inpudence [v.r. Impudence] Insolence . . . and many another twig.' Shakespeare in *All's Well That Ends Well*, Act II, Scene I, has 'Taxe of impudence, A strumpet's boldnesse, a divulged shame'. The 1682 *Hereford Diocese Register* records that 'This deponent, blushing to see soe much impudence betwixt the said persons, immediately went out of the same Chamber.' And in 1712, J. Digby's translation of Epicurus has 'Tis very well known, that Crates and Diogenes have made profession of Beastly Impudence, even in public places.'

In a good or neutral sense the word also meant freedom from shamefastness; cool confidence. The playwright Thomas Fletcher in *The False One* (1619) had 'Off, my dejected looks, and welcome impudence! My daring shall be deity, to save me.' A later playwright, Thomas Shadwell, famous for his risqué aphorisms and his stage-Irish priests like Teague O'Divilly, has, in *The Squire of Alsatia* (1888), 'Learned lawyer of little practice, for want of impudence'.

My friend the late Augustine Martin heard yet another meaning of impudence in his native Leitrim. Quite by accident I saw this in a

Cumbrian glossary recently; it is Gus's meaning: 'Impudent. In good spirits. The idea intended to be conveyed is much weaker than that of impertinence or of shamelessness, for it is used in reference to a person recovering his spirits after illness.'

Imperence is a corruption of *impudence*, common in Donegal writers. 'Yer too knowlegable a man for me to have the imperence to tell ye what to do afther,' wrote Seumus MacManus in *Billy Lappin*. And I see that Dickens used the corruption in *Pickwick*: '"Let me alone, imperence," said the young lady.'

✦ INCONY

Ever since I came across this word in college, reading Tudor and Jacobean literature, it has fascinated me. It means fine, fair, delicate, pretty, 'nice'. It is a useful word, and I wonder why it hasn't survived. The last time it is seen in literature is in Ben Jonson's *Tale of a Tub*, in 1633: 'O super-dainty Chanon! Vicar incony! Make no delay, Miles, but away; And bring the wench and money.'

Oxford says it is a cant word, which may account for its early demise and for its uncertain pedigree. One theory is that perhaps it is from *in* = not, and *con* = connected with Old English *cunnan*, to know.

But I wouldn't discount the suggestion of Robert Nares in his *Glossary of Words, Phrases, Names and Allusions to Customs and Proverbs*, published in 1822, with a new edition by Halliwell and Wright in 1888. Nares suggested *in* as an intensive and *canny*, pretty. This sense of *canny* or *conny* has come to be applied as a general term of approbation or affection to persons or things, e.g. Robert Burns's 'Couthie fortune, kind and canny'. Compare Christopher Marlowe's *Jew of Malta*: 'Love me little, love me long, let music rumble / Whilst I in thy incony lap do tumble.'

Shakespeare in *Love's Labour Lost*, Act III, Scene I, wrote, 'My sweet ounce of man's flesh! my incony Jew, / O' my troth, most sweet jests! most incony vulgar wit.'

Well, wherever the word came from it has now joined the words dubbed *obsolete* in the dictionaries, if they can find room for it at all.

✦ IRIS

Most people know the *iris* as what the French call the fleur-de-lis or the flower-de-luce, a genus of plants, the type of the natural order *Iridaceæ*, natives of Europe, North Africa, and the temperate regions of Asia and America. In 1667 Milton in *Paradise Lost* sang of 'Each beauteous flour, Iris all hues, Roses, and Gessamin'. In 1850 Tennyson, in *In Memoriam*, which by the way he finished while on holiday in Bray and read aloud to the nuns in Ravenswell convent to see what they thought of it, has 'We glided winding under ranks / Of iris, and the golden reed.'

Another meaning, the anatomical one, is also well known: the flat, circular, coloured membrane suspended vertically in the aqueous humour of the eye, and separating the anterior from the posterior chamber; in its centre is a circular opening, called the pupil, which may be enlarged or diminished so as to regulate the amount of light transmitted to the retina. Jerome of Brunswick wrote a surgical manual in 1525, and showed that he knew about the origin of the word *iris*, and was familiar with a meaning of the word now forgotten by most people: 'There be iij. materyall circles yt ronne about the iye, and because they be so different of colours they be callyd yride[s] or rain bowys.'

Many writers have referred to the rainbow as *iris*, from Caxton in 1490 in *Eneydos*: 'Yris is the rayen bowe wyth hir fayr cote of dyuerse fygures.' In 1601 Shakespeare in *All's Well That Ends Well* has 'What's the matter, That this distempered messenger of wet, The many colour'd Iris rounds thine eye.' The word was used figuratively by Shelley in *Hellas* in 1821: 'If Liberty lent not life its soul of light, Hope its iris of delight.'

Unknown to most of those who know the iris as a flower, as part of the eye, and possibly even to those who know that the poets sometimes referred to the rainbow as *iris*, is the ultimate origin of the word. It's to be found in Greek mythology.

Iris was the goddess who acted as the messenger of the gods, and was held to display as her sign, or appear as, the rainbow. Hence, allusively, *iris* meant a messenger. Shakespeare knew about her: In 1593, in *Henry VI, Part 2*, Act III, Scene II, he has 'Wheresoere thou art in this world's Globe, I'll have an Iris that shall find thee out.'

✦ JACK STRAW

A young friend of mine from Waterford, Jack Roche, wrote to me recently about another famous Jack, Jack Straw. His grandmother used the phrase to describe any man she didn't approve of, to denote a ne'er-do-well, a good-for-nothing. Master Roche tells me that his granny is the only one he knows who uses the word. I'd well believe it; I haven't heard it myself in years.

No, this wasn't the English politician, a friend of Tony Blair, and by extension of the late lamented George Bush of Iraq war fame. Our Jack Straw was a friend of Wat Tyler, leader of a peasants' revolt against King Richard II in 1381, a revolt mainly against poll taxes and restrictions placed on pay increases for working men. Richard ignored the peasants' demands, and Wat Tyler was killed by the Mayor of London during a meeting to discuss what to do.

Don't run away with the idea that Mr Tyler and his accomplice, Jack Straw, were nice people. Mr Straw was particularly destructive and vicious, and became so unpopular that he left his name stamped on anybody who was seen as a ne'er-do-well.

My own grandmother, who lived in Ross, some fifteen miles from where Master Roche lives, used the word too, telling me more than once that I would end up a Jack Straw if I didn't do my homework.

◆ **JAGGER**

I have been asked more than a few times, and always by infatuated old girls who should have more sense, where the bould Mick Jagger's surname originated. The honest answer to that is that I don't know for sure, but when pressed for a guess, my answer always tended to displease.

A *jagger* in the old days was applied to a travelling pedlar; a hawker. The word was not confined to Scotland and the northern half of England, as some dictionaries will tell you, but was found in Dublin's fair city once upon a time, and still is, according to my friend the late Ronnie Drew of The Dubliners. I heard him refer to a Greystones man who delivered coal as a jagger. I asked him if he thought our Mick of Rolling Stones fame knew that he might be descended from coal, fish or hay peddlers; he said that he knew all right: 'I told him one night in London, and he nearly broke his arse laughin' at the idea.'

Walter Scott in *The Pirate* (1822) has this: '"I am a jagger," replied a stout vulgar little man, who had indeed the humble appearance of a pedlar.' Jamieson's nineteenth-century Scots dictionary says that 'the word properly signifies a person who purchases goods, chiefly fish contracted for by another'.

A *jagger* was also a carter or carrier who would lease you his horse and cart for a day to remove furniture or the like. Tomás de Bhaldraithe, UCD lexicographer, once told me of leasing a horse and cart from a jagger to bring his books from the north side of the city to the south. He was young then, in his first university job and broke, and he wasn't used to driving a horse in city traffic. Still, all went well until he came to O'Connell Bridge, where the old horse decided that he was tired of life, lay down and died.

I mentioned hay. Yes, some jaggers went around selling hay, not fish or coal, in places. They bought the hay cheaply in summer and kept it until the hard winter arrived, when they transported it to coal-jaggers who lived in the towns.

There was another *jagger*, a Scottish one, whose job it was to place penitents in the *jag*, which consisted of an iron collar fastened by a padlock which hung from a chain secured in a church wall near the door. An offender sentenced to the jag was compelled to stand locked in this collar for an hour before service on a Sunday to teach him the error of his ways. The jag was usually reserved for fornicators. Such was the power of the kirk that people owned up and delivered themselves to the care of the jagger without being compelled to do so.

No, I don't think our Michael would own up to being descended from these jaggers, whatever about the other ones mentioned above.

✦ JIMP

I don't think I have ever heard this adjective south of the Border. It meant slender, neat, and was used by men as a compliment to women. I was surprised to hear recently that the word is hard to come by nowadays around Ballymoney in Co. Antrim and in the Ards peninsula in Co. Down, where I heard it many years ago. The word had another meaning in Antrim (I'm not sure about Co. Down)—'scarce'. An Antrim lady, Mary Craig, who corresponded with me frequently, sent me the word in the 1970s. God look to her, she went to her reward since then. She was a friend of the Ulster folklorist Brendan Adams, to whom she transmitted many words and phrases in the Ulster Scots dialect.

Jimp was imported from Scotland. The Lass of Lochroyan enquired, 'O wha will shoe my bonny foot / And wha will bind my middle jimp [my slender waist] / Wi' a lang, lang linen band?' Burns knew the word. He has 'Thy waist sae jimp' in *O, were I on Parnassus's Hill*. Hence *jimpy*, used by Rhymer Rab to describe Bonnie Ann, and by a lesser light, Ballantine, in a poem of his from 1856: 'Bawbee dolls the fashions apit, / Sae rosy cheekit, jimpy shapit.' [A bawbee was a Scots coin, the equivalent of an English ha'penny.]

Jimp can also mean scanty; tight, narrow; deficient in quantity. The word was sometimes spelled *gimp*. The *Ballymena Observer* of 1892 has 'gimp measure'. Hence the adverb *jimply*, scarcely. Lynn Doyle has 'Jimply a mile from here' in one of his stories.

The word travelled to the north of England as well as to Ulster. *The Northumberland Glossary* of 1893 defines the word as 'thin, neat in figure'.

The origin of *jimp* is a bit of a mystery. Oxford says, 'Known in Scotland since c1500; origin obscure. It has been compared with *gim*, adjective, "smart, spruce", of the same age, and with *jump*, adjective, "exact, precise", which appears later; but in neither case is the sense congruous.'

The DSL gives no etymological information, except to say that the word was in Old Scots as *gymp* since about 1500.

✦ JOUK

This word was once common in Ulster, Scotland, and in England in Northumberland, Cumbria, Yorkshire and Cheshire. It has also found its way to America. As a verb it means to duck, or stoop so as to avoid a blow; to dodge, evade, shrink from. It is also used figuratively. It has many variants.

W.H. Patterson has it in his 1880 glossary of Down and Antrim words. 'Juke and let a jaw flee,' was sent to the EDD by a correspondent from Co. Antrim. It means 'Take no notice of angry words, stoop and let it pass over you.' Robert Burns in *Pastoral Poetry* has 'Thou need na jouk behint the hallan [an inner wall, partition or screen erected in a cottage between the door and the fireplace to act as a shield from the draught of the door], A chiel [a child, a boy or girl] sae cleever.' The Donegal writer Seumas MacManus, in a story called *Billy Lappin*, published in the *Century Magazine* in February 1900, had this: 'He went jookin' an' creepin' roun' be the ditches.'

It was used figuratively of a stream: to run in and out, meander. 'Where burnies jouk an' flowerets bloom,' sang the fine dialect poet Alexander Orr from Lanarkshire in *Laigh Flights* in 1882.

Hence the word *joukery*, trickery, double dealing, deception. *The Ballymena Observer* has this word in 1892. Hence also the compound *joukery-pawkerie*. Christopher North in *Noctes Ambrosianae* has this: 'Lord Althropp is a fule, or warse, an' has been playin joukery-pawkerry wi' that chiel O'Connell.' Yes, our Dan.

To jouk also meant to mitch from school. 'My pow got mony a knock, When frae the school I strave to jouk,' is a line in *Original Scottish Rhymes* by David Webster from Renfrewshire (1835). Hence *jouker*, a mitcher.

The word is in Old Scots from 1456 as *jouk* and *jook*. The DSL says that the origin of the word is somewhat uncertain but that the similarity of many of the forms and meanings to English *duck*, Middle English *douke*, Old English *ducan*, to dive (like a duck), to stoop, etc., suggests that the word may be a palatalised variant of the Scots form *dook*.

| K 〜

✦ KEECH

I heard this word in Limerick city a few years ago. Two men were surveying the talent which had entered a hotel lounge at what the place had advertised as 'the cocktail hour', and appraising it. One woman was described as a *keech*, a word I had heard in my home town of Ross (only blow-ins call it *New* Ross) once or twice. I wonder if the word is still alive in both places.

The behaviour of the two gentlemen was not above reproach, but I was interested in the word they used. One dialect dictionary says that the word is a variant of *cake*, and maybe it is; certainly there is a Northamptonshire *keech*, described by A.E. Baker in his glossary of 1854 as 'a large, oblong or triangular pasty, made at Christmas, of raisins or apples chopped together'. But the word, meaning fat, is found in many places in England from the North Country south to Northamptonshire, Warwickshire (I note that Shakespeare knew it), Shropshire, Gloucestershire, Hampshire, Somerset, and Dorset.

In these places *keech* is a noun meaning a lump of congealed fat; in the old days, the fat of a slaughtered beast rolled up and ready for the chandler. Hence the Hampshire *keechy-belly*, a fat man.

The word is also found as a verb. Of melted fat: to set hard in cooling. William Barnes, the Dorsetshire poet and lexicographer who first published Poole's glossary of Forth and Bargy words, has the verb in his glossary of Dorset words (1863).

Shakespeare was very fond of the word. In *Henry VIII*, Act I, Scene I, he has 'I wonder that such a keech can with his very bulk, Take up the rays of the beneficial sun, And keep it from the earth.' And in *Henry IV, Part 1*, Act II, Scene IV, he has, relating to you-know-who, 'Thou obscene, greasy tallow-keech.' He applies the term contemptuously to the wife of a butcher in *Henry IV, Part 2*, Act II, Scene I, and to the son of a butcher in *Henry VIII*, Act I, Scene I.

Keech is of obscure origin, Oxford says. I have nothing to add to that.

✦ KEEL

The lovely jazz singer Cleo Laine and her husband John Dankworth once got together to make a marvellous recording of Shakespeare's songs. The CD is called *Shakespeare And All That Jazz* and as I was listening to it in the still hours of the night recently, I wondered if the word *keel*, used by the great playwright in *Love's Labour's Lost*, is still alive anywhere: 'To-whit, to-whoo, a merry note, / While greasy Joan doth keel the pot.'

Keel, according to Oxford, means to cool (a hot or boiling liquid) by stirring, skimming, or pouring in something cold, in order to prevent it from boiling over; hence the phrase 'to keel the pot'. It is also used figuratively.

Langland used the word in *Piers Plowman* in 1393: 'And lerede men a ladel bygge with a long stele, That cast for to kele a crokke and saue þe fatte aboue.' The *c.* 1420 *Liber Cocorum* has 'Whenne hit welles up, thou schalt hit kele With a litel ale.' In 1602 John Marston in *The History of Antonio and Mellida* has 'Boy, keele your mouth, it runnes over.'

Figuratively to keel also meant to grow cold, in feeling, etc.; to become less violent, fervid, or ardent, to 'cool down'; to diminish in intensity. In a *c.* 1325 *Metrical Homily* we find 'Mi soru sal son kele.' Hampole's *Psalter* of *c.* 1340 has 'He gars sa many kele fra godis luf.' The Countess of Richmond's translation of *De Imitatione* (1504) has 'Vnto me . . . that so often synnes, and so soon keles'. An 1891 *Sheffield Glossary* Supplement has 'The door never keels of beggars'.

A friend in Sheffield University tells me that keel is used here and there around that city still, but that it is obsolete everywhere else. A pity. It had survived from ancient days.

Of Common Teutonic origin, says Oxford. The Old English was *célan* = Dutch *koelen*, Low German *kölen*, Old High German *chuolen, kualen*, German *kühlen*, Old Norse *kœla*, Danish *køle*, Swedish *kyla*.

✦ KELD

Once upon a time I was called on to drive two old north-west Donegal ladies to Letterkenny to pick a headstone for a relative who had died the previous year. That done, we headed home, but I was asked to take a wee detour to Doon Well, a place of pilgrimage for many centuries past. Off the two went to pray for the dead, and when they returned one of them thanked me, and said that to visit the holy *keld* gave her great spiritual strength. She was surprised that I didn't know that a *keld* was a holy well; indeed any spring of water, holy or not.

These two ladies had spent a considerable amount of time in Great Yarmouth and other places in Yorkshire when they were in the bloom of youth, gutting fish and packing them, and I'm certain that they picked up the word there. The EDD recorded *keld* in Yorkshire, Cumberland and Northumberland; no trace of it was found in Scotland, and no Irish glossary that I know of recorded the word either. Hence *kelly*, applied to land containing small springs which dry up in summer.

There are compounds. A *keld-head* is the head of a spring; a fountain in north Yorkshire; and in the Lakeland they have, or had, *keld-syke*, a field containing a spring of water.

Keld is used of the still part of a river or lake, which has an oily smoothness while the rest of the water is ruffled. *Notes and Queries* Series 3 (1867) says that *keld* is used in the North Country of a deep hole in a stream. A correspondent of the EDD said that 'The watermen about Heworth Shore call the smooth, oily, and unrippled parts of the surface of the Tyne by the name of *kelds*.'

I asked Gweedore teacher Proinsias Ó Maonaigh once if the word, used of a holy well, was common. 'Twice in my lifetime I've heard it, and from old people long gone from us now,' he replied.

It is, I hear, well on the way to extinction in England as well. It was introduced there by the Vikings. The Old Norse has *kelda*, a spring well, the Icelandic lexicographer Vigfusson tells me. Swedish has *källa*, and Danish *kilde*.

✦ KELP

This is a noun once found in Southern Irish English and in many dialects of the north of England. It means the iron hook from which pots were hung over an open fire in country kitchens. I was sent the word by a north Co. Dublin man, Paddy O'Neill, in the 1960s. The word was on the verge of extinction by then, because the open fire was no longer the means of cooking. The distinguished archaeologist and medieval historian Liam de Paor gave me the word two decades later. 'Some of the Clare workmen who helped with the dig called a pot-hook a kelp.'

The EDD has the word from Yorkshire. One correspondent wrote this bit of Big-House folklore: 'When a pot is taken from the kelps the latter begin to vibrate, and the maid is anxious to stop them, for while they are in motion "the Virgin Mary weeps".

In Northern England a *kelp* is also the movable or detachable handle of a metal pot, and also the hook of a dress. And in Lincolnshire there is a phrase used of children, *to hang a kelp*: to drop the lip previous to crying.

Oxford has *kilp* instead of the EDD's *kelp* and defines the word thus: 'The movable or detachable handle (pair of clips) of a pot or cauldron; also, a pot-hook or crook from which a pot is suspended; the bail or hoop-handle of a pot or kettle; rarely, a hook in general.'

It gives the origin of the word as Old Norse *kilpr*, handle, loop.

✦ KELPIE

Children love monsters and all sorts of weird beings, and a few years ago I was witness to the disappointment of two little west Waterford girls when they heard on the television that the Lough Ness monster didn't exist. I suppose that most children in the province of Ulster don't believe in the existence of the Kelpie any more either, and for the same reason: wonder has been vanished from their lives with the coming of the television.

The Kelpie came from Scotland to Ulster. I heard about the creature in north Donegal, and his inclusion in the fairly recent CUD shows, I think, that he still figures in the folk belief of parts of Ulster. But for how much longer, I wonder.

It wasn't just the wains who were afraid of this monster. Jamieson the early-nineteenth-century Scots lexicographer and folklorist regarded the Kelpie as a water spirit . . . 'the spirit of the waters, who gives previous intimation of the destruction of those who perish within his jurisdiction, by preternatural lights and noises, and even assists in drowning them'. Captain Grose mentions him in 1790. He appears in many folklore studies, including the *Folk Lore Record* of 1879: 'The Kelpie is a sly devil, he roars before a loss at sea, and frightens both young and old upon the shore.' Many accounts give it the appearance of a young black horse, just like the Irish *Púca*, anglicised *Pooka*. One Scottish account of how the Kelpie carried off a toper from a wedding, and drowned him in a mountain lake, is uncannily like Mr and Mrs Samuel Carter Hall's account of the naming of the Wicklow placename *Poll a' Phúca*, or *Poulaphooka*, in their book *Ireland, Its Scenery and*

Character. But most accounts say that the Kelpie is a woman, every bit as fearsome as the *Bean Sí*, or *Banshee*, or as she is called in my part of Ireland, *The Bow*, from Irish *Badhbh*, described by Dinneen as, among other things, 'a female fairy or phantom said to be attached to certain families, appearing as a scald-crow or royston-crow'. Yes, and in Wexford and other places, as a woman who could be a sister of the Banshee.

The CUD describes the Kelpie as a mythical creature which takes the form of a woman and inhabits fresh water. In Scotland she doesn't confine her evil-doing to rivers and lakes, but appears on the seashore-line at times, as well as racing over the waves to appear to those poor wretches about to be drowned as the result of storms.

An Ulsterman I asked recently about the Kelpie said that the only way of preserving its memory would be for some enterprising hotelier or pub owner to persuade, for a consideration of course, a few prime-boys to encounter one and to spread the news. 'Bedad,' he suggested, 'she'd bring as many tourists as old Nessie brings to Scotland.' An interesting thought indeed.

The CUD says that the word *Kelpie* is from the Scottish Gaelic *cailpeach*, a colt or heifer.

✦ KEMP

When I was a lot younger than I am now I spent a lot of time in the company of sheepmen in Co. Donegal. They had their own good words relating to their pretty arduous calling; most of those I knew were mountainy men who had to deal with rain, snow and frost, and who didn't know the meaning of the word holiday. One of the words from their private vocabulary was *kemp*. I first heard it from John Gallagher of Dunlewey, at the foot of Errigal; he was my father-in-law and I used to travel to fairs with him and, on occasion, to help him find lost sheep on the mountainside in inclement weather.

Kemp was a coarse wool appearing in a fleece, and tending to spoil it. Another sheepman, Jack Bell, from the southern side of the mountain guarding the Poisoned Glen near Dunlewey, told me of his difficulty with some English buyers: 'They wouldn't look at my wool. Too much kemp in it for their liking. Kemp is rough old wool you find in mountainy sheep.' In one of the bibles of the woollen trade, Luccock's *Wool*, an early-nineteenth-century publication, you'll find 'Its staple was perfectly free from kemps and wild hair, so common on the backs of northern sheep.'

Jack Bell also used *kemp* to describe matted, tangly human hair, and long before his day old Chaucer thought of kemp as coarse, hairy eyebrows in *The Knight's Tale*: 'Lik a grifphon looked he aboute, With kempe heeris on his browes stout.'

The word comes from the Old Norse *kampr*, a beard, moustache, the whiskers of a cat, etc.

✦ KEMPLE

A sheepman from down Glenties direction arrived at my father-in-law's house one night in the 1960s, a little the worse for wear after a trying day at Falcarragh fair. He was asked to stay the night, a bed was made up for him, and I was impressed with the way in which he went to look after his horse in the stable before he himself sat down to his supper. His horse watered and fed, he said that he was glad to see a good bed of straw under him: 'a nice kemple of straw' was what he called it.

You won't hear *kemple* in Donegal or anywhere else in Ulster any more, or so I'm told. It is an import from Scots and it is thus defined in the DSL: 'A bundle of straw, a certain quantity of straw varying in weight between 14 and 19 stones tron (21 to 29 stones avoirdupois).' In the Lothian *Farmer's Magazine* of August 1814 we are informed that 'In the vicinity of Edinburgh, it is calculated that a boll, or 4 bushels of wheat, produces a kemple of straw, which, by the regulations of the Edinburgh market, should weigh only 15 stones; but the farmers generally give about 18 stones.'

An account from Caithness dated 1907 has 'A bundle or load of hay or straw made up in a particular way, a truss of straw prepared for thatch'. In that northern county they used the word figuratively to mean a stout lump of a girl.

The word also came to mean a lump of food, 'a piece of cheese broken off'. There are also the intensive forms *kimplack*, *kimplock*, 'a very large piece', and the diminutive *kimplet*, 'a piece of anything solid of moderate size'. In extended meaning a *kemple* is an icicle in Scotland's northern counties.

And where did our visitor's word originate? Not an easy question to answer, because it may have come directly into Scots from Scottish Gaelic *ciomball*, a bundle of straw or heather, or directly from Norwegian *kimbel*, a large bundle of grass, a truss of hay. However, both the Norwegian word and the Scottish Gaelic *ciomball* are from the Old Norse *kimbill*, a truss, a little bundle.

Perhaps Paddy Joe Gill's old word still survives in places at the foot of the Donegal hills, but I doubt it. It is, I fear, a good word gone from us forever.

✦ KENSILL

This word, found in Cumberland and in England's Lakeland, is sometimes written *kensel*. It is a verb meaning to beat. From it comes a noun, *kenselin*, a thrashing, a beating.

I'm reliably informed, by a friend of mine who spent some time practising medicine in what I suppose I may call Wordsworth's country, that the word is not yet dead there. A lady came to him one day about a persistent cold, but he noticed a bruising on her cheek. Correctly guessing that the bruising was the result of a domestic tiff, he asked her about it. To his surprise, she laughed the question off, saying that her man was right in giving her a kenselin. 'You see, doctor, she said, 'I refused him his martials to which he was entitled, so he gev me a bit of a kenselin.' From the same lovely part of England a dialect dictionary recorded this: 'Thoo'll git a kenselin if thi mudder catches thi smiuken bacca.'

The word originally meant to instruct, to give a lesson to. The meaning to discipline was added over the course of time and the word became associated with schoolmasters batin' larnin' into childer. Well the word had an old association with the classroom. It comes from the Old Norse *kennsla*, teaching, and the old language also has *kennslu-piltr*, a schoolboy, according to the Icelandic lexicographer Gudbrand Vigfusson, and he should know.

✦ KENSPECKLE

This is an adjective and noun once used all over Scotland and Ulster, and in England, in Northumberland, Durham, Cumberland, Yorkshire, Lancashire, Lincolnshire and Shropshire. It means conspicuous, remarkable; easily recognisable owing to some peculiarity or oddity. *The Ballymena Observer* of 1892 had this: 'He was a very kenspeckle man and regular in the markets, and it was not likely the plaintiff would be mistaken.' W.H. Patterson recorded the word in his Antrim and Down glossary of 1880. And as late as 1998 Rab Sinclair, a frequent correspondent of mine from Antrim, heard the word from an old-timer who was living near Ballymoney, in the 1970s. He told me that the word is dead and gone now.

One of the letters written by Robert Burns from Ayr in 1795 contains 'My phiz is sae kenspeckle that the very joiner's apprentice . . . knew it at once.' The word was commonly used in Scots literature. Scott had this in 1818 in *The Heart of Midlothian*: 'She had little, as she said, to make "her kenspeckle when she didna speak."' D.M. Moir's popular *Mansie Wauch*, published in Edinburgh in 1828 and reprinted many times until 1898, and which is given credit for attracting a lot of the snobs to the potential of dialect Scots, has 'I have heard tell, that his speech was so Dutchified as to be scarcely kenspeckle to a Scotch European.' As late as February 1950 the *Scots Magazine* of Fife used the word: 'Peter Smith is a kenspeckle and popular figure in the narrow streets . . . of Cellardyke and Anstruther.'

The word had another meaning once: a mark by which a person or thing can be known or recognised. From West Yorkshire, where the word was *kensback*, it was reported to the EDD that 'Of a person with a hump-back or a crooked nose it would be said, "He's varry kensback."'

In Yorkshire they also had the word *kensmackle*, conspicious from some mark or spot. It was used only of cattle, sheep or horses: 'It's varra kensmackle is that cow.'

As to this old word's origin, Old Scots has *kenspecke* from 1614, *kenspeckled* from 1684, and *kenspekil* from 1538. Apparently a derivative of English dialect *kenspeck*, conspicuous, probably of Scandinavian origin. Cf. Norwegian dialect *kjennespak*, Swedish *känspak*, quick at recognising, Old Norse *kennispeki*, faculty of recognition.

✦ KEOUT

Sometimes spelled *kewt*, and in Wexford *khout*, this word is, according to the EDD, found only in Ireland and Wales, and in the English counties of Cheshire, Warwickshire and Shropshire. As a verb it means to bark like a dog.

As a noun it means the short, snarling growl of a dog. It also means a snarling little dog, an ill-tempered cur. The word is also found as a compound: *keout dog*. Joseph Philip Robson has the compound in his valuable *Songs of the Bards of the Tyne*; his 800-word glossary is often quoted by lexicographers.

Captain Grose heard the word in Wales in 1790 and included it in his *Provincial Glossary*. From Shropshire a correspondent sent the EDD this: 'A keout is a little, sharp, vigilant, barking dog.' The same correspondent reverts to dialect, adding, 'Snap's a rar keout, 'e ooana let nobody goo nigh the 'ouse, athout lettin' them know.'

Figuratively the word means a mean rascal; a sneaky cur of a fellow. A correspondent from Wexford sent Wright the sentence 'Go 'long ye kyout'; and Patrick Kennedy in *Evening in the Duffrey*, published in 1869, has 'More than one young khout'. The Duffrey is the northern part of the town of Enniscorthy, and the scene of a bloody battle in 1798, before what Heaney called 'the fatal conclave' at Vinegar Hill across the river. I doubt very much if anybody in the Duffrey would know nowadays what a *khout* is.

I have no idea where the word is from. The EDD doesn't say, and Oxford doesn't record the word.

✦ KEVEL

This rare word has a lot of different meanings, many of them found in Ireland, particularly in the North and Midlands. Often spelled and pronounced *keivel*, first of all it is used of animals: to kick out or to leap awkwardly; to sprawl or gambol; to move restlessly; to paw the ground or toss the head, as a restless horse does.

Used of the human race, to which most of my readers belong (Chesterton's gag), *to kevel* is applied to women who toss their heads. 'Watch the way yon girl keivels her head' was recorded in Antrim and Down by W.H. Patterson in 1880. 'Lang sair they kevelled, danced and sang,' wrote the Cumberland dialect poet John Stagg in one of his *Collected Poems*, dated 1807. I've heard *kevel* used by Wexford and Kildare Travellers to describe a restless horse dropping his head and raising it suddenly. Some of them called this action *caving*.

As a noun *kevel* means an awkward, blundering manner or action. Used of horses mostly, this noun is known to Irish Travellers of the old school. There aren't many of them left in today's world. These *kevels* are possibly variants of the noun *cave*, a toss of the head, or the verb *cave*, to stand on the hind legs and toss the fore legs; to rear; to lower the head and bring it back up suddenly. The DSL asks us to compare Old Norse *kaf*, a plunge, *kafa*, *kefja*, to dip.

Kevell also means to bungle, carry out a piece of work badly and clumsily, and as a noun, clumsily done work; a muddle. This is found in

Shetland and in other northern districts and its origin may be traced to Norwegian dialect *keivla*, to work clumsily and to the adjective *keiv*, awry, crooked.

✦ KIBE

What has befallen the good old word *kibe*, a chilblain, a crack in the skin, that it has been deemed in a recent survey of dialect words to be on the brink of extinction? It is still fairly secure among the older generation in many places in England and Ireland, but its use is not as regular as it was even ten years ago, it seems, in Scotland, Ulster, Derbyshire, Northampton, East Anglia, Somerset, Devon and Cornwall.

'There's kibes upon your dozened heels,' wrote the Perthshire poet Ferguson in *Village Poet* in 1897. 'His shins are dotted over with the fire blisters, black, red and blue—on each heel a kibe,' wrote Tyrone's Carleton in his *Traits and Stories of The Irish Peasantry*. In that marvellous treasury of Ulster words and phrases, *The Ballymena Observer*, edited by J.W. Knowles in 1892, we find this gem: 'Kibes is a sort of disease. Those suffering from it get rid of the kibes by going at night to some one's door and knocking. When anyone asks "Who's there!" the person who knocked runs away calling "Kibey heels, take that!" Then the kibes are expected to leave the person who has the disease and pass to the one who called "Who's there!"'

Hence we got *kibbed* and *kibby*, sore, afflicted with chapped heels or chilblains.

Master Shakespeare was familiar with the word *kibe*. You'll remember *Hamlet*, Act V, Scene I: 'The toe of the peasant comes so near the heel of the courtier, he galls his kibe.'

As to origin, the great Skeat in his *Etymological Dictionary* refers us to the Welsh word *cibi* (*y gibi*), a kibe, chilblain.

✦ KINTRA-COOSER

Kintra is Scots for 'country,' a variant form of *countra*, and it has spawned many agreeable compounds. The DSL lists many of them, such as *kintra-clash* and *kintra clatter*, the gossip of the countryside; *kintra-cleadin*, rustic dress; *kintra fock*, country people; *kintra-claver*, a fiction; *kintra-side*, countryside; *kintra-crack*, friendly country chat, and the headlined *kintra-cooser*.

Robert Burns, in *Here's His Health* (1796), has the couplet 'I'm slighted sair / And dree the kintry-clatter.' *The Northern Muse* of 1897 has the line 'The auld blue Hell he thinks a haiver; The auld black Deil a kintry claver.' The Edinburgh poet Crawford in a 1798 verse has 'Wi' kintra-cleadin', hame-spun grae'. A reader's letter to *The Shetland Advertiser*, back in September 1862, complained, 'Every een at reads da papers kens at da editors aye ca's demselves "we", an sae shurely whan ony een is wraetin ta ony o' dem dey ocht ta pit *kiuntrymen* an no "country man."' 'And no a perfect kintra-cooser,' sang Burns in 1796.

Well *kintra* is country; so what's *cooser*? The word is Scots for a stallion, a corruption of English *courser*; the Old Scots is *courser*, *cursour*. But the compound means not just 'country stallion', but figuratively a rake, a debauched rustic gentleman. Just what Burns had in mind. John Mactaggart's *Scottish Gallovidian Encyclopedia* of 1824 defines the word as 'a human stallion, a fellow who debauches country girls'. John Jamieson entered the compound in his famous nineteenth-century dictionary of Scots, thus giving it the aura of respectability. Well, almost. It joins many great Scots terms which some English lexicographers consider risqué, such as Burns' wonderful *houghmagandie*, fornication. In *Holy Fair*, drawing on his own experience, no doubt, he has the memorable lines 'Monie jobs that day begin, / May end in Houghmagandie ...'

Kintra-cooser, too, deserves to live.

✦ KISH

Also found as *kesh* in south Leinster, the once very popular word means a basket, a pannier made of sally rods. Maria and Richard Lovell Edgeworth have the word in their *Essay on Irish Bulls* published in 1802: 'A train of their companions leaving their cars loaded with kishes of turf.' *Paddiana*, two anonymous volumes published in 1848, defines kish as 'an oblong basket commonly placed upon a rude country car, and used in bringing baskets of turf from the bog'. A. Hume in his *Remarks on the Irish Dialect of the English Language*, and first published in the *Transactions of the Historic Society of Lancashire and Cheshire* in 1874, came on the word in Co. Antrim: 'there is an old kish on the ground.'

In the south-east of Ireland, in central Co. Wexford, the important nineteenth-century folklorist Patrick Kennedy, in *The Banks of the Boro*, published in the year of the Fenian troubles, wrote, 'sitting on a pillion behind you going to a fair or market to look after your kish'. I see that Mrs Samuel Carter Hall has *kesh* in *Irish Life and Character*, published in London in the 1840s: 'An old lady had taken undisputed posession of a kesh of potatoes.' Mrs Hall's old lady came from south Wexford, near Bannow, a district our author knows intimately.

Emily Lawless published *Grania, the Story of an Island* in two volumes in 1892. Emily wrote about Co. Mayo, and in volume two of *Grania* she has 'From the time she was the height of that turf kish there, she could not be bid by anyone.'

Donnchadh Ó Conchubhair, a wordsman from Durrow in Co. Laois, sent this to *Éigse, a Journal of Irish Studies*, in 1945, in reference to Durrow: 'Durrow must have been always *in the heel of the kish*, that is, it was never of any great account.'

And where would we leave Mr Joyce, who has in *Ulysses* 'ignorant as a kish of brogues'?

The diminutive *ciseán*, anglicised *kishaun*, is very common still all over rural Ireland. Our words may be traced to Medieval Irish *ces*, a basket, pannier. Whether this is related to Latin *cista*, an ark, a chest, which corresponds to Old English *cest* and Old Norse *cista*, a chest, is a moot point.

✦ KISSING BUNCH

The venerable academic journal *Notes and Queries*, over a century and a half old now, has given us accounts of many old customs, and many old words associated with them. *Notes and Queries* was first published in 1849 as a weekly periodical edited by W.J. Thoms. It was founded as an academic correspondence magazine, in which scholars and interested amateurs could exchange knowledge. Very frequent contributors include the Rev. Walter W. Skeat, one of the most important figures in the field of English etymology, and Eliza Gutch, founder of The Folklore Society. The journal is now published by Oxford University Press.

Browsing in a volume dated 1887 in Trinity College library I came across an account of the *kissing bunch*. We had kissing bunches in south-east Wexford in days gone by: so old Mike Flynn of Kilmore and Elizabeth Jeffries of the same village told me. Wexford is not mentioned in *Notes and Queries* but here is an account of this charming Christmas custom from Derbyshire:

This Derbyshire *kissing bunch* is always an elaborate affair. The size depends on the couple of hoops—one thrust through the other—which forms its skeleton. Each of the ribs is garlanded with holly, ivy, and sprigs of other greens, with bits of coloured ribbon and paper roses, rosy-cheeked apples, and oranges. Three small dolls are also prepared, and represent Our Saviour, the mother of Jesus, and Joseph.

These dolls generally hang within the kissing bunch, by strings from the top, and are surrounded by apples and oranges tied to strings, and various coloured ornaments. Occasionally these dolls are arranged in the kissing bunch to represent a manger scene. Generally a bit of mistletoe is obtained and this is carefully tied to the bottom of the kissing bunch, which is then hung in the middle of the house-place.

Mike Flynn informed me that the Kilmore kissing bunch wasn't as elaborate as the Derbyshire one. They were more like the Devonshire one in that they consisted of small furze bushes dipped in water, powdered in flour and studded all over with holly berries. Every time a kiss was given, a berry was plucked from the bush. I don't recall old Mike mentioning either the mistletoe or the dolls of Derbyshire.

The *kissing bunches* were no more than an old man's memory when he mentioned the word to me forty years ago. Has the old custom survived in Derbyshire, I wonder.

✦ KIST

This ancient word, found in remote places in Scotland, Ulster, and in many northern and southern dialects of England, means a chest, a trunk; a chest of drawers, a coffer. It is, I'm informed, not as widely used as it was even twenty years ago.

'The size o' a kist o' drawers', wrote W.G. Lyttle in his story *The Adventures of Paddy M'Quillan* around 1890. Lyttle, a native of Co. Down, published this book in Bangor. He never dated his books except for his most famous work, *Betsy Gray or Hearts of Down*, reprinted from the *North Down Herald* of 1894.

W.H. Patterson has the word from his 1880 glossary of Antrim and Down words; and in our own time, the word was sent to me by David Hammond of Belfast and by a long list of people from all over Co. Donegal. Mrs Rae McIntyre, the great lady who taught school outside Coleraine in Co. Derry, sent me this, collected by one of her pupils: 'a kist of whistles, an organ'. This meaning was once found all over Scotland. In 1889 Bernard Shaw in *London Music in 1888–89* referred to 'M. Gigout, who was performing on the "Kist o' whustles"'. In 1891 Scotsman R. Ford in *Thistledown* assures us that 'There was no such thing as an organ, or "kist o' whustles", in any Presbyterian kirk in the land.'

The word is ancient. It's in *Havelok the Dane* around 1300: '. . . in arke or in kiste'. And, Oxford tells me, it is in common use in the English of South Africa. It quotes these advertisements of *The Star*, the first from a Johannesburg paper: 'Heavy bowfronted kists price cut to £15:19:6'; the *Cape Times* had 'Furniture and effects . . . walnut bedroom suite, easy chairs . . . several large teak glass fronted cupboards, 2 carved Zanzibar camphor-wood kists.'

The word was also applied to the 'ark' of bulrushes in which Moses was placed; and to Noah's ark. In about 1300 *Cursor Mundi* has 'A rescen kyst sco did be wroght . . . In þis kist þe barn sco did.' In an Early English alliterative poem of ante 1300, we find '"Now Noe", quoth oure lorde, "Hatz þou closed þy kyst with clay alle aboute?"'

I myself have come across the word only in my county, Wexford, in Counties Antrim, Donegal and Derry, in Scotland on a recent trip to visit Robert Burns's Ayr, and on my frequent trips to Cornwall, where my son resided. He remarked to me, 'You'd be surprised at how many old Cornish people keep their money in a kist, as they call it, rather than trust the banks with it.' Oh wise, foreseeing Cornish people!

I can't resist adding this from Gregor's *Folk Lore* of 1881, a Scottish book which should be republished: 'A cure for toothache was to go to a running stream, lift from it with the teeth a stone, put it into the kist, and keep it. When the stone began to waste so did the tooth.'

Well, the old word is from the Old Norse *kista*, a chest. The Danish is *kista*. From Latin *cista*. Corresponds to Old English *cest*, which gave chest. The Irish *ciste*, a chest, a treasury, is from the Latin.

✦ KITCHEN

A word once found in Co. Wexford this, but I very much doubt if it is heard there today. It means to season, to give relish to, and it was used extensively in Scotland, in northern England, and in parts of Ulster. In *Traits and Stories* William Carleton from Tyrone has 'Instead of drinking his little earnings in a sheebeen house, and then eating his praties dry, he'd take care to have something to kitchen them.' In his good book *The Banks of the Boro* from mid-Wexford, Patrick Kennedy has the word. He wrote that people were 'without a single bit of meat to kitchen our potatoes'. Kennedy was an important folklorist who, apart from his books, contributed to many journals, notably the *Dublin University Magazine*, in the middle to the end of the nineteenth century.

The word was a great favourite among Scots writers, great and small. A love-lorn lassie in a poem published in Chambers' *Popular Rhymes* (1870) says, 'His heart this night shall kitchen my bread.' A minor poet from Lanarkshire, Nicholson, in a verse in his 1895 collection *Kilcuddie* liked his potatoes 'weel kitchened wi' dab at the stool' [pepper and salt]. And the great Rhymer Rab frae Ayr used the word in a poem on Scottish drink: 'His wee drap parritch, or his bread, Thou kitchens fine.' A good Northumberland poet, Donaldson, writing at the beginning of the nineteenth century, has 'Bessie's butter made me up, / it kitchens roots sae fine.' In 1935 Victor McClure in *Scotland's Inner Man* remarked, 'With the work-a-day people, to whom a light and casual repast was of little use, and who could not get home until work was done, the tea meal had to be of a sustaining nature. It was accompanied by some sort of "kitchen", which is Scots for relish or garniture. And so was instituted the "high tea".'

To kitchen also meant to serve out sparingly. W.H. Patterson has it from Down and Antrim in his glossary of 1880 and the nineteenth-century Scots lexicographer Jamieson gives us 'Kitchen weel!' This kitchen reached Northumberland as well: the EDD has 'We mun kitchen the broth or it'll not gang roon' [round].

It seems that the kitchens I've mentioned are somehow connected with the noun *kitchen*, the place we cook in, and so, they are ultimately from Old English *cycene* = Old Low German **kukina*, which gave Middle Dutch *coken(e)*, *koekene*, *kuekene*, Dutch *keuken*; Danish *kökken*. The vulgar Latin is *cucina*, *cocina*, variant of *coquina*, from *coquere*, to cook.

✦ KNAB

A very useful word this, but now obsolete, the EDD tells me. It was used in Scotland in the eighteenth and nineteenth centuries, and its adjective *knabby* was heard in Antrim by David Hammond, one of Ulster's leading authorities on folk song, in our time, used by an old man from near Cushendal. Why these words died out I can't even guess; they would still be useful in our day to describe both a man of importance or wealth, and a conceited, self-important ass. The man described to Davy Hammond was one of the latter.

Jamieson's nineteenth-century dictionary of Scots gives this definition of a *knab*: 'One who is wealthy in a middling line, who possesses a small independence; a term often applied to those otherwise called "little lairds". Obviously this carries with it a degree of contempt, however small.

I sense the same in some citations from the *English Dialect Dictionary*. 'The herds of many a knabby laird / War trainin' for the shambles,' is a quotation from a poem by the Renfrewshire poet Picken around 1809. In Ayr the adjective was 'spoken of one who dresses rather above his station', according to Jamieson.

According to the Scandinavian lexicographer Molbech, *knab* comes from the Danish dialectal word *knabe*, a man of importance, a landed proprietor.

✦ KNOWE

Talking to a gaggle of Donegal schoolchildren in a Dublin art gallery recently, I was surprised to find, when I told them in jest that Errigal was only a *knowe* compared to the peaks of the great Alpine range, that they didn't know what this word for a hillock, a small mound, meant. The EDD has the word from Scotland, Cumberland, Yorkshire, Lancashire and Derby. It does not mention Donegal, where I heard it many's the time, but it does say that W.H. Patterson included it in his dialect glossary of Down and Antrim words of 1800. Seemingly the *Ulster Journal of Archaeology* (1853–62) thought it rare enough to include it in a glossary of Ulster words.

There is a charming Ulster song called *The Maid of the Sweet Brown Knowe*. An ancient teacher of mine, a kindly Christian brother called J.A. Egan, used to sing it to himself. My mother knew the song, a classic *pastourelle*, in which a young man fails to seduce a fair maiden with flattery. He had the last word, however: 'The young man said, "My pretty maid, / How can you answer no; / Look down in yonder valley where my crops do gently grow; / Down in yonder valley / I have horses, men and plough, / And they're at their daily labour / For the maid of the sweet brown knowe."/// "If they're at their daily labour, / Kind sir, it's not for me. / And I've heard of your behaviour / I have indeed" said she. / "There is an inn where you call in / I hear the people say, / Where you rap and you call and you pay for all / And go home at the break of day." /// "If I rap and call and pay for all / The money is all my own. / Nor do

I seek your fortune / For I hear that you have none. / You thought you had my poor heart broke / From listening to you now, / But I'll leave you where I found you, / At the foot of the sweet brown knowe.'" Marie Heaney sings the song beautifully.

'The path rose and came at last to the head of a knowe,' wrote Scott in *Catriona*. 'Upon a knowe they sat them down,' wrote Ayrshire's Burns in *Twa Dogs*. The word reached the Shetland Islands as well. In a book I read recently for its dialect content, *Klingrahool*, written by a man who signed himself 'Junta' as he desired anonymity, there is this: 'The night mist shrouds the very knowe where she and I last met and parted.' Isn't it strange that lovers were very fond of knowes?

This good word, which is in Scottish literature since 1513, when Gavin Douglas wrote in his *Æneis*, 'From a hyll or a know / To tham he callis,' seems to have fallen from grace. What a pity this is.

Oxford speculates that the Old Scots word *know* is a variant of *knoll*, which comes from Old English *cnol*, a hill top, summit, hillock. May I be so bold as to suggest that it comes from the Old Norse *knauss*, defined by the great Icelandic scholar Gudbrand Vigfusson as 'a knoll, crag' recorded in *Diplomatarium Norvagicum* (v. 620), whence the modern Danish *knös* and *bonde-knös* = 'a boor knoll', a boorish youth. But where did the Norse ending in *ss* go? I think the English thought it a plural and removed it, leaving us with *knowe* as a singular.

| L ∿

✦ LADY ABBESS AND OTHER GROSE WORDS

The name Francis Grose (1731–1791) pops up from time to time in this book. He was a soldier, antiquarian, classical musician of note, and lexicographer who thought that the language of the poor merited research. I have a first edition of his great work *The Vulgar Tongue*, thanks to my friend the late Séamas Ó Saothraí, bibliophile and historian of Ireland's Presbyterian legacy.

Captain Grose's book shocked the fainthearted with words such as *Lady Abbess*, or simply *Abbess*; a bawd; the mistress of a brothel and expressions such as *Stand Moses*, 'a man is said to stand Moses when he has another man's bastard child fathered upon him, and he is obliged by the parish to maintain it'. He was the first to collect and publish a phrase which has survived since his time, *Birthday suit*: 'He was in his birth-day suit, that is stark naked.'

He has many words connected with brothels. *An Academy* or a *Pushing School* was a brothel. Many's the man who was summarily evicted from one for vomiting into the lap of one of the girls or one of the other customers—he was known to sailors as an *Admiral of the Narrow Seas*.

Grose himself had little time for apothecaries. *To talk like an apothecary* meant to the poor man 'to use hard or gallipot words; from the assumed gravity and affectation of knowledge generally put on by the gentlemen of that profession, who are commonly as superficial in their learning as they are pedantic in their language'. He tells us that *bolus* was a nickname for an apothecary.

It was claimed that the churches found Grose's book extremely offensive. For instance, the head of the Jesuit order in England told all Catholics not to purchase the book, probably because of the entry under *To Box the Jesuit*: 'a sea term for masturbation, a crime, it is said, much practised by the reverend fathers of that profession'. But, as if to even the score, Grose has *ballocks*, 'a vulgar nick-name for a parson'.

Francis Grose loved Ireland and came here often. He published a worthy book called *The Antiquities of Ireland*. I regret that he confined his lexical studies to the north, particulary Co. Antrim. He described himself as 'the idlest fellow living', but this embodiment of Falstaff wrote seventeen books on a variety of topics. To forestall any charges of immorality against *The Vulgar Tongue* he wrote in the book's introduction that he did not seek indecorous or indecent words, and could with great truth make the same defence that Falstaff ludicrously argued in defence of one engaged in rebellion, viz that he did not seek [indecorous words], but that like rebellion in the case instanced, they lay in his way and he found them. He apologised to the professions and trades which were hard done by in the book, and begged his readers not to consider the sentiments expressed as his own, but as the sentiments of the persons by whom they were used.

An Irish phrase, or so he claims, and still used today, is *To Catch A Tartar*, of which he wrote, 'To attack one of superior strength or abilities. This saying originated from a story of an Irish soldier in the Imperial service, who in a battle against the Turks, called out to his comrade that he had caught a Tartar, "Bring him along then," said he. "He won't come," answered Paddy. "Then come along yourself," replied his comrade. "Arrah," cried he, "but he won't let me."'

Grose died while dining with an artist friend in Dublin in 1791. He is buried in Drumcondra.

✦ LAITS

More often used in the plural than in the singular *lait*, this good Scots word, once so popular, has disappeared from both literature and the speech of the people, and nobody can tell why. It was also spelled *leats* around Perth, and *leets* in Robert Burns's country, Ayrshire. It meant manners, demeanour; habits, customs; specifically, in many cases, bad habits, pranks, tomfoolery that would annoy the pious or the elderly.

The word has been used by some of the major Scots poets, including Allan Ramsay in his *Gentle Shepherd* in 1725. Another good poet, though a little too didactic for my taste, Alexander Nicol of Perthshire, preached in 1766, 'Be advis'd to mortify / Your youthfu' laits by piety.' He tended to preach a lot to the young, and in another poem he remarked, 'A rackless youth may prove a man riht wise, / And may like you the leats of youth despise.'

The word was still being used at the end of the nineteenth century. Hew Ainslie's *A Pilgrimage to the Land of Burns*, written in Ayr in 1878, says, 'Some o' your saints . . . found it easier to lay down their life than their ill leets.' It pops up for the last time in Scots literature in 1913, in H.P. Cameron's *Imitation of Christ*: 'Unlearn a' ill-laits.' It's remarkable how most of the citations have been written by the unco guid, as Burns called them; *lait(s)* became a preacher's word, and it has been suggested to me that that's why the common man eventually discarded the old word from his lexicon.

Lait(s) is from Old Scots *late*, outward appearance or manner. The Northern Middle English was *lates*, from Old Norse *lát* (plural), manners.

✦ LAKE

Last year as I drove through the Cornish rain towards Newquay I went astray in the Bodmin Moor mists. I hailed a man who was beating his way home on his bike and he gave me directions. I wasn't too far away from where I should be, he said. His instructions were, 'Keep going on this road for a mile or so, and then turn right at the lake.' Off I went and found no lake. What I did find was a little stream, and my adventure brought me back to Carne, Co. Wexford, where, in 1970, a ninety-year-old man named Phil Wall referred to a little stream as a lake.

As I searched for the word in the dialect dictionaries, I discovered that it is found in Cumberland, England's Lakeland, Glamorgan, Pembroke, Devon, Cornwall, Dorset and Somerset: quite a spread, but no trace of it on the east coast. A Lakeland source said that 'running streams are of three kinds, the smallest being a lake'. A Somerset source said that 'the word is not applied to a large pond or sheet of water, but to running water'.

I was surprised at the word's absence from the territory of the Danelaw in the east of England, and equally surprised to find it in Wales and Cornwall, where the Vikings left little or no influence on the native languages. Any word of Scandinavian origin you may find in Welsh or Cornish English, a hundred to one it came directly from English; this one is an exception.

The word is from Old Norse *lækr*, a stream. Wexford is a town founded by the Vikings so I suppose it is reasonable to expect that some of their words might survive in its hinterland. Old sailor Bill Blake from Kilmore Quay had the word, as did Peter Byrne, a scholarly school-master still fondly remembered in the Baronies of Forth and Bargy, the Anglo-Norman enclave whose own distinctive dialect survived until the nineteenth century. It is not, however, among the numerous old words I collected from a host of other people in the 1970s. It has gone out of use by now, forty years on.

✦ LAMITER, LAMIGER

Once found throughout Scotland, the North Country of England, Northumberland and Ulster, *lamiter* seems to have lost its popularity in recent years, possibly due to people thinking, quite mistakenly, that the word was not politically correct. It was also spelled *lemeter* in Scotland and northern England, *lyemittor* in Northumberland, and *laimeter* in Ulster. It means 'a lame person, a cripple; a deformed person', according to the EDD.

The *Ballymena Observer* of 1892 has *laimeter* and so does W.H. Patterson in his 1890 glossary of Down and Antrim words. Sir Walter Scott has 'Though you think him a lamiter' in *Black Dwarf* (1816); 'Jenny Hirple, a lameter woman, who went round the houses of the heritors of the parish with a stilt', wrote the Ayrshire novelist Galt in *Entail*, a few years later. 'Am I going to be for life a lamiter?' complained a character in Christopher North's *Noctes Ambrosianae*, published in Selkirk in 1856.

The word must be related to the southern English dialect word *lamiger* or *lammiger*, found in Devon, Somerset and Dorset; a word that has the same meaning and that has suffered the same fate as *lamiter*. Thomas Hardy has it in *The Mayor of Casterbridge*: 'What can we two poor lamigers do against such a multitude!' Sweetman's *Wincanton Glossary* of 1885 has the word, as has James Jennings' *Observations on some of the Dialects in the West of England, particularly Somersetshire, with a glossary of words now in use there* (1825). From the same county a correspondent sent this to the editor of the EDD: 'Poor old fuller, he's a come to a proper old lamiger [pronounced laam.ijur] wi' two sticks.'

Oxford says that both words are from *lame*, adjective, and that the formation is obscure.

✦ LAMMER

Some years ago I was in a house in Co. Donegal where a young lassie was getting ready to go to her first dance. She wore a very fetching necklet of amber, and I was surprised to hear her mother call the substance *lammer*. The mother had been a long time working in Scotland in her youth, and I'm fairly certain that it was there that she heard the word; it may be found elsewhere in Ireland, but I've never seen it in any glossary. The *Concise Ulster Dictionary*, I see, hasn't recorded it.

Amber is a word even lovelier than *lammer*, and just as lovely as the Irish *ómra*. But as to *lammer*, the Scots seem to have taken a great liking to it, and their folklore has abundant references to the substance. In 1584 the Bishop of St Andrews wrote about the spiritual efficacy of 'Halie water and the lames beidis'. Gregor's *Folk Lore* of 1884 spoke of 'an amber bead vernacularly called lammer [which] was commonly used to remove the chaff from the eye both of man and beast'. Jamieson, the distinguished nineteenth-century Scottish lexicographer, wrote that 'In olden time, the present made by a mother to her daughter on the night of her marriage was a set of lammer beads to be worn about her neck, that from the influence of the bed-heat on the amber, she might smell sweet to her husband.' Brown's dictionary of 1845 assures us that 'lammer beads and red thread are a charm with power to repel witchery'. Henderson's *Folk Lore* of 1889, a book from England's North Country, echoes this: 'Black luggie, lammer bead, / Rowan tree and red thread, / Put the witches to their speed.' The *luggie* was the horned owl.

Lammer-wine was an imaginary liquor of great virtue. Hislop, a Scottish antiquarian of the latter part of the nineteenth century, wrote that this imaginary liquid 'was esteemed a sort of elixir of immortality, and its virtues are celebrated in this infallible recipe: "Drink ae coup o' the lammer-wine, an the tear is nae mair in your e'e."'

A woman's amber hair was praised above all other by Irish song makers in both English and Irish. The Scots, too, delighted in 'lammer hair's full glory'. 'Her locks that shine like lammer' is a line by Allan Ramsay in his *Tea Table Miscellany* of 1734 that will stand for the army of poets who loved the colour and the texture of lammer hair.

Lammer is from French *ambre*, with article prefixed.

✦ LAMMIT

I was immediately enraptured by this address of endearment ever since Veronika Bonaa, a Norwegian scholar, mentioned it to me a year or so ago. Don't get any ideas, reader dear; Veronika and I have never met, but she kindly let me consult a thesis she wrote about surviving words from Old Norse and modern Norwegian in the dialect of the Orkney Islands.

Lammit is also found as *lammiet* in places in Orkney and Shetland. The old scholar Jakob Jakobsen, in his classic *Det Norrøne Sprog på Shetland*, published in Copenhagen in 1897, has 'Lamit! my lamit!' The EDD gives an example of the use of the word. It's from J.J. Haldane Burgess's *Shetland Sketches and Poems* (no date but *c.* 1900): 'Yea, my lammit, I widna say bit what de'll be someen comin dis lent da nicht.'

The extraordinary thing about this tender word *lammit* is that it has survived for so long. It was introduced to Orkney and Shetland by the Viking invaders, to whom *lam mitt* meant 'my lamb'.

✦ LANE

I was surprised to learn in a note from an old friend of mine from Liverpool that the verb *lane*, deemed obsolete by the EDD around 1906, is still alive, even if only barely so, in parts of rural Lancashire. It means to conceal, keep secret, connive at, according to the EDD, and was once used extensively in Scotland, as well as in Northern England.

It was used as well in north Co. Dublin, around Lusk and Swords, before the Great War, according to Paddy White, an old soldier who lived in Swords, as far as I remember, and who gave me a lot of interesting words from his native place. 'What I'm telling you now, lane it,' was an example Mr White sent me, meaning 'Keep it to yourself, a secret between us.'

Why it died out is a mystery; it had survived for a long time. 'Lady . . . layn not yf ye knowen,' is from Langland's *Piers Plowman*. In more recent times, in Jamieson's *Popular Ballads* from around 1806, there is the line 'Tell us, May Margaret, And dinna to us len.'

I am delighted that the word, which came with the Vikings, still survives, although it is at death's door. I wonder if any reader remembers it from Yorkshire or Cumbria, or from north Co. Dublin, where it once was common. The Scandinavian marauders had *leyna*, to hide, conceal.

✦ LAVENDER

'Enuye . . . is lauender. In the grete court always,' wrote Chaucer in the *Legend of Good Women* around 1385. He was referring to a laundress. The word was commonly used once for both a laundress and a washerman, but this sense seems to have become obsolete since the end of the sixteenth century. About 1310 in one of the early English *Lyric Poems* edited by Wright we have 'Prude wes my plowe fere, Lecherie my lavendere.' One of the publications of the Roxburghe Club in the mid-nineteenth century has a line from a 1430 poem, 'The lauenders she saw in the floode, Ful besilie washing a shert.' Oxford gives the following as the last mention in writing of this meaning of lavender. It is from 1567 and it reads, 'Lauandrie. Margaret Balcomie, lauander.'

Well, the word describing the occupation of Margaret Balcomie is from Old French *lavandier* masculine, *lavandiere* feminine. (The modern French is *lavandière* feminine.) It has cognates in many Romance languages, the Spanish *lavandero* masculine, *-era* feminine, Portuguese *lavandeira* feminine, Italian *lavandaio* masculine, *lavandaja*, *lavandara* feminine. All are from late Latin *lavandarius*, *-aria* from *lavanda*; originally neuter plural 'things to be washed,' but in Romance used as feminine singular: cf. Italian *lavanda* washing, from *lavare* to wash.

Lavendry is a Middle English form of 'laundry'. Langland used it in *Piers Plowman* in 1377. Some have suggested that *lavendry* and the modern *laundry* have been influenced by Middle English *laund*, a lawn, on which newly-washed clothes were spread out to dry, but that's debatable.

I was once asked if this lavender is etymologically related to that other lavender, a fragrant plant *Lavandula vera* (family *Labiatæ*), a small shrub with small pale lilac-coloured flowers, and narrow oblong or lanceolate leaves; a native of the south of Europe and Northern Africa, but cultivated extensively in other countries for its perfume. The jury is out on this question. Hearken to Oxford.

Lavender is from Anglo-French *lavender*, from Old French **lavandre*, from Medieval Latin *lavendula*. The current hypothesis is that *lavendula* is a corrupt form of *lavandula*, which appears in Italian as *lavanda*. This is commonly identified with Italian *lavanda*, 'washing', the supposition being that the name refers to the use of the plant either for perfuming baths (so already in sixteenth-century writers) or laid among freshly-washed linen.

I have my doubts. On the ground of sense-development this does not seem plausible; a word literally meaning 'washing' would hardly, without change of form, come to denote a non-essential adjunct to washing. Besides, the earliest form appears to be *livendula*; if this could be connected with Latin *livere*, to be livid or bluish, the sense would be appropriate, but the formation is obscure. Oxford quotes the linguist M. Paul Meyer, who suggests as a possibility that the original form may have been *livindula* for *lividula*, from *lividus*, livid.

No matter where the name of this fragrant plant came from, and nobody seems certain, remember that it has wonderful properties apart from smelling nice. According to Nicholas Culpeper's famous *Pharmacopeia Londinensis, or the London Dispensatory*, published in 1653, 'two spoonfuls of the distilled waters of the flowers taken, helps them that have lost their voice, as also the tremblings and passions of the heart, and faintings and swoonings, not only being drank, but applied to the temples, or nostrils to be smelled into'. Great stuff this lavender! You have been told.

✦ LAVEROCK

The laverock is the lark, *Alauda arvensis*. What a lovely word it is, and once used all over Scotland from Orkney and the Shetlands in the far north to Selkirk in the south. It has been recorded in England from Yorkshire, Cumberland, Westmoreland and Lancashire down to Northamptonshire, Warwickshire and Suffolk. The word was common in Ulster as well, recorded by W.H. Patterson in Down and Antrim in the closing quarter of the nineteenth century, and by Simmons in south Donegal around the same time. Seumus MacManus in a story called *Phelim Ruadh*, published in *Pearson's Magazine* in May 1900, has 'The blackbird sings there, and the laverock.' It was recorded in Wexford by Jacob Poole in the latter part of the eighteenth century, and Liz Jeffries gave me the word in the form *larock* in Kilmore in Co. Wexford in 1975; she pointed out a field known to old-timers as the 'trapeen hye larocks', the little stile of the field of larks.

The word had many variants, and Mrs Jeffries's *larock* was also known in north Yorkshire. *The Shetland News* of 24 July 1897 has 'Laevericks and plivers', a variant that interested me greatly: in the Kerry Gaeltacht a *leábhairic* is a prankster, a trickster.

English poets preferred to praise the lark; it was left to the Scots to sing of the laverock 'piping out his blythe gude morrow', as one of them wrote. 'The lav'rocks they were chantin,' wrote Burns in *Holy Fair*. The laverock has entered folklore as well as poetry. Ramsay's *Scottish Proverbs* of 1737 has 'Live upon love, as laverocks do on leeks.' Christopher North's charming *Noctes Ambrosianae*, the 1856 edition of which I picked up in a Glasgow shop for half nothing many years ago, advises us to 'rise wi' the laverock an' lie doun wi' the lintie [the linnet]'.

What a pity it would be if *laverock* disappeared from the people's speech. A friend of mine from Yorkshire told me recently that her daughter was 'corrected' by her teacher when she wrote 'laverock' in an essay extolling the beauty of her native county. This is one example of the depradation the educational system of a country can do on dialect speech. Old Chaucer, who wrote *Romaunt of the Rose* over 700 years ago, must have turned in his grave. He sang of 'many flokkes of turtles and of laverocks'.

The word is from Old English *láwerce*, also written as *laferce*.

✦ LEED

Whenever we see the description 'now mainly poetical' in a dictionary, we may safely assume that the word in question is close to becoming obsolete. Such a word is *leed*, which has many variant spellings, *leet*, *lied*, *leid* among them. The word means a language or dialect, particularly one's native tongue. It can also mean a song, rhyme or tune; a long rambling speech or tale; and as a verb it means to speak a lot but with little meaning.

I first heard the word twenty-five years ago from a rugby player who lived near Ballyclare in Co. Antrim. He told me that the auld Scots lied had died out in his place in his father's day. At least he had one word of it in *lied*. In Scotland too the word seems to be in danger, although the DSL has many examples from recent times. In 1926 Hugh McDiarmid, in *A Drunk Man Looks At the Thistle*, has 'Nor cared gin truth frae me ootsprung In ne'er a leed o' ony tongue That ever in a heid was hung.' And in 1936 J.G. Horne in *Flooer o'Ling* has 'I could for very joy ha'e sung To hear again the lallan leid.' Whether or not these poets were being deliberately archaic here, I don't know; they both were often accused of using a long-dead lied for patriotic purposes. The EDD was sent the word from Perthshire just before 1900: 'Has'n the Glasca fowk an' awfu' queer leid?'

Leid meaning a song, a tune, is very rare in Scotland now. Buchan's *Ballads* of 1875 has the couplet 'I will to yon small window, / And hear yon birdie's leed.' The meaning, a long rambling speech, one particular line of conversation or argument, seems to be alive and well still in places. In 1949 the *Forfar Dispatch* had 'Weel, ye've mebbe herd auld

fowk on this sonnet yersel, so I'll no' gie ye nae mair o' thatten leid.'
And from Aberdeen in April 1959, the DSL recorded 'She jist has a leed
aboot it.'

Oxford gives the history of *leed* thus: 'Old English *lǽden*,
representing a Celtic or early Romanic pronunciation of *Latinum*, Latin,
was confused with the native *léden*, *lýden*, *léoden* language, from *léode*
people. The confusion seems to have originated with the compound
bóc-léden "book-language", which was fashioned by popular etymology
as a more intelligible synonym for *lǽden*.'

✦ LEEP

I heard this word once, and only once, in a house in Meenbanad, in the
Rosses of Donegal. The old woman who used it, Mary Sweeney, was
approaching her 104th birthday and was in full possession of her
faculties. She could read and write English, an extrordinary accom-
plishment for a woman of her time; she thanked her mother for this, a
woman who had heard the great O'Connell speak at a Glasgow rally. A
knowledge of English, she told her daughter, would ensure that she
wouldn't be exploited when she went to work in Scotland. Wise woman.

I don't know where she picked up the word *leep*, which means to
parboil, warm hastily; to boil for a short time, to scald. Probably in
Scotland, where, like most of her friends, she had to go to gut and cure
herrings before she was ten. A useful word, and now almost obsolete, the
Concise Ulster Dictionary has it from Donegal, which only proves that old
Mary wasn't the only one there who used it in her kitchen. It is also found
in Scotland and in Northern and Midland English across the water.

'We say that a thing is leeped, that is heated a little, or put into
boyling water or such like for a little time,' wrote Ruddiman in his
valuable glossary to Gavin Douglas's *Eneados*, in 1710. The EDD quotes a
correspondent from Cumbria: 'To boil for a short time with a view to
keeping for ultimate cooking. Generally of newly-caught salmon not
meant for immediate use.' I remember distinctly that Mary Sweeney
instructed her daughter to leep a salmon which a neighbour, a
fisherman, had brought her as a present.

Those expert fishermen, the Vikings, presented English with *leep*.
Modern Norwegian still has it in *løpa*, to scorch milk; in the older
language *hleypa* meant to curdle milk by heating.

✦ LIAISON & OTHER CULINARY WORDS

Some words have entered the English language through the kitchen and some have become generalised over time. *Liaison* is a good example of what I have in mind. That boyo Byron was one of the first to use it in the sense of illicit relations. In a letter written in 1816 he has 'She is by far the prettiest woman I have seen here. I believe I told you the rise and progress of our liaison in my former letter.' He also has it in *Don Juan* in 1821: 'Some chaste liaison of the kind . . . I mean / An honest friendship with a married lady.' Shelley in an 1821 letter commented that 'He [Byron] has a permanent sort of liaison with Contessa Guiccioli.' In 1849 Thackeray in *Pendennis* has 'If it were but a temporary liaison, one could bear it . . . But a virtuous attachment is the deuce.' In 1853 Greville in his *Memoir of George IV* wrote, 'He was always much addicted to Gallantry, and had endless liaisons with women.'

What, you might ask, has the kitchen to do with illicit hanky panky? Well, *liaison* was a French cookery term. It came from the Latin *ligari*, to bind, and in the kitchens of France eggs were the means by which the *liaison*, or thickening of sauces, came about.

In *To the Lighthouse* Virginia Woolf has a cook in the Ramsay household who seemingly mastered at least one example of French cuisine and Virginia described her *boeuf en daube*, a delicious stew cooked from cold, and named after the *daubiere*, the special, fat-bellied, narrow-necked pot used in the cooking. Mrs Ramsay gives a recipe of her grandmother's and remarks, 'Of course it's French. What passes for cooking in England is an abomination. It is putting cabbages in water. It is roasting meat until it is leather. It is cutting the delicious skins off vegetables.'

Resistance to French cuisine was usually vociferous until the travellers of the nineteenth century brought back words such as *gourmet*, which originally meant a wine-taster, and *ratatouille*, a ragoût, in full, *ratatouille niçoise*, a dish, originating in Nice, consisting of aubergines, tomatoes, onions, peppers, and other ingredients stewed in olive oil. The English cooks also tried *bouillabaisse*, and liked it. This was a dish from Provence, a word which shows its components: boiling, and then reducing (*abaissement*). They also discovered *brioche* in the nineteenth century, a kind of cake made of flour, butter and eggs; a sponge-cake, and also the *éclair*, which means lightning in French, and *croutons*, from *croûte*, crust, a small piece of toasted or fried bread used in soups and to garnish stewed dishes and minces. *Chef* quickly supplanted the old word *cook*. This new snobbery in the kitchen had the French *aubergine* supplanting the English *eggplant*. Oxford gives the word's origin as a diminutive of *auberge*, variant of *alberge*, 'a kind of peach' according to Littré's monumental *Dictionnaire de la Langue Française*; from Spanish *alberchigo*, *alverchiga*, 'an apricocke' according to John Minsheu's delightfully eccentric study of the comparative etymology of words in eleven languages, published in London in 1617. Other examples are given in Henry Hitchings' *The Secret Life of Words*, a book which I can heartily recommend.

Hitchings mentions that the late British foreign secretary Robin Cook, in a lecture he gave extolling Britishness and Britain's capacity to absorb foreign cooking and cooking terms, gave as an example 'the most popular of all Indian dishes, *chicken tikka masala*'.

The dish is completely unknown in India. Ouch.

✦ LINTWHITE

This is a Scots word for a linnet or lintie, *Linota cannabina*, and is, I'm told, getting rarer by the day. How I hate this onward rush towards conformity in language! *Lintie* is thriving in both Scotland and Ulster and thank goodness for that, but *lintwhite* simply isn't.

It is very old, as old as the *c.* 725 *Corpus Glossary*. It is found too in the 800 *Erfurt Glossary* and in *Ælfric's Glossary* of *c.* 1000. In 1400 or thereabouts *Morte Arthure* has 'With lowde laghttirs one lofte for lykynge of byrdez, Of larkes, of lynkwhyttez, þat lufflyche songene.' The great Scots poet Gavin Douglas has the word in his *Æneis* in 1513: 'Goldspynk and lyntquhyte fordynnand the lyft.' In 1785 Robert Burns in a poem *To William Simpson* wrote, 'When lint-whites chant among the buds'. Tennyson must have found the word in northern England. He was fond of dialect and gave us the couplet 'The lintwhite and the throstlecock / Have voices sweet and clear.'

W.H. Patterson recorded the word in his glossary of Antrim and Down words in 1880, as does our modern *Concise Ulster Dictionary*. *Lintie* is not as old as either *linnet* or *lintwhite*, and is from *lint* in *lintwhite*, ravellings or scrapings of linen cloth used for dressing wounds, medicinal lint, plus the diminutive ending *ie*. (*Linnet* is from Old French *linette*, from *lin*, flax.) Figuratively *lintie* also means a sprightly, young girl in both Scotland and Ulster; also in a bad sense, a malevolent or depraved woman. It can also mean a song, ditty. *The*

Buchan Observer of 28 November 1950 had 'Every encouragement was given towards the establishment of sessions of song and story; and . . . some of these illiterates had a fine opportunity to score if they could "come aff wi' a wee bit lintie".'

I almost forgot the *white* part of *lintwhite*, the word in grave danger of becoming obsolete everywhere. Well the word is from Old Scots *lyntquhyte*, from *lint* as I've explained, + the unattested *quhyte*, a variant of onomatopoeic *twite*, from its call. So says the great DSL.

✦ LIPOGRAM

I have once or twice been asked about this word, which is defined by Oxford as a composition from which the writer rejects a certain letter or letters. The word is a backformation from a Greek adjective meaning 'wanting the letter'. The word may have come through French, which has *lipogramme*. You may wonder why a writer would shun a certain letter in the composition of a story or poem, but I'm not the one to ask about this: try a psychiatrist.

Addison was the first to use the word in English literature in *The Spectator*, Number 62, 1711. Not all writers who composed lipograms were bonkers. Some regarded the thing as a literary frivolity, and didn't lose their sense of perspective in the matter. Certainly the first practitioner, the Greek lyric poet Lasus, who flourished before 600 BC, was as sane as they come; and so was the great Pindar, his pupil, who wrote *Ode Minus Segma*. Whoever wrote the *Odyssey of Tryphiodorus* took the biscuit. This work contains twenty-six books. There is no A in the first book; no B in the second; no C in the third. Some contemporary wag suggested that the work would have been immeasurably better if he had omitted the other letters as well.

Who else have we among the lipogramaniacs? The great Spanish playwright Lope de Vega in his novels is one. Then there is Ronden's *Pièce Sans A*, written in 1816, and influenced by the German poet Gottlob Burmann, who died in 1805, having to his credit, if that's the word, 130 poems without the letter R. For seventeen years he never used the letter B, and he never spoke his own name because it had a B in it. But as an antidote to all this lunacy the great American humorist James Thurber wrote a very funny piece about a country where the letter O was banned.

Yes, it's a mad world, my masters.

✦ LITHER

The adjective *lither* was once found in the form *luther* in Caithness in northern Scotland, and as such I once heard it used by a Donegal sheep farmer in Rogers' pub at the back of Muckish mountain to describe a young fellow who was, he said, bone idle and lazy. The farmer had spent the best years of his life in Scotland, and he had probably picked the adjective up there. The word is also found in England's North Country, in Lancashire, Yorkshire, Derby, Lincolnshire, Northamptonshire, Shropshire and Sussex—quite a spread.

'The horses are grown so lither fat / They downs stir out o' the stall,' is a line from a song in Scott's *Minstrelsy* of 1802. 'A laughing-faced lad makes a lither servant,' is a saying in Henderson's *Scottish Proverbs* of 1832. 'Long and lither is said of a tall, idle person,' a correspondent from Cheshire told the EDD.

Hence the following words, obsolete now, according to Scottish and English dialect scholars: *Lidderie*, adjective, feeble, lazy; *litherly*, adverb, lazily, idly; *lithermon's load*, phrase, a lazy man's load, a load piled up to save the trouble of a second journey; *litherums*, *litherness*, nouns, idleness.

The noun *lither/lidder* means idleness, laziness. Jamieson has in a supplement to his Scots dictionary of 1808: 'Ill! He's just ill with the lidder.'

I hate to see old words die out, and this word is very old. It's the same word as Middle English *lither*, bad, wicked, a word used by Hampole in his 1330 version of the Psalms: 'Thai ere many ill men & lithere deuels.' The Old English is *lyðre*, bad, base.

✦ LITTLE WILLIE

Since I mentioned Little Willie in an *Irish Times* article some years ago I have had a lot of letters about the man who gave his name, or part of it, to the grisly little quatrain with a trick last line. Little Willies are known in America as *grues*, and Robert Hendrickson, an American lexicographer, says that *grue* was coined by Robert Louis Stevenson from *gruesome*.

The verb *grue* is far older than Stevenson. Not recorded in Old English or Old Norse, it is cognate with the synonymous Old High German *in-grûên*, Middle High German *grûwen*, modern German *grauen*, Dutch *gruwen*, Danish *grue*. *Grue* means to feel terror or horror, shudder, tremble; quake; to shrink from something; to be troubled in heart. It is as old as *Cursor Mundi* (ante 1300) which has 'Dauid . . . thoght on his fas philistiens, Gladli wald he þam confund, To ger þam for him gru and grise.' But what about this fellow, Willie? Who was he, this mysterious bloke who gave his name to verses such as this one I remember from the recitation of some of my school friends:

> Willie pissed in his oul' lad's tay,
> His oul' lad died, I'm sorry to say.
> His oul' wan looked extremely vexed:
> 'For fuck sake, Will,' she said, 'What next?'

It has been suggested to me that the term Little Willie was first used of Crown Prince Friedrich Wilhelm Viktor August Ernst of Germany (1882–1951) and applied to persons as a term of disparagement and to weapons. It seemed to me that it is unlikely that the gruesome little verses took their name from an artillery piece mentioned in a letter from the trenches by D.O. Barnett in May 1915: 'At intervals of about twenty minutes last night they fired a Little Willie on to our trench.' *Ibid.* 8 June: 'Our fieldgun H.E. shell is a very fine thing, more powerful than the German one (otherwise known as Little Willie).'

Whether the name was suggested by that of the German prince or not, the Little Willie verses were first seen in a book by Harry Graham called *Ruthless Rhymes For Heartless Homes*. I see that my New Ross version appears in it, but without the bad language it had accrued. Here are a few more disgusting Little Willie verses:

> Little Willie hung his sister.
> She was dead before we missed her.
> 'Willie's always up to tricks.
> Ain't he cute! He's only six.'

> Willie bashed open baby's head
> To see if brains are grey or red.
> What a naughty boy is he.
> He shall have no jam for tea.

William in a nice new sash,
Fell in the fire and burned to ash.
Now, although the room grows chilly,
I haven't the heart to poke poor Willie.

And that's enough about gruesome Willie.

✦ LOODER-HORN

The persistent screeching of a boisterous French couple at a table nearby prompted my companion, Jack Devereux, an old seaman from Kilmore Quay, Co. Wexford, to whisper in my ear that we both should go across the street to another hostelry, 'away from them looder-horns'. A *looder-horn*, he explained to me later, was a fog horn, defined by the EDD as 'a large horn with which each fishing boat is furnished, to be blown occasionally in foggy weather and during the darkness of night, in order to ascertain the relative position of all boats in the same track'. Obsolete except in Shetland and Orkney, the great dictionary observed a hundred years ago. It was a revelation to find it alive and well and living in my native Wexford.

But where does this *looder-horn* come from? As you might expect from the maritime connection, from the Old Norse. The Vikings' word for a bugle or trumpet was *lúðr*. The lexicographer Aasen also points us to the modern Norwegian dialectal *lur*, a cowherd's horn.

I have enquired about the word's health in south Wexford since my meeting with the old Jack Devereux. Not a trace of it anywhere. It has gone with Jack to the grave, I'm sorry to relate.

✦ LOPPER

This useful word was once widely known in Ulster, where it was found as *lapper*, in many parts of Scotland, and in northern England, Lincolnshire and East Anglia. As a verb it means to coagulate, curdle, congeal, clot. 'The blood's lappered,' said the *Ballymena Observer* of 1892. A Lincolnshire contributor sent 'Th' milk was all lopper'd wi' th' thunner,' to the EDD. 'Bluid was lapper'd on its broo,' sang Murdoch the Lanarkshire poet in *The Doric Lyre*, in 1873. By extension, it means to besmear with something moist and sticky, especially blood, to dabble, to become covered with blood or the like; to have a blotched or mottled appearance, said of the sky. Scott in *Rob Roy* has 'They may lapper their hands to the elbows in their hearts' blude.'

As a noun *lopper* means a clot, a coagulated mass; a clot of blood. Jamieson, the Scots lexicographer whose dictionary of his language appeared in many editions from 1808 until the end of the century, has 'the milk's into a lapper'. The word also meant sour or curdled milk, and there is a compound, *lapper-milk*. Scott in *The Antiquary* (1816) has 'It will set ye better to be slaistering at parritch and lapper-milk than meddling wi' Mr Lovel's head.'

Lopper/lapper has one other meaning, snow in the act of melting; slush. This is, as far as I know, confined to Dumfries and Galloway in Scotland.

The *Concise Ulster Dictionary* has the word, but I'm told that the word is rarely used nowadays. It's an old word of Scandinavian origin. The *Catholicon Anglicum* of 1489 has *lopyrde mylke*. Compare the Old Norse phrase *hleypa mjólk*, to curdle milk, and the Norwegian dialectal *løypa*, also *lopen*, coagulated.

✦ LOSSET

It would be a pity to lose homely words connected with the kitchen, the most important room in the house according to Dr Johnson and, indeed, according to most domestic cooks.

The word *losset* is confined to Ireland, where it was once found all over the country. It means a kneading trough or board, and comes from the Irish *losad*. The estimable Fr Dinneen gave this definition: *Losad*, genitive *loiste*, feminine, a kneading trough, a 'losset'; figuratively a table spread with food; in Co. Cavan the farmer calls his well laid-out field his fine *losset*. It was also found as *lossel* in one eighteenth-century source, but this may have been a spelling error. Andrew Carpenter's *Verse in English from Eighteenth-Century Ireland* has, on page 121, 'Then four great swine . . . / Came in, on brawning shoulders born, / And laid in lossels to be torn.'

In the course of a letter to me, Mrs Ann Whyte, a friend of Jackie Bolger, wife of the great racehorse trainer Jim Bolger, told me an intriguing story about this *losset*. She and her husband paid a visit to a place called Whyalla in the Australian outback many years ago, and in the course of the visit she saw a friend, a native Australian, prepare to make a 'damper' for her barbeque. This was almost identical with the Irish griddle bread, and Ann got a bit of a land when the native cook said that he must first find a losset. He came back with a metal basin, almost identical with the one Ann had seen used in Clare by her mother-in-law. How, she wonders, did the word reach the outback and find its way into the native lexicon? Through convicts or early settlers, she supposes.

Yes, words are indeed great travellers. To think that the homely Irish *losad*, through its anglicised form *losset*, is used by native Australians as a word of their own. The mind boggles.

✦ LOST

I met Paddy the Cope, not the politician but his grandfather, at a party given to celebrate the 104th birthday of a Meenbanad woman, Mary Sweeney, some time in the late 1950s. Meenbanad is not far from Dungloe. Paddy himself was, as they say in the west, trushtin' towards the ninety himself at the time; he had founded an immensely successful co-operative society and written a fine book on his life which is still in print. I read his book again lately and found many interesting words in it including *lost*, which to Paddy, and to Peadar O'Donnell, his friend, and to old Mary Sweeney, meant very hungry. This is, apparently, an importation from England's North Country.

This is what Paddy has in his book: "'Did you not make yourself a cup [of tea]?" I told her I had not. She said: "God save us, you are lost."'

There is another Donegal *lost*, a word I heard Peadar O'Donnell, among others, use. It means miserable from being cold and wet. This *lost* is not, I have read, used anywhere outside the north of Ireland.

The ordinary meaning of *lost* is one which, I am sorry to say, must be applied to the recording made by my old friend the late Seán Mac Réamoinn of Paddy the Cope's reminiscences. So my RTÉ spies tell me. The story goes that at the end of the session a delighted Mac Réamoinn extended his hand in thanks to his guest, and mentioned that there would be a small fee for his services. At which the old man, who, though next to illiterate, had beaten the combined forces of church, state and the local gombeenmen to found a co-operative empire, said, 'That's all right, my friend.' He put his hand in his pocket and handed Mac Réamoinn a half-crown.

✦ LOUP

A lady from near Cashel, Co. Tipperary, Jane O'Brien by name, tells me that she is a horsewoman and interested in strange words that are rarely heard outside the realm of the horseman, or woman.

One such word, in grave danger of becoming extinct, my corre-spondent heard from a Traveller. She was putting a newly broken young hunter through his paces, and the Travelling man cast an expert eye on the animal. His assessment was that 'there's a fair oul loup in him, I'd say'. He explained to Jane that by *loup* he meant a jump. I wonder was he a Wexfordman: the word is in Poole's glossary of the dialect of Forth and Bargy. I heard the word from Miley Connors, a Wexford Traveller. I wrote down at the time Miley's opinion of a horse he sold: 'A dangerous hoor to put a youngster up on, though. He'd even shy at sheep in a field a mile away. They'd make him loup out of his pelt with fright. I tould the woman who bought him that plenty of the holly would cure him.' Miley also used *loup* in the context of servicing mares. 'He's charging five hundred pounds a loup from his oul' nag.'

This is not from Sheldru, or Minker's Tawrie, or whatever else you'd like to call the secret cant of Travelling people. The word is still found in places in rural Scotland, and in Northern England, and is common in the literature of Scotland. In 1375 the poet Barbour in his great poem *The Bruce* wrote, 'A lowp richt lychtly maid he than.' Four centuries later, another fine Scottish poet, Alan Ramsay, in *The Gentle Shepherd*, wrote of advice given to a poor young eejit driven to thoughts of suicide by a love affair that had gone agley, 'Yonder's a craig, since ye have tint all hope, Gae till 't your ways, and take the lover's lowp.' Scott in *The Black Dwarf* has a character in similar dark mood: 'I could find it in my heart to . . . loup ower the scaur into the water to make an end o' it.'

The word was recorded by W.H. Patterson in the Antrim of 1880, and it is still used there by a few old people. It's from Old Norse *hlaup*, a jump, *hlaupa*, to jump.

✦ LYCANTHROPY

A darlin' word, Captain. It was mentioned to me recently by one of that class of medical men described with a charming lack of political correctness by Bertram Wooster as *loony doctors*. I hasten to say that that man in question is a son of mine, and that I was not consulting him in relation to the heading above, which refers to somebody who thinks he's a wolf. No, I'm not yet that far gone.

Blount's seventeenth-century *Glossographia, or a Dictionary Interpreting such Hard Words as are now Used*, described the condition under discussion as 'frenzy or melancholly wherewith some being haunted, think themselves turned into wolves, fly the company of men and hide themselves in caves and holes, howling like wolves'.

Oxford has this definition: 'A kind of insanity described by ancient writers, in which the patient imagined himself to be a wolf, and had the instincts and propensities of a wolf. Now occasionally applied as a name of those forms of insanity in which the patient imagines himself a beast, and exhibits depraved appetites, alteration of voice, etc., in accordance with this delusion.'

Lady Morgan, in her story *Florence Macarthy* (1819), wrote, 'I am not well, surely, Sir, and thinks betimes that it's the lycanthropia I have got, which Maister Camden saith was common to the ancient Irish.' Maister Camden wasn't too far wrong, according to William Baldwin in his 1561 *Beware the Cat*. Said he, 'There is also in Ireland one nation whereof one man and woman are at every seven yeeres end turned into wolves, and so continew in the woods the space of seven yeers; and if they happen to live out the time, they return to their own forme again . . . and that this is true witnessed a man I left alive in Ireland, who had performed this seven yeeres penance, whose wife was slain while she was a wulf in her last yeer.' But then, Camden lived in a time when it was almost obligatory to tell whoppers about the inhabitants of foreign countries.

Still, the condition did exist in all European countries since classical times, when it was mentioned by Herodotus the Greek and the Roman poet Ovid, who wrote of King Lycaon, who was turned into a wolfman for challenging Jupiter's divinity.

The story is still running, even if the disease is no longer in vogue. Witness all those wolfman films and the film cult of the werewolf.

| M ～

✦ MAKING BEDS, DOORS, SOULS; MAKING MUCH OF

A Cork lady, Hannah Burke, put me working on these phrases, because she is sure they all come from Irish. Well, I don't agree with her, except for *making one's soul*.

As far as making a bed goes, there is no such concept in Irish; no native speaker ever said '*leaba a dhéanamh*'. It was, however, in English since about 1290, where it is to be found in *The South English Legends of the Saints* in a reference to St Brendan. Geoffrey Chaucer, some hundred years later, has 'I had men shulde my couche make.' This is almost certainly Germanic in origin. Consider the Modern German *das Bett machen*, to make the bed. The Low German *maken* is apparently from *maka*—fit, suitable; and Oxford suggests that the primary sense of *make* in 'to make the bed' would be to fit, arrange. Many scholars say that the French *fair un lit* is also of Germanic origin.

To make the door means to close it and I can assure Miss Burke that there is no direct equivalent in Irish. She tells me that she heard the phrase, not in Cork but in the West. I also heard the phrase there, in Sligo, from two good men, both gone from us now, Peter Kivlehan, a Sligo county councillor who was a member of the Governing Body of UCD, of which I was also a member at the time, and journalist Seán Kilfeather, also a Sligoman, of *The Irish Times*. This usage is also found in *The South English Legends of the Saints*, referring to Beket; and Shakespeare has it 300 years later in the *Comedy of Errors*: 'Why at this time the doors are made against you.'

In the last phrase on her list Miss Burke is on surer ground. *Making one's soul* is from Irish. Fr Dinneen has 'ag déanamh a anama, making his peace with God; preparing for eternity'. The English translation is found all over the country. Patrick Kennedy in *The Banks of The Boro* has 'Maybe it would be bether for me to think of mekin' me sowl. It's ten years since I was at a priest's knee, and I'll have a hard job of it.' Closer to our own time, Rev. William Forbes Marshall, a Tyroneman who died in 1959, mentioned the phrase in his famous *Me an' Me Da*: 'So I'm livin' in Drumlister, / An' I'm getting very oul', / I creep to Carmin wanst a month / To try an' make me sowl./ The diel a man in this townlan'/ Was claner reared nor me, / An' I'm dyin' in Drumlister / In clabber to the knee.'

To make much of is in English since about 1300. *Cursor Mundi* has 'Quen noght es mad of crists word.' In *c.* 1305 *St. Dunstan* in *Early English Poems*, edited in 1862, has 'A gret ordeynour he was And makede moche of gode reule.' That should, I think, dispel Miss Burke's notion of its having an Irish origin.

✦ MALISON & BENISON

Malison, unlike the equally old and lovely *benison*, is still alive and used in parts of Scotland as well as in remote parts of Cumbria, Lancashire, Northumberland and Westmoreland. Whereas *benison* means a blessing, *malison* means the direct opposite, a curse, a malediction. The word has survived the centuries in Scots literature. It appeared in 1989 in Anna Blair's *The Goose Girl of Eriska*: '"Threttie golden pounds paid I for my coal-black horse, and more faith have I in her, than in your malisons." And the last she heard was the thunder of hooves.'

Later still, in 1999, James Robertson in *The Day O Judgement* has 'Ma malisoun an curse gang wi ye: I lay upon ye pyne an gloom. / In hell-fire ye sall roast for aye: An this I dae pronoonce for doom.' The word is still used for the Evil One, the devil, in Scots.

The word has been in English literature since the *Cursor Mundi* was written sometime before 1300: 'His malison on þam he laid.' In *Havelok the Dane*, *c.* 1300, we find 'Haue he the malisun today Of alle þat eure speken may!' Forward to 1865 when Charles Kingsley's *Hereward the Wake, Last of the English* has 'Farewell, and my malison abide with thee!'

Both Oxford and the DSL give the Norman French *maleison* from Latin *malediction* as its origin.

Benison, regrettably, did not fare as well. In 1775 Dr Johnson said that it was 'not now used except ludicrously'. This after an innings that lasted from just before 1300, when it appeared in *Cursor Mundi*: 'On morn wit godds beniscon Was mai rebecca lede o ton.' In the same Northern work we find '[He] sal haue pardon / And part of cristes benison.' In 1605

Shakespeare wrote in *King Lear*, Act IV, Scene VI, 'The bounty, and the benizon of Heaven / To boot, and boot.'

The meaning, the pronouncing or invocation of a blessing, a benediction, lasted longer than Shakespeare's time, until the nineteenth century in fact, and then seems to have disappeared from literature as well. In 1815 Robert Southey's *Roderick, the Last of the Goths* has 'Short interchange of benison / As each to other gentle travellers give.' In 1828 Sir Walter Scott in *The Fair Maid of Perth* wrote, 'I have slept sound under such a benison.'

The old ecclesiastical meaning, grace before meals, lasted in literature no longer than *Havelock the Dane*, about 1300; thereafter, silence: 'Thanne [he] were set, and bord leyd, And the beneysun was seyd.'

Well, the lovely word is now classified in the dictionaries as obsolete. It is from Middle English *beneysun*, etc., from Old French *beneiçun*, *-çon*, *-sson*, *son*, *zon*, from Latin *benediction-em*.

✦ MANABLE

It must be fifteen years since a Galway correspondent sent me the above word. She overheard a conversation between two Travellers in a shop, which wouldn't, she thought, go down well in the Irish Countrywomen's Association. No, nor in many's the women's association besides, methinks. The conversation between the women went something like this: 'Wha' age is the Mongan young wan now?' 'I don't know the hell. I'd say she must be manable, anaways.'

My correspondent knew the word because of her dealings with Traveller women as an unpaid teacher of the three Rs, and she knew that there was nothing coarse about its use: *manable* meant simply 'of an age to get married'.

My friend Pádraig Mac Gréine of Ballinalee, Co Longford, who died a few years ago at the age of 106, knew the word. He was a national teacher, and contributed a seminal article on Travellers' cant, Sheldru or Shelta, to the folklore journal *Béaloideas* in 1935. The word was common in Travellers' speech until quite recently, he told me, but had suddenly been dropped by the women, for no apparent reason. A Traveller, Rosie Keenan, with whom I have the occasional pint in an Abbeyside, Dungarvan, hostelry, tells me that no Travelling women use the word nowadays; 'somebody must have told them that it was dirty or something', she thought. She was probably right in that.

I don't think the word has ever been recorded in the speech of settled people anywhere in Ireland. It was known to at least two Jacobean dramatists. In 1607 Thomas Middleton, in *The Familie of Love*, Act IV wrote, 'Had you not been so manable, here are some would have saved you that labour.' And in 1623 John Fletcher & William Rowley in *The Maide in the Mill*, Act II have, 'She's manable, is she not?'

✦ MANÈGE

I was sitting looking down at some children getting a riding lesson in an enclosed arena one day last year, when a lady sat alongside me and began to shout at her offspring, who was sitting petrified on her pony. My companion was unmistakably American, and I felt I had to tell her to desist for the child's sake and to leave the instruction to the instructor. I was informed that she had paid good money to have her child taught in this expensive manège and that the instructor was useless. The situation went from bad to worse and finally the instructor, who owned the arena and was one of the best in the business, took the child off the pony's back and told the mother that she could have her child and her money back at the office. The child, looking relieved, left with an attendant and the lesson resumed.

Still and all, *manège* was a fine old word the lady used, and it is still common in the States for a riding school. It was once common in this part of the world. John Evelyn in his Diary for 1644 wrote that 'The Prince has a stable of the finest horses of all countries . . . which are continually exercised in the manège.' Horace Walpole in a letter dated 1756 wrote, 'The horseman Duke's manège is converted into a lofty stable.'

The word also has the meaning, the movements proper to a trained horse; the art or practice of training and managing horses; horsemanship. Thackeray in *The Newcomes* (1854) wrote, 'For all her bitting and driving, and the training of her manège, the generous young colts were hard to break.'

The word was also used figuratively and by transference. Byron, in Moore's *Life*, was reported to have said, 'Taste is sometimes found restive under the pedantic manège to which it is subjected.'

The word is from the form of the word earlier adopted as *manage*, noun, the art of training and managing horses; from Italian *maneggio*. The ultimate origin is Latin *manus*, a hand.

✦ MANISHEE

I heard an interesting word from a Traveller lady who has now settled in Dungarvan. My friend has a fine command of gammon, sometimes called Sheldru or Shelta, the secret language of the Travellers, now, alas, dying out among the men. The word she told me about was not in her own lexicon, but she learned it from an old woman, now gone from us. The word is *manishee*, a woman, and my friend asked me if it came from Irish; the word *bean sí*, or *banshee* in Irish English, came to her mind, and mine.

I looked in all the sources for it, but devil a trace of it could I find. And then I tried the Romany glossaries, and I was delighted to find it in one of them, a booklet compiled outside Glasgow in the late nineteenth century. *Manishee* had no known connection with Scottish Gaelic, but came directly, it would seem, from a far more ancient language, Sanskrit, the ancient religious language of Hinduism, and one which also has an extensive philosophical and scientific literature dating from the first millennium BC. It is still one of India's official languages. It is the oldest recorded member of the Indic branch of the Indo-European family of languages, of which Irish is one of many.

At any rate, *manishee* is from Sanskrit *manúsí*, a woman.

✦ MAWK

An old acquaintance of mine, Jane Harte, asks me if I've ever heard the word *mawk*, the Scots word for a maggot, especially the larva of the bluebottle fly. It has been designated obsolete by many dictionaries.

Mawk is a very old word. It appears in a tract of 1425, edited by Wright and Wülker in that golden era of lexicography, the nineteenth century; the text reads 'Hic simex, mawkes'.

It has been recorded many times in the literature of Scotland; an old book I picked up years ago in Glasgow for a few bob, Christopher North's *Noctes Ambrosianae*, has 'I saw her carefully wi' a knife scrapin' out the mawks.'

William Gaskell in his *Two Lectures on the Lancashire Dialect* (1854) says that the word was confined where he grew up to the maggots used for fishing. A Lancashire friend tells me that *mawk* is used in his place for the disgusting bluebottle larva. In Donegal I once heard a woman tell her daughter to put the cheese in the fridge before the heat turned it *mawky*.

Before it made its appearance in English it was in Old Norse as *maðkr*, a maggot. The Danish is *madike*.

✦ MAYO WORDS

I was delighted to get a letter from Fr Leo Morahan, who many years ago gave me permission to use his collection of local words published in his Louisburgh, Co. Mayo, parish magazine, *An Choinneal*, over the years. I included many of these words in my book *A Dictionary of Anglo-Irish, Words and Phrases in Irish in the English of Ireland*. He wrote now about the Mayo word *saraft*, the time just before Lent, when people all over Europe tended to go a bit mad, even madder than they did in Ireland, with drinking, wild parties and the devil knows what else. *Saraft*, in other places *shraft*, comes from *shrift*, 'the imposition of penance implying absolution; the word came to be apprehended in certain contexts as = absolution', as Oxford defines it.

Carleton in *Traits and Stories* (1843) has 'Will you have my new big coat made agin shraft?', and Wexfordman Patrick Kennedy in *The Banks of the Boro* (1847) has 'I was in Iniscorfy (sic), you see, on Shraft Tuesday'. We'd call the day Shrove Tuesday. In Louisburgh the following Sunday used to be called *Puss Sunday*, from the sour expressions allegedly seen on the faces of those ladies who hadn't been asked to marry before Lent brought a temporary end to their hopes.

I hope Fr Morahan is still collecting words. Has his extraordinary parish journal survived?

✦ MEAGRE

I read recently that the adjective *meagre*, meaning sickly, ghostly, rather than scanty, deficient in quantity or goodness, had long departed from English, but I was very glad to hear it used in this way by a friend from Co. Down recently. He did say that very few people in the Mournes would still use the word, and that they were all old-timers like himself.

The word made its appearance in English around 1300 in the Romance of *Cour de Lyon*: 'the lyoun was hungry and megre'. Milton wrote of 'Blue meagre hag or stubborn unlaid ghost', and John Keats has 'Thou shall see the field-mouse peep / Meagre from its celléd sleep.' The most poignant use of *meagre* in this sense is in Shakespeare's *King John*. During Queen Constance's great lament for the doomed Prince Arthur, she says, 'There was not such a gracious creature born. / But now will canker sorrow eat my bud, / And chase the native beauty from his cheek, / And he will look as hollow as a ghost, / As dim and meagre as an ague's fit, / And so he'll die . . .'

King John was written late in 1596. In August of that year Shakespeare's only son, Hamnet, died in Stratford-upon-Avon, aged eleven. Ivor Brown the Scottish lexicographer said that if ever a poet wrote after a personal loss and from a broken heart, surely it was here.

Co. Down may not be the only place in Ireland where Shakespeare's usage still survives. When I taught school in south Kilkenny in the early 1960s I made its acquaintance through my pupils, to whom the word meant '*ainnis*, sick-looking', as one of them glossed it. They pronounced the word *mayger*.

The word is from Middle English *megre*, from Old French *meigre*, from Latin *macrum*, thin, skinny.

✦ MEAR

A lady who farms near Naas, Co. Kildare, and who breeds fast horses, wrote to me about the word *mear*, a word meaning to border on, and the noun *mearing*, a marked boundary between fields, farms, and strips of bogland.

Patrick Boyle, apart from writing very good fiction, was a kindly, understanding bank manager in Wexford town in the sixties. I used to have a pint with him every so often, and I recall having seen the word in a short story of his called *Pastorale*: 'It is a scraggy strip of land which would graze a goat, but it mears on the Bennett property.'

The noun *mearing* seems to me to be more widely used than the verb, and it has many variants. It is found all over Connacht and in places as far apart as Monaghan and west Waterford. Lady Gregory had *mering* from Galway in one of her less than memorable plays. 'It's little temptation there was for my poor beasts to cross the mering'; George Moore had *marin* in his *Muslin* (1936). 'There is a fall into the marin stream betwixt your honour's property and the Miss Brennans'; Lady Morgan, formerly Owenson, had *mearing* in *The O'Briens and the O'Flahertys* (1846). 'A mearing of loose stones marked the separation of this favourite bit of bog from the turlough through which its red veins ran'; Marrie Walsh had *mayren* in *An Irish Country Childhood* (1966); *Mearing Stones* is the title of a collection of prose essays by Joseph Campbell (1936).

The word first appeared in literature around 825, in an Old English psalter. Edmund Spenser wrote this in *The Fairie Queene*, between 1590 and 1596: 'So huge a mind could not in lesser rest, / Ne in small meares contain his glory great.'

We depend more and more on the countryside to preserve ancient words. It is heartening to know that the ancient *mear* and *mearing* are used in parts of rural Ireland. The question is, how long more will they survive? They are now unknown in Ireland's cities and towns, as you might expect.

The origin of the two words is the Old English *mœre*, a boundary, a landmark. It is found in Middle Dutch as *mere* and *meer*, and cognate with Latin *murus*, a wall.

✦ MELTITH

Found only in Scotland and in England's North Country, the word is now in grave danger of extinction. It means a meal. The word is found in Scots literature since the eighteenth century.

James Kelly's *A Complete Collection of Scotish Proverbs, explained and made intelligible to the English reader* (1721) has 'A hearty hand to give a hungry meltith,' which he glosses as 'An ironical Ridicule upon a niggardly Dispenser'. Fergusson's *Poems* of 1773 has 'A heartsome meltith, and refreshing synd O' nappy liquor, o'er a bleezing fire'. Fergusson, an important Aberdeen poet, was edited and republished by the Scottish Text Society. Another important poet and storyteller, James Hogg, known as the Etterick Shepherd, has in his 1811 *Poems*, 'Auld Geordie sat beside a board Wi' routh o' hamely meltith stored.' Walter Scott in his 1821 book, *The Pirate*, has 'Mair like a mash for horse than a meltith for man's use'. In the 1880 edition of *The Border Counties Magazine* there is 'I'll do it for a meltith o' meat.' J. White's *Eppie Gray*, published in 1910, is the last citation in the DSL: 'An' though a humble meltith, Feth, a better coodna be.'

Hence the compounds: (1) *meltith-buird*, a table, the board where meals are served; (2) *meltit time*, mealtime; (3) *meltith hale*, able to eat heartily. P.H. Waddell's charming translation of the Psalms (1871) has 'Yer weans, round about yer meltith-buird, sal growe like the olive wands.'

A. Balfour's *Contemplation* of 1820 has 'For milk, an' bread, an' sowens, an' kail, Were never missed at meltit time.'

R. Clark's *Random Rhymes* of 1842 has 'To see gin a' be meltith hale, An' thrang at wark.'

The OED dismisses the word as simply a Scots variant of *meal-time*. This is undoubtedly true, but the DSL gets a little more mileage from it. It is, it says, from Old Scots *meltydit*, first recorded in 1493, afterwards *melteth*, = obsolete English *mealtide*, from *meal*, a repast, + *tide*, from Old Norse *máltið*.

✦ MENSE

This ancient word, once found in profusion in its different shades of meaning in Scotland, Ireland and all the northern counties of England, seems to be becoming obsolete by the week according to recent surveys. It means honour, respect, reverence.

'Ye rin frae ae thing tae anither, Wi' mad intent, the Diel's ain brither, Till mense is lost,' wrote an Ayrshire dialect poet, John White, in *Jottings in Prose and Verse*, a book still consulted by scholars of Scots, though it was written in 1879. The word also means profuse hospitality or liberality; a liberal amount, a great deal. A Durham man who was a correspondent of the editor of the EDD at Oxford told Joseph Wright that in relation to funeral extravagance as a token of respect, 'mense is a great thing in this country'. A south Lincolnshire correspondent wrote to Wright, 'What a mense of folks there was!' 'Oh dear, it runned a mense.' 'He's gotten a mense out of it.' 'The rain has done a mense of good.'

Our word also meant recompense, reward; thanks, kindness. 'We've fed him, cled him—what's our mense for it all?' asked a peeved man from Renfrewshire.

Perhaps the most widespread use of the word was in its meaning of decency, propriety, decorum; good manners, politeness. Scott in *Rob Roy* has 'We hae mense and discretion.' A correspondent of Wright's sent him from Ulster, 'You have your mense and your meal,' used when a favour has been offered and refused. The *Ballymena Observer* of 1892 had the word, meaning thanks, kindness. And the *Concise Ulster Dictionary* also has the word.

Neatness, tidiness, order, is still another meaning. In Yorkshire 'He has no mense of himself' means 'He doesn't keep himself respectable.' 'You've spoiled his mense,' was said of a horse the tail of which was cut too short.

A credit, an ornament, is another use which has survived. I was recently sent a cutting from a Scottish newspaper which said that their tennis player Andy Murray was, whether he won or lost, a mense to his country and to the town of Dunblain.

I like the compound *mense-money*, sent to me by a Glasgow friend. It was, he said, money kept in his pocket by a Scotsman, just to rattle, to show that he has some lolly; this money was not for spending! I also savoured a phrase I heard in Skye, *to mense the table*, to preside over a meal.

As for origin, the SND points to the Old Scots *mense*, honour, from 1438, a reduced form of English *mensk*, courtesy, dignity, ornament, from Old Norse *mennska*, humanity, kindness. There is also the Old Norse *mennskr*, human, belonging to man.

✦ MENYIE

This extraordinary word, still around in places in Scotland and in northern England south to Derbyshire, is with us in a variety of forms and spellings since medieval times. *Menzie* is a Scots form, *menya* is found in north Yorkshire, *meeny* is the norm in north Lancashire and Derbyshire, and *meany* was once found in the Barony of Forth in south-east Wexford, where Jacob Poole recorded it towards the end of the eighteenth century. It meant, first of all, a family, a household. It also meant a retinue, a train of followers; a procession; a crowd, throng, multitude.

'Engaged in the same joyous revel as the menyie of old Sir Tom o' Lynne', wrote Walter Scott in *Redgauntlet* in 1824. In his vicious polemic *Papistry Stormed*, published in 1827, William Tennant from Fife has 'The menzie o' that German loon Hae pykin been at this my gown.' A Lanarkshire law of 1710 read 'It is provyded . . . that none hold more [victuall] than will sustain themselves and their meinzie till neu corn.'

Ramsay in his 1736 *Scots Proverbs* contains this: 'If the laird slights the lady his menyie will be ready.'

W. Gregor's treatise on Dunbar's works, published by the Scottish Texts Society, has 'It is still used in Banffshire = a number, and pronounced *maingeh* (*ng* nasal); also by way of contempt to a family or a particular set of people, as "She's mairriet in amon a queer maingeh."' There is a line in a Northumberland ballad which runs, 'Then the Percy out of Bamborowe came, With him a mighty meany.'

The word is still used by people in Orkney. This is from W.T. Dennison's *Peace's Almanac* of 1885. I must thank Norwegian linguist Veronika Bonaa for the reference: 'The drinking cogs at a feast were divided into two kinds, the "menye-cogs" and the "cogilt-cogs"; the first were passed through and drunk from by all the company; the second were confined to their respective cogilts [ordinary cogs]. The "menye-cogs" were distinguished from the others by having every alternate stave made of dark wood, so that the vessel had a variegated appearance ... The "menye-cogs" were the guid-man's cog, the priest's cog, and the bride's cog.'

Wyclif, in 1388, wrote this: 'In thi seed all the meynes of erthe shulen be blessid', as far as I know the earliest use of the word in English literature.

I had thought that the word might be of Norse origin, but no. The DSL gives this: 'The Old Scots was *men(h)e*, an armed troop; by 1375, it meant a retinue, and by 1438, as *menzie*, a multitude. From Old French *meyné, mesniee*, a household, from unattested Latin *mansionatia*, from *mansio*, a dwelling, a house.'

A long journey it had from ancient Rome to remote Orkney in the north, and to the Anglo-Norman Barony of Forth at my own doorstep.

✦ MERLE

The one and only time I heard this word in Ireland was in Dunlewey, Co. Donegal, at the foot of Errigal, that lovely cone-shaped mountain which takes its name from the Latin *oraculum*, a place of prayer. The lady I heard the word from was a singer in Eddie McGeady's pub, clearly a native of Donegal, but no local: she was a visitor, home from Scotland, and she sang a plaintive ditty about a young man bound for the army, who had a voice sweeter than the mavis (thrush) or the merle. I had to ask her what a *merle* was and I was told that it was a word used by Scots poets for the blackbird, *Turdus merula*. Dead right the singer proved to be.

The Scots have been singing the praises of the merle for quite a while now. Their great Dunbar led the chorus in a 1510 poem: 'This joyfull merle so salust scho the day.' But before that date Caxton refers, in 1483, to 'a blacke byrde that is called a merle'. In 1791 Burns celebrated the bird in a love poem: 'The merle, in his noontide bow'r, Makes woodland echoes ring.' 'The hazle groves rang with the blythe merle's sang,' wrote the lesser poet Cunningham, twenty years later. Another Scots poet of the nineteenth century, Archibald Thom, frae Aberdeen, who called his book *Amusements of Solitary Hours in Poetry and Prose*, must have been love-lorn when he penned the lines 'There's nae a sound in yon bower / Merle's sough nor Mavis singin.' Another minor figure in Scots literature, but still important because of his rich vocabulary, is Crockett, author of the engaging *Bog-Myrtle* (1895). He has 'Fairet and rarest ever was seen / Sing the merle and laverock merrily.'

Swainson, chronicler of birds of the British Isles, heard the *merle* singing in Ireland. It seems to Oxford that *merle* wasn't used much by the ordinary folk in Scotland, but was confined to verse, good and bad. It attributes the word's popularity to Caxton and Drayton, who wrote, in an *Eclogue* of 1593, of 'The jocund Mirle perch'd on the highest spray.' The DSL agrees. 'Found only in verse,' it says.

I suppose that puts paid to any notion of a revival of the word. A pity. I like it.

It comes from French *merle* masculine (in Old French also feminine), from Latin *merulus, merula*, blackbird or ousel.

✦ MINNIE

This word, meaning a mother, used to be in general use in Scotland, Northern England and Ireland, but is in decline according to the latest surveys. Its first apearance in literature is in a poem by the Scots poet Dunbar some time after 1500: 'Sen that I borne wes of my mynnye, I nevir wowit weycht bot yow.' In 1790 Robert Burns in *Tam Glen* wrote, 'My minnie does constantly deave me, / And bids me beware o' young men.' If they were anything like the bould Rab, that was sound advice. In a poem *To His Auld Mare* he used the word again: 'When first I gaed to woo my Jenny / Ye then was trottin wi' your minnie.' In 1816 Scott wrote nostagically, 'Light loves I may get mony a ane, / But minnie ne'er anither.' In 1858 Charles Kingsley in *Andromeda* had 'My minnie bad me bide at hame until I won my wings.'

Many's the time and oft have I heard the word in Ireland, from Wexford to Donegal. When I made enquiries from my friends the schoolteachers about the present health of the word, the prognosis was very bad indeed. Only the very old have the word, was the general comment.

In Shetland, whose English has always fascinated me, *minnie* means a grandmother. And in Lothian they have it as a verb meaning to join each lamb in a flock to its own mother; and of a lamb, to run to its mother. The *Edinburgh Magazine* of January 1772, in an indictment of a farmer, had 'the said twelve ewes being separated from the rest, and having bleated or cried, four or six lambs broke off from the flock of eild sheep and ran to the ewes and minnied or mothered themselves by sucking'.

The DSL says that the word possibly originated from infant utterances or in baby talk. That makes sense.

I wonder if the Irish word for a she-goat, a nanny-goat, *minseach*, is related. This word has entered the English of West Cork as *meenshuch*.

✦ MIRAAM

My old friend Jack Devereux sat in his kitchen in Kilmore Quay waiting for me. I had heard he had been in hospital and I was worried about him. He was closer to ninety than he was to eighty. To my question as to how he was he shrugged his massive shoulders and replied, 'I'm miraam, boy, miraam.' I didn't quite know what that reply meant, and seeing the query in my eyes, he smiled at me and said again, 'I'm miraam, I'm as you see me.'

The old fisherman, and former lifeboatman, who had given me a few hundred old words from the Anglo-Norman Barony of Bargy, and who had been given an M.A. degree for his work in securing the place of the famous Kilmore Carols in the life of his parish, carols which have been sung every Christmas since 1728, looked at me and asked me where the word *miraam* originated. 'It doesn't sound like French,' he said. 'I wonder is it an old form of English?'

When I got back to Dublin I asked the opinion of my colleagues in UCD, Rick Caldicott of the French department and Alan Bliss of Old and Middle English. I drew a blank. But Tomás de Bhaldraithe, the expert on Irish lexicography, thought he had the answer. 'I think it is a corruption of Irish *mar atháim*,' he ventured, emphasising that it was only a guess. *Mar atháim*, as I am: or as Jack put it, as you see me.

For what it's worth, I think Tomás was right. Both he and Jack Devereux have by now gone from us, and so has the word *miraam*. In a recent visit to Kilmore, of the many people I enquired about the word, only Jack's son, John, ever remembered hearing it, and that from his father.

✦ MIRK

This old word was once in general use in Scotland and in many of the counties of England, particularly in the north. It is, I suppose, simply a variant of *murk*.

Murky is common as an adjective. We might speak of somebody's murky past. But the noun *mirk* seems to be in decline, and I notice that the *Concise Ulster Dictionary* doesn't record it. It means darkness, gloom; the close of day, night. I was surprised at the CUD's omission, because I've heard it in Co. Donegal. I remember an old woman bumping into me on the loanin (lane) one dark night. 'Mother of God,' she said to me, 'I nearly knocked you down. I never saw you in the mirk.' It struck me that she had picked the word up in Scotland, where she, like many another from the district, worked for many years. 'Thou would be found deep drown'd in Doon; Or catch'd wi' warlocks in the mirk,' wrote Rhymer Rab in *Tam o' Shanter*.

The EDD has the noun *mirk* meaning darkness, gloom, from Jane Barlow's best-known work, *Irish Idylls* (1892), stories set in Lisconnel, a fictitious village in the heart of Connemara. Miss Barlow has 'Nowhere else, one imagines, does mirk swooping from overhead so mingle with mirk striking up from underfoot.'

Hence the Scots have *mirklings*, adverb, in the dark; *mirkiness*, noun, darkness; *mirksome*, adjective, somewhat dark; *mirky*, adjective, dark, gloomy, dusky. There is also a Scots verb *mirk*, which means to darken, cast a shadow over, which is also used figuratively. 'In my hert love's licht is mirked by sorrow's nicht,' wrote the Lanarkshire poet Thomson in a downcast mood. In Ray's dialect dictionary of 1691, assembled just to the south of the Scottish border, 'to be merk'd' is explained as 'to be troubled or disturbed in one's mind, to be startled'.

Mirk is a word I like since I came across it in a striking line in some long-forgotten Scots poem: 'where saughs and osiers mirk the face of day'. I'm a sucker for gloomy words. I'm sorry this one is not used much any more.

It's from Middle English *mirk(e, myrk(e, mirc* (thirteenth century), from Old English *mirce* = Old Norse *myrk-r*. The Swedish is *mörk*, the Danish *mørk*.

✦ MISCAWN

Also found as *miscaun, miskin, mischaun* and *muscawn*, this word means 'a lump of butter'. Long gone are the days of the *miscawns*, when the country buttermakers brought their produce into the big town and city markets to be inspected, tasted and bought by traders from cities as far apart as Bristol and Liverpool, as well as by native wholesalers. The word and its variants are corruptions of the Irish *meascán*, defined by Fr Dinneen as a ball or lump; a pat of butter.

William Carleton from Tyrone in a footnote in *The Party Fight and Funeral* has 'a portion of butter, weighing from one pound to six or eight, made in the shape of a prism'. In one of the *Stories from Carleton*, edited by Yeats, there is 'I remember the flitches of bacon, the sacks of potatoes, the bags of meal, the miscawns of butter and the dishes of eggs.' And in *The Legend of Knockgrafton* he has 'Throw me up fifteen or sixteen tubs, or the largest miscaun you've got.'

William Robert Wilde in *Irish Popular Superstitions* has 'Curious and many are the means taken by the peasants' wives to ensure success, and to gather a plentiful mischaun of butter, when the milk cracks.'

Jacob Poole's glossary of the dialect of Forth and Bargy, Co. Wexford, collected in the late eighteenth century and first edited by William Barnes in 1867, has the line 'Aar was a miscaun of buthther,' and in *Lays and Legends of the North of Ireland* (M.H. Gill, Dublin, 1884), we are told that 'plates wir heap'd up with miskins av butter, an' praties, an' tea'.

Notes and Queries, in 1854, gives this from Ireland: 'She tauntingly replied that his large oatcake, his quarter of beef, and his "miscawn" of butter would amply suffice a better man.'

Yes indeed, and two men, such a short time after the Great Famine. No mention of the praties here, you'll notice, and yet spuds and butter served us well until the blight struck. When Sir John Carr visited rural Wicklow in 1806 he noted that a family lived six days a week on potatoes and buttermilk (*bláthach*) kept after the *miscawn* was made, and related that when an English visitor saw a number of fine florid children in a hovel, he asked the father how he contrived to have so many of them. He replied proudly, 'By Jasus, it is the potato sir!' He might have added the *bláthach*, the rich product of the *miscawn*.

A friend of mine from Mitchelstown, Co. Cork, told me of the procession of country carts which used to come into the town in the old days, laden with miscawns of butter in casks and tubs which were set out on the streets ready to be tasted by buyers from the great Buttermarket in Cork city. One celebrated buttermaker was Alie Daly, a Limerickwoman. Her butter was so good that one day, so the story goes, she allowed some buyers to engage in a blindfold testing competition, and when a buyer from the Cork city Buttermarket gave his verdict on

Mrs Daly's keg, he proclaimed it to be 'the real Alie Daly'. The phrase survived to describe the very best of anything.

✦ MOLLYCODDLE

Even the latest scholarly surveys have shown that this word has not been recorded in Ireland, and is confined to Scotland, Wales, and most of the dialects of England from the northern counties south to Somerset, Devon and Cornwall. It has also reached the United States. This is very strange given that the word is used in Ireland in every county even if it is showing signs of being on the wane. Having said that, I notice that Terry Dolan hasn't got it in his *Dictionary of Hiberno English*, and that all our literary men have ignored it; there is no sign of it in Richard Wall's *Irish Literary Dictionary and Glossary*.

I think I'm right in saying that it is usually used as a verb in Ireland. It means to pamper; to spoil by over-care and attention. From Somerset this piece of conversation was sent to Joseph Wright at Oxford: 'I can't abear to zee nobody a mollycaudled up in this farshin; better put the boy in a glass case to once. No wonder the children be wakely, always molly-caudled up like that there; must'n ever go out o' doors 'thout girt coat and shawls . . .'

Of a man it means to do such household work as is usually done by a woman. The verb is not always used in a derogatory way, as is evident from this example sent to Wright from mid-Yorkshire: 'His wife's an ailing body [person] so he mollycoddles himself a bit.'

Mollycoddle, the noun, is defined by Wright as 'an effeminate person, especially a boy; one who takes excessive care of his health; a valetudinarian'. The noun also means a man who does household work; one who interferes with women's business. A Yorkshire lady is reported to have said, 'He's a regular mollycoddles; yer can't see him for coats and comforters.' In Oxford Wright heard, 'Jane tells me her husband scrubs all the house for her. What a regular mollycoddle she has made of the man, to be sure.'

So, where does the word come from? I can only guess because the dictionaries duck the issue. *Molly* is an old generic name for a woman. *Coddle* is more of a problem. But I think it's from the old dialect verb meaning 'to cover, wrap up; to shrink, wither, wrinkle by contracture, to lie in bed with drawn-up limbs', according to the EDD, which has it from east Yorkshire. I'll run with that.

✦ MOONSHLAY

The late Alan Bliss, irascible professor of Old and Middle English at University College Dublin, did not, regrettably, live long enough to demolish the work of many linguists, some of them home-bred, who in recent years have taken to treat as irrelevant the work of those scholars who think that the influence of the Irish language on Irish English is of great importance. Bliss himself learned Irish in the Mayo Gaeltacht; many of these linguists I refer to ply their trade either in continental Europe or in Japan, and not having enough Irish to put the cat out, would have no interest in words like the lovely *moonshlay*, sent to me fifteen years ago by a Cashel, Co. Tipperary, woman.

The Suir basin, particularly the fresh-water stretch of it, is often hit by flash floods that swamp the land, and even make angling impossible. These flash floods, which start in the Galtee mountains very often, used to be called *moonshlays* in south Tipperary, from the Irish *madhm slé* [*sléibhe*], a mountain burst or eruption.

The late Liam Clancy, the balladeer, knew the word from old people in Carrick-on-Suir, but he assured me that I could search every parish along the banks of the lovely river nowadays without coming on a single person who used the word. I did my best to test his assertion, writing to various schools in the region, and although I freely admit that this is not a scientific method of doing things, the responses I got led me to believe that the folk-singer was correct. The pupils of all thirty-five schools I wrote to had never heard of the word. Another expressive word gone from both the Irish and the Irish English of Tipperary.

✦ MORAL

I've heard this word, which once was in general dialectal use in Scotland, Ireland and England in Counties Sligo, Leitrim, Fermanagh, Donegal, Louth, Mayo and Galway. I'm told that it is now in decline, and that it is unlikely to survive. It has been defined as the exact likeness, counterpart; model, pattern.

E. Owens Blackburne, in a story in *Irish Stories, Humourous and Tragic*, published in London without a date, but in the late nineteenth century, has 'The back av it was the very moral av an ould sack.' Carleton in *Traits and Stories of The Irish Peasantry* wrote, 'You're the moral of a Methodist preacher.' In the West of Ireland Emily Lawless picked up the word and used it in *Grania*, published in 1892: 'A fine big girl she was, just the moral of that Grania there.' *The Century Magazine*, November 1899, in a piece set in Co. Donegal, has 'Private families . . . known and respected as morals of family affection . . .' The late Augustine Martin, my friend and colleague in UCD, showed me that the word had nothing to do with the concept of morality, by telling me that he heard in his native Ballinamore, Co. Leitrim, a man described as 'a moral of a bastard'.

This word has been used in 'respectable' English literature a few times. In 1757 Smollett, in his comedy *The Reprisal or the Tears of Old England*, has 'Och! the delicate creature!—she's the very moral of my own honey.' A century later Frances Smedley in *Frank Fairlegh, scenes from the Life of a Private Pupil* wrote, 'He's the very moral (as the old women call it) of Sir John.' 1890 the Australian reformer T.A. Browne writing under the name 'Rolf Boldrewood' has in his *Colonial Reformer,* published in 1891, 'He's . . . the very moral of a horse the whipper-in rode.'

The EDD has many examples collected all over England. (Only one of its contributors reported hearing the word in Scotland, and the DSL doesn't record it at all.) The oldest citation in both the EDD and the OED is this, representing a symbolic figure, from one of Constable's *Sonnets*, from 1584: 'Fooles be they that inueigh gainst Mahomet, / Who's but a morrall of Ioues Monarchie.' In 1599 Shakespeare in *Henry V*, Act III, Scene IV, has 'Fortune is painted blind to signify to you, that Fortune is blind. Fortune is an excellent Moral.'

Shakespeare probably had the word from his childhood. The EDD has 'He's the very moral of his father,' from near Stratford.

Origin? Several of the uses are wholly or in part suggested by the corresponding late Latin *morale* neuter singular, *moralia* neuter plural, manners, customs, or French *moral* masculine, *morale* feminine. So says Oxford.

✦ MORT *var.* MURT(H)

This little word, once in general dialect use in Ireland and England, is, according to the most recent research, in mortal peril. As a noun it means a quantity, a great deal; abundance; a large number, a great many; it is also used adverbially in the phrase *a mort*, or *a murth*, much.

'I hear he was left a mort of money,' I heard in Donegal. Indeed, all over Ulster you could have heard it until recently, and it was alive and kicking all over the south as well in my father's time, and used not just in relation to money. My father heard, in relation to a funeral in Dungarvan, 'There was a murth of people there; he was very well known.' Further west, near Killeagh, in Co. Cork, a farmer told him that there wouldn't be a murth of spuds this year on account of the damnably wet spring.

Over in Leicestershire they have a saying, 'Wan or tew's a few; three's a mainy; foor's a mort.' I came on this in the Northamptonshire poet John Clare's *Village Minstrel* (1921): 'Hodge went drunk to bed, and morts / Of things were done.' Indeed, there is no scarcity of the word in literature. The earliest citation known is from Echard's translation of Plautus, 1694: 'They had a mort o' Prisoners.' In 1775 Sheridan's *The Rivals* has: 'Here's a mort o' merry-making, hey?' Dickens has the word in *David Copperfield*: '"We have had a mort of talk, sir", said Mr. Peggotty to me.'

There has been a mort, or a murth, of argument among scholars about the etymology of *mort/murth*. Oxford says that 'The suggestion that it is derived from Old Norse *mart*, neut. of *margr* great, as in *mart manna* a great number of people, is not supported by the form, chronology, or locality of the English word. It is possibly a dialectal corruption of *mortal* used as an intensive (e.g. with such a noun as 'deal'). The existence of the northern dialect *murth* (Old Norse *mergð*) in the same sense may have assisted its development.'

The EDD offers as a more immediate source: the Old Norman French *mort*, in the phrase '*a mort*, en grande quantité: Le prunier a des prunes à mort,' with Henri Moisy's glossary of Anglo-Norman (1889) as its source.

It's a handy little word wherever it came from, and it's a pity we are abandoning it as being crude or rustic or 'un-cool'.

✦ MORTACIOUS

I first heard this word walking towards Hayes's hotel in Thurles after a Munster hurling final many years ago now. It was uttered by a very disappointed Limerick supporter who had just witnessed his native county, heralded by the press as being a team of greyhounds about to be let off the leash to show the rest of Ireland what great hurling meant, doing just that to Cork until, in the second half, Willie John Daly from Carrigtohill moved out to centrefield and ensured that an aging hurler named Ring got, at last, a supply of the ball. In a matter of six minutes or so he had scored three goals, and a few points as a tilly, to deprive a stupefied Limerick of a famous victory.

What the sporting Limerick supporter said was that Christy Ring was 'a mortacious great hurler'. Recently I heard the word used in Cahir, Co. Tipperary, so I looked up the EDD and some younger glossaries to see where else it has survived. It is alive and well as an adjective and adverb in England's North Country, Cheshire, East Anglia, and Kent, where it means bad, terrible, troublesome. As an adverb it survives in all those districts, and means extremely, exceedingly, 'mortal' (q.v.). The EDD gives some examples of the word's use: 'Mortacious bad', from Cumbria; 'I am mortacious hungry,' from Suffolk; 'He was so mortacious hungered he tumbled in de street,' from Sussex; 'My old sow's mortacious bad, surelye,' also from Sussex.

The EDD didn't record the word in Ireland. Nor have I come across it in Irish literature written in English; neither does Richard Wall have it in his *Irish Literary Dictionary and Glossary*. Is Limerick and south Tipp its last remaining habitat here?

✦ MORTAL

This word was used as an intensive in many parts of Ireland until quite recently, so much so that many people think that it was confined to this country and not used in Britain at all. Not so. What its status is in Ireland at the moment I'm not sure; but I've heard it used in Donegal, Monaghan and Louth, as well as in many counties in the south and south-east, but only by the ancients. I have a feeling that it may have fallen out of use by now.

First of all let's take its use as an intensive adjective: very, exceedingly, extremely, greatly. From Ayrshire the EDD recorded 'The wife is geyan carefu' w' the crockery . . . she is mortal grippy.' It has 'mortal weary' from Galloway. 'Mortial' seems to have been extensively used in Ireland. 'Thin the wife tuk sick and was mortial bad,' wrote Jane Barlow in her *Bogland Studies* of 1892. 'The song at night is mortial hard to raise,' is a line from Moira O'Neill's 1900 *Songs of the Glens of Antrim*. 'Mortial' was also recorded in some places in England, but 'mortal' was more common by far. 'Q', Sir Arthur Quiller Couch, a Cornishman, has 'I must ax'ee to bear a hand wi' thicky portmanty o' yourn, 'cos 'tes mortal heavy' in his engaging *Troy Town* of 1888.

I've heard *mortal* meaning dead drunk, completely ossified, from a Mayoman. It is common in England and in Scotland, and perhaps my friend heard the word where he worked, in Manchester. John Mactaggart's *The Scottish Gallovidian Encyclopedia* of 1824 has this comment: 'He was often carried home . . . on a hand-barrow, just mortal.' In Northumberland the EDD recorded this: 'The Pilgrim was drunk when he went oot, and he came back mortal.'

In Forfarshire they used the word *mortallacious* for 'extremely drunk'. And further south the *Newcastle Evening Chronicle* of 8 August 1898 reported that 'She boldly charged the charging officer with having been drunk, and not only drunk but *mortallacious*.' A delicious word.

There is also a phrase, *be the mortial*, an expletive, used by Yeats in his *Folk Tales* in 1888: 'Be th'mortial! ye could ha' rung parspiration out o' the hair.'

I am told that the adverb *mortally*, very, exceedingly, may still be found in places in southern Ireland, but I've never come across it either in my ramblings or my reading. The EDD doesn't have a citation from Ireland, but that doesn't mean much. Apart from Ulster, Ireland doesn't feature much in the great dictionary.

✦ MOSKER

An old friend of mine from Lincolnshire, a retired policeman who comes to Ireland regularly to enjoy coarse fishing on our midland lakes and on the lower stretches of the river Shannon, gave me this word. It means, he told me, to decay, rot, crumble away. He had been stricken with muscular disease and he laughed his condition off with the comment that he was *moskering* away slowly like an old tree trunk.

The verb is found in Ayrshire in Scotland, in England's North Country, Yorkshire, Lincolnshire and Westmoreland. It hasn't been recorded in Ireland by the EDD, but many years ago Peadar Ó Casaide sent me the word from Co. Monaghan and Mary Reilly sent it from north Louth. Both my Irish correspondents used it of a diseased tree.

I see that old Captain Grose collected the word in the North Country back in 1790; he noted 'a moskered tree' and 'a moskered tooth'. In Yorkshire's venerable *Bairnsla Annual*, a treasury of Yorkshire dialect words and phrases, there is 'agean t'moskard walls were hung soards, shields etc'. The same journal has 'Whear creeking doors an moskerin lime daan fall'.

The word also means to smoulder; to burn slowly. The Yorkshire newspapers use the word with reference to house fires, and my friend tells me that the police have no hesitation about using it in court-room evidence, although the odd git of a supercilious magistrate pretends not to understand the word.

I have no doubt that this word is of Scandinavian origin. Compare the Danish dialect words *musk*, mustiness, mouldiness, and *musken*, mouldy, words found in C. Molbech's *Dansk Dialect Lexicon*, assembled in Copenhagen in 1841 and never superseded.

✦ MUCKINGER

Back in my home town, New Ross, Co. Wexford, recently, I met an old lady who had been in the lingerie business when I was young. Her shop was studiously avoided by all adolescent boys for fear of instigating gossip about our relationship with whatever female we were close to, or thought we were, at the time. She reminded me of this, telling me about the harassment suffered by one unfortunate chap, a keen angler, who bought some elastic to mend his cane rod, and was caught doing so, the poor devil. Whose knickers elastic was he replacing, his school pals wondered aloud, to his great embarrassment. At any rate she told me of a box she had kept from her days in business; it was marked *Muckingers*. It had been in the shop since her mother's day; and that's not today or yesterday. The box was empty, and she had no idea what it once contained; its cover gave nothing away, showing a demure, smiling young lady, wearing clothes that, at a guess, would have been fashionable when Gladstone was looking after his fallen women.

Muckinger is not in the Standard English dictionaries, but the EDD has it from districts as far apart as Cumberland and Dorset. Captain Grose collected the word in the North Country in 1790, and Ray, in his South Country glossary of 1691, defines the word as 'a cloth hung at children's girdles to wipe their noses on'. Ben Jonson used the word in his *Tale of a Tub* in 1633: 'Be of good comfort; take my muckinder (*sic*) And dry thine eyes.'

The EDD has another interesting word, found only in Shropshire: *mucketer*. It must be related to *muckinger*. The word was mentioned by Cotgrave in his 1611 French–English dictionary: 'Baverette, a mucketer to put before the bosom of a slavering child.' John Florio in his engaging Italian–English dictionary, *Queene Anna's New World of Wordes*, dedicated to his pupil Anne of Denmark (1611), also has the word, while Baret, in 1580, defined *mucketer* as 'a bib'.

The EDD hazards no guess as to origins; in all probability *muck*, mud, dirt, has something to do with it, but what about the rest of the word?

✦ MUSICAL TERMS

I could scarcely believe what I had just read in a review published by a respected American college. The English faculty, in an unofficial questionaire, had asked all its undergraduates to define certain words, one of which was *madrigal*. Not one, not a single one, knew what madrigal meant. There were some interesting answers, though; I like the one which confidently said that the word meant a South American or New Orleans street festival. Yes, I'm afraid it has come to that. I wonder if our bright young things would do any better.

Were all Elizabethan poets musicians too, I wonder? They certainly seem to have had the ability to work technical music terms into their works, and to good effect. *Descant* stood for the earliest form of counterpoint. Shakespeare used it as a verb to mean talk or comment. In *Two Gentlemen of Verona* Julia is said 'to mar the concord with too harsh a descant'.

That unattractive word *diapason* is the concord through all the notes of the scale, and Drayton used it in a poem which could have been written by some love-sick music teacher: 'My hollow sighs the deepest bass do bear / True diapason in distincted sound: / My panting heart the treble makes the air, / And descants finely on the musick's ground; / Thus like a Lute or Viol did I lie, / Whilst he, proud slave, daunced galliards in her eye.'

A musician friend, once associated with Hans Waldemar Rosen's RTÉ Singers, is passionate about the madrigal, defined by Oxford as 'a kind of part song for three or more voices (usually five or six) characterized by adherence to an ecclesiastical mode, elaborate contrapuntal imitation, and the absence of instrumental accompaniment; also applied loosely to part songs or glees not bound by these conditions'. My friend knows of course that not every scholar agrees with Oxford that the word *madrigal* may be from the early Italian *madriale*, *mandriale*, from *mandria*, a herd, from Latin *mandra*, from a Greek word meaning a fold. The primitive sense, according to this view, would be 'pastoral song'.

Well, Morrison Boyd in *Elizabethan Music*, and another renowned musicologist, E.H. Fellows, do not agree, and say that the word simply means 'a composition in the mother tongue'. Perhaps Oxford should consider Boyd's and Fellow's alternative to the source of the word which is given to the enchanting music of Boyd, Dowland, Morley and company.

The Scottish lexicographer Ivor Brown wrote that Gilbert and Sullivan are to blame for making us think of the madrigal as merry, whereas the Elizabethans' addiction to melancholy admitted sighs and groans to this form of writing. But *madrigal*, because of the exquisite sound of the word, passed into general poetic usage as a synonym for sweetness of sound. Marlowe's birds sang madrigals, but Ivor Brown contended that madrigals might be said to ring the bells of heaven too, and called Wren's spires of London city 'madrigals in stone'.

N ❧

✦ **NEB**

Mary Jane Rogan wrote to me from Northern Ireland about the word *neb*, still used there in a variety of senses. 'In my schooldays we called the nib of a pen the *neb*. Was this a mispronunciation?' she asks, 'or was it one of the many nebs we used in our everyday conversation? For example, we called a bird's beak the neb, likewise the human nose, and we used phrases such as "to dip yer neb into other people's porridge," to stick your nose into other people's business. *To neb* also meant "to kiss"; *nebbin'* was kissing.'

Well, Mary Jane, since *neb* meant the tip or point of anything, I'd say your *neb* used for a nib was no mispronunciation. Its original meaning in English was the beak of a bird; the other nebs found all over Scotland, England and Ulster were just humorous applications of the word. *Neb* meaning nib is found in Galt's *Gilhaize* (Ayrshire 1823): 'Thou's got a tongue in thy pen neb,' and in that delightful book from Selkirk, Christopher North's *Noctes Ambrosianae* (1856), a treasury of Scots words and phrases, which I picked up for a few bob in Glasgow many years ago, he describes a man 'mendin' the slit in the neb o' his pen'.

Neb in all its meanings came across the Sea of Moyle from Scotland to Ulster, as did some phrases: *A black neb* is a man who takes a striker's place during a strike, a blackleg. *More red nebs than midges* is a phrase used in very cold weather. *The neb of the mire snipe*, the last extremity. *To cock up one's neb*, to turn up one's nose. *To dight (clean) the neb an' flee awa*, figuratively, to take one's departure.

The phrase 'the neb o' the mornin' was written off as obsolete by the *English Dialect Dictionary*, but it has been recorded in recent days from farmers bringing their produce to the Edinburgh markets. It means the time between dawn and sunrise, according to the EDD (I had always thought sunrise *was* the dawn). The great dictionary quotes John

Mactaggart's *The Scottish Gallovidian Encyclopedia* of 1824: 'There are few who do not love to keep the bed until the neb gangs aff the morning; it is when the neb is on the morning that the hoar frost is produced.'

Nebs of all description are from Old English *nebb*, *rostrum*, to you Classicists, *beak* to the rest of you.

✦ NIEVE

Defined by the EDD as the fist; the closed hand; the hand, it is spelled *neive* and *neif* in that great dictionary. It was found in Scotland, Ireland, the northern counties of England, in Gloucestershire, and strangely enough in Devon, where Kingsley had it in *Westward Ho* in 1855: 'Come, give us thy neif and let us part in peace.'

I first heard the word in north-west Donegal, and no doubt it arrived there from Scotland, where a large proportion of the population have either worked themselves or have friends and relations who have settled there on a semi-permanent basis, returning to their native Donegal in summer. But I was surprised to find the word in Mayo, Sligo and Dublin. An old man told me in Kimmage not long ago that the master he had in school 'would cut the nieve off you with a skelper of a rod' if you didn't perform up to his expectation of you.

The word hasn't been neglected in literature since its first appearance in *Havelock the Dane* around 1300. Barbour has it in *The Bruce* in 1375; in about 1400 *The Destruction of Troy* has 'He nolpit on with his Neue in the necke hole.' Around 1400 Gavin Douglas in his masterpiece *Æneis* wrote, 'Mesapus . . . in hys left neif haldis all redd.' Nor did Shakespeare neglect the word. In *A Midsummer Night's Dream*, Act IV, Scene I, he has 'Give me your neafe, Mounsieur Mustardseed.' Burns has the word in *Death and Dr Hornbook* where he speaks of 'An honest Wabster to his trade, Whase wife's twa nieves were scarce well bred'.

In Ireland, I know that Peadar O'Donnell from the Rosses of Donegal was fond of the word, and a much less prominent figure, W.G. Lyttle of Co. Down, noted it in *The Adventures of Paddy M'Quillan*, self-published in Bangor in 1892 and important in that it, like other Lyttle books, contains a lot of dialect words: 'They kept hemmerin' the table with their neeves.'

I once saw a Donegal woman playing a game with her very small children. She called it *Knievy-knievy-nick-nack*. Later I found that the game is played in Scotland, in northern England, and in Devon, where Madox-Brown mentioned it in *Dwale Bluth* in 1876: 'The beadle, finding a small unowned boy playing surreptitiously at 'nievy-nievy-nick-nack' (with marbles), hurried the offender out of the sacred precincts.' Here is Chambers' *Popular Rhymes* (1870 ed.) on this guessing game: 'Some small article, as a marble or comfit, is put into one hand secretly. The boy then comes up to a companion with both hands closed, and cries as he revolves the two fists before his friend's eyes, "Nievy-nievy-nick-nack, which hand will ye tak? Tak the right, tak the wraong, I'll beguile ye if I can." The fun is in the challenged person choosing the hand in which there is nothing.'

I was glad to hear from the nice people in the SND that the game is still a favourite with Scottish kids, but disappointed to learn that in recent years it has fallen into disuse somewhat in many areas in both Ulster and Scotland.

The origin of *nieve* is the Old Scots *newe*, *nave*, fists (from 1375) from the Old Norse *hnefi*, a fist, *knefa*, to clasp with the fist.

✦ NITHING

I first came across the word *nithing* in Freeman's *History of the Norman Conquest* (1877): 'The king and the army publicly declared the murderer to be Nithing.' In the same work he has 'The shameful name of *nithing* was to be the doom of every man . . . who failed to obey this summons of his lord.' *Nithing* was glossed by Oxford for me as 'a vile coward, an abject or despicable wretch, a villain of the lowest type'. It adds, 'A mean or miserly person'.

The great dictionary's first citation is from Liebermann in *Die Gesetze der Angelsachen* (*c*. 1000). The word is found in many medieval works and then seemed to die out for no obvious reason; Freeman, quoted above, was perhaps the last to use the word in literature, but he was, after all, a medieval scholar, and perhaps he thought that the word should be familiar to the rest of mankind.

This was a useful word, and God only knows why it lost its appeal and died out.

It came with the Vikings. Norwegian, Swedish and Danish have *niding* still; the Old Norse is *níðingr*, villain, scoundrel, vile wretch, from *níð*, contumely, derision. The Old English negative form *unníðing* corresponds to an Old Danish *úníþingr*, which occurs on a runic stone (of the early part of the eleventh century) found in 1905 at Aarhus in Denmark.

✦ NOMINY

I was very sorry to hear that the Carne Mummers are no more, having been in business for a couple of hundred years, on and off. For about half a century they were commanded by Leo Carthy, who has sent me many good words over the years; I am glad to say that I featured his mummers in a few programmes I wrote for RTÉ television and the BBC. The mummers were once brought before the court of justice and fined, under Mr de Valera's Dance Hall Act of, as far as I remember, 1935, for dancing in a public place without a licence, or in other words, without the permission of the parish priest. Their solicitor said that they were mumming, not dancing, to no avail. Leo introduced me to an old man in Carne back in the early 1970s who gave me the word *nominy* for the rhymes in the mummers' performance. The word has now gone from local speech.

In Yorkshire and Pembrokeshire the word is still alive, but is now used only to describe a longwinded, tiresome speech; a rigmarole. It used to mean, apart from a mumming rhyme, a complimentary doggerel used at weddings, and an uncomplimentary doggerel used during the ceremony of 'riding the stang', a rural punishment for wife, or husband-beating, which was comprised of the culprit being carried around tied to a pole, while being pelted with dung and drenched with buckets of water and worse. Here's a stang nominy from early-nineteenth-century Yorkshire: 'With a ran tan tan on my old tin can, Mrs — and her old man, she banged him, she banged him, For spending a penny when he stood in need. She upped with her three-footed stool. She struck him so hard and she cut so deep, Till the blood ran down like a new stuck sheep.'

Poor English girls knitting for a living made up their own nominies to relieve the boredom. This is from the Northampton of the 1880s: 'Needle to needle and stitch to stitch. Pull the old woman out of the ditch. If you ain't out by the time I'm in, I'll rap your knuckles with my knitting pin.'

The word represents the Latin *nomine*, in the invocation to the Trinity, *In nomine Patris*, etc. ('In the *name* of the Father, etc.')

✦ NOT IN WEATHERBYS

If you are not interested in horse racing, you may not know what Weatherbys is. Let me tell you something about it.

For over 200 years the firm of Weatherbys (they dropped the apostrophe a century or more ago) have undertaken the formal registration of mares, foals and stallions, both Thoroughbred and Non-Thoroughbred, to ensure the integrity of bloodlines upon which breeding and racing industries worldwide depend. The definitive ancestry record for Thoroughbreds is *The General Stud Book* (GSB). Published by Weatherbys every four years since 1793, it records all Thoroughbred matings and births in Britain and Ireland. In contrast to its historical perspective, the Stud Book Department has been instrumental in securing notable scientific advances in the integrity of the Stud Book information, including the introduction of bloodtyping and, later, DNA testing for parentage verification and since 1999, the microchipping of all foals to assist with identification.

Weatherbys organises and hosts the International Stud Book Committee—a body representing sixty-seven countries whose objectives are to ensure that horses are accurately and consistently identified and to ease the movement of racehorses and breeding stock between countries. It is a venerable and absolutely essential institution then for ensuring the quality of the thoroughbred.

The late Willie Evans of Greystones was a very handsome Byronic figure. He was lame and depended on a walking stick, because of being a haemophiliac who neglected his doctor's advice not to ride horses for fear of a fall. He was injured, and started a riding school in a small way in Greystones, Co. Wicklow. He taught both my sons, John and Barry, to ride, and used to have a drink with them and me after the meets of the Bray Hunt. He was the epitome of a country gentleman, and never used coarse language in front of women.

I remember him saying to a fellow who liked to shock women by the coarseness of his language, 'Well, the ladies present will take no notice of you; they won't find you in Weatherbys.' A very elegant way of saying he was badly bred. If he had hit your man across the butt of the ear with his walking stick, he wouldn't have looked so shocked. He knew what Weatherbys represented. He departed hurriedly.

Willie Evans died as a result of a contaminated blood transfusion. He was mourned far beyond his native county as a gentleman, and as a man who would not have been denied a place in any human Weatherbys.

O ~

✦ OMELISH

It must be ten years since a lady who lives in Kilmacthomas at the foot of the Comeragh Mountains in Co. Waterford sent me the word *omelish*. This is what she wrote: 'Here in the district around Kilmacthomas the children at Hallowe'en go out on the omelish, the modern trick or treat. The word is not known in Waterford city, nor indeed is it known in Dungarvan or in the countryside around these places. Only around Kilmacthomas does it survive.'

I did my own bit of detective work recently. I enquired of a man who used to teach in Kilmacthomas, and he told me that the word is no longer used by children there. Gone like the snows of yesteryear on the Comeragh's peaks, he assured me. Gone too around that district with the beautiful name, Cúil na Sméar, the hidden place of the berries, not far from Kilmacthomas. Unknown too to the children in the lovely coastal villages between Bunmahon and Clonea. I enquired of children who came knocking on my door in Dungarvan, and they had never heard of the word. Not a trace of it in Knockanore, Clashmore, Grange or An Seana Phobal. What a pity.

Father Dinneen's dictionary has *alamuis*, undoubtedly the word's immediate origin. He has: '*Alamuis*, excitement, merrymaking, extravagance; *alamuis cainte*, wild, extravagant talk; dainties got on Hallowe'en; *oíche alamuise*, a name for Oíche Shamhna in Waterford.' *Alamuis* becomes *omlish* through metathesis, the transposition of two words or letters in a word.

But is the word of Irish origin or is it a borrowing? My friend and former colleague in UCD, Nicholas Williams, convinced me that a borrowing it is. *Omlish/alamuis* is simply *Hallowmass* in disguise, a word used as far back as the fourteenth century for the Feast of All Saints.

✦ ON THE PIG'S BACK

I must thank Tomás Ó Duinn from Athlone for his contribution to the debate on the phrase *ar mhuin na muice, on the pig's back* in the English of Ireland. His letter was one of many I received on this subject recently and because my reading had been brought almost to a halt due to eye problems, his letter was overlooked by me.

He points out, quoting a well-known Co. Kildare saddler, that pig skin was used in the old days as well as calf skin. Pigs grow their hair from the inside out and the leather has lots of little perforations and would wear for a very long time. But nowadays pigs are slaughtered at a much younger age and the skin is too thin for saddlers to use. A pig-skin saddle was always expensive, and this, I find, was attested to by Jack London and by writers and historians of the old American West. Tomás suggests that as only well-off people rode horses in Ireland, and that as they fancied the expensive pig skin saddle, so they were *ar mhuin na muice*, or, *on the pig's back*.

Has Mr Ó Duinn solved the problem for us? I think so.

✦ OOSLIFIED

You won't find this word in any dictionary; believe me I've tried them all. I heard it only once, used by a Co. Wicklow farmer who lived near Rathnew; a delightful man named Billy Clements who bred horses, and whose daughter now hunts the Bray Hounds, I believe. He sported an enormous ginger-coloured Royal Air Force moustache, and to those who asked about it he would spin yarns of which Baron Münchhausen would be proud. His real reason for growing it, he told me, was to honour his own contribution to the Hitler war, which consisted of walking all the way to Belfast along the railway line with a friend who had been expelled from school, to enlist; they were both turned down for not having parental permission. The kind Flight Lieutenant gave them five bob each, and but for the apple orchards they robbed on the way home, they would have starved to death.

Ooslified was his word for 'gentrified'. A stuck-up lady with an anglicised accent would be 'an ooslified bitch'. He himself, a Protestant with a Wicklow accent so genuine that I once asked my friend Augustine Martin to get him to record one of Synge's plays for the UCD's English department, certainly didn't come from the Gaelic tradition, but the only explanation I have for the etymology of his strange word is that it comes from the Irish *uasal*, adjective, noble, or *uaisleacht*, noun, nobility. *Uasal* can at times have a slight pejorative slant to it, jumped-up.

Billy and his friend Robert Collis, the eminent paediatrician, and also a good horseman, spent years trying to entice Cearbhall Ó Dálaigh on to the hunting field, but the latter, an eminent jurist in Europe at the time, thought it mightn't be politically correct to do so, even with an outfit like the Brays who followed an artificial scent. Ó Dálaigh loved hunting, and one day as I was waiting for the off at the Willow Grove pub, he came over to adjust my girth, and said to me, '*A Dhiarmaid, is geal lem chroí tú a fheiscint ag dul amach ag sodar leis na h-uaisle. A Thiarna, ná rabhamar fada go leor ag sodar ina ndiaidh.*' '*Ag sodar i ndiaidh na n-uasal*' is a phrase meaning, literally, trotting after the gentry; being subservient, in other words. A translation of what he said is 'It does my heart good to see you going out trotting with the gentry. Lord, weren't we long enough trotting after them.'

He came from a humble background, and he disliked ooslified people as much as Billy Clements did. And he thought his friend's word a wonderful invention, and that it deserved to live.

✦ ORKNEY WORDS

I would like to meet Gregor Lamb from Orkney, now living, I am told, in Italy. He is the author of a very important book, which began, he says, in 1968 while in exile in England. To quote from his book's preface, he found odd words and phrases from his childhood days still being used as tools in his thought process. No longer of any value in communicating, the purpose for which they had originally emerged, they had been relegated to his private world, where, before long, they would atrophy and disappear. To forestall this inevitable fate, Mr Lamb began to collect his island's disappearing word hoard, and *The Orkney Wordbook* is the result. It is published by Byrgisey, in Birsay, Orkney, and I bought my copy over the internet, not the cheapest way, perhaps, for about £25.

Orcadian, the language of Gregor's island, was a Norse dialect, now almost extinct, alas. A sampler: *Smoosk*: To smile in a sly manner. From Norwegian dialectal *smuska*. *Skyran*: A glittering of the sky. Also applied to a girl. From Old Norse *skirr*, bright. *Polt*, a small, chunky person, the man who was lowered over a cliff to gather seabirds' eggs; he had to be small and strong. From Norwegian *bult*, a chunk of wood. *Heevie*, a woven straw basket carried on the back. From Scots *haev*, a fisherman's hand-basket, related to Old English *hyf*, a hive, and Old Norse *háfr*, a bag-net.

Had in Orcadian means 1. To hold. 2. To protect. Lamb quotes a pre-Reformation 'bonie-words prayer': 'Mary Mither had thee hand / Roond aboot wir sleepan band / Had the lass and had the wife / And had the bairnies a their life.' *Boona* means a variety of things; a harness for a horse; equipment in general; the male sex organ. From Old Norse *bunaðr*, equipment; Scots has *bouney*.

As one would expect, sea terms abound here. *Andoo* is a verb meaning to row a boat against wind and tide so that it keeps in position for fishing. The verb is from Old Norse *andoefa*, to keep a boat in position by rowing.

I hope Mr Lamb is *in his ludgy pot*, in the best of health (from Old Scots legal jargon *liege poustie*, in full possession of one's faculties). He has done hero's work in collecting this splendid treasury of a beautiful Norse dialect, now on its last legs. What happened to Orcadian? As the Irish scholar T.F. O'Rahilly said, not of Orcadian but of Manx, when a language surrenders itself to foreign idiom, and when all its speakers become bilingual, the penalty is death.

✦ ORRA

I was sent this word by a lady from Co. Down whose mother came from Forfarshire in Scotland, and as I haven't come across it anywhere else in Ireland, I suppose it's fair to jump to the conclusion that the word is not, as they say in parts of Wexford, 'agree to this country', that is, not native here.

It has various meanings. First of all it means spare, additional to what one requires, extra, supernumerary, odd, superfluous. In John Buchan's story *John Burnet* we find 'We've an orra bed i' the house for the maister, and plenty o' guid saft straw i' the barn for the man.' Closer to our own time *The Border Magazine* of August 1937 has 'I'm no saying that if the laddie had a sair throat or the auld man needed something to his tea, I couldna find an orra eke [something extra] if need be.'

Another shade of meaning is, one of a pair: not having the other, unmatched, odd. *Notes and Queries*, Fifth Series 1856, tells of a woman who described a set of tea china as 'embracing twelve cups and saucers and an orra cup—meaning that it was unmatched, that is without a saucer corresponding to it'. R. Chambers' *Traditions of Edinburgh* (1856) tells of 'a shop kept by an eccentric personage, who exhibited a sign bearing this singular inscription—Orra Things Bought and Sold—which signified that he dealt in odd articles, such as a single shoebuckle, one of a pair of skates, in short, any unpaired article'.

Yet another shade of meaning is miscellaneous, sundry. The *Elgin Courant* of 6 November 1953 said that 'a tractorman is expected to drive and to maintain his machine—or at least to keep it clean and serviced. A tractor-orraman is only expected to drive the tractor and can be called upon to do orra work as the rest of his job'; and the *Southern Reporter* of 6 October 1995 carried the advertisement 'Orraman (married) or Orrawoman required for Hillhead, attend some cattle in winter.'

Of persons or things *orra* can mean worthless, rejected, shabby, dirty, slatternly, low, coarse, unseemly, disreputable. G. Michie's *Glen Anthology* of 1959 has 'My auld bauchlit shoon they are orra and dune, The sutors [cobblers] declare, and they'll mend them nae mair.'

Orras also mean odd jobs, or the part of a job not yet completed. In J.G. Horne's *Flooer o' the Ling* (1936) a man with more than fresh air on his mind says, 'Come, lassie, lay your orries by! Let's daun'er [stroll] doon the clearin.'

A very versatile word indeed is this word of ours. The DSL says that it's from Old Scots *orray*, unmarried. A reduced form of *o(w)eraa*, over all, over and above, extra, supernumerary. The word is equivalent to English *odd*, with similar extensions of meaning.

✦ ORT

This little word I came across while re-reading George Eliot's *Silas Marner*. The word, generally used in the plural *orts*, means leavings of any description; remnants, scraps, fragments, especially of food, broken victuals; the refuse fodder left by cattle and horses. Eliot wrote, 'Besides, their feasting caused a multiplication of orts, which were the heirlooms of the poor.'

As far as I remember George Eliot was a Warwickshire woman, but her word was once in general dialect use all over Scotland and England, as well as being recorded in Antrim and Down. The EDD has recorded many examples. 'Save up those orts for the cat,' was recorded in Devon. From Leistershire a poor man praising a charitable woman said that 'she'd used to gi' me orts and sups'. From Gloucestershire came the following: 'He's well served for he has oft made orts of better hay, is applied to a woman who refuses good offers of marriage when young, and often ends up with an inferior partner later on, perhaps not as good-looking as the one she has rejected.' I've heard the word myself in a pub in Cornwall's Newquay.

As for Ireland, W.H. Patterson has the word in his glossary of Antrim and Down words collected in the 1880s, and Captain Grose collected the word in Antrim back in 1790.

There was a related word in Antrim, Down and Donegal, *ortins*, which also meant the leavings of food, indeed the leavings of anything, as is evident from Patterson's reference to an Antrim man laying down the law about who his daughter would, and would not, marry: 'Other wemmin's ortins shan't be Sally's pick.'

I regret to say that *orts* and *ortins* are now dying out.

They still use the phrase *orts and ends* for odds and ends in East Anglia. I heard it from my friends Peter and Neila Drake, who farm near Norwich.

Everywhere *ort* was used, you'd have found the verb *to ort*, to pick out the best part of food and leave the rest; to crumble or waste food; and also used figuratively. This is from a western Scotland correspondent of the nineteenth-century lexicographer Jamieson: '"The lasses nowadays ort nane of God's creatures"—the reflection of an old woman as signifying that in our times young women are by no means careful in their choice of husbands.' Jamieson also gave us this from Ayrshire: 'When a father gives away any of his daughters in marriage without regard to the order of seniority, he is said to ort his dochters.'

The word is in literature since *c.* 1440, when the glossary *Promptorium Parvulorum Sive Clericorum* gave us 'Ortus, releef of beestys mete'. The *Catholicon Anglicum*, an English–Latin wordbook of 1483, has 'Ortys'. Shakespeare was very fond of the word. In 1593, in *Lucrece*, he wrote, 'Let him have time a beggar's orts to crave', and in *Timon of Athens* (1607) he has 'It is some poore Fragment, some slender Ort of his remainder.'

As to origin Oxford says that our word is cognate with early modern Dutch *oor-aete*, *oor-ete*, remains of food, with Low German *ort*, Swedish dialect *oräte*, *uräte*, refuse fodder; and notes the North Frisian *ôrte*, to leave fragments; from *or-*, *oor-*, privative + *etan*, to eat. There may have been an unrecorded Old English **or- t*, cognate with the continental forms, but the absence of Old English and Middle English examples is noteworthy.

✦ OUT OF FACE

I first came across this phrase, which is translated from the Irish *as éadan*, in D. Patterson's *The Provincialisms of Belfast and the Surrounding Districts Pointed Out and Corrected*, published in Belfast in 1860. This Patterson is often confused with William Hugh Patterson, who gave us *A Glossary of Words in Use in the Counties of Antrim and Down*, published by the English Dialect Society in 1880, and incorporated by Joseph Wright in his monumental EDD, published by Oxford University Press in 1898. W.H.'s glossary is a very important work, while D.'s is a pain in the neck, particularly the 'corrections' he suggested. But at least his words and phrases are good, even though they made him wince.

This upset him: 'To do a thing out of face is to do it right through from first to last without stopping.' To give him his due, he interpreted the phrase correctly. P.W. Joyce's *English As We Speak It in Ireland*, a seminal book on Irish English published in 1910, has 'Do that out of face i.e. begin at the beginning and finish it out and out.' The EDD defines the phrase thus: 'Out of face: incessantly, straight through without stopping.' It states that it was recorded by an Ulster correspondent.

Michael Traynor's *The English Dialect of Donegal*, assembled for the most part in, of all places, Tasmania, in the 1950s, has 'To do, take, work out of face—to do it methodically, in an orderly manner.'

I had come to the conclusion that the phrase wasn't known outside the province of Ulster until I overheard in the bar of a hotel in Tuam, Co. Galway, a man who had just attended a local hurling match say to the barman, 'They were too good for us all over the field. They hurled us home; they beat us out of face.' That same year, some time in the early 1960s, I came across the phrase in the Galway playwright M.J. Mulloy's *The King of Friday's Men*, which I was directing for an amateur theatre group in east Limerick: 'We'll fight and beat them out of face at last.' I was surprised to find that the phrase was in my actors' own vocabulary. Much later I found out that the phrase was used in south Tipperary, in the midlands, where my good friend Séamas Ó Saothraí, scholar and bibliophile, had recorded it in his native Co. Westmeath, in Roscommon and south Carlow.

I hope it still lives on, if not in its origin form *as éadan*, then in its Irish English garb. The prognosis is not too good, I'm sorry to report.

P ~

✦ PAD

In Northumberland and in Yorkshire, and across the border in Berwick, Edinburgh and Galloway, they refer to a frog as a *pad*. By extension, a member of any French rugby team may also be referred to as a pad. This is not a slang word, as I've seen written, but a very old word: it first appeared in the *Old English Chronicle* of 1154, where reference is made to 'nadres & snakes & pades'.

Henryson's 1470 *Moral Fables* (Frog & Mouse) has 'The fals ingyne of this foull carpand pad', and in 1570 Peter Levins' *Manipulus Vocabulorum, a Dictionarie of English and Latine Wordes* has 'A Padde, tode, bufo'. Around 1585 Montgomerie's *Flyting* has 'That this worme . . . some wonders may wirk; And, through the poyson of this pad, our pratiques prevaile.' There seems to be no further mention of the pad in literature after that, though the word is given in the 1876 *Whitby Glossary*: 'Pads, frogs'; and in the 1876 *Mid-Yorkshire Glossary*: 'Pad . . . a frog.'

The variants *padda* and *paddo* are also found. Robert Chambers' *Popular Rhymes of Scotland* (1870) gives 'A paddo then came loup-loup-louping out of the well.'

Yes, you'll still hear the word in many of the places I've mentioned, but it's not as *flúirseach* as it was even twenty years ago.

Here we have another word of Norse origin. The Old Norse for a toad is *padda*.

✦ PAJOCK

This is a term of contempt used by Shakespeare in *Hamlet*, Act III, Scene II: 'For thou dost know, O Damon dear, / This realm dismantled was / Of Jove himself; and now reigns here / A very, very pajock.'

Oxford thinks that it is a misprint. 'The spelling *peacock* or *peacocke* is found in the First Folio in the 5 other places where the word occurs, and there seems no reason why Hamlet should here use a stray dialect word. The context suggests that Hamlet was going to say "A very, very Ass", but checked himself at the last word and substituted this.'

That said, there are other conjectures offered by scholars down the years. One wrote, 'I have often heard the lower classes in the north of Scotland call the peacock the *peajock*, and their almost inevitable name for the turkeycock is *bubblyjock*.' Another suggested *patchcoke*, as applied by Spencer to a ragged Irishman, a raggamuffin. The great Skeat says that Shakespeare's word is connected with *patch*, a motley, a fool; hence *pajock*, a king of shreds and patches.

It has been pointed out that *pajock* would have been pronounced *payjock*, and that *peacock* might have been pronounced *paycock*, as O'Casey had it, and as it is pronounced in places in rural Shropshire and Warwickshire to this day.

I feel that the misprint theory is the most plausible one. A writer in the *Edinburgh Review* for October 1872 says that in the natural history of Shakespeare's time the peacock was the accredited representative of inordinate pride and envy, as well as of unnatural cruelty and lust, and that the word here expresses in a concentrated form the odious qualities of the guilty king.

✦ PALINODE

Trawling through old books and journals for words and phrases which might be of interest to the multitudes who, I'm told, eagerly await my words of wisdom about the language of my native county Wexford to be spoken in a lecture in the autumn, I came across this in Patrick Kennedy's *Evenings in the Duffrey* (1869): 'The intruder thus commenced his *palinody*.' This is a good word that was familiar to a people who had learned their English from people who had learned theirs from books—the hedge schoolmasters, justly famed, many of them, for their learning in the Classics.

Palinode was an ode or song in which the author retracts something he had previously written in a former poem; hence generally, a recantation. In 1599 Ben Jonson, in *Cynthia's Revels*, Act V, Scene III, had 'You, two and two, singing a Palinode, March to your several homes.' The following year in the Recantation or Palinode of a Scot named John Colvill, we are assured that 'he doth penitently recant his former proud offences, specially that treasonable discourse against the undoubted and indeniable title of king James the sixt unto the crowne of England'. In Bell's *Dictionary and Digest of the Laws of Scotland* (1838) we find that *palinode* had become a law term: 'In actions for damages on account of slander or defamation raised in the Commissary Court . . . , it was formerly the practice to conclude not only for damages, expenses, and a fine, but also for a judicial recantation or palinode by the defender.' But it had not been abandoned by the people on the other side of the bar. In 1898 R.L. Stevenson in *St. Ives* wrote, 'I abounded in palinodes and apologies.'

Palinode or *palinody* also means 'a rambling discourse calculated to deceive the masses', according to the EDD. We have been subjected to many of them in recent years by our political masters explaining away the financial mess they have got us into.

From Old French *palinodie*, from Latin *palinodia*, from a Greek word meaning singing over again, repetition, especially recantation, a name first given to an ode by Stesichorus, in which he recants his attack upon Helen.

✦ PALTHOGUE

I've seen the word spelled *polthog* and *polthogue* as well, all corruptions of the Irish *paltóg*, which means a blow, a thump, a wallop. It used to be found in many parts of Ireland from Ulster to Cape Clear, from the Midlands to west Clare. In Ulster it has the added meanings a slap, a cow-pat and a blackthorn stick—a versatile word and no doubt, yer honour.

In the first sense, *Lays and Legends of the North of Ireland* has 'The peats flew through the house and whack came a polthogue on the farmer's back.' The word was, and is, popular in Co. Donegal, and Seumas MacManus was quite fond of it. In his story *Bold Blades of Donegal*, written towards the end of the nineteenth century, he has 'I reached a polthogue that took the fellow between the two eyes and toppled him.' In another story, *A Lad of the O'Friels*, he has 'After being struck a polthog fit to kill a bull . . .'

In the parish of Louisburgh, Co. Mayo, and the district which surrounds it, a *paltóg* is a large stone, ideal, I suppose, to use in emergencies in the bad old days of faction fighting. This meaning was given to me many years ago by Fr Leo Morahan, or Leon Ó Morcháin, a Mayoman. In that lovely part of Ireland a *paltóg* also means a big word, a 'jaw-breaker'.

By extension, if that's what it is, a heavy shower of rain is also called a polthogue. That dreadful novelist Jane Barlow has the word in her *Bogland Studies* (1892): 'Wid the storms an' the mists an' the polthogues o' rain.' The same lady in *Irish Idylls* (1892) also has the word, again from Connacht: 'Polthoguin' fit to drown a water-rat.'

I feel sure that our word is from the English dialect word *polt*. Found in dialects of England from Derby to East Anglia, Gloucestershire, Kent and the Isle of Wight, it means a knock, thump; a hard driving blow. 'I levelled him with a polt on the head,' was recorded in Norfolk. In the south-west cider country, the word has the specific meaning, to knock down fruit from the trees with a long pole. The pole is called a *polting lug*.

So, the only part of the excellent Irish English *polthogue* that is native Irish is the suffix *óg*.

Dying out now, my spies, the schoolteachers, tell me.

✦ PARAMOUR

When, dear reader, did you last refer to somebody as so-and-so's paramour, when you meant lover, sweetheart? The word seems to have disappeared from the modern lexicon; the last Oxford citation is from 1871, from Ellis's rendering of *Catullus* (lxi, 44): 'Lord of fair paramours, of youth's Fair affection uniter.' Oxford does not mention the American poet Wallace Stevens, who, in our time, gave one of his poems the title *Final Soliloquy of the Interior Paramour*.

What has happened to the lovely word? Why is it not used in common speech any more? It has been in English as a noun since the Middle Ages, when it meant both sexual love and a lover. In Chaucer's *Cook's Tale* (1386 or thereabouts) we find 'He was as ful of love & paramour As is the hyve ful of hony sweete.' The Scots poet Henryson, in his *Fable of the Cock and the Fox* (1470), recently translated admirably by Heaney, has 'In all this warld was thair na kyndar thing; In paramouris he wald do ws plesing.'

Paramour, in the sense love, was in devotional use since about 1300, when in the Vernon MS we find a poet address the Blessed Virgin, 'Heil puyred princesse of paramour, Heil Blosme of Brere.' Men applied the word to the Virgin, women to Jesus. And in medieval verse we find Christ addressing his mother as his paramour, while she returns the compliment. In a carol of *c.* 1475 we find 'To his moder he [Christ] say,

My swete moder, myn paramour.' In a poem of 1492 Mary says to Christ, 'Myne owne dere sonne and paramoure.'

The word is from Middle English, from the Old French adverbial phrase, *par amur*, *par amour*, by or through love. From an early date the phrase was written as one word, and came to be treated in English as a noun, both in sense of love and lover, as I've said. What a pity it is that the lovely word is now described in the dictionaries of English as 'obsolete', gone from common speech forever.

✦ PAUT

I collected many good words from a Wexford Traveller named Miley Connors. He was a horse dealer in a small way and he used words which couldn't be classified as belonging to Sheldru, the secret language of his nomadic people. He used to travel a lot in his young days, both in England and Scotland; perhaps it was in those times, working for farmers, that he picked up the verb *paut*, which has many meanings; Miley's one is, of a horse, to paw the ground, to stamp, to kick lightly.

This is found in Scotland and in the northern counties of England, according to the EDD. 'I pautit wi' my foot, Master, Garr'd all my bridles ring,' is from a collection of Scots ballads published in 1827. An EDD correspondent from Cumbria wrote that 'if a horse paws gently with his fore feet, we say he pauts'. From Nottinghamshire a correspondent wrote that 'a horse pawts the ground'. From Lincolnshire, where the word was in common use until quite recently, a man wrote to the EDD that 'pawting about he [a horse] got his foot fast in a fence'.

Lincolnshire was a Danish stronghold, one of the most formidable in England, and the influence of Scandinavian is still to be seen in the dialect of the place (I'd recommend Streatfield's work *Lincolnshire and the Danes* if this topic interests you; your library should be able to get it for you as the last edition is long out of print). *Paut* is one of the good Old Norse words which has survived the centuries since the Viking marauders got fed up with pillaging and settled down to farming. The EDD says that the word is still in use in modern Norway in their dialect word *pauta*, to push, poke.

I have often thought that *to paw* wasn't a very good verb to use of a horse stamping the ground with his fore feet. Here in *paut* we have the ideal word.

✦ PEND

The word *pend*, noun and verb, is still found in the odd place in Ulster, where people often drop the *d* in the word and pronounce it *pen*. Ben Kiely, the Tyrone writer, gave me the word many years ago, but I've heard it as well in Co. Donegal. It was almost certainly imported from Scotland, where it meant, first of all, an archway; an arched or covered gateway or passage. This was the meaning I heard attached to it by Kiely and by Mrs Nora O'Donnell from the foot of Errigal.

In 1893 Robert Louis Stevenson in *Catriona* wrote, 'We took shelter under a pend at the head of a close or alley.' A lesser novelist, Beatty from Edinburgh, had the word in his story *Secretar* in 1897: 'The Secretar oxtered the lass out from the courtyard and through the pend into the street.' The word *pend* had by then been accepted in the jargon of architectural journals; one of them, as far back as 1792, contains the following: 'Under the ceiling at the West End of the pend, whereon the great steeple stands . . .' Hence the architectural terms *pen-mouth*, the entrance to a pend or covered gateway, and *pend-stone*, the irregularly cut stone from which the arch of a bridge springs.

The Scots, as we all know, were famous for their fireball preachers and their sermons and polemics. The vault of heaven was frequently mentioned by them. In 1663 Sir G. Mackenzie, a zealot if ever there was one, wrote a book called *Religious Stoic* in which he used the poetic phrase 'The stately fabrick of Heaven's arched Pend'. And in 1819 W. Tennant's *Papistry Storm'd*, which still reeks of brimstone, had 'Throu' Aurora's gildet gate, . . . And up the pend, at furious rate'.

There is one other *pend*, this one recorded in Ulster by the EDD. It means an arched conduit, or, according to Jamieson's Scots dictionary, 1880 edition, 'a covered sewer, small conduit; also, the entrance to, or the grating over, a conduit or sewer'. Mactaggart's *Gallovidian Encyclopedia* of 1824 described *pend* as a sewer.

The word is now deemed to be either obsolete or archaic. It's from Norman French *pendre* or Latin *pendere*, to hang.

✦ PEPPER

This word, both noun and verb, I first heard from Ned Cash, the well-known and respected horse dealer, in his home in Moate, Co. Westmeath. Ned was an honest man, and made an excellent living selling point-to-point horses to English racing men; one of his clients was Fred Winter, the great jockey turned successful trainer. I went to see him hoping he'd have a child's pony to sell me. What he had he refused to part with because the animals were too good for my son, who was then only six, as far as I remember. He told me that he wouldn't be responsible for getting the child hurt or for giving him such a fright as would ensure that he was put off riding for years. Eventually he found an old piebald called Treasure for me, and he proved ideal: quiet and dependable, and I'm sure that an exploding bomb on the roadside wouldn't put him out in the least.

Ned gave me the word *pepper*, an English dealer's word for a thief, a cheat, especially a cheating horse-dealer. They are to be found in Yorkshire especially, and not only among itinerant horse-dealers, he emphasised; they were to be found as well among those employed at 'respectable' auction houses which held occasional children's pony sales. They were known as *peppers* because of their method of pepping up a jaded animal and making an old nag behave as friskily as a young, newly-broken colt or filly. This miracle came about by the insertion of a good dollop of really hot pepper in the animal's rectum. The verb *to pepper* meant to cheat as a *pepper* or rogue horse dealer does.

Before I left his hospitable house, a convent he bought to accommodate the clients of a riding school his wife wanted to set up, he told me about his impoverished beginnings under canvas on the side of the road, about being able to buy a caravan for his aging father to die in comfort, of his growing success as a dealer, and of one of the crowning moments of his life, the day he saw his son riding for Ireland in the Aga Khan competition in Ballsbridge, 'with the green white and orange flag on the saddle cloth under his arse'.

I had the temerity to ask him if he would permit me to write a documentary television programme on his life. He and his family, whom he consulted about the matter, assented. But when I enquired at that station, the powers-that-were showed no interest whatever in his story.

✦ PILL

'Come out of there, until I pill the effin hyde offa ye,' the rather obese lady, very much *maith go leor*, or under the weather, shouted in the door of the pub in Ireland's midlands. She was answered by another female who it seems had escaped inside; the owner of the place or one of his staff closed and locked the door through which yours truly had intended to enter to meet on old friend. So I hung around until the coast was clear and the vituperations of the large lady had ceased, as she made her way across the street to another hostelry, her shawl billowing like the sail of a full-rigged ship.

Pill, meaning to peel, was a verb I hadn't heard since my youth, when people pilled the skins off potatoes. An old word this is, and still in use here and there in England both as a noun and as a verb. The EDD lists it from the northern shires as well as from East Anglia, Warwickshire, Lincolnshire, and from Somerset in the south-west, where they pill the crusts off loaves, and sheep are put into fields to pill them, to graze them closely. Ray's *Proverbs* from 1678 gives this advice from northern England: 'Pill a fig for your friend, a peach for your enemy.'

Pill, noun, means peel, rind, skin, bark. Holland's translation of Pliny's *Historie of the World, commonly called the Natural historie*, book xix, i. has 'Now that part thereof which is utmost and next to the pill or rind is called tow or hurds.' That important glossary with the forbidding name, *Promptorium Parvulorum Sive Clericorum, lexicon Anglo-Latinum princeps*, assembled about 1440, has 'Pyllyn or pylle bark or oþer lyke, *decortico.*' And the great King James Bible, *Genesis* xxx, 37, has 'And Jacob took him rods of green poplar, and of the hazel and chesnut tree, and pilled white strakes in them.'

There are many unrelated pills recorded in Ireland and Britain. Along the length of the tidal reaches of the Barrow, Suir and Nore a pill is a creek. I learned to swim in one near Ballyanne, close to New Ross. The people who live along the banks of the Severn think the word is their very own. From Herefordshire a correspondent told the EDD that a pill was 'a small creek capable of holding barges for unloading. The word is used on the Severn, and is probably peculiar to that river.' Sir Arthur Quiller Couch, 'Q', critic, essayist and novelist, had the word in his Cornish tale *Troy Town* (1888): 'Pyll, sir, otherwise a creek.' The word also meant a fishing village with a creek. From Somerset the EDD has 'You will have noticed Pill, Bristol Pill—the word is found all over the Somerset coast, and means a fishing village with a creek.' From Old English *pyll*, with the same meaning.

Another *pill*, found in Orkney, Shetland, and the northern counties of England, is often found as *pillock*, and *pillick*, and used as a derogatory term to describe a man. Think of 'a bad pill', and Del Boy

Trotter's 'Rodney, you pillock,' in the television series *Only Fools and Horses*.

Ivor Aasen, the great Norwegian lexicographer, tells us that this *pill* is from the Norwegian *pill*, a penis.

✦ PIXILLATED

This lovely word, thought to be imported to the United States from England in the eighteenth century if not before that, seems to have changed its meaning since the dictionaries gave it their blessing and elevated it from slang. Oxford defines the word as 'mildly insane, fey, whimsical, bewildered, confused, intoxicated, tipsy'. The journal *American Speech* (1941) XVI records it from 1848: 'You'll never find on any trip That he'll be pix-e-lated.'

What does that mean, exactly? Which of Oxford's wide spectrum of meanings fitted the bill? Nor am I sure what E.L. Bynner in his 1886 story *Agnes Surriage* meant exactly when he wrote, '"See now wher' we ha' come to wi' yer talk, Job Redden!" cried Agnes, waking suddenly to their situation. "We'll be pixilated 'n' driven on to th' rocks an ye don't wake up."'

The 1937 *Notes and Queries*, 2 January, published this: 'As a native of the state from which "Mr. Deeds" is reputed to have come permit me to comment on "pixilated". To use the word in the sense of "crazy" is not correct. A Vermonter would not hesitate to use "crazy" if that conveyed his meaning. A "pixilated" man is one whose whimseys are not understood by practical-minded people. More nearly a synonym of "whimsical".'

In 1952 the *New York Times* reported that the United States diplomatic corps was pixilated to a man by the young English queen. Well, we in Co. Wexford used *pixilated* as a more genteel substitute for *pissed*, and I suppose that it was a sense of adoring intoxication which affected the American diplomats.

At any rate the word is from *pixie*, plus *-lated* as in 'elated', 'emulated' etc. *American Speech* (1941) XVI tells us, 'The word *pixilated* is an early American expression—derived from the word "pixies" meaning elves. They would say, "The pixies have got him," as we nowadays would say a man is "balmy".' All right, but I wonder where the notion of pixilated = drunk came from? Some lexicographers say London town, and maybe they are right. Puritanical America would never approve their lovely word being used in such a vulgar manner.

I haven't come across the word in this country in years. It used to be in vogue in my home town, meaning drunk, but a recent enquiry found no trace of it.

✦ PLACK

An old friend of mine from Alice Marie O'Connor's friendly tavern in Abbeyside, Dungarvan, Maurice Fraher, died a few years ago aged eighty-seven, while I was away. One of his many interesting words was *plack*, a small amount of money, a farthing: 'The poor man never had a plack to his name,' he said of a mutual friend who had died.

Obsolete now except in dialectal phrases in northern England and Scotland, according to Oxford, it is found in Alan Bliss's edition of part of *The Irish Hudibras* (1689) in *Spoken English in Ireland* (1979): 'What though of Ready nere a Plack / Yet many a plugg of good Toback / It cost me to come to this Port . . .' *Ready*, cash, is still with us in the plural; as for *plack*, Bliss says we might compare the Irish *plaic*, defined by Dinneen as 'a coin'. This is from Flemish *placke*, *plecke*, a small coin of Brabant and Flanders, current in the fifteenth century, of varying value. The Medieval Latin (from 1481) was *placca*, 'a flat disk, tablet'; so Flemish *plak*, French *plaque*. Oxford invites us to compare the *Journal d'un Bourgeois de Paris*, dated 1425: '*En ce temps couroit une monnoie a Paris, nommee plaques, pour douze deniers parisis, et estoient de par le duc de Bourgogne.*' [At that time there were coins called plaques in circulation in Paris worth twelve Parisian denars, issued by the Duke of Burgundy.]

Maurice Fraher's speech was littered with obscure words. For a man who came from the foot of the Comeragh Mountains, and who had little formal education, his English vocabulary was truly amazing. I miss him.

✦ POLTER, POUTHER

As far as I'm aware this verb was found in this country only in Ulster, and in the north of Co. Louth. It was also found in Scotland, and in England in Yorkshire and the Lake District. There are many variant forms, the Donegal and Scots *pouther* among them. It means to poke about, to rake, as among ashes; to stir with the finger or some instrument, and it is also used figuratively. Sir Walter Scott in *Waverley* (1814) has 'There's no the like o' him ony gate for powthering wi' his fingers amang the hot peat-ashes and roasting eggs.' John Service in *Notandums, Being the Literary Recreations of Laird Cantycarl of Mongreymen of little Memory*, an attempt at comedy written in Ayr in 1890, has 'He powthered aboot the dresser and in the press.'

The verb also means to work in a careless, unskilful manner; to patch and mend, to do little easy jobs. *Pearson's Magazine* of May 1900, in a story by Seumus MacManus, has 'Masther M'Grane called shame on Neil to let Phelim Ruadh, who was only poutherin' through the books, bate him like that.' This meaning has been recorded in Selkirk and is quite common in the Lake District; but it has not been recorded elsewhere in England. And the EDD also has the meaning 'to go about aimlessly or so as to cause annoyance or confusion; to walk backwards or forwards; to trifle'. It has 'he was polterin' on' from north Yorkshire.

Polther in the west of Ireland meant to rain heavily and with a great noise. Jane Barlow has the word in her *Bogland* of 1892: 'It settled to polther an' pour, and the sky overhead grew as black as the bottomless pit.'

The word is also found as a noun meaning a poking, a stirring. Jamieson, the great Scottish lexicographer, has 'Gie the fire a pouter,' from Aberdeen. Miss Barlow, in her *Irish Idylls*, set in Connacht around 1892, has the noun meaning a downpour: 'You're abroad in great ould polthers.'

The noun also means 'a careless or messy worker, an inefficient untidy person, an aimless and ineffectual muddler', according to the DSL.

Oxford doesn't have the word; the EDD gives no etymology. The DSL hazards a guess that the word is a Scots form and usage of the English verb *potter*, itself from *pote*, to push, thrust, from Old English *potian*.

In all its meanings it seems to be in decline everywhere.

✦ POMANDER

A friend of mine who teaches English in a big school in Cork city asked her pupils recently on my behalf if they knew what a pomander was. Not a single girl had ever heard the word. My friend asked them to ask their mothers if they knew, and the following morning only two girls out of forty replied that their mothers knew a pomander as a piece of fruit, such as an orange, stuck with cloves and usually tied with ribbon, which is hung in a wardrobe to give the clothes a nice fresh smell. People didn't use them any more, they said; they bought sprays in shops instead.

So it seems that the lovely old word is on the way out. Originally the pomander was a perfumed ball or powder carried in a case in the pocket or worn suspended from the neck or waist. The name was sometimes applied to the case for holding the perfume. In olden times the ladies wouldn't dream of buying the article; it was considered part of a young lady's education to learn how to make one. The following is a recipe for making a pomander from an anonymous play written in 1607 and called *Lingua, or a Combat for the Tongue*:

'Take an ounce of the purest garden mould, cleansed and steeped seven days in rose water. Then take the best labdanum, benjoin, ambergris, civet and musk. Incorporate them together, and work them into what form you please. This, if your breath be not too valiant, will make you smell as sweet as my lady's dog.' (*Labdanum*, or *ladanum* is a resinous balsamic substance; *Benzoin* is a dry and brittle resinous substance, with a fragrant odour and slightly aromatic taste, obtained from the Styrax benzoin, a tree of Sumatra, Java, etc. It is used in the preparation of benzoic acid, in medicine, and extensively in perfumery. *Ambergris* is a wax-like substance of marbled ashy colour, found floating in tropical seas, and as a morbid secretion in the intestines of the sperm-whale. It is odoriferous and used in perfumery; formerly in cookery; *civet* is another name for chives; *musk* is an odoriferous, reddish-brown substance, secreted in a gland or sac by the male musk-deer. It has a very powerful and enduring odour, and is used as the basis of many perfumes.)

Drayton referred to pomanders in *Quest of Cynthia*: 'And when she from the water came / Where first she touched the mould, / In balls the people made the same / For *pomander*, and sold.' Pomanders were also used against infection. Drayton again, in *Polyolbion*: 'Her moss most sweet and rare / Against infectious damps for pomander to wear.' And Shakespeare had the word in *The Winter's Tale*: 'I have sold all my trumpery; not a ribbon, glass, pomander, brooch ...'

The word is from Old French *pomme d'embre*, an apple of amber.

✦ POOK

This good word was once common in Ulster as well as its place of origin, Scotland. It is still in use in the odd place, but is thought to be in danger of extinction. It was recorded in the *Concise Ulster Dictionary* as well as in Joseph Wright's EDD. It means to pull with nimbleness or force; to pull gently; to pull the hair; to pluck a fowl. It is also used figuratively.

Burns, in *Death and Dr Hornbook*, has 'The weans haud out their fingers laughin, And pouk my hips.' Jamieson has the word in his great dictionary of Scots, and there is a proverbial saying: 'Pookin' an' pooin' is Scots folk's wooin'. 'Pooin'' means 'poking', I'm assured by Scottish friends; I have failed to find it in the Scots dictionaries.

To pook also means to pluck fowl. I was recently asked to quote the famous tongue twister about the pheasant plucker by a seven-year-old Donegal child who described it as the one about 'the man who was pookin' the birds'. Quite a forward child this. I mean, I didn't learn the verse until I was ten. Unless you've had a sheltered upbringing you must have heard it yourself: 'I'm not the pheasant plucker. I'm the pheasant plucker's son. I'm only plucking pheasants till the pheasant plucker comes.'

At any rate *pooking* was mentioned in many nineteenth-century Ulster literary sources. *The Ballymena Observer* had it in 1892. 'Sanny pookit my coat tail,' complained Lyttle in his *The Adventures of Paddy McQuillan* (no date but probably *c*. 1892). The same writer has 'A pookit the Meer's coat tail' in *The Adventures of Robin Gordon of Ballycuddy, Co. Down* (again no date, but *c*. 1893).

To pook also means to moult. Shetland and Orkney children used to be told that falling snowflakes were the angels pooking. In Roxburghshire *pooks* are also the short unfledged feathers on a fowl when they begin to grow after moulting; also down or any other similar substance adhering to one's clothes; the end of threads; unconsidered trifles. There is a Scottish phrase, *pooking and rooking*, which means to pillage. Another phrase, *to be in* or *on the pook*, means to be in declining health.

The ultimate origin of *pook* is unknown. The main thing is that the word is still alive, and as an Antrim friend put it to me lately, if the schools told their pupils that the word was one of their own and a legacy of their Scots linguistic heritage, they wouldn't be afraid to use it, and it would survive.

✦ POSS

Some time in the early seventies I earned a crust translating the news into Irish in the RTÉ newsroom. I found it exciting and challenging work. One of the newsreaders was Pádraic Óg Ó Conaire, who was confined to the radio studio both because of his age and because of his endearing habit of inserting prayers for any deceased person mentioned in the bulletin: 'The Russian general Dimitry Zuchov died today in Moscow aged eighty-four.' Then came the unscripted 'May his soul and the souls of all the faithful departed, through the mercy of the ever-loving and forgiving God, rest in peace, Amen.'

Well, one day Pádraig Ua Maoileoin from the Kerry Gaeltacht, a grandson of Tomás Ó Criomhthain, author of the classic *An t-Oileánach*, The Islandman, wrote the verbal noun *pasáil* in the script to be read by Pádraic Óg, and the latter beamed with delight at seeing the word. He hadn't heard it for many years, he said.

I was asked if my father had it in his west Cork dialect and I said that I heard it from him and that it meant to him what cows do to a field when they gather near a gate: churning the place up by stamping on it. To the amazement of my audience I told them that in south-east Wexford people also had it in their rich English as *possing*, the verb being *poss*.

Further enquiries led me to find an interesting pedigree for this old word, which has various shades of meaning. 1. To drive or thrust with a forcible or violent impact; to dash or toss with a blow or stroke; to knock: often expressing the action of waves on a boat, etc. In the *Legend of Good Women* Chaucer has 'The se . . . possith hym now vp now doun.' Chaucer's *Romaunt of the Rose* has 'Thus am I possed up and doun With dool, thought, and confusioun.'

To some old New Ross people *possing* meant to pound clothes in water in the process of washing them. This meaning is found to this day in Scotland and in England's North Country. Cotgrave in his 1611 French–English dictionary has 'Mettre à la flac, to . . . squash, clap, or posse downe.' Gervase Markham's *The English Hus-wife* of 1615 advises his readers to 'Take it forth, posse it, rinse it, and hang it up.'

There is also the noun *poss*, to shove, push, a noun familiar to Cotgrave. In his dictionary he has, '*Culassé* . . . that hath receiued an arse-posse, or fall on the arse.'

Origin? The OED suggests that it is possibly a modification of the Old French verb *pousser*, to push.

✦ POSY

A few years ago I devoted two paragraphs of a book to the little word *posy*, regretting that it had gone out of fashion since my grandmother's time. I regretted too that the little word, which once meant a line of verse written to a loved one in patterned language expressing love and devotion, is now regarded as rustic, and doomed.

We are told that in medieval times boys, when they departed for the wars, gave their girls posies written on knives, just to remind them to be good while they were away. My mother did not like the French word *bouquet*, introduced in the eighteenth century; she used to ask what was wrong with carrying a *posy*, as she did on her great day. The Irish language borrowed the word as *pósae* and *pabhsae*, and used it figuratively; a lovely word for a lovely girl.

Well, after I mentioned the word in my scribblings, the postmen were kept busy delivering letters from old people, throwing posies of gratitude at me for championing a beautiful word used by Christopher Marlowe and my mother. You'll remember the line in *A Passionate Shepherd to his Love*: 'And I will make thee beds of roses /And a thousand fragrant posies.'

Yes, a hundred poets from Kit Marlowe to Robert Burns; from John Clare to John Synge, from the Irish folk-poet Anthony Raftery to the Dorsetmen Hardy and Barnes, have written lovingly of posies. Burns, in *The Posie*, writes, 'An a' to pu' a posie to my ain dear May.' From Northamptonshire, the ailing John Clare writes wistfully in *The Village Minstrel* in 1821, 'On this same bank I bound my posies up.' Figuratively a posy meant a cluster; a small collection. So Reid, a Dumfries poet who flourished around 1900, sent a lady this dedication: 'I send you this wab o' my weavin—this posie o' sangs.'

A posy also meant any single flower. A word collector from Cumberland sent the EDD's editor a note which said that posy 'is well-known here as a single flower, the first by which a country child used to hear of a flower'. The use of the poets is chiefly on the side of its being plural, but not exclusively so. 'He promised to buy me a garden of roses, He promised to buy me a garland of posies.' You will probably recognise the song, 'Oh Dear, What can the Matter be?'—the matter being that the singer's boyfriend, Johnny, is too long at the fair, and, she thinks, up to no good. A garland, he says, was 'a garland of varied flowers, not bunches of them'. This would complement my mother's version of the English folksong: 'He promised to buy me a basket of posies. A garland of lilies, a garland of roses. A little straw hat to set off my blue ribbons, That tie up my bonny brown hair.'

I'm not forgetting the garden *posy*, known to botanists as *Paeonia officionalis*; and there is, too, the *posy* or aroma of freshly mown hay or grass.

I am fond as well of the north of England adjective *posey*, which means gay with floral patterns, used to describe print dresses and gowns. Hence *posey jacket*, the holiday jacket of a pitman, of curious patterns and displaying coloured flowers, worn at church on Sundays before Thatcher closed the mines.

I see that even Oxford considers the lovely word to be 'somewhat archaic and rustic'. It is, it says, a syncopated form of *poesy* (which, even when written in full, was often pronounced in two syllables).

✦ PUNANN

As every schoolboy and girl used to know, *punann* is the Irish word for a sheaf of corn. It is a very old word, coming into Medieval Irish from Old Norse *bundin*. It has remained unchanged in modern Norwegian. *Punann* made its first appearance in Irish literature in *Saltar na Rann* in the tenth century, and as far as I know the linguist Alexander Brugge was the first to attest to its Norse ancestry in an article entitled *Norse Loan Words in Irish*, published in 1912.

Some years ago I went astray as I was travelling from Limerick to Greystones, Co. Wicklow, on a foul night of rain and hail. I decided to stay the night in Cappoquin, Co. Waterford. I found lodgings for the night in a comfortable bed-and-breakfast and made my way in the rain to a nearby pub which had a welcoming fire, not of the *spiochaid* variety of three wet sods of turf, but of the kind which would roast an ox. There was a television above the bar showing the film *Some Like It Hot*; a lone farmer by the looks of him, and slightly the worse for wear, was admiring Miss Monroe as she sang that famous song, and purring lasciviously as he watched. When she had finished he turned to me and gave as his opinion that there wasn't on the face of the earth such a lovely punann of a woman. Here, the Medieval Irish word which meant a sheaf, which had come to us via the Vikings, had entered Southern Irish English and now meant a beautiful woman. And why not! Think of the golden head, the narrow waist, the lovely shape . . .

A week later I met my golfing friend Niall Tóibín, and told him about the new Irish English word I had found in Co. Waterford, and remarked on the genius of a people who had so subtly changed its meaning from a sheaf of wheat to a woman of dazzling beauty.

He looked at me, sipped his coffee, and uttered gravely one of the best puns I have ever heard. 'You know what they say: *punann* is the lowest form of wheat.'

Last year after a hunt near Cappoquin I heard the word again in a similar context. A man referred to my grandaughter, Mary, aged ten, who had been hunting all day with the Dungarvan Foxhounds, as 'a great little punann'. She has hair the colour of November sloes but no matter. The word I had heard in Cappoquin for a beautiful woman has survived.

Try as I might, I haven't been able to find the word used in that context in any other place in Ireland.

Q 〜

♦ QUAT

Many long years ago, when I was jung and easily freudened by people of the opposite sex, if I may steal Mr Joyce's pun, I heard a lassie telling another that she needed to go and quat. I was appalled, shocked, by the realisation that in my favourite part of Co. Wexford well-bred young women used such a vulgar word as *quat*, which I correctly took to mean *squat*. Sixty years and more later I found out the word has disappeared from the people's speech in my home place.

Quat was once known all over our neighbouring isle from Leicestershire and Warwickshire, Glamorganshire, and Pembrokeshire, Berkshire, East Anglia, Kent, Sussex, the Isle of Wight, to Dorset, Somerset, Devon and Cornwall. The EDD defines the word as 'to squat, sit; to crouch down, especially of game; to hide; generally used with *down*'.

Well, *quat* is not a derivative of *squat* but is the closest of relatives of that equally old word. More of that anon. Jefferies' famous book on wildlife, published in 1879 and reprinted many times since, had this to say about the elusive corncrake: 'He will then, after a short time, if still hunted, "quat" in the thickest bunch of grass he can find in the ditch.' That was written from Wiltshire. From Dorset, Thomas Hardy in *Under the Greenwood Tree* has 'How the blood do get into my head whenever I quat down like that.' In Cornwall a child might *quatty* on the floor, not for the same purpose as did the Wexford girl of long ago, but to rest.

The word also means collapsed, quiet, dead; also used figuratively and in the phrase *to go quat*. From Devon, a correspondent sent this to Joseph Wright's dingy little office that the Oxford dictionary powers-that-were lent him to finish his great dialect dictionary: '"Politics be a-go quat," meaning that nothing is now heard of them. Also, "Old Jack is a-go quat," meaning that he has lost his position, either socially or financially.' A Cornish correspondent told Wright, 'He was perky enough in his speech but when he was questioned he was quatty and hadn't another word to say.' The phrase *to go quat* means to collapse in Cornwall. Jerry-built houses are apt to go quat; so are banks, to judge by recent events.

Quat is from Old French *quatir, quattir, catir*, to press down, sink, hide; to crouch, to squat. *Squat* is from Old French *esquatir, esquater*, from *ex-* plus *quatir*. The relationship between *quat* and *squat* could scarcely be closer.

✦ QUAW

Also found as *qua, quaa, quagh* and *quah*, this old word, an importation from Scotland, reached the great Ulster dialect dictionaries of the nineteenth century, W.H. Patterson's, which recorded the word in Antrim and Down, and Simmons's, which recorded the word in Armagh and south Donegal. The estimable Capt. Grose recorded the word in Co. Antrim back in 1790. I'm glad to report that the word is still alive in Donegal. I heard it in Rogers' pub at the back of Muckish mountain and I see that Michael Traynor has it in *The English Dialect of Donegal*, published by the Royal Irish Academy in 1945. C.I. Macafee also has it in her more recent *Concise Ulster Dictionary*. It means a quagmire, and I'd bet my trousers on it that not more than a handful of people in the north-west have ever heard of the word.

Let's look at the word's Scots ancestry. The Perthshire Session Papers of 1762 has 'The large Dam of Water which supplies the Mill-lead of Errol, called the Quaa'. In 1824 MacTaggart's engaging work the *Scottish Gallovian Encyclopedia*, an important source of post-Burns dialect, has 'Some think they sank in a snaw wride, and afterwards into a Qua.' I don't know what a *wride* is. J. Nicholson's *Tales* from the same county, published a few years after MacTaggart's book, has 'He hadna gane far till down he plumpit in a quaa to the saddle laps.'

The Scots Magazine of March 1847 was the first publication to bring the compound 'quakkin' quaa' to our notice: 'Just below the crest, in a quakkin quaw the river was born.' Crockett's 1894 story *The Raiders* has 'Green, deceitful, "quakkin-quas", covered with a scum that looked like tender young grass, but in which, at the first step, one might sink to the neck'.

The word also means a disused and overgrown pit, and a hole from where turf has been dug.

The Scotsman of 5 Jan. 1952 reported 'A rash-infested quaakin-qua that will ultimately extend on both sides of Devon'.

According to the DSL the origin is Old Scots *quawbog*, from 1409, *qwhawe*, from 1420, a quagmire. Of doubtful origin, perhaps from an unattested *quall*. *Quallmyre* is recorded once in English, in 1553. There may be some connection with Early Middle English *cwellen*, to well up, as a spring (cf. German *Quelle*), or alternatively the word may be onomatopoeic as *quag* is in *quagmire*.

✦ QUEAN

Where have all the Scots *queans*, who have enlightened literature for centuries, gone? The word is rarely heard nowadays in Scotland. Why have queans never crossed the sea to Ulster? This lovely old word, found in a variety of forms, *quine* being the most popular, in Scotland, northern England, and in Somerset and Devon in the south-west, means a woman, a damsel; a term of endearment for a little girl. It also means an immoral woman, and is used as a term of reproach for a dirty woman.

It is to be found in profusion in Scots dialect literature since 1728, when a poem by Ramsay published by the Scottish Text Society gave us 'Blaw up my Heart-strings, ye Pierian quines.' Burns's masterpiece, *Tam o' Shanter* (1790) has 'Now Tam, O Tam! had thae been queans, A' plump and strapping in their teens!'

Selkirk's Hogg, in his *Winter Evening Tales*, has 'You delve a garden like him, and like him have been bilked by a lusty young quean.'

Scott, Hogg's friend and mentor, has this in *Redgauntlet*: 'If ye expect to be ranting among the queans o' lasses ...'

The word was also recorded in the far north, in Orkney, where in 1880 Dennison's *Sketch-Book* has 'Ye witless impident quine . . . I'me aften telt you tae close the door efter you.'

Burns used the word as a term of endearment, as did many a poet after him; and he also knew the word as a term for a female child, a girl up to the end of her schooldays. *The Scots Magazine* for February 1930 has 'Rob spoiled them both, the wife and the quean.'

The word also means a maid-servant. Scott has it in *Rob Roy*: 'My servant quean, Mattie'. So James Hogg in *The Brownie of Bodsbeck* (1818): 'He had hired a wastlin, auldish quean.' In 1884 a crofter gave evidence before a committee that 'I couldna get a quine either in Tomintoul, Grantown, or Forres to keep the hoose an mak my brose.'

As a derogatory term for a woman, a concubine, a person of loose morals, it was very popular among writers. W. Finlay's *Poems* from the 1840s has 'Twas said, when a stripling, his feelings had been Storm-blighted and rent by a false-hearted quean.'

A.J. Cronin's *Hatter's Castle* (1831) has 'That's a bold looking quean ye have about the house.' One of the Childe Ballads, *Laird o Drum*, has the couplet 'For I'm our low to be yer bride, An yer quine I'll never be.'

J. Thomson's *Poems* of 1819 has 'Solomon for wives had haill three hunder queans.'

Old Scots has *qwen*, a girl, lass, from 1420; Middle English has *quene*, Old English has *cwene*, woman, serf, prostitute. Compare if you will Old High German *quina*, Old Norse *kvenna-*, woman, female. The short vowel Old English form is in ablaut relation to Old English *cwén*, which gave *queen*.

✦ QUEEM

Mary Sweeney from Meenbanad, in the Rosses of Donegal, at whose hundredth birthday party I was a guest, gave me many extraordinary words, picked up in Scotland during her childhood, where like many another she was sent to supplement the family income gutting herrings in winter and working in the potato fields and helping with the harvest in summer and autumn. She was, I need hardly say, a native speaker of Irish, but whenever possible she went to school, and could write flawless English. I have letters from her, one written on her 103rd birthday, and I since found difficulty in persuading people that this particular one was written by a a woman of her great age. Somebody from RTÉ radio interviewed her not long before her death at 104. She spoke of her youth in both languages. Then RTÉ destroyed the tape, just as they did with Seán Mac Réamoinn's talk with her friend Paddy the Cope.

Queem was one of the words she used. It means pleasant; calm; smooth. The word is also found in Ulster in the Montiaghs, a soggy district on the shores of Lough Neagh. It was recorded in *Montiaghisms* by Lutton, mentioned below.

The Scots Magazine of May 1893 has 'Whan the year grown auld brings winter cauld, We flee till [to] our ha's [halls] sae queem.' In 1863 a poem by J. Hamilton from Lanarkshire gave us 'Yer wee shilpt weanie's a pityfu' prufe That yer bosom's as dry an' as queem as my lufe [hand].'

Lutton's *Montiaghisms* defines *queem* as 'affectedly nice, over fastidious'. It can also mean smooth, calm, tranquil. Hence *queemly*, defined as smoothly by Lutton.

In that marvellous book of odds and ends, MacTaggart's *Scottish Gallovidian Encyclopedia* (1824), he has both *queem* and *queemly*, 'At length his restless pulse mair queem grew' and 'The gled glides queemly alang.'

As an adverb the word can mean exactly, neatly, snugly. It also means smoothly, pleasantly, without snags or hitches. The EDD says that it was written of an engine in Kircudbright in 1900, 'She's rinnin' as queem as silk.'

To queem also means to fit snugly, fall into place. Its derivative, *queemer*, means a person skilled in fitting joints, etc., a joiner; figuratively it means a toady, lickspittle, a 'yes-man'.

Queem is an ancient word, first seen in *Havelok the Dane* in *c.* 1220: 'þat hire kin be ful well queme.'

The word is in Old Scots as *quem*, pleasing, quiet, pleasantly, from 1400; meaning closely, smoothly, from 1513; meaning to join closely from 1501. The Old English is *cwéman*, to please.

✦ QUICKEN

This name for the mountain ash, *Pyrus Aucuparia*, was in general dialectal use in Ireland, England and Scotland not long ago, but in many places people have discarded it in favour of *rowan*, and indeed *mountain ash*. P.W. Joyce has *quicken* in his *English As We Speak It In Ireland*, and *Henderson's Folk Lore* of 1879, speaking of Leinster, mentions its mysterious powers: 'In Leinster when witchcraft is suspected in the dairy the doors are shut and the plough irons thrust into the fire and connected with the churns by twigs of mountain ash or quicken-berry.' Quicken was regarded as having supernatural powers far from Wexford, where I first heard of it; in Lincolnshire the scholarly journal *Notes and Queries*, Series 3, viii, 1865, has this: The (q)wicken tree, or mountain ash, is represented as having the power of deterring evil spirits from where it grows.' From Cheltenham direction a correspondent told the EDD, 'A piece nailed over the door is supposed to keep off witches.'

In Chester as elsewhere, the quicken was considered to be a sacred tree, and was thought to constitute one of the most infallible charms for the cure of the whooping cough. The EDD's correspondent there also said that he had 'noted an objection on the part of Cheshire labourers to cut one down'.

The origin of the word *quicken* is elusive, and many have tried to explain where it came from. Scott in *The Antiquary* (1816) said it was 'so named because of its lively nature; as every joint of the root, which is left in the ground, springs up anew'. Not likely, Sir Walter.

The EDD offers no etymology. The *Concise Ulster Dictionary* doesn't record the word. Oxford says that *quicken* is 'the northern equivalent of *quickbeam*, and presumably from *quick* adjective, but the exact nature of the ending is not clear: in early use always in combination with *tree*'. It adds that 'In Old English glosses, *cwicbeam* usually renders Latin *cariscus*, which seems to be otherwise unknown, and is perhaps an error for *tamariscus*.' Collins makes no mention of it. Perhaps it considers it a dialect word. The DSL offers this: 'Middle English *quicken*, juniper; a derivative of *quick*, as in *quickbeam*, the service-tree, Old English *cwictrow*.'

Whatever its origin, the quicken tree, with its magical powers against witches and the dreaded whooping cough, deserves to live in our lexicon. Is it now confined to the south-east of Ireland, and to a receding number of dialects in England. The Irish is *caorthann*, famous in ancient lays and stories, defined by Dinneen as 'the rowan or quicken tree, mountain ash, held sacred by the Druids'. A magical tree in any language.

R ∽

✦ RAIK

A lady interested in folk song emailed me to enquire about a word she found in a few old broadside ballads, *raiking*, the verbal noun of *raik*, to wander. The gentlemen who went raiking in the old adventure songs, a legacy the French left our literature, were usually up to no good, as many a tearful maiden on both sides of the Irish sea was left to relate in song. Mind you, some of them were fly enough to send the raikers packing; I remember one lassie bidding a boyo adieu with the explanation 'For I have heard along the road that you were fond of raiking'. Now, the point of my correspondent's letter was to enquire if *raiking* was merely a misprint made by the old printers when they meant *raking*, which is what *rakes*, men of loose habits, did: rambling around country roads and sitting in inns searching for demure lasses to accost and, as the old phrase had it, to pleasure.

Raik is as old a word as *rake*, verb, and is found in literature as early as 1300. As a noun it came to prominence around 1400. In Scotland it meant simply a walk, a journey. Wyntoun, who wrote the Chronicles of his country around 1420, has 'To the dure . . . Scho tuk hyr rayk rycht hastyly.' Around 1440 *Promptorium Parvulorum Sive Clericorum* gives the definition '*Reyke*, or *royt*, ydylle walky[n]ge abowt, discursus, vagacio'. Gradually, *raik*, verb and noun, died out in England but persisted in Scotland and in Ireland, In Scotland, we find James Hogg, 'the Etterick Shepherd', Sir Walter Scott's friend, saying in *The Queen's Wake*, 1813, 'Lang haif I raikit the world wide.'

I am informed that although you might find *raiks raiking* in the odd remote place near the Scottish border with England, it hasn't been recorded in that area since 1920. As for Ireland, we have long given up raiking in search of young innocent *cailíní*.

Raiks and *raiking* are from Old Norse *reika*, to walk about, stroll, wander. In Middle English it is distinct from *rake*, in which it was subsequently absorbed.

✦ REAVE

Sometimes spelled *rief*, this word used to be common in the west of Ireland, and I've heard old people use it in rural east Wicklow. It means to rob, steal, plunder, and it was also common in Scotland and in Northumberland, Cumberland and Yorkshire.

I heard the word from old John Vines from Kilpedder, with whom I had many a pint. 'That fellow would reave the eyes out of your head.' This he said of a neighbour of his. A member of the Garda, a Mayoman, once told me of an acquaintance who was in trouble for 'reaving bags of coal out of the parish priest's shed'. Jane Barlow had this in *East into West*, published in 1898 and set in the west of Ireland: 'We'd riefed th'oul bags off him.'

The word is very common in the Scottish literature of the eighteenth and nineteenth centuries. Nicholson, a dialect poet from Galloway who flourished around 1815 and is read nowadays mainly by pillagers like me interested in his dialect, has in one of his tear-jerkers 'I've seen her reaved o' all her charms, / Her helpless offspring in her arms.' Robert Burns has the word in *Death of Mailie*: 'To slink thro' slaps, an' reave an' steal / At stacks o' pease, or stocks o' kail.' In 1813 Scott in a poem wrote, 'A wild resemblance we can trace, / Though reft of every softer grace.' And in 1884 Tennyson's *Becket* has 'We fear that he may reave thee of thine own [eyes].'

But *reave* is older far than those. It is to be found in the Lindisfarne Gospels before 950; by Wulfstan in a Homily around 1020; in *Cursor Mundi*, the great Northumbrian poem of around 1300: 'Lok þat þou ne reue ne stele.'

How it got to Kilpedder and Mayo God only knows, but it is from Old English *réafian*.

✦ ROSE OF SHARON

I'm a keen gardener, but I've never been good with roses. No matter what I do to care for them, one fungus after another attacks them, and no matter how often I spray them, greenfly and other pests devour them. So perhaps Jennifer Greene, an American living in West Cork, should have addressed her query to a botanical expert and not to me.

She wants to plant a *Rose of Sharon* in her seaside garden, and wants to know where she could find one. My friend is Jewish and she says she has consulted about every rose grower's catalogue in Britain and Ireland, north and south, but they don't mention the Biblical beauty.

No wonder. The Rose of Sharon is not a rose at all, Mrs Greene, but one of about twenty-five varieties of flowers or shrubs so named, and the Biblical variety has never been positively identified. Varying scholars have suggested that the biblical Rose of Sharon may be one of the following plants. A crocus that grows in the coastal plain of Sharon is the New Oxford Annotated Bible's guess; *Tulipa montana*, a bright red tulip-like flower, even today prolific in the hills of Sharon, according to Harper's Bible Dictionary; *Tulipa agenensis*, the Sharon tulip, a species of tulip suggested by a few botanists; or *Lilium candidum*, more commonly known as the *Madonna Lily*, a species of lily suggested by some botanists, thought likely in reference to the 'lily of the valleys' mentioned in the second part of *Song of Solomon*. Sephardic Hebrew poetry from the tenth to the fifteenth century demonstrates prolific use of a word translated into English consistently as *Rose of Sharon*; there are a few renderings as *lily*. In the seven-branched Menorah of the Jewish Temple, the branches were designed in the shape of the Madonna Lily. In King Solomon's Temple there were designs of Madonna Lilies on the columns. The Metsudot says that the word 'lily' is synonymous with six, because it always has six petals. Six petals of the flower form is a shape that resembles the Star of David, and this is a source of importance of the Star of David in Judaism. The term and trope are found throughout much of the poetic corpus of the Golden Age of Iberian Jewish *belles lettres*.

To confuse the issue further, many botanists believe that the *Rose of Sharon* was a flowering shrub, possibly *Hypericum calycinum*, an evergreen flowering shrub native to southeast Europe and southwest Asia, and the plant generally referred to in British and Australian English as 'Rose of Sharon'; or *Hibiscus syriacus*, a deciduous flowering shrub native to east Asia, the plant generally referred to in American English as 'Rose of Sharon' and the national flower of South Korea. The specific epithet indicates that the plant was thought to originate from Syria. The flower's name in Korean is *mugunghwa*, meaning 'immortal flower'. Neither of these is thought by most authorities to be the Rose of Sharon of the Bible.

Mrs Greene tells me that she has friends in Israel. Perhaps she should get one of them to get her a cutting of a rose from a garden in Sharon. She might be happy to eventually have a rose *from* Sharon, if not a Rose *of* Sharon. I'm sure somebody in the Israeli Department of Agriculture would help her in this matter. Good hunting!

✦ ROUT

Forty years ago, my notebook tells me, I heard the word *rout* in a pub in Falcarragh, Co. Donegal, used by a visitor from Co. Tyrone in describing the efforts of a singer from Tory Island who had to raise his voice to be heard above the din in the pub. I remembered being annoyed myself because I had never heard a Toryman singing in Irish before, and because his song was new to me, a beautiful love song which didn't lend itself to shouting.

Rout may have been imported to Ulster from Scotland, but it is also found in England in Shropshire, Yorkshire, the North Country, Lincolnshire and Lancashire, and in the Isle of Man, and as far south as Devon. It has many spelling variants, *raut*, *rowt*, and *route* among them. The verb *rout* originally meant to bellow, as a bull does; and of humans, to make any loud noise. 'Nae mair thou'll rowte it out ower the dale,' wrote Burns in *Ordination* in 1786. 'She's come home routin,' is a line from Henderson's *Popular Rhymes* of 1856; the poet wasn't talking about a cow or a bull, but of his lady wife. *The Ballymena Observer* of 1892 has 'I wud rether hear my ain coo routin,' used of a lady singing. A correspondent from Shropshire sent this to the EDD: 'Did'n you fother them beasts well las' night? They wun routin' till I couldna get a wink o' sleep.'

Router, noun, was given to me by Benedict Kiely from Tyrone. He defined it as a loudmouthed man or woman. *Routing* is a participial adjective found in Co. Down. George Savage-Armstrong has this in his *Ballads of Down*, published in 1901: 'Remarkable and dangerous eddies under Bankmore, at the entrance to Strangford Lough, named for their loud and ominous roaring sound: "the Routing Rock".'

The verb also means to snore. Walter Scott in *Guy Mannering* wrote, 'Jock, ye villain, are ye lyin' routing there, and a young gentleman seeking the way to the Place.' And Joseph Wright, in his great dialect dictionary, informs us that in parts of bonny Scotland the verb means 'to break wind from behind'; and that in England's North Country they have a phrase *to keep a rowt*, to make a noise.

The noun means the prolonged roar of an animal; any loud noise; an outcry; bustle, confusion, disturbance, commotion. A Northamptonshire correspondent told Wright, 'If a person is needlessly annoyed or excited by any particular circumstance, it is commonly said, "What a rout she's making over it!" "She needn't make such a rout about such a trifle."'

The origin of this old word, still alive in Ulster, but only barely so, is the Old Norse *rauta*, to roar.

✦ **SACRED FISH**

In a recent book on the lore of An Rinn, Co. Waterford, fisherman Mícheál Turraoin, or Maidhc Dháith, there is a short piece in which the grand old man says that the older generation prized above all the other fish in the sea the haddock (*cadóg*), the John Dory and the sea bream (*deargán*), because these fish were the ones chosen by the Saviour to be fed to the Apostles at the Last Supper, and that they have ever since borne the marks of the Lord's fingers and thumb. Women made the crosses on rosary beads from the bones of the haddock, he said.

Maidhc Dháith was one of the late Risteard B. Breatnach's informants in his outstanding studies *The Irish of Ring* and *Seana-Chaint na nDéise II*. He was also a friend of the Celticists Heinrich Wagner, Myles Dillon, James Carney and David Greene. They would, I feel, have been delighted at Micheál Verling's collection of old Maidhc's reminiscences in beautiful Irish, unspoiled by the bogey of standardisation, about every subject under the sun, including the almost sacramental one about the three sacred fishes. How sad it was to hear that Mr Verling died, a young man, not long after his wonderful book was given to us.

As I was recently browsing through a book on phrase origins by the American Robert Hendrickson, I was surprised by a piece he had on the John Dory, one of the old Waterfordman's sacred fishes. John Dory, Hendrickson tells us, is most likely a humorous designation for some real or imagined person, perhaps a notorious privateer of that name active in the sixteenth century, and the subject of a popular song of that time. That much I already knew, but his next paragraph surprised me. 'Like the haddock,' he says, 'which also has a dark spot on each side, the golden-yellow John Dory has the reputation of being the fish from which the Apostle Peter extracted money. In France it still bears the name "St Peter's cockerel"; its oval spots are said to be the finger marks left when Peter held the fish to take the coin from its mouth.'

I note that Maidhc Dháith had no Irish word for the John Dory. *Ní fheadar mé canathaobh*. Dinneen has *deoraí*, which seems to be a translation.

✦ **SALVOR**

This is an obsolete form of *salver*, which Oxford defines as formed (with suffix -*er* after *platter* or some other word of like meaning) on French *salve*, a tray used for presenting certain objects to the king, adopted from Spanish *salva*, primarily 'a foretasting, as to a prince', the 'assaying' of food or drink, and hence a tray or salver on which the cup was placed when the tasting had shown that its contents were free from danger. Minsheu's *Spanish Dictionary* of 1623 has the phrase *hacer salva*, 'to taste meat or drink, as they do with princes'.

Medieval kings and princes were very worried about being poisoned, especially by arsenic. The poor devil who had the job of tasting from the cup placed on the salvor was also called the *salvor*, which originally meant *saviour*, and came from the Latin *salvus*, safe, and which also entered English in *salvage*, *salvation*, and *salve*. It was believed in many European courts that to serve drinks in expensive Venetian crystal glass would save the poor salvor's life; it was claimed (by Venetian glass-makers among others) that the quality of the glass would ensure that it would break into smithereens as soon as it came into contact with baneful *Aqua Tofana*, which contained the dreaded arsenic.

Not until the middle of the seventeenth century was it considered fairly safe to dispense with the services of the taster and so *salvor*, by then generally spelled *salver*, became the platter on which the food and drink was carried to ordinary mortals as well as to princes. The *salvor/salver* now had a new purpose according to Thomas Blount's 1661 *Glossographia, or a Dictionary interpreting such Hard Words as are now Used*: he described a salver as 'a new fashioned peece of wrought plate, broad and flat, used in giving beer or other liquid thing, to save the carpit or cloathes from drops'. Slobberers all, those seventeenth-century topers.

Nowadays one has one's letters brought to one on a salver, doesn't one?

But it is interesting that the old meaning of *salve* is retained in another *salvor*, a maritime word meaning 'one who saves or helps to save vessels or cargo from loss at sea; one who effects or attempts salvage'; also, 'one who saves or attempts to save some one from drowning'. Oxford cites the 1890 *Daily News* (16 Oct.): 'Among the cases of saving, or attempting to save life from drowning . . . there are thirteen in which the salvors' ages ranged from eight years to sixteen.' The word is still in use in maritime circles, I am told.

✦ SAUP

An old friend of mine worked as a medical practitioner in rural Lancashire some years ago. He sent me many interesting words from there, including *saup*. On a beautiful, hot summer's day, when he had attended to a patient, he went with the woman of the house to see what we in Ireland would call a *meitheall*, a voluntary band of men and women, working in the hay fields. The farmer's wife carried with her a bucket of buttermilk for the thirsty workers. She called the refreshing liquid not buttermilk but *saup*.

The EDD hasn't got the word, but I have come across it in a glossary of words from rural Yorkshire. It comes from the Old Norse *saup*, buttermilk, according to the Icelandic lexicographer Zoëga. What an interesting survival this is; but the sad thing is, it is already obsolete in Yorkshire, and at death's door, like so many country words, in Lancashire.

The late Beryl Bainbridge, the novelist, gave me the word from Lancashire. She said it was a rural word and unknown in the towns and cities.

✦ SAUVAUN

Sauvaun is an acceptable Irish English spelling of the Irish *sámhán*, a lovely word for a short nap, collected in the Baile Bhúirne district of West Cork by the schoolmaster Mícheál Ó Briain. *Sámh* is an adjective meaning tranquil; a goodnight greeting is *codladh sámh!*

But *sauvaun/sámhán* was not confined to West Cork. Michael Banim the Kilkenny novelist had in *The Croppy*, written not long after the '98 rebellion, 'I was in a raal sauvaun of a sleep.' He glossed the word as 'comfortable drowsiness'.

An old man from a neighbouring parish to mine in west Waterford once told me after I woke him one evening from a nap he was having before his fire, 'Whatever about apples, a sauvaun a day keeps the doctor away.' Many doctors would agree with him.

I also heard the word from east Limerick. A man who meant that his sick wife was having a little sleep said, 'There's a sauvaun on her; I hope it won't take the night's sleep on her.'

Hence *sauvauning*, recorded in north Kerry, and glossed by the man who sent it to me as 'taking life easy without fuss or bother'.

I came across a related word in Co. Monaghan. It is *sámhas*, which could be acceptably written as *sauvas* or *sawvas*, and it was sent to me by Peadar Ó Casaide and by my friend of many years Tomás Mac Gabhann, both gone from us now. It was glossed by both men as a nap after a meal.

It may still be alive among the old people. I doubt if the young know of it.

✦ SCALTEEN

This is an acceptable Irish English spelling of the Irish *scailtín*, sometimes *scaillín* and *scaoiltín* according to Fr Dinneen's *Irish-English Dictionary*, which defines it as 'a tansey, a mixture of boiled whiskey, butter, sugar and hot milk as a cure for a cold in the chest; rum often takes the place of whiskey'. With respect to Fr Dinneen, one should never boil the whiskey. As a Kerryman he should have known that; that's what a lifetime in the Jesuits does to one's knowledge of strong drink.

I have asked I don't know how many Irish chefs to include *scalteen* in their dinner menus as a starter. I can assure my readers that the modified version I make myself is very palatable. It consists of hot whiskey poured into strained consommé of beef, with a little salt and cream added. Not one of them would consider it: 'Oh, it's Irish, is it?' was the attitude I always encountered. If I had said that I picked up the recipe from an Inuit fisherman's wife or from a Mongolian fur dealer's ditto, no doubt they would have expressed a keen interest.

Scalteen was denounced by the temperance crusader Fr Mathew in no uncertain terms and by his follower Mr Mac Namara Downes from Co. Clare, a very bad temperance poet who formed the rather unsuccessful Irish Water Drinkers Association. This boring gentleman went to Dan O'Connell to invite him to become a patron of his association, but Dan showed him the road.

I remember encountering the word *scalteen* in George A. Little's *Malachy Horan Remembers*.

> They always had scalteen ready at the Jobstown Inn. Men, in weather like this, out from morning till night without a bit, would be coming in with the mark of the mountain on them. Scalteen would make a corpse walk. It would put the life back in them, but make them

drunk too. It was taken red hot. They made it from half a pint of whisky, half a pound of butter, and six eggs. You should try it some time, but when you have it down go to bed while you are still able.

The German prince with the fairytale name, Hermann Heinrich Ludwig von Pückler-Muskau, tried the beverage at a dinner after a hunt near Cashel in 1828. He slid under the table after a while and was licked awake in the morning by some foxhounds and terriers.

Try the following recipe. I assure you, it's the best remedy for the symptoms of a cold you'll ever find. I recommend it particularly to my Norwegian friend Per Egil Hesla, to whom this book is dedicated. There could be nothing better than a flowing bowl of scalteen after a day hunting elk in winter. It was sent to me by a man who drinks in the famous Tipperary hurling pub Mary Willie's: 'Add half a bottle of whiskey, two whisked eggs, a lump of butter, to a pint and a half of strained beef broth to which salt and black pepper has been added. Heat the mixture well but do not boil.' He adds, rather unnecessarily, 'consume'.

✦ SCART

Scart, *skort*, *scorth*, and *scort* are corruptions of the Irish word *scairt*, a loud laugh, a guffaw. Dermot O'Byrne, a Donegal novelist, in *Children of the Hills*, has 'He'd be left in the latter end with the skin cracked in his foot bones with scairts of laughter they'd take out of him.' I've heard the word in Limerick, Waterford, west Cork and south Carlow; Dr Patrick Henchy, the Clare scholar, director in his time of both the National Library and the Chester Beatty Library, sent me the word, which he had sent in a valuable glossary to the *North Munster Antiquarian Society Journal* in 1975. But on enquiry recently my spies, the scholteachers, have told me that the word is now in danger of becoming obsolete in these counties.

This word was also used of the diaphragm, and in this case as well, the word seems to be in danger. Dr Henchy again: 'In a local cure carried out by a blacksmith the words used were: "D'ucht a bheith socair is do scairt a bheith réidh, in ainm an Athar agus an Mhic agus an Spioraid Naoimh." [That your chest might be settled and your diaphragm at ease, in the name of the Father, the Son and the Holy Spirit.]'

There is a third *scart*. It means a covert, a thicket. The Kerry playwright George Fitzmaurice has 'My legs all scrope from scorts of briers' in *The Pie Dish*. The word is found in the diminutive in many Munster placenames, notably in the placename Scarteen in Co. Limerick, appropriately the home of the famous Scarteen Black and Tan foxhounds, hunted by the Ryan family for centuries. It would be a pity, though, if the word survived only in placenames, as now seems likely to happen.

✦ SCOOT

The late Ginette Waddell, actress and member of a distinguished literary and scholastic family, once gave me the word *scoot*, which she had heard in the Belfast of her youth. She remembered that her kinsman Rutherford Mayne, the dramatist, used the word in one of his plays. It was, she said, a word reserved for the most contemptible people of either sex. It does not sound like a word that borders on the taboo, but she assured me than when women ran out of epithets to insult other members of their sex, *scoot* got an airing. I'm assured that the word has also reached parts of Donegal and that it is reserved there for insulting members of the fair sex accused of being a little weak in the carnalities, to use Seán O'Faoláin's phrase.

It came to the north from Scotland. It is also found to this day in Lincolnshire, a fact that points to its origin, but I know of no connection between the speech of that English shire and Co. Antrim. The EDD has the word, as does Jamieson in his earlier Scots dictionary. A Moray correspondent told Jamieson that 'scoot is a term of the greatest contumely, applied to a woman. A Celt or Highlander can hardly receive greater disgrace than to be thus denominated.' But men were also called a scoot. The Scot Robert Leighton in his satirical work *Scotch Words and the Bapteesement o' the Bairn*, published in London in 1869, reserved *scoot* to insult a parson: 'The learned, pious, but unworthy skoot / Neglects his pious trust to catch a troot.' George Henderson in *The Popular Rhymes, Sayings and Proverbs of the County of Berwick* says that 'applied to a woman it means a trull, or camp-trull; applied to the other sex, a braggadocio'.

The speech of Lincolnshire has no connection with the speech of Co. Antrim, but our word is still in use there. The Lincolnshire lexicon contains a vast number of words of Scandinavian origin, and Johan

Ernst Rietz the Swedish lexicographer asks us in his *Svenskt Dialekt-Lexicon* to consider the Swedish dialect *skjut*, also *skut*, a horse; also a wanton man, as the origin of the word given to me by a lovely lady and a fine actress in the green-room of that fine company of radio players in Henry Street almost fifty years ago.

✦ SCRAT

An old friend of mine from south Co. Carlow who now lives in Norfolk sent me the above word, which she says is used extensively in East Anglia. Her trouble with the word *scrat* is that it has a variety of meanings: a small person; a 'maneen' who likes to throw his weight about; a small potato; an undersized, scrawny animal.

Many dictionaries have ignored the word, but the EDD has it from the North Country, from the Lake District, from Gloucestershire and Cheshire, as well as from East Anglia.

In a collection of folklore from the north of England, published between 1846 and 1849 by the important scholar Michael Denham, we find mention of 'scrats, gnomes and sprites', which gives us a pointer to its origin.

This rare word is also found in Scotland, from where it was imported to Donegal, Fermanagh and west Tyrone. Back in the early 1960s I heard a Donegal sheep farmer say of a belligerent young man who was the worse for wear in a Falcarragh pub, 'He throws a lot of shapes for such a wee scrat. You'd see bigger at night comin' out of a *lios* [a fairy fort].'

As to the word's origin, there is little doubt that it came from Scandinavia over a thousand years ago. Old Norse has *skratte*, a wizard, goblin, monster; modern Icelandic *skratti*, a devil; Swedish *skratte*, a goblin.

✦ SEVENDIBLE

This word of unknown origin is, it would seem from the EDD, found only in Ulster. It also appears in *Montiaghisms*, a little book first published in Armagh in 1923. This glossary of Ulster dialect words and phrases was assembled by William Lutton, who died in 1870. It was reprinted by The Linenhall Library, Belfast, in 1976. The glossary was introduced by Francis Joseph Bigger, who has some interesting things to say about it and its compiler.

The Montiaghs is a district adjoining Lough Neagh, and is pronounced Munchies. It's from the Irish *móinteach*, adjective, boggy.

Lutton spent some years as a medical student in Paris before some curious conscientious objections compelled him to return home and become a surveyor, a profession he excelled in. He worked for Lord Lurgan and for the Great Northern Railway, and his survey maps are minor works of art, decorated with artistically drawn insets, houses, scenery, etc.

Bigger says that the number of items included by Lutton contains about twenty-five per cent of purely Gaelic origin, and that 'the character of the users is shown in the use of abusive epithets, which amounts to over 13%, while terms of endearment do not reach half that figure'. Oh dear!

The word *sevendible* is defined by Lutton as 'thorough, complete', and has been given a place in the EDD, glossed as 'very great, thorough, severe'. It is reserved to describe beatings. *Notes and Queries*, Series IV, for 1873 has 'I have heard a groom threaten to give a boy a sevendible good beating.' The *Ulster Journal of Archaeology* V for 1853–62 has 'Hee tuk the wee fella by the scruff o' the neck and beat him most sevendibly.' Patterson also has the word in his 1880 glossary of Antrim and Down words.

As I said, the word's origin is a mystery. Neither Oxford nor the DSL has it, and it certainly is not of Irish ancestry. But the *Concise Ulster Dictionary* has this: '*Sevendible* is also found in Orkney; a form of Scots *sevendle*, itself an altered form of Scots *solvendie*, from Latin *solvendo*, solvent.' The DSL has *solvendie* and agrees that it comes from Latin *solvendo esse*, to be solvent, with later extensions of meaning. Perhaps one of these is Lutton's 'thorough, complete'; perhaps *sevendible* is a variant of *solvendie*.

✦ SHIFFIN

I've also heard *shifeen*, which is closer to the origin, the Irish *sifín*, which means a stem of corn, hay, straw or rush.

The word is common in Irish folklore, where it is associated with the Liberator, Daniel O'Connell. There are stories galore about the *Sifín Siúil*, the travelling straw, *Oíche na Sifín*, the night of the straws, or *Lá na Sifín*, the day of the straws.

Michael Traynor in *The English Dialect of Donegal*, published in the mid-1950s, has this to say about the word's appearance in Donegal folklore:

Dan O'Connell boasted that he could rise Ireland in one day, or send a message from end to end in twenty four hours. On that night (oíche), from various headquarters, a man went forth from a house with a straw to the next house. He of that house had immediately to pull a straw from his thatch and start off to the next house, and so on; each man going to the nearest house to his own. Thus word was passed all round Ireland in one night.

I came across the rare word near Kilpedder, in east Wicklow. Old John Vines and I were watching a soccer match in which Ireland were playing and were being hard pressed by their opponents. We were in front, with not much time left to play, but we were giving away free kicks near the goal. John was doubtful about the outcome, and said to me, 'We're leaning on a shiffin now,' meaning that we were now depending on something untrustworthy or dangerous: he had Lady Luck in mind. But as it happened, she was on our side that night.

I've also heard the word *sifín* used by a woman near Dungarvan, Co. Waterford, to describe a feckless, untrustworthy person. And my friend Pádraig Collins, a Clareman and distinguished diplomat who died tragically young, once described the hurling team representing my own Co. Wexford as 'a team of bloody shifeens'. Alas, I had to agree with him.

✦ SHOOLER

An American student at my old alma mater, Trinity College Dublin, e-mailed me about whether the word *shooler*, also found as *shuler* and *shuiler*, is still used in Ireland.

If it is, I haven't heard it. It is an Irish English word for a beggar or vagrant, and is common enough in nineteenth-century literature. James Joyce played with it in *Finnegans Wake* in the twentieth: 'Any of the Zingari shoolerin may pick a peck of kindlings yet from the sack of auld hensyne.'

My friend the late Richard Wall gave a list of the word's appearances in nineteenth-century literature in his very valuable *An Irish Literary Dictionary and Glossary*. Carleton in his *Traits and Stories* has 'What tribes of beggars and shoolers.' Lady Morgan wrote in her dreadful *The O'Briens and the O'Flahertys*: 'When the poor wild shuler comes to the bawn, the curs bark and the garlaghs [Irish *gárlaigh*, babies] cry.' And in

1842 Samuel Lover in *Handy Andy* has '"Throth, you do me wrong", said the beggar, "if you think I came shooling".'

Later in the century Patrick Kennedy from Wexford, a far more reliable guide to dialect, wrote in *The Three Crowns*, 'It was a big shuler of a fellow that took up employment from me yesterday.' Padraic Colum wrote *What the Shuler Said As She Lay by the Fire in the Farmer's House*, a poem as bad as its title. Joseph Campbell wrote a sentimental piece called *Every Shuler is Christ*. *The Shuler's Child* is a play by Seamus O'Kelly.

I must confess to being surprised at seeing so many citations of the verb *shool* from the literature of England in the Oxford dictionary, where it is defined quixotically as 'of obscure origin; hardly identical with *shool*, variant of *shovel*'. It redeems itself to an extent when it adds, 'In Ireland it seems to have been associated with *siubhail*, to go, travel. *Shooler* seems to correspond to *siubhlach*, vagrant.'

It citations are more interesting and more accurate. First of all *shool* in English literature means to go about begging; to sponge; to acquire some advantage by insidious means; to skulk. It cites the following, one, you will note, from Ireland: 1736 J. Lewis *Isle of Tenet* (ed. 2): 'Shooling, begging, to go a Shooling'. In 1748 Smollett in *Roderick Random* has 'When they found my hold unstowed, they went all hands to shooling and begging.' In 1785 Grose in his *Dictionary of the Vulgar Tongue* has 'Shoole, to go skulking about.'

Oxford also defined *shool* as to carry as a pretense, quoting John Clare in his 1820 *Rural Life*: 'Who takes delight to shool her knitting out at night.'

We must forgive Oxford for their 'of obscure origin' gaffe. Their Irish *siubhlach* does mean a traveller, a vagrant, but they might consider *siúbhlóir*, now spelled *siúlóir*, defined by the great lexicographer Fr Dinneen as 'a wayfarer, a *shuler*'.

✦ SILLY

This meaning foolish, lacking in common sense, empty-headed, is comparatively new, first appearing in literature in 1576 in Abraham Fleming's *Panoplie of Epistles*: 'Wee sillie soules, take the matter too too heauily.' In 1598 John Florio in his Italian–English dictionary has 'Zane, A sillie Iohn, a gull, a noddie'. Shakespeare had this meaning in *Love's Labour's Lost* in 1588: 'By vertue thou inforcest laughter, thy silly thought, my spleen.'

But the word had a variety of other meanings: deserving of compassion or sympathy; helpless, defenceless, especially of women and childen, a meaning now obsolete. But Shakespeare knew this *silly*. In *Two Gentlemen of Verona* he has 'Provided that you do no outrages / On silly women, or poor passengers.'

Silly was also used of people and animals to mean weak, feeble, frail. In 1633 George Herbert was a bit hard on himself in *Temple, Sighs & Grones*: 'Thou onely art / The mightie God, but I a sillie worm.' It also meant poor, rustic, unsophisticated, and was often used by poets in contrasting the unease of the courtier's life with the safety of the poor man's cottage. Campion wrote, 'Yet for all your pomp and train / Securer lives your silly swain.' And Shakespeare, echoing Campion's misgivings, also used *silly* in the poetic convention of the time relating to frail animals, especially sheep; in *Henry VI, Part 3*, he has the King say, 'Ah what a life were this! How sweet, how lovely! / Gives not the hawthorn bush a sweeter shade / To shepherds, looking on their silly sheep / Than does a rich-embroider'd canopy / To kings that fear their subjects' treachery . . .' This meaning hadn't changed when Burns wrote about the silly walls of the field mouse's house.

All these meanings of silly other than the usual one of foolish, lacking in sense, were known in south Wexford until fairly recently. I heard both old Phil Wall of Carne and Liz Jeffries of Kilmore speak of the silly kind of life the fishermen endured in the bad old days; silly sheep are mentioned in an old Kilmore carol. You won't find those meanings of the word there any more. The tide has gone out forever, alas, leaving so many old words from the Anglo-Norman baronies whitening on the sea shore, if I may steal Aidan Mathews' metaphor.

Silly is a later form of Middle English *sǽli*, happy, good, innocent (often in contemptuous sense) from Old English *(ge-) sǽlig*, from *sǽl*, happiness, related to Gothic *séls*, good.

✦ SKEEL

One of my tutors in Trinity College long ago was Gordon Quin, who was responsible for the Royal Irish Academy's *Dictionary of the Irish Language*. He told me many interesting stories about his schooldays in Dublin's High School, including how he was taught Latin by an eccentric master who used macaronics to teach the language; this master was considered completely daft by all the staff, but what could they do about him when the exam results showed that every single student, year in, year out, got between ninety-five and one hundred per cent in the Honours Leaving Certificate Paper? Gordon gave me some of his father's words: he had been a cooper in Guinness's brewery.

One of the words he remembered from the old man was *skeel*, a shallow, flat, wooden tub used in some testing process. I don't think *skeel* is used anywhere else in Ireland, and it has probably become obsolete at St James's Gate by now.

There were many types of skeels. In Durham a skeel was described as a peculiarly shaped wooden bucket, used in colliery villages to carry water for household use. The women carried them on their heads.

In the farms of Shakespeare's country the *butter skeel* was used for working butter in, by pressing it with the hand, as the *dough skeel* was used for kneading bread by hand. In the farms around Cheltenham race track, skeels were used for setting milk in, to stand for cream. Marshall's *Rural Economy* (1789) informs us that skeels were made in the tub fashion, with staves and hoops, and two stave handles, and that there were various sizes from 18 inches to 2 feet 6 inches in diameter, and from 5 to 7 inches deep. In both Gloucestershire and Northumberland, the skeel was also used to cool beer. In Orkney and Shetland, you drank your beer from a *skell*, a wooden drinking cup with a handle.

The word, now on the verge of becoming obsolete everywhere, is an old one. It came with the Vikings, whose language had *skjóla*, a pail, bucket.

✦ SKRIKE

Also as *screik* and *scraik* in Scots literature, this verb means to scream, shriek, screech; to cry out loudly. It was once found in many of the dialects of England from the Border to Yorkshire, Lancashire, Cheshire, Staffordshire, Warwickshire, Leicestershire and Gloucestershire. Hence the word *skriker*, or *The Skrikin' Woman*, one of the most feared apparitions of northern England, the counterpart of our banshee. She was feared particularly in Lancashire until recent times. James Bowker in his *Goblin Tales of Lancashire* (1882) says that 'it is supposed that only the relatives about to die, or the unfortunate doomed persons themselves, ever see the apparition'. *Notes and Queries*, First Series, ii. 1850, tells us that the *Skrikin' Woman* could change appearance: 'Many hundreds of people there are in these districts who place implicit credence in the reality of the appearance of a death sign locally termed *trash* or *skriker*. It has the appearance of a large black dog with shaggy hair and eyes as big as saucers. The second appellation is in allusion to the sound of its voice when heard by those parties who are unable to see the appearance itself.'

The verb also means to weep, cry. From a correspondent in Cheshire the EDD received this: 'I can tell by yur een as yo'n bin skrikin.'

The noun *skrike*, and its variant *scraik*, a scream, screech, a loud outcry, has been recorded in many places in Scotland and in the English dialects mentioned above; it was also recorded in Co. Antrim. Whether the Antrim *scraik* came from Scotland or is from the Irish *scréach*, a scream, screech, I'm not sure. *Scréach* is, in any event, a cognate word, and from the same ultimate source. Hence the compound *skrike-owl*, the screech owl, *Strix flammea*; and the phrases *no great skrikes*, not much to boast of, and *skrike of day*, dawn, cockcrow.

The word has been in literature since about 1300, when *Coer de Lion* was written. It contains the line 'The Crystene men gunne make a scryke: Anon they wunnen ovyr the dyke.' In around 1400 *The Destruction of Troy* has 'A wonderfull noyse Skremyt vp to the skrow with a skryke ffelle.' In 1548 Nicolas Udall's *The First tome of the Paraphrase of Erasmus upon the Newe Testament* (Mark xv. 37) has 'Jesus . . . gaue a great skryke, and therwith yelded vp the ghost.'

As to origin, it is probably of Scandinavian origin: cf. Norwegian *skrika* (strong verb), Danish *skrige*; from Old Norse *skrǽkja*, probably echoic.

✦ SLACK

This noun is found in places in Scotland and in Ulster, but I don't think it has penetrated south to Leinster, Munster or Connacht. The word was once widely used in northern England and as far south as Warwickshire and Sussex and it unexpectedly (because of its ultimate origin) turns up in Devon, Cornwall, Dorset and Somerset. It means a hollow, especially one in a hillside; a shallow dell, a glade. 'Till the hill that tuk the way. In a slak thame enbuschit thai,' sang Barbour in *The Bruce* in 1375, the earliest citation from Scots literature. The word lived on. In Buchan's *Ballads* of 1828, a fine repository of Scots, there is this couplet: 'Then she became a gay grey mare / And stood in youder slack.' Buchan's contemporary Walter Scott wrote in *Guy Mannering*, 'I see some folk coming through the slack yonder.'

I heard the word in Gweedore, Co. Donegal, from teacher and fiddle-master Proinsias Ó Maonaigh. Looking across from Hudie Beag's pub where we were having a pint, I told him I liked a new house, built on traditional lines, that had just been completed. He agreed, but said, 'The trouble with that house is that it's built in a slack, and a house built in a slack like that could be a wee bit damp, and even prone to flooding.'

Slack hasn't found its way into the placenames of Ulster, but England's Lakeland has many of them: Ashslack and Nettleslack are but two.

I mentioned my surprise at finding this word in England's south-west, because the word is of Norse origin, and the Vikings did not leave a rich legacy of words to Cornwall, Devon and Somerset. The Old Norse is *slakki*; the Danish is *slank*, a hollow or sinking in the ground.

✦ SLAMMICK

I had a hard time trying to persuade a Dun Laoghaire correspondent that the word *slammick*, which she heard from her uncle, is probably not a native word but one imported from our neighbouring island. This lady does not say where her uncle came from, but I would guess that he may have been a west Cork man. I have heard the word *slaimice* in the Irish of west Muskerry many's the time, and I know for a fact that the Tailor Buckley of Gúagán used it, not to his wife Ansty, you may be sure, but when he was describing local women. He said once that words were great travellers, and in that he was right. How the word came to his part of the world I have no idea.

Ó Dónaill's dictionary defines *slaimice* as an untidy person, a messy eater, a gobbler of food. But the English dialectal equivalent *slammock* and its many variants were recorded in many counties in England, and defined by the EDD as 'A dirty, untidy person, a slattern, a hulking, lazy, contemptible fellow, an awkward, waddling person or animal.' It also has *slammockin*, noun, 'a dirty, sloveny woman; an ungainly, burly person'. Hence the adjective *slammocky*, untidy, dirty, slatternly.

The EDD, the only one which gives the word, as far as I can see, does not offer an etymology. I can only guess that it's onomatopoeic and that it survived in so many places in England because it sounds good. Tantalisingly, the EDD says that *slammock* is found in Ireland, but it doesn't say where.

✦ SLEEK & SLAKE

The verb *sleek* was once common currency in the counties of Ulster. It means to lick; also to kiss in a slobbering manner.

W.H. Patterson defined *sleek* as 'lick' in his glossary of Antrim and Down words in 1880. Tom McCuaig, a journalist from Rathlin Island, off the Antrim coast, also had the word: 'The dog is supposed to be a watch dog, but the aul' fool would sleek a burglar instead of taking a lump out of him.' He also commented on a neighbour's boy who had done spectacularly badly in his Leaving Certificate exams: 'Well, what would you expect? Out sleekin' women all night instead of being at his books.'

A friend of mine, Rosemary Greene from near Stranorlar in Donegal, told a young lassie preparing to catch the bus to take her to school, 'Wash your face properly, and don't just sleek it with the towel.' The EDD has this from Lancashire: 'An' th' doctor's dog slakin its great long tong o'er mi face.' One of my valuable correspondents from Yorkshire, Tim Carmichael, wrote, 'I barely had time to sleek my face.'

This old word has a long pedigree. It comes from the Old Norse *sleikja*, to lick. You may compare the Irish *slíoc*, smooth.

There is another *sleek* or *slake*, to appease hunger, thirst, desire; also to extinguish a fire. Once very common in Ulster, I found this in *Crugh-a-Leaghan and Slieve Gallion, Lays and Legends of the North of Ireland* (1884): 'Feelin his drout in need of a sleakin'. Walker, in his *Bards Bon Accord*, published in Aberdeen in 1887, a good repository of Scots, has 'Ye'r baith hungry and dry, But ye'r nae vera far frae the slakin' o' t.'

To slake meaning to extinguish was first seen in print around 1566 in *Merie Tales of Skelton*: 'The fire being quickly slaked, Skelton cam in with his frendes.' Here in Ireland Lover has the word in *Handy Andy* in 1842: '"Only for two days," said Charlotte, trying to slake the flame she had raised.' The word may still survive in Irish dialects.

We also owe this *slake* to the Vikings. The Old Norse is *slokna*, to be extinguished, to expire, die.

✦ SMOOLYINS AND SMIGGERS

I once heard the word *smoolyins* from a woman who lived between Fintown and Glenties in Co. Donegal. The word, according to the *Concise Ulster Dictionary*, is found only in Ulster; it hadn't come to the notice of Joseph Wright's great EDD. It means both a small heap of stones, grains, etc. and a small amount of liquid.

It is Norse in origin. Compare the modern Norwegian *smule*, a fragment, and the Shetlandic and Orcadian verb *smuil*, to break into smithereens. There is also the Norn noun *smule*, a fragment, still used in Shetland by the older people.

The suffix in the Donegal word is, I think, the Irish diminutive *ín*, little.

The interesting little word *smigger* came my way from the Tyrone writer Benedict Kiely. A *smigger*, he informed me, was a man who was perhaps a little too fond of women for his own good. I'm not sure what exactly he meant by that, but I gathered that he meant a womaniser. I had heard the verb *smig*, to kiss and cuddle, in Donegal, and the verbal noun *smigging*, kissing and cuddling. Ben Kiely wondered if these words originated in the Irish noun *smig*, chin, but no. A far more likely origin is the Old Danish *smege*, to caress. Yet another little gem from the Viking word hoard we plundered.

✦ SMOOR & SMOORICH

Smoor is both a verb and noun, once found in general dialect use in Scotland, Ireland, and in England from the Borderland down to Leicestershire and Derbyshire, and in East Anglia as well.

It means, first of all to smother, suffocate, stifle; to oppress by heat; to drown.

'They wad hae seen my father's roof-tree fa' down and smoor me,' wrote Walter Scott in *St. Ronan* in 1824. In *Tam o' Shanter* (1790), Robert Burns has the couplet 'By this time he was cross the ford, / Whare in the snaw the chapman smoor'd.' The word travelled to both Wexford and Antrim. Poole has it in his glossary of words collected in Forth and Bargy in the late eighteenth century and W.H. Patterson recorded it in Antrim in the 1880s. Hence the Yorkshire *smoor'd i' the keld*, or *smooredikeld*, caul-smothered; suffocated in the amnion; used of new-born foals.

Smoor can also mean to conceal, hide, suppress. A woman praised in one of the Scots ballads collected by Jamieson in around 1800 was described as one 'wha's praise should not be smoor'd'. Edinburgh wasn't called Auld Reekie for nothing; an essayist of the early twentieth century, a man named Beatty, wrote of 'watching the reek from the Toun lums [chimneys] smooring the golden lift [sky]'.

To smoor also means to extinguish a light. This has reached Antrim and Donegal, where I've heard 'smoor the candle'.

The noun also means a stifling, smoky atmosphere in many places of Scotland. In Crockett's rattling good yarn *The Raiders*, published in 1894, he has 'our cave was full of the white smoor of gunpowder smoke'. Hence *smoor-thow*, 'a heavy snow, accompanied with a strong wind, which threatens to suffocate one', according to Jamieson's dictionary.

I have little doubt that *smoorich* is from the same source as *smoor*. It means to kiss, and as a noun, a good hearty smooch, a word which also may be related.

Hence *smooriken*, a stolen kiss. These words are found to this day in both Fife and Shetland, where Burgess in his *Sketches* wrote, 'Yon nicht I juist hed a smooriken at dir door, an sae left her.'

I think that the connection between both *smoor* and *smoorich* and the Old English *smorian*, to choke, suffocate, is pretty obvious.

✦ SNARL

This noun is, or was, found in Scotland and in Ulster. It means a snare or noose. Sometime in the 1960s I first heard the word in Donegal from a man who boasted of making his own snarls during the war years, when rabbits were fetching good prices, and hordes of buyers crossed over from the Six Counties, sent by butchers who just couldn't get enough of the creatures. A sheep-farmer's daughter from the back of Errigal mountain told me of helping her father during a winter blizzard as they searched for a prize ram: 'We found him trapped in a gully, but we were lucky to have a wee bit of a rope with us, and we made a snarl out of it to pull him out of the hole.'

The word probably came from Scotland. The EDD gives many examples of the use of the word, which editor Wright thought to be on the brink of extinction. One from Cumbria reads, 'When they see a trout lyin' they put this snarl or snirrup roond the gills an' click t'fish oot.'

The noun was also used of a tangle or knot in the hair. 'Curle not the snarles that dwell upon these brows,' said a character in *Everie Woman in Her Humour*, an anonymous play of 1609.

The verb *snarl* was, of course, once common as well. They snarled rabbits in Donegal; dirt snarled hair in Scotland.

The word is related to *snare* in both being from Old Norse *snara*, a noose, properly a hard-twisted cord.

✦ **SOULT**

Also found in the forms *sowlth* and *soulth*, all from the Irish *samhailt*, a spectre, an apparition. P.W. Joyce's *English As We Speak It In Ireland* defined the word as 'a formless, luminous apparition'. Yeats took a particular interest in stories relating to soults, and he wasn't the only one to do so. Their existence was firmly believed in in rural Ireland and during the dark nights, when perhaps only a candle, an oil lamp and firelight illuminated the country kitchen, the old storytellers used to frighten the life out of their listeners with rumours of soults which haunted the boreens. Many's the man waited until the clear light of day dispersed the apparitions before heading home from a rambling house or a wake house.

Yes, even the youngsters were believers. When in the full bloom of youth I asked a girl if I might see her home, she thanked me for the offer, but wondered would I myself be all right on my way home. She lived in a place a few miles from town, and, she said, the place was often haunted by soults of the redcoats who were killed there in '98. 'It isn't you I'm afraid of at all,' she said kindly, 'but *them.*'

Heroically I accompanied her and encountered no soults either going or coming other than her mother, who berated me for keeping her daughter out so late.

'The sowlth was seen upon the Black Lake last week, and few are fond of crossing the bridge since then,' wrote Gerald Griffin in *The Collegians*. James Joyce in *Ulysses* has 'Tare and ages what way would I be resting at all, he muttered thickly, and I tramping Dublin this while back, with my share of songs, and himself after me the like of a soulth . . .' The late Richard Wall pointed out in *An Irish Literary Dictionary and Glossary* that the quotation from *Ulysses* is one of a number of parodies in the work of the rendering of folk speech by Synge and others. The phrase 'share of songs' appears twice in *The Twisting of the Rope*, Lady Gregory's translation of Douglas Hyde's very bad play *Casadh an tSúgáin* (1901).

Samhailt, soult, etc. has another, figurative meaning, 'a man who has grown thin and wasted from illness', according to a mid-Tipperary correspondent of mine: 'He's gone in a soult.'

Rural electrification, someone said, killed off all the *soults*. However, New Ross youngsters who were taught local history might still feel a bit anxious about venturing on foot around the blood-soaked Lacken Hill at night, as I did nearly sixty years ago.

✦ SPARKS OF LOVE

A Kilkenny broadside ballad of the macaronic kind, dating from the beginning of the nineteenth century, tells of a young fellow getting into serious trouble for pleasuring a young lady without benefit of clergy, and being caught in the act by the law. His excuse was that *creasa an tSamhraidh*, the sparks of summer, led them both to stray from the paths of virtue.

A Pembrokeshire man of my acquaintance tells me that in his part of the world young scamps don't try to knock sparks out of young ones, rather did they try to knock a *vonk* out of them. *Fonk* was used in my young days in south Kilkenny by boyos up to no good in haysheds with *cailíní óga*. When I once asked a contemporary how he got on with a girl I saw him shifting from Mullinavat Hall one night, he replied, 'Begod you sir, I couldn't knock a fonk out of her.' *Vonk/fonk* means a spark, and is either from the Dutch *vonck*, a sparkle, or Middle High German *vanke*, a spark. The words are related to one sent to me by a woman who lives in Norfolk but who grew up with me on the banks of the lordly Barrow, *funk*, a spark. You might compare the German *Funke*, a spark.

Speaking of sparks of love, I once came on the word *selemnic* in a glossary by William Barnes, the Dorset dialect poet and scholar of the nineteenth century. He it was who first edited Poole's glossary of the dialect of Forth and Bargy, Co. Wexford, by the way, and hence my interest in him. Barnes knew his Greek mythology, and I think he may have coined the word *selemnic*, for 'in a state of oblivion'. I asked the late Bedell Stanford, the Trinity classicist, who was once my tutor there, about the word's existence, coined by Barnes or not; he led me to a delightful story told by Pausanias in the second century AD. It is set in the Northern Peloponnese:

Selemnos was a beautiful shepherd boy and Argyra was a lovely sea-nymph who fell in love with him. They say that she used to come from the sea to visit him and to sleep with him. But time took its toll on the mortal shepherd boy, and the sea-nymph would visit him no more. So he lost his Argyra, and he pined away and died of love. But Aphrodite, the goddess of Love, pitied him and gave him immortality by turning him into a river. Even then Selemnos pined for his lost love; so Aphrodite bestowed on him a priceless favour: Selemnos forgot his Argyra completely. And I've heard it said that the waters of

Selemnos are equally good for man or woman to cure the wounds of love, and if you wash in that river you'll forget the hurt and the pain that attend the breaking of the bonds of love. If there is truth in this, the water of Selemnos is worth more to mankind than all the money in the world.

Amen.

✦ SPRIGGAN

When a lady from Penrith in Cornwall wrote to me many years ago about *spriggan*, a word used in her lovely seaside village with its wonderful golden beach, I was able to tell her that I had the word from the Barony of Forth in Co. Wexford, but that it was known only to a few old people there.

A *spriggan* to my friend, schoolmaster Peter Byrne from Tacumshane, meant an unruly child; Peter, who had retired when I met him in the 1970s, heard it from old men, his neighbours. The word *spriggan* means an imp, a fairy, a goblin. He is a Cornish *cluthracán*, an unruly Irish sprite who does mischief in kitchens and dairies, turning milk sour and stealing butter. Here's what Hunt's *Popular Romances of the West of England* (1865) has to say about spriggans:

> They appear to be offshoots from the family of the Trolls of Sweden and Denmark. They are found only about the cairns, coits or cromlechs, burrows or detached stones, with which it is unlucky for mortals to meddle. They are a remarkably mischievous and thievish tribe. If ever a house is robbed, a child stolen, cattle carried away, or a building demolished, it is the work of the spriggans. Whatever commotion took place in earth, air, or water, it is the work of these spirits. It is usually considered that they are the ghosts of the giants of old; they have the charge of buried treasure.

The English *Folklore Journal*, vol. 4, 1886, recorded another piece of folklore regarding the spriggans of Cornwall. Sad to say, the poison of anti-Semitism had reached the Cornish tin mines: 'Knockers and Spriggans and all underground spirits . . . always heard working where there is tin, and who are said to be the ghosts of Jews who crucified Christ.' In 1891 J.H. Pearce's Cornish novel *Esther Pentreath* has 'She found Aichel watching her as closely as if he were some gruesome spriggan set to guard the old mill or herself.'

The Wexford word *spriggan* doesn't seem to have any meaning outside an unruly child. I suppose it came to south-east Wexford on board Cornish fishing vessels.

Oxford says that the word is probably of Cornish origin and leaves it at that.

✦ SQUINNY

Until I read a piece by the late Sir John Mortimer on certain practices in the English law business which he held to be in need of urgent reform, I had never come across the verb *squinny*; it means to solicit for business.

I used to meet Sir John and his wife Penny at *The Oldie* literary lunches in London, and he said that as a young barrister he had to squinny a lot, both on the courts and in certain wine-bars, restaurants and pubs frequented by the successful members of the Bar, as they did in the fictional Pomeroy's in the *Rumpole of the Bailey* stories. Am I right in thinking that in our legal slang the practice is called *devilling*?

In Joseph Shipley's *Dictionary of Early English* the word is defined as 'to look sidelong or invitingly, as a prostitute'. Strangely, the verb is not in Oxford, but the online Merriam-Webster has it, both as noun and verb. It is a dialectal variant of *squint*, and was used by many satirists in Tudor times, to describe the activities of both whores and lawyers, who made a practice of promenading outside churches and places of entertainment, looking for business.

Squint is an aphetic form of *asquint*, of uncertain origin, but corresponding to Dutch *schuinte*, slope, slant.

Squinny is dead now, outside of legal slang, I'm afraid. The London working girls no longer squinny; they leave that to the lawyers.

✦ STOT

The man from Ballyclare, Co. Antrim, was talking to me in the bar of a Dublin hotel after a rugby international about, would you believe it, the game of hurling. Ballyclare is not exactly a GAA stronghold. He had asked me where I was from, and I told him. 'Do you know Nicky Rackard?' was his next question. I said I did, and Bobby and Billy as well. He said that he had come south to see both Christy Ring and Nicky play a good few times. 'Man dear,' he said, 'it must have softened the dung in many's the full back to see that big man bearing down on him like a maddened stot, and letting fly.' I think Nicky would have been amused at your man's earthiness, and with the comparison with a stot, maddened or otherwise, because *stot*, a word fast disappearing from the lexicon of Ulster, means a bullock.

Stot is an old word and is found in Scotland and in northern England as well as in Ulster. 'Stotte, *bucculus*', glossed the *Catholicon Anglicum* in 1483. Burns had the word in *The Calf*: 'Forbid it, every heavenly Power, / You e'er should be a stot.'

You may still hear the word in Northumberland, although recent research shows that the word is not as much used there as it was. Brand's *Popular Antiquities* (1813) makes mention of a stot-plough being put to illegal use at Christmas. Speaking of the dress of the sword dancers, he says, 'Others, in the same kind of gay attire, draw about a plough, called a stot-plough [a plough drawn by a bullock], and when they receive a gift, make the exclamation Largess!; but if not requited at any house for their appearance, they draw their plough through the pavement and raise the ground of the front in furrows.'

The origin of *stot* is the Old Norse *stútr*, a bull. The suggested derivation, from Old English *stott*, a poor horse, seems very unlikely.

✦ STROAN, STRONE

Just as often written *Strone*, the word is found in Ireland, Scotland, Northumberland and Cumbria. I remember a mother writing to me once from the Glens of Antrim telling me that her little girl was told off by her teacher for asking permission to go out to stroan. It was, the lady said, a vulgar word that young ladies should not use. God help her head.

You'll have guessed that *stroan/strone* means to make water. Rab Burns tells us in his poem *Twa Dogs* that he and they 'stroan't on stanes and hillocks' together. Another worthy Scots writer, John Service, in *Notandums*, published in 1890, asks, 'Do ye no ken that on Halloween the deil stroans on the haws?' I wonder what the gentleman described in the Perthshire *Chronicles of the Atholl and Tullibardine Families*, written in 1735 and published in 1908, was up to: 'He stron'd over Mrs Wat's hand into a basone that was too yeards off.' Not much wrong with his stroop (q.v.) in any case.

The verb *stroan* also means to milk into, to milk laboriously; and as a noun *stroan* means the stream of milk drawn from a cow at one pull; a very small quantity of milk. The *Ballymena Observer* of 1892 noted this.

And the noun can also mean simply a stream, or as a Yorkshire correspondent put it, 'a runlet of water but not having much force'.

The DSL says that the word is of obscure origin. Not a bit of it. The origin of the word is the Scottish Gaelic and Irish *sruth*, a stream; diminutive *sruthán*. That invasive *t* is common in words derived from Irish. Compare another Ulster word for making water, *strool*. Its Irish origin is *srúill*, a stream.

✦ STROKE

My father had this word from his native west Cork. He was surprised to find, he told me, that his Wexford neighbours among whom he spent most of his adult life didn't know what he meant when he praised a youngster for eating up his dinner, by telling him that he had a great stroke. By stroke he meant appetite. I am told that the word used to be found in north Tipperary (my father heard it in the Commons, near Thurles), in Kilkenny and in west Waterford once, but that it is now, if not obsolete, quite close to it.

It first appears in literature in 1669 in a travel book by William Dampier called *A New Voyage Around the World*. He wrote, 'Neither can any man be entertained as a soldier, that has not a greater stroke than ordinary at eating.' Jonathan Swift had the word as well. In *A Complete Collection of Genteel and Ingenious Conversation*, better known as *Polite Conversation*, he wrote, 'Lady: God bless you, Colonel, you have a good stroke with you.' After Swift, not a trace of the word is to be found in English literature. It doesn't seem to have been known in any of the dialects of England or Scotland: the EDD only records it once, from Northumberland: 'The bairns hes a gran' stroke,' meaning the child has a good appetite.

Oxford doesn't record this meaning and its etymology is obscure. The great dictionary does have *stroke* meaning a stroking movement of the hand, which, it has been suggested to me, does fit the bill as it conjures up the picture of a hungry person busily mixing his food in his bowl or trencher. If this makes sense the word may be connected with Old English *strácian*, corresponding to Middle Low German, and Middle Dutch *strêken*, modern Dutch *streeken*, Old High German *streihhôn*, Middle High German and modern German *streichen*.

This, when I heard it from an esteemed German lexicographer, seemed far-fetched to me. It still does.

✦ STROOP

I heard this word for the first time from a Travelling woman, Annie Wall, who used to visit me at my house in Wicklow many years ago asking me to fill her kettle for her. I used to oblige her, and to boil the water for her after we had a *taoscán* of Jameson together. I got many words from her, most from her cant, Sheldru, and I used to forward them to the expert on that language, former schoolmaster Paddy Greene, of Ballinalee, who died a few years ago aged 106. He was glad I used to give Annie the drop of whiskey. She was old for a Travelling woman, and she lived alone. He attributed his own long life to drinking a glass of the stuff every night since he was a boy, mixed with milk, not water, mind you.

This word *stroop* is not a word from the Travellers' secret language, but is found in Ulster, in Scotland, and in Northumberland and East Anglia. It means, in all these places, the gullet or windpipe, and the spout of a kettle. Annie, when the Jameson had loosened her tongue a little, confided that *stroop* was also used of the penis.

All the dialect glossary compilers in Ulster recorded the word; I've been sent it as well by correspondents from Sligo, Westmeath, Louth, north Tipperary and Clare. W.G. Lyttle the Co. Down writer has 'He put the stroup of the taypot in his mooth,' in his *The Adventures of Paddy McQuillan*, no date, but probably a little ante 1900.

In East Anglia they have a verb *to stroop*, to bawl out or cry aloud; and *stroop* is used figuratively for a mischievous child: 'You little stroop!' Where then did Annie Wall's word come from? The Middle English is *stroup, strowpe*, found in *Promptorium Parvulorum Sive Clericorum*, the Latin–English glossary of *c.* 1440. The Old Norse was *strúpe*, throat.

✦ STUCKER

I have heard this word so often over the years in Co. Donegal that I am amazed that Caroline Macafee hasn't recorded it in her excellent *A Concise Ulster Dictionary*. Well, nobody sent it to her, so let's not blame her; *sceinneann gráinne ón scilligeadh*, as they say, or used to say in the Muskerry dialect of West Cork: a grain may shoot or escape from the milling.

I have always heard the word in public houses at sheep fairs, used by men who resented interlopers who insinuated themselves into company without being asked, with the all-too-obvious purpose of cadging free drink. Michael Traynor records the word, spelled *stuccour*, in his 1953 *The English Dialect of Donegal*. As a verb, he defines it as 'to follow a person in the expectation of getting something'. As a noun it means, he says, 'a person who, though uninvited, goes to a place in expectation of something'. It also means 'a dog that sits watching a person at meals in expectation of getting food'.

Traynor's book is remarkable in that it was finished in extraordinary circumstances. He relied heavily on the collection of Henry Chichester Hart, a famous Trinity College-trained naturalist and botanist, who went with Admiral Markham to the North Pole in 1875 and with Hull and Kitchener's geological survey to Sinai and South Palestine in 1885. He became a lecturer in Natural Science in Queen's College Galway in 1885–6. Not content with publishing works on the natural sciences, he found time to edit some of Shakespeare's plays for the Arden series, and *Notes on Ulster Dialect, chiefly Donegal*, which was published by the Philological Society in 1899.

Michael Traynor emigrated to Tasmania, and had to finish his book and read its proofs there. Professor J.J. Hogan, one of UCD's most scholarly presidents, found him a publisher in the Royal Irish Academy. He rightly derived our word from the Irish *stocaire*, an interloper, a sponger.

✦ STUGUE

This is an Irish English form of *stua*, and as far as I know seems to have been known only in the south-east, in the neighbouring counties of Carlow and Wexford.

Stua is an arch, an arc, a bow, a loop.

Patrick Kennedy's works, both his novels and his anonymous contributions to the *Dublin University Magazine* during a great part of the nineteenth century, are valuable repositories of words since disappeared from the speech of the people. I found *stugue* twice in his writings, in *Evenings in the Duffrey* and in *The Banks of the Boro*. In the former he has '. . . to beg some good Christian to give him a drink of could wather, or he'd stugue up'. In the latter book he has 'He began to think that his inside would all be gone, and that he'd fall in a stugue on one of the big diamond-shaped flags of the floor.'

I have made extensive inquiries about this word in my native county in recent times, but friends and family and my host of schoolteacher informants have not heard the word in years. Two men, one from

Campile, the other from Horeswood, both places within a few miles of one another, did remember the word, but said that it was no longer used.

It was used in a hurling context. 'He was no softie, I can tell you. He would take so much blackguardin' from an opponent, and then, all of a sudden he would make a stugue of him with the hurl.' The other example was almost identical: 'He made a stugue of your man with the hurl, and if any mortal deserved it, he did.'

Fr Dinneen in his *Irish-English Dictionary* has the same idea in the phrase '*Do ghním stuagh de*,' glossed as 'I double him up with a blow.'

Stuadh is the form in Scottish Gaelic, and it means, as it does in Irish, a bow, arch, indeed anything curved or bow-shaped, such as a wave, a rainbow, or, I suppose, the shape of a man who has just got a knee where it hurts.

✦ STYGIAN

I was as surprised as my friend Peter Byrne was to hear of the existence of this word in south Wexford. Peter was a schoolteacher of the old school, wise, well-read, and respected; he lived in Tacumshane in the Barony of Forth. One miserable, gloomy November morning, with black rainclouds rolling threateningly in from the sea, a neighbour greeted Peter as he was making his way to his schoolhouse. 'What ails the weather at all, Master,' said the man. 'Such awful weather. Wet, miserable, cold: bloody stygian.'

Now Peter was keenly interested in the words used around his village, which was in the heart of the Anglo-Norman Barony of Forth, but this adjective he used was not a word from the old dialect of English spoken there until the beginning of the nineteenth century, but a book word, as he termed it: a word that had its origin in Greek mythology. Peter had come to the conclusion that it was a word bequeathed by some hedge schoolmaster of the nineteenth century which had miraculously been passed on.

South Wexford had some famous hedge schools, or Latin schools as they came to be known after the hedge schools gave way to the National Schools after 1831. Some of the better hedge schoolmasters started up these Latin schools to prepare pupils for entrance to Catholic seminaries, and to prepare Protestant pupils for the Trinity College entrance examination. It has been attested to that Tommy Maher's school at Goff's Bridge produced farmers who could read and speak

Latin fluently; there was another one near Tacumshane and another at Carne that I know of. How else could this word, which means black as the river Styx; dark or gloomy as the region of the Styx, have entered the vernacular?

Master Byrne's friend's adjective was used in 1599 by John Marston in *Antonio's Revenge*: 'Will I not turn a glorious bridal morn / Unto a Stygian night?' Milton's *Comus* (1634) has 'Mysterious Dame, That ne're art call'd, but when the Dragon womb / Of Stygian darkness spets her thickest gloom.'

The stories about the best of those old hedge schools were not, as W.B. Stanford of Trinity, once, for his sins, my tutor there, pointed out in his study *Ireland and the Classical Tradition*, romantic nonsense. They taught Burke and Goldsmith; they taught Sylvester O'Halloran, pioneer ophthalmic surgeon, who is credited with being the *fons et origo* of the idea that a Royal College of Surgeons be set up in Dublin; they were non-sectarian and they tolerated no class distinction, and their standards were so high that, as Stanford pointed out, their ordinary pupils could speak Latin perfectly. He wrote of one pupil, a Waterford city shopkeeper, who had an advertisement in his window about the quality of his eggs—in Latin. And an impoverished soul from my father's district in West Cork wrote a charming love song in Irish for his girl from Glenflesk, in which he used a striking image from Lucan's *Pharsalia*.

I suggested to Stanford that Trinity should erect a plaque in the Library to the memory of those old teachers who gave Ireland so much and he agreed. Alas, he died before he could do anything about it.

And I think it's time that Dublin's College of Surgeons remembered Sylvester O'Halloran, a nephew of the poet Seán Clárach Mac Dónaill, who paid for his medical training abroad.

✦ SUB ROSA

This Latin phrase means 'under the rose', privately, in secret, in strict confidence. So early modern Dutch, *onder de roose*, Middle Low German *under der rosen*, German *unter der Rose*. It entered English in the middle of the seventeenth century, but was in use all over Europe since before the time of Christ.

There was a lovely Greek myth which was probably its origin. According to this story Harpocrates, afterwards the Greek god of silence, went out for a ramble one day. What did he see but a son of Cupid making passionate love to the goddess Venus. She saw him, and entreated him to keep his mouth shut about what he had seen. He swore he wouldn't utter a word, and in thanks Venus created a lovely new flower, the rose, and gave it to him as a token of appreciation of his silence.

And so it came to pass that in the diplomatic councils of Europe, for more than a thousand years, men sat under a rose carved on the ceilings of halls and chambers, *sub rosa*, a reminder that their discussions were secret. The rose became a symbol of secrecy, and in medieval times was carved on the confessionals in churches.

I hate to spoil a lovely story, but the Greeks got the idea for their legend of Harpocrates' rose from a picture of the baby Egyptian god of silence, Horus, sitting under a lotus; he had a rose in his hand and he was sucking a finger, which he had probably pricked with the rose.

✦ SURFEIT

This is one of Lutton's words from the Montiaghs, a boggy district on the shores of Lough Neagh. He defines it as 'an illness, generally pleurisy, occasioned by excessive fatigue. A chill after profuse perspiration.' The *Concise Ulster Dictionary* hasn't recorded the word; it may well be obsolete by now.

The EDD recorded it in a combination *surfeit of cold*, a severe cold, in Scotland, Northumberland, Durham, Cumberland, Yorkshire, Lancashire and Cheshire. A Cumbrian correspondent to the EDD defined the combination as 'A cold that is difficult to get rid of; a cold that shows itself by outward signs, as cracked lips &.'

There is also the past participial adjective *surfeited*, recorded in south Cheshire, and meaning 'unwell'.

Oxford has a particularised sense of surfeit, 'The morbid condition caused by excessive eating or drinking; sickness or derangement of the system arising from intemperance; also applied more widely to fevers or fits arising from other causes.'

All surfeits are from Old French *sorfait*, *surfait*, *surfet*, excess, surplus, from popular unattested Latin *superfactum*, from unattested *superficere* (cf. late Latin *superficiens* excessive, Old French *sorfaisant* intemperate, immoderate), from *super-* + *facere* to do, act.

✦ SUTLERY

Marjory Blake e-mailed me about a word which she found in an American thriller she had been reading. This book is set in the seamier sections of the lower east side of Manhattan, and two detectives who are chasing a murderer notice a sign which reads 'Clothing and Sutlery'. They have no idea what *sutlery* means, and neither does Marjory.

As far as I can see, the word, and the noun it comes from, *sutler*, have now almost disappeared from English. Oxford defines *sutler* as 'One who follows an army or lives in a garrison town and sells provisions to the soldiers'. It is an old word and came into English in the time of the first Elizabeth. In an ordnance of 1590 we find 'The Provost Mareschal and Sergeant Maior of euery garrison shal keepe a perfect rolle of all such English victuallers (called in dutch Sutlers) petimarchants, and other loose persons of the English nation.' Shakespeare knew the word. In *Henry V*, Act II, Scene I, he has 'I shall sutler be unto the camp, and profits shall accrue.'

Gradually the word came to mean simply one who furnishes provisions, and not necessarily to the army. In 1793 the Earl Dundonald's *Description of the Estate of Culross* wrote about 'Many of the Scots Owners of Collieries acting as Sutlers, and supplying their workmen with Oatmeal.' Long before that *sutler* had become underground slang. The 1790 *Dictionary of the Canting Crew* has 'Sutler, he that Pockets up [steals] Gloves, Knives, Handkerchiefs, Snuff and Tobacco-boxes, and all the lesser Moveables.'

The Tudors knew that the word came from early modern Dutch *soeteler* (modern Dutch *zoetelaar*), small vendor, petty tradesman, victualler, soldier's servant, drudge, sutler in an army, which had cognates in Middle Low German *sut(t)eler*, *sudeler*, from *soetelen*, to befoul, to perform mean duties, follow a mean or low occupation or trade. Compare Low German *suddeln* and early modern German *sudeln*, to sully.

The Manhattan word, noted, let it be said, by the thriller writer Peter de Jonge, was first seen in print in a 1606 comedy by Marston called *Parasitaster, or the Fawne*: 'Has my sutlery, tapstry, laundrie, made mee be tane upp at the Court?'

Why did this good and useful word fall from grace, I wonder?

✦ SWANK

I could scarcely believe it when I read in a reliable American academic journal that both *swank* and *swanky* were on the verge of being classed as 'obsolete' by the dictionary editors preparing their next editions. I rang a friend who works for the great Webster; he confirmed that *swank* and the adjective *swanky* were being replaced in the people's speech by *posh*, and that his own people had made no decision on the demotion of *swank* just yet.

It would, I feel, be a great pity to lose the word, which was first seen in print, as a noun, in Baker's Northamptonshire glossary of 1844: 'Swank: An ostentatious air, an affectation of stateliness in the walk. What a swank he cuts.' I am tempted to deduce from that that the word is ultimately related to Old High German and Middle High German *swanc*, a swinging motion, and to Middle High German *swanken*, modern German *schwanken*, to sway or totter. The verb was first seen in print in a Bedfordshire dialect dictionary of 1809, which gives 'Swangk: to strut'.

Swank, noun is defined by Oxford as ostentatious or pretentious behaviour or talk; swagger, pretence. In a 1913 letter, Vita Sackville-West wrote, '[He is] a swank, more swank than you could ever dream of.' In R. Crompton's *William Again* (1923) her millions of schoolboy readers saw 'He was a pariah, outside the pale, one of the "swanks" who lived in big houses and talked soft.'

The adjectives *swank* and *swanky* can be traced to Middle Low German *swank* and Middle Dutch *swanc*, and originally meant supple, active, agile. This is what Burns had in mind in describing his Auld Mare in 1776.

To Dunbar in 1508, Ramsay in 1715 and Jane Elliot in 1756 *swanky* meant strapping, smart, active. All three used the word of young men, Elliot as a noun. Mourning the Scots dead she wrote in her great farewell to the young soldiers,

E'en in the gloaming nae swankies are roaming,
About stacks with the lasses at bogle to play:
But ilk maid sits drearie, lamenting her dearie—
The Flowers of the Forest are a' wede away.

Has the growing dislike of dialect (*swank* is a dialect and not a slang word), helped to put it in such a precarious position in America? I remember Ted Hughes saying, 'Whatever other speech you grow into, presumably your dialect stays alive in a sort of inner freedom . . . it's your childhood self there inside the dialect and that is possibly your real self or the core of it . . . Without it I doubt if I would ever have written verse.'

That is a good reason to cherish dialect; the educational establishment should remember it.

| T ～

✦ TAAM & GILFER

Two old acquaintances of mine, both Irish Travellers, gave me an old word which can be traced to the Vikings. Annie Wall, who travelled around Co. Wicklow in a horse-drawn caravan, was telling me one day that she never had a bit of trouble bringing up her daughter, who, incidentally, was one of the most beautiful women I have ever laid eyes on. But, she said, among Travellers, where chastity in women is considered all-important, 'you'd want to keep the young wans that's growin' up nowadays on the *taam*, I'm telling you.' Another Wexford Traveller, Miley Connors, a noted horse dealer in his day, also gave me the word. Its origin is the Old Norse *taumr*, a bridle. How, you might ask, did it come to be in the Travellers' lingo? Your guess is as good as mine.

As far as I can judge—and I have been in touch with many Traveller acquaintances—the word is not used any more. Last year in St Stephen's ancient cemetery in New Ross, I was one who attended the annual pattern at which graves are cleaned up. There were hundreds of Travellers there, and I got a chance to enquire about the health of their words. Only one, a woman named Brigid Cash, remembered *taam*. 'The only place you'll find it now, boss,' she said to me, 'is down there,' pointing to the rows of Travelling people's graves.

Thomas Greene, another Traveller I met on that occasion, asked me if I had ever heard the word *gilfer* in my travels. A gilfer, he said, is a foul-mouthed woman, given to destroying people's characters. Yes, I told him, I had heard the word in the south of the county Wexford, from an old woman who lived close to where my mother taught school.

The word is also found in various places in England, from the border country to Lancashire and East Anglia. This good word is also from the Norse word hoard. Their *gylfra* means, according to the great Icelandic scholar Vigfusson, an ogre, a she-wolf.

✦ TALLAMACKA

Every so often letters are sent to me from old people who live between the bogs around Thurles and the banks of the lovely Suir, asking where the word *tallamacka*, also spelled *tallymacka* by some, comes from. I was first sent the word by an old man from Thurles direction back in 1997 and I remember him writing that the word was used by his mother, who, as mothers tended to do when he was young, threatened to give him tallamacka if she caught him smoking. Try as I might, I couldn't find even a hint as to the strange word's origin in any of the dialect dictionaries; all that happened when I asked help from the readers of my *Irish Times* column was that readers from south Tipp were prompted to write telling me that they had heard the word used by old-timers; one woman told me that her father used the word to describe the intensity of the exchanges between Mickey Byrne and Christy Ring in the 1950s: 'they ruz tallymaka'.

I tried another journal I wrote for, and still write for, Richard Ingrams' *The Oldie*. The word was remembered if not used in Cornwall; a Newquay woman said that her mother used to threaten to raise tallamacka if she and her brothers misbehaved while she was out.

And then came a letter from B.H. Sharp, a clergyman of Cymbach, near Aerdare in Wales.

> Would tallamacka have a religious connection? [he asked] St Telemachos (his Greek name; he is Almachius in Roman Catholic calendars) was martyred in Rome about 400 AD. He was a monk from the East who sought to put an end to gladiatorial contests. One day he ran into the arena to separate the contestants. There was a riot, and poor Telemachos was killed in the affray. Nobody is sure who killed him. Perhaps it was the mob who didn't want their fun ruined. Perhaps it was the gladiators on the orders of the city prefect, who thought such unruly scenes bad for business. Anyway, it is said that as a result of the affray the emperor Honorius abolished such barbarous shows. Did the saint give his name to the uproar?

What do you think?

✦ TATTER

This is a verb, noun and adjective, once used extensively in Ireland, Scotland, and, in England, in Lancashire, Yorkshire, Northumberland,

Northamptonshire, Lincolnshire, Somerset and Kent. First of all the word means to chatter, to tattle. A Somerset correspondent sent this to the EDD: 'Come now, there's too much tatterin' by half, let's have less noise and more work,' and 'Her's a tatterin kind of a thing; better fit her'd look arter her chillern and keep 'em to school, and tidy like.'

The verb also means to scold, chide; to be furious or cross. Samuel Lover has 'I never seen him in such a tattherin rage,' in *Handy Andy* (1840). Hence the nouns *tatter-can*, which can mean both a kicking cow and a termagant; *tatterer* and *tatters*, a scold. *Tatter*, noun, is a rage, a long-continued condition of grumbling discontent. Hence *tattery*, adjective, cross, peevish, ill-natured, ill-tempered.

In 1579, Samuel Twyne in his translation *Phisicke Against Fortune*, has 'His two wiues, most tatter and testie olde women,' and from the same book we come across 'When a man maketh hym selfe seruiceable and subiect to a tatter olde foole ...'

In 1736 John Lewis's *Isle of Thanet in Kent Glossary*, republished by the English Dialect Society in 1874, gave us 'Tatter, ragged, cross, peevish: 'He is a very tatter man'. And in 1887 *The Kentish Glossary* has 'The old 'ooman's middlin' tatter today, I can tell ye.'

This tatter doesn't seem to have reached Ulster; at least the CUD hasn't recorded it. Oxford has no idea where it originated, and I can't even hazard a guess.

✦ TATTHERATION

This is a mild expletive like *botheration* and *tarnation*, used to express annoyance or frustration. It may be related to *tatter* (q.v.), one meaning of which is 'a rage; a long-continued condition of grumbling discontent'; the trouble with *tatter* is that nobody knows its origin.

I have never heard *tattheration* myself anywhere in Ireland, its only home, according to the EDD. 'It is used', it says, 'to express annoyance in the phrase "tattheration to some one or something."'

It cites two Irish writers who lived far apart. Tyrone's William Carleton had this in his *Traits and Stories*: '"Tattheration to me," says the big Longford fellow.' The EDD's second citation is from Wexfordman Patrick Kennedy's *Fireside Stories*, published in 1870: 'Oh, tattheration to that thief of a gardener.'

I wonder is this innocuous curse still in use anywhere? I doubt it, somehow.

✦ TAUGH

When I first came to Vienna I was introduced to one of their famous *Heurige*, those traditional restaurants which serve wholesome Austrian food at prices that would make Irish restaurant owners hang their heads in shame, and which sell only the restaurant's own wine. Some of them date to the reign of Maria Theresa; she granted farmers the privilege of selling their wine in town during two specified weeks in the year. Nowadays these places are open all year round.

I was amazed to find on their menus a starter which they call *Bratenfett*, the fat which drips off a roast. Nobody seems to care about the menace of cholesterol, just as nobody cared about it during the war in Ireland, when people rendered *dripping* from roasted or fried meat, and queued up at the butcher's to buy *lard*, the rendered fat from a pig. In Austria, as in Ireland, the dripping, or Bratenfett, is spread on bread.

I was telling this to Scottish friends, and one of them told me that she heard her grandmother speak of *taugh*, or *tauch*. It was a delicacy of the poorer people, and it contained tiny specks of meat unavoidably mixed in during the slaughtering of the cattle or sheep—an important source of protein, especially to growing children in those hard times. John Jamieson's great nineteenth-century dictionary of Scots has *tauch*, and says that this is 'properly the name used by butchers before it is melted; after this operation it is given the name of *tallow*'.

Taugh or *tauch*, obsolete everywhere in Scotland now, is from the Danish *talg*, tallow, according to Larsen's *Dansk-Norsk-Engelsk Ordbog*. By the way, *dripping*, properly the fat that exudes from meat while it is being roasted or fried, is from Old English *dryppan*, from *dropa*, drop. And *lard* is, via French, from Latin *laridum*, bacon fat.

So, if ever you go to Vienna, do visit a *Heuriger* and sample the *Bratenfett*, to which they add wild spices to give it a delicious aroma and taste, and to blazes with cholesterol for that night.

✦ TAUPIE

Holly Henderson from Sandycove, who is of Co. Antrim stock, sent me the word *tawpie*, a foolish, giddy, slovenly, idle girl. W.H. Patterson has it in his Antrim and Down glossary, which he sent for inclusion in Joseph Wright's great *English Dialect Dictionary*; and it is also in Simmons's South Donegal glossary of 1890.

A dialect word which has been found in Scots literature this. In *St Ronan*, Sir Walter Scott has 'She formally rebuked Eppie for an idle taupie.' The word was also quite common in the northern counties of England, where it was also used of a male blockhead. The word is of Scandinavian origin. Compare the Swedish *tåp*, a simpleton.

The latest reports from linguistic surveys tell me that the word has had its day everywhere. I hope these pessimistic surveys are wrong.

✦ TEACH

It must have been around 1970 when I first set foot in The Lobster Pot, in Carne, my favourite Co. Wexford hostelry. I had a pint with old Phil Wall there; he was over ninety at the time. Two pints were set down on the counter, but Phil's drink was beyond his reach. 'Teach me that pint, like a good man,' he said to me. He must have seen that I didn't quite understand him, so he explained. He wanted me to reach across and hand it to him.

To my surprise I found this meaning of *teach* in Poole's glossary of the Dialect of Forth and Bargy, collected towards the end of the eighteenth century, and edited twice since. The EDD quotes the word from Poole, and gives the meaning 'to hand or give'. This *teach* is from the Old English *taecan*, in the sense 'to show something to somebody'.

In a radio broadcast not long after my meeting with Phil Wall I mentioned that if I came back to Carne in thirty years' time I wouldn't find the word in the place. Well, I did return, and asked people from twenty to eighty if they knew what 'teach me that thing over there' meant, and they had no idea what I was talking about. A link with Anglo-Saxon English is dead and gone, I'm sorry to say.

✦ TETTER

Many years ago I heard this word from a Travelling woman of Wexford stock. It was her word for ringworm. She used the word only in the plural, *tetters*. The EDD makes no mention of Ireland in its entry relating to it, and I wrongly thought that it was confined to Travellers. In this I was wrong; when I wrote a note about it I got many letters from south Tipperary and from Limerick telling me so.

In England the word is found in the dialectal English of Yorkshire, Lancashire, Chester, East Anglia, Gloucestershire, Hampshire and Cornwall. In many places the word also means a small pimple or pustule; any small boil; the 'spots' which are the bane of many teenagers' lives.

Cornwall had a cure for tetters, or so it was claimed in a delightful book, Hunt's *Popular Romances of the West of England*, published in 1865 and reprinted many times since. It is still possible to pick up copies of it in second-hand bookshops; I bought mine for ten bob in a bookshop in Truro six years ago. The 'cure' I mention is in the form of a charm, and here it is: 'Tetter, tetter, thou hast nine brothers. God bless the flesh and preserve the bone. Perish thou, tetter and be gone. In the name of the Father and of the Son and of the Holy Ghost. Tetter, tetter, thou hast eight brothers. God bless the flesh etc. Thus the verses are continued until tetter, having no brother, is imperatively ordered to begone.'

My schoolteacher friends tell me that the word is dying out in Tipperary and Limerick. A pity this. It is a very old word, coming down to us from Anglo-Saxon times. The Old English is *teter*, ringworm.

✦ THIEVELESS

This useful word is found only in Scotland and in Ulster, *thaveless* being the general Ulster spelling. It means, first of all, listless, wanting in energy, aimless, ineffectual. 'A thieveless excuse, one that is not satisfactory' is the Scots lexicographer John Jamieson's gloss. Fergusson the Perthshire writer wrote in *The Village Poet* (1897), 'He had a broken-down look and appeared listless, or, as he himself expressed it, *rale thieveless*.' Hugh McDiarmid has this in *The Drunk Man Looks at the Thistle* (1926): 'You left the like in Embro' in a scunner To booze wi' thieveless cronies sic as me.'

A correspondent sent Oxford this from Ulster: 'A thaveless body; a thaveless bit of work; I was thaveless at her—meaning I regarded her as acting or talking foolishly.'

The dictionaries give another meaning: cold, bleak. Also used figuratively to mean shy, reserved; cold, frigid in manner, forbidding. In *The Brigs of Ayr* (1787) Burns has 'Wi' thieveless sneer to see his modish mien'. Jamieson's dictionary has 'to look thieveless to one—to give one a cold reception'.

From Renfrewshire the EDD has this: '*It's a thieveless morning* is a phrase used by old people. *Thieveless* is applied to weather in a sort of inter-mediate or uncertain state. Thus a thieveless day is one neither properly good nor bad. Used also to denote frigidity or insipidity of manner.'

The DSL thinks that *thieveless* is a variant of *thewless*, giving the word the following pedigree: Old Scots *thewless*, immoral, from 1513; Middle

English *theweles*, id.; Old English *þéaw*, a characteristic, an attribute. Modern English has *thewless*, from *thew*, bodily strength + *less*.

Thieveless is still alive and well in parts of Scotland. The *Concise Ulster Dictionary* has recorded it as well, but I gather that like many another good word it is not thriving among the younger generation.

✦ THIG

To thig in Scotland meant to beg or borrow. I had thought it long dead, but friends from Glasgow tell me that it can still be heard there; as for the rest of Scotland it hasn't been heard in years, the surveys say.

Young lads going to a match in Glasgow thig a few pounds from their mithers. In the old days *to thig* also meant so solicit gifts on special occasions, such as setting up house and the like. 'Maun gang thigging and sorning about on their acquaintances,' wrote Scott in *Rob Roy* in 1817. The Highlanders were fond of thigging, so Alexander Hislop tells us in *The Book of Scottish Anecdote* (1874): 'At a young Highlander's first setting up for himself . . . he goes about among his near relations and friends; from one he begs a cow, from another a sheep . . . till he has procured for himself a tolerable stock. This they call thigging.'

They had an interesting custom in Shetland, which was known as *thigging nine mothers' meat*. John Spence in his important work *Shetland Folk Lore* (1899) has this: 'The mother is further instructed to thig the nine mothers' meat for the bairn's restoration, i.e. nine mothers whose first born were sons are each solicited for an offering of three articles of food, to be used during the convalescence of the patient who has been thus snatched from the power of the trows.'

Hence *thigging*, begging, borrowing; *thigger* and *thighster*, a beggar. Lorimer in *Leaves from the Buik of the West Kirke* (1885) refers to 'Scotch penal enactments against sturdy beggars, thiggers, sorneys, and such like'.

The word *thig* reached England's North Country, but the *Concise Ulster Dictionary* hasn't recorded it. It was in Middle English. *The Destruction of Troy* has it *c.* 1400: 'And now me bus, as a beggar, my bred for to þigge At doris vpan dayes, þat dares me full sore.' The word is Germanic in origin. Compare the Old English *þicgan*, to take, receive, accept, and the Danish *tigge*, to beg.

✦ THRONG

When I was living in Co. Wicklow a man knocked at my door and asked me if I had any odd jobs for him to do. He had an Ulster accent, an

Antrim one, I guessed. He was interested in fixing anything on the roof that needed fixing, he said; he had noticed that one of the drain-pipes was loose. I wasn't interested, but I did ask him if he would do a bit of gardening for me at a fixed price. He looked around, and told me that this was a big job and that he was too *throng* to attempt it; the roof job wouldn't take long. He went his way.

I hadn't heard the word *throng* in a long while but I had come across it in books. It's in Bernard Share's *Slanguage* and is in *The Concise Ulster Dictionary*. I'm told that it is rarely heard in Ulster any more.

Used of a place it means crowded, very busy; of a person, busy, fully occupied. The Donegalman Seumus MacManus in his engaging story *The Rocky Road to Dublin* (1938) has this: 'Because Billy had no help foothering with his farm and wrestling with cattle, he had been too throng ever to go courting.' Another Ulster writer, Lynn Doyle from the east of the province, has this in his charming *Ballygullion* (1908): 'And the market day, being a throng day for the polis in Ballygullion, it was generally Billy's throng day outside av it, delivering a wee keg here and there.'

It would seem from the evidence of literature that *throng* was once used in the south and west as well as in Ulster, but if it still exists there I'm not aware of it. Somerville and Ross, the creators of the Irish R.M., have 'We were as throng as three in a bed,' in *Some Irish Yesterdays*. Samuel Lover had 'Mighty throng it was wid the boys and the girls,' in *Legends and Stories of Ireland* (1848).

The Scots form of the word is *thrang*. From Middle English *þrang*, *þrong*. Cf. Old Norse *þrœngr*, narrow, close, crowded. The Swedish is *trång*, Danish *trang*, strait, narrow, close, tight.

✦ TINE

Rab McAllister from Co. Down has corresponded with me frequently over the years and his missives always contain an interesting word or two. *Tine*, sometimes spelled *tyne*, is a word he sent me a few years ago, and it undoubtedly arrived here in Ireland over four hundred years ago with the Scottish Planters. It means to lose. Rab tells me that Ulster has now tined the old word, and more's the pity.

Sir Walter Scott had it in *The Heart of Midlothian*: 'Better tyne life since tint is gude fame.' 'He's on the sea—they've tint him,' wrote Haliburton in his translation of Horace in 1886. Robert Burns recorded in his great *Tam o' Shanter* that the bould Tam 'tint his reason a' thegither' when he shouted encouragement to the lassie who danced in her cutty sark. Burns also had the word with the meaning to perish, cease to be, in his poem *Here's a Health*: 'May tyrants and tyranny tine in the mist.'

They still use a lovely proverbial phrase in many parts of Scotland: *tine heart, tine all*, which urges the necessity of not suffering the spirits to sink when one encounters difficulty.

The word travelled south across the English border, I notice; either that or it came to England directly from its source in Scandinavia. I found it in that charming book Streatfield's *Lincolnshire and the Danes*, where it means a forfeit.

It has been in literature since around 1300 when *Havelok the Dane* was written: 'That he ne tinte no catel.' Around the same time we find in *Sir Beues*: 'Treitour! now is þe lif itint.' In 1340 Hampole's *Psalter* lxi. teaches that 'It is a harmefull winninge to win cattell & tine rightowsnes.' And in 1460 in one of the *Towneley Mysteries* we find, 'Oure love is tynt.' Ramsey, that excellent Scots poet, has the word with the meaning to fail to win in his *Prospect of Plenty*, first published in 1721: 'She grasps the shadow but the substance tines.'

The word is from Old Norse *týna*, to lose. The Norwegian, older Danish and Swedish dialect is *týne*, to destroy, lose, to perish, derived from *tjón*, loss, damage; cognate with Old English *téon*, injury, etc.

✦ TIN-EGIN

This is a compound, a corruption from Scottish Gaelic, from the Western Isles. It means forced fire, and I've come across it in my forays into the languages of Britain and Ireland and their connections with the language of the old Vikings. The Vikings had a profound influence on the Western Isles of Scotland, and at first I thought that perhaps this was one of their words. In this I was mistaken.

Martin Martin, in his *Description of the Western Isles*, written in 1716, had this explanation:

> The inhabitants here did also make use of a fire called Tin-Egin, i.e. a forced fire or fire of necessity, which they used as an antidote against the plague, or murrain in cattle; and it was performed thus: All the fires in the parish were extinguished and then eighty one married

men being thought the necessary number for effecting the design, took two great planks of wood, and nine of 'em were employed by turns, who by their repeated efforts rubbed one of the planks against the other until the heat thereof produced fire; and from this forced fire each family is supplied with new fire, which is no sooner kindled than a pot full of water is quickly set on it, and afterwards sprinkled upon the people inflicted with the plague, or upon the cattle that have the murrain. And all this they say they find successful by experience. It was practised on the main land opposite to the south of Skie within these thirty years.

No doubt this was the remnant of some Druidic practice, and it is believed that it continued on the islands long after Martin wrote the above account of it. The ecclesiastical authorities denounced the practice but it survived in places until the end of the eighteenth century.

The origin of the compound Tin-Egin is given by the Scottish Gaelic lexicographer Macbain as *teine*, fire + *éiginn*, genitive, of necessity.

✦ TIRL

There is an Ulster noun and verb *tirl* which has long intrigued me. Because I have never heard it in the south I guessed, correctly it seems, that it came with the seventeenth-century Scots Planters to Ulster, and indeed it is found to this day in Dumfries, Perthshire, Caithness, Ayrshire, and in Shetland and Orkney. It is, however, also known in Northumberland and Yorkshire, and also in the deep south of England on the Isle of Wight. It is glossed in the EDD as a twirl, whirl; the act of rotating; a short turn at anything, especially dancing. As a verb it is glossed as to cause to twirl or move rapidly; of the wind, to tear the slates off a roof. Burns in his *Address to the Diel* (1785) has 'Whyles on the strong-winge'd tempest flyin, Tirlin the kirks'.

In the north of this sainted isle I've heard the word used in the sense to dance; to move a girl around the dance floor, so that in Tyrone, the late Benedict Kiely informed me, 'to give a girl a tirl' meant to dance with her. One of the EDD's citations from Dumfries has 'Nane o' thae whirlin', tirlin', close-claspin' lustfu'-lookin' dances.' Back in 1697 the poet Cleland said of a girl he wanted to dance with that 'she would far rather had a tirl of an aquavitae barrel'. A few years ago on a trip to Ayr, a man standing beside me in a bar named *Tam o' Shanter* remarked that he would dearly love to give a passing statuesque blonde, a pilgrim from Scandinavia to Burns's haunts, a tirl amang the sheets. She looked as if she would break the *spriosán*'s back in two if he as much as suggested it to her.

I was surprised to find that the word is not etymologically related to *whirl*, but is a metathetic form of *trill*, to turn around, to cause to rotate, and is of Scandinavian origin. We may compare the East Frisian *tireln*, *tirlen*, to turn about quickly, and the Danish *trilde*, *trille*, to roll, trundle a wheel.

A Donegal girl once told me that I tirled her with all the grace of one of Messrs Arthur Guinness's dray horses. I need hardly remark that that gratuitous insult to my dancing skill ended our budding relationship there and then, and that I left her where I found her, at the foot of the sweet brown knowe.

✦ TOADY & TOAD-EATER

I'm sure you remember the days when people were seriously concerned that both George W. Bush and Tony Blair might be awarded the Nobel Peace Prize. Many articles were published about these two pacifists in the serious press in which Blair was referred to as Bush's toady.

Toady seems to me to be the perfect word for a fawning, sycophantic person. It hits the mark, and is far superior to the innocuous *poodle*, which admittedly was used to effect by cartoonists both here and in Britain in their depictions of our two heroes.

Toady is an interesting word. It is an abbreviation of *toad-eater*, who was a common sight in seventeenth- and eighteenth-century England. He was a side-kick of the quack-doctors who infested the towns, cities and fairs, selling patent medicines. Now in those days, toads were considered poisonous, and the quack's assistant had to eat one in full view of the audience, and then, after he had rolled around a bit, pretending to be in danger of death, he would be given a sup from the doctor's magic bottle, and in no time at all appeared to have recovered his health and vigour.

Toad itself was a term of contempt, dislike or disgust in Scotland, England, Wales and Ireland in the eighteenth and nineteenth centuries. In a scurrilous novel published anonymously, and with good reason, in Edinburgh in 1798, and called *Carlop Green*, we find a politician of the day called 'a swindling, hen-pecked, poisonous toad'. The EDD has many citations from correspondents from Ayr to Cornwall, where in a novel by Baring-Gould, published in 1893 and called *Curgenven*, we find a man calling his darling wife 'a dirty ou'd toad, hasn't swept'n up fitty this mornin'. And our own Jane Barlow in her *Ghost-Bereft*, published in 1901, has 'Och the bould little toad, did you notice the dhrive, mam, she hit Murty Doyle?'

Toady, which originally meant a little or young toad, was introduced into literature by Benjamin Disraeli, Earl of Beaconsfield, in *Vivian Grey* in 1826: 'You know what a Toadey is? That agreeable animal which you meet every day in civilised society.' And in 1883 W.J. Stillman, a friend of Shaw, wrote in *The Century Magazine* in October 1883 of 'A toady to the superior and a bully to the inferior grades'.

Toad-eater first appeared in 1629 in J. Rous's *Diary*: 'I inquired of him if William Utting the toade-eater . . . did not once keepe at Laxfield; he tould me yes, and said he had seene him eate a toade, nay two.' In the sense a fawning flatterer, a parasite, a sycophant, the compound entered literature in 1742 in a letter of Horace Walpole's: 'Lord Edgcumbe's [place] is destined to Harry Vane, Pulteney's toad-eater.' The American Washington Irving in *Salmagundi* (1824) has 'Encouraged by the shouts and acclamations of toad-eaters'. And in 1876 George Eliot in her *Daniel Deronda* has 'The toad-eater the least liable to nausea, must be expected to have his susceptibilities.'

A fine word, and still useful today.

✦ TOICE

I haven't heard this word *toice* outside a Gaeltacht in years, nor seen it in print, even in the excruciatingly ugly anglicised spellings of *teeka*, *thwacka*, *thecka*, *hecka*. The diminutive is *toicín*, anglicised *tuckeen* in places. *Toice* means simply a wench, but it has accrued a veneer of contempt in many places.

Many years ago I set out to find out where the word survived outside the Gaeltacht areas. In south Tipperary the world was common and meant simply a young adolescent girl. Further north in the same county, around Thurles, a correspondent informed me that 'the word was used both affectionately and contemptuously, and very often ironically to describe mutton dressed up as lamb'.

Across the Suir in north Co. Waterford I was told that *thecka* and *hecka* were terms of contempt for a young woman: 'That hecka is as bould as brass.'

James Joyce has the word as *thwacka* in *Finnegans Wake*. My old friend Liz Jeffries from Kilmore, Co. Wexford, informed me that a *thuckeen* was a girl who is full of herself, the female equivalent of a *gorseejack*, a word I have failed to find elsewhere, and whose origin I can only guess at. The nineteenth-century folklorist Patrick Kennedy from mid-Wexford, in *Legendary Fictions of the Irish Celts*, has 'When I was a thuckeen about fifteen years of age . . .'

Fr Dinneen defines *toice* as 'a girl, a wench (either affectionate or contemptuous)' and adds the name for a girls' school in Cork (he doesn't say which of the county's Gaeltachtaí): *Scoil na dToicí*. My father, who came from Baile Bhúirne direction in west Muskerry, had *toice*, 'a young girl of marriageable age'. Last year on a visit there I asked a young waitress what a *toice* or a *toicín* was, and she said that it meant 'a brazen strap of a young girl'. 'A bit like myself,' she added with a wink.

✦ TRIG

Hazel Byrne of Brickfield Lane, Wicklow town, was reading a book called *Fairytales from Erin's Isle* by Marie Baynes recently. The book was published in 1910, a time when Irish fairies attained great popularity all over the world. Anyway, Hazel's book contains references to a leprechaun and described him as 'a trig little man in a green coat and britches'. She is puzzled by the word *trig*.

May I digress for a minute? It might surprise even some Irish people to know that belief in fairies persisted in places until quite recently. My friend Dick Walsh (R.B. Breatnach), a fine linguist who wrote memorable studies of the Irish of Waterford, told me of visiting an old man who was supposedly dying. The poor man, a monolingual Irish-speaker, had just made his confession to a young priest who didn't know any Irish, and appeared confused and upset, and turning to the window he expressed his worry that he might not be accepted out there with *them*. There appeared to be nothing out there except a field and a fairy fort or *ráth* at its end. This man held as an article of faith that when he died his soul would reside with the fairy folk, enjoying music, drink and all the good things he couldn't afford in this life, until the Lord took him to heaven. He was worried about the validity of his confession, because one had to have a clean slate to get into the *ráth*. He did not believe in the Purgatory the priests spoke of.

As to Hazel's trig fairy, I remember my friend and colleague in UCD the late Gus Martin being puzzled as well when I dropped the word into a casual conversation about a colleague we both disliked. *Trig* to me meant smartly dressed, spruce, brisk, nimble, while Gus knew it as faithful, trustworthy, which did not match the character of the man we were bitching about. According to Oxford Gus's meaning was the older one, and now found only in the northern dialects of England, in Scotland, and, although Oxford didn't know it, in my friend's native Leitrim.

The word is as old as *The Ormulum* (c. 1200). My meaning of *trig* first appeared in Henryson's *Moral Fables* (The Lion & The Mouse) in 1470: 'Ane trip of myis . . . Richt tait and trig, all dansand in ane gyis.' Oxford considers trig a dialect word now. Tell that to ee cummings, who described the sadistic officer in *I Sing of Olaf* as 'a trig westpointer most succinctly bred'.

Trig is from Old Norse *tryggr*, faithful, trustworthy. How the meaning changed to nimble, brisk, spruce and tidy between 1200 and 1470 nobody has yet explained.

✦ TRIST

Some of the old-timers I knew down around Carne in south-east Wexford used the verb *trist* for *to trust*. It was found too in Somerset and Devon, and also in Yorkshire and Lancashire. The EDD has this: 'Back may trist but belly won't,' which it explains as 'the saying of the thrifty in dear times—dress may be deferred but hunger cannot'. The adjective *tristy*, trustworthy, was found in nineteenth-century Yorkshire.

Trist comes from the Old Norse *treysta*, according to the Icelandic scholar Vigfusson. It is not the same word as *trust*, noun, although it is etymologically related; *trust* is from early Middle English *trost(e)*, *truste*, from Old Norse *traust*.

The prognosis is not good, I'm afraid. It is no longer heard in Carne, probably the only place in Ireland it survived; and only the very old remember it in Yorkshire and Lancashire.

Peter Byrne of Tomhaggard, barony of Forth, Co. Wexford, a retired schoolmaster, first drew my attention to the word's existence back in the 1970s. He predicted that it wouldn't live past the year 2000. He was right.

✦ TUMMERIL

I doubt if they use *tummerils* on the farms of Wexford and Kilkenny any more. This was a cart so constructed that the body tilts backwards to empty out its load of manure. I enquired recently from schoolteachers in the region and they failed to find anybody who still uses the word. Farming methods have changed a lot in the past forty years, I suppose.

I heard it in south Co. Kilkenny in Moulerstown, near Glenmore, about eight miles from New Ross. A small farmer named Tommy Greene gave me the word. I heard the word as well both from Mike Flynn of Kilmore and from Phil Wall from Carne, two very old men when I met them in the early 1970s.

The word is found in some parts of England under a variety of guises. They have *tumril* in Lincolnshire, *tumberel* in parts of East Anglia, and *tumbril* in Yorkshire, Cheshire, Nottinghamshire, Warwickshire and Shropshire. Yes, this is the *tumbril*, the cart in which so many went to meet their doom during the French Terror.

It's an old word and first appeared in the *c.* 1440 glossary *Promptorium Parvulorum Sive Clericorum*: 'Tomerel, donge cart.' It also had 'Tumrel, donge carte, *fimaria, titubatorium*.'

In 1494 the *Fabyan Chronicles* show that the French had used the tumbril as people-carriers long before the Revolution: 'He was sette in a tumbrell, & therunto fastenyd with chaynes of iren, and so conueyed, bareheded, with dynne and crye, thorough the hyghe stretes of Parys tyll he came vnto the bysshoppes palays.' In 1700 Dryden's *Cock & Fox* has 'My corps is in a tumbril laid; among / The filth and ordure, and enclos'd with dung.'

The word is from medieval Latin *tumb(e)rellum*. The Old French had *tumb-*, *tomberel*, *tummerel*, *tumerel*, *-il*, etc., fall, chute, tip-cart, dung-cart. The modern French is *tombereau*, 'a Tumbrell or Dung-cart', according to Cotgrave's French–English dictionary of 1611. Apparently there is no record in French of its use in punishment. Imagine that!

✦ TUP

This is a true story. I know of a Co. Wicklow sheep-farmer's daughter who was reprimanded for her use of what they termed 'a crude, vulgar, expression' in an essay she had submitted in some nursing exam. The offending word was *tup*, which any young person of her background would use instead of *sexual intercourse*. I suggested she write a letter to her supervisor explaining the situation and the origin and use of the word in rural Ireland. That's me. Ó Muirithe coming once again to the rescue of maidens in distress. To be fair to her examiner(s) she was rewarded honours in that particular paper.

The verb *tup*, of a ram to copulate with a ewe, and by transference in the coarse earthy slang used by the gurrier class, of a man to copulate with a woman, is younger than the noun *tup*. It seems that Shakespeare was the first to use the verb in *Othello*. 'An old black ram is tupping your white ewe.' This coarse verb was, I see, used by B.W. Aldiss in *The Hand-Reared Boy*, published in 1970 and immediately banned in this isle of saints: 'In Derbyshire's dull dorms . . . when lesser souls abused themselves, outclassed, Our Dancer, saint and patron, he upped and tupped the matron.'

The verb is from the noun, which originally meant a ram, and after a time transferred to a man. The word is first recorded in a ballad of the Scottish Wars around 1300, and in its crude sense in James Shirley's *Honour and Mammon* in 1659: 'Cuckolds' sconce, Or haven, to which all the tups strike sail.'

But as to origin we have a problem. Oxford is not sure, but quotes Skeat's suggestion that it may be a transferred use of Norwegian and Swedish *tupp*, 'cock', said to be the same word as *top*, the crest or 'topping' of a bird; the forelock of a horse, etc. Skeat's word is Common West Germanic in origin, found in Old English *top*, Old Frisian *topp*, Old Norse *toppr*, top, tuft, Swedish *topp*, top, pinnacle, Danish *top*, point, modern Norwegian *tupp*; all from a supposed Old Teutonic *tuppoz*; not known in Gothic, and outside Teutonic known only in Romanic derivatives.

In many cultures, including our own, the ram was a potent symbol of virility. In Derbyshire they had a pastime in which a wild ram's tail was thoroughly greased before the local swains were let loose to chase the fleeing animal in a bid to prove their manliness. The first to hold on to the tail and knock the ram was adjudged the winner, and the possessor of superior virility, which, of course, made him appealing to the young ladies of the place. By all accounts a great time was had by all, except perhaps by the unlucky gentlemen whose ribs and other bodily parts were smashed by the horns of the infuriated Derby ram.

Ram by the way is from Old English *ram*, perhaps related to Old Norse *rammr*, strong.

U ∾

✦ **UZZLE PIES & DAINTIES**

I was looking through the *Oxford Book of Nursery Rhymes* the other night, and found myself wondering if today's children are as fascinated as we were long ago by these little poems, the first we ever learned. I doubt it somehow.

I learn something new every time I dip into this treasure of a book; I now know that the line in *Sing a Song of Sixpence* 'When the pie was opened the birds began to sing' is explained by a recipe in a translation of an Italian cookbook of 1549 'for making pyes so that the birds may be alive in them and flie out when it is cut up'.

The crust was made in the usual way, but then filled with fruit or dried beans to weight the bottom crust down while the pie was being baked. When the pie had cooked, songbirds such as blackbirds, finches and thrushes were tethered inside without being harmed; when the dish was brought to the table the upper crust was removed and, if we are to believe the rhyme, the birds began to sing. John Nott, an eighteenth-century commentator, tells us that the fun was greatly increased at the dinner table when the birds were not tethered in the pie, but flew around the room putting out the candles, 'and so causing a diverting Hurley Burley among the guests in the dark'.

This pie was called *uzzle pie* by the old writers. *Uzzle* is a dialectal variant of *ousel*, an old name for the blackbird, *Turdus merula*. From Old English *ósle*, which is related to Old High German *amsala* and Modern German *Amsel*; its ulterior etymology is unknown.

Uzzle pies were certainly a dainty dish to set before a king, but in using the word *dainty* we don't have in mind those alluded to by Shakespeare in *Love's Labour's Lost*: 'He had never fed on the dainties of the book.' If we are to believe the stories about Shakespeare poaching deer in his youth, he probably ate *dainties*, which were deer testicles set in a sweet and sour sauce. I ate them only once, in a great restaurant in Halifax, Nova Scotia, called Fat Frank's. I had not considered eating there because its name didn't appeal to me, but poet and academic Deirdre Dwyer told me that the restaurant, housed in a lovely old town house, had been lauded by the *New Yorker* as one of the best in North America. Its food was reasonably priced, and Fat Frank himself introduced me to *dainties*, which I found delicious.

Dainty, in the sense anything pleasing or delicious to the palate, is from French, through Middle English. In *Beket, c.* 1300, we find this holy man being served *deyntes*. The Old French source was *deintié*, *daintié*, *dainté*, pleasure, pleasing morsel, from Latin *dignitatem*, worthiness, worth, beauty, from *dignus*, worthy.

| W ～

✦ WAPPERED

What a pity this great dialect word has gone out of fashion in all but a few places in England. At a luncheon hosted by Richard Ingrams, editor of *The Oldie*, for which I write a column on words, I was given the word by Sir John Mortimer, barrister and novelist, and creator of the immortal Rumpole of the Bailey. When I asked him how he was he confessed to being *wappered*, which he explained meant tired, fatigued, or, as we might say, knackered. On enquiry later, I found that the word had disappeared everywhere except in Gloucestershire and Warwickshire. I don't believe it has travelled to Ireland.

Captain Grose in his *Provincial Dictionary* of 1790 recorded the word in Gloucestershire and explained it as 'restless or fatigued'. I found it as well in J.A Gibb's *A Cotswold Village*, published in 1898; I picked it up for a pound in a Cheltenham second-hand bookshop the year Arkle won his last Gold Cup; I smiled when I found in it the sentence 'Thou'll not see Stratford tonight, sir, thy horse is wappered out.' He gives a footnote: '*Wappered* = tired. A Cotswold word.' *Unwappered* appears in *The Two Noble Kinsmen* in 1612; this is one of the Shakespeare Apocrypha, edited again in 1908.

The origin of the word? John Mortimer, who proclaimed himself to be a bit of an authority on these matters, bade me consider the word *wap*, in the old sense of 'to have sexual intercourse with'. He quoted me *Timon of Athens*, Act IV, Scene III. Could your man from Warwickshire have had this in mind when he wrote, 'This [gold] it is / That makes the wappened (sic) widow wed again'? Oh, chivalrous people like me would say that the lady was just tired.

✦ WAYZGOOSE AND BEANFEST

In England they once had a celebration called *wayze goose*, a party given by the bosses to printers and their families. The eighteenth-century lexicographer Nathan Bailey described this party as 'entertainment given to journeymen at the beginning of winter'. He suggests that *wayz* once meant a bundle of straw, and that the goose in the title was one reared and fattened late in the year on stubble fields. Shipley, in our own time, was a far more reliable source, and he thought that the entertainment took place in late summer, 'around Bartholomew-tide (August 24th), marking the beginning of work by candlelight'.

The practice was ancient by Bailey's time; Chaucer referred to it in the *Cook's Prologue* in the fourteenth century. The practice lasted until the end of the nineteenth century. In 1875 Southward's *Dictionary of Typography* has 'The wayzgoose generally consists of a trip into the country, open air amusements, a good dinner, and speeches and toasts afterwards.' In 1895 the *Surrey Mirror* 23 August reported that 'The members of the typographical staffs of the *Surrey Advertiser* (Guildford) and the *Surrey Mirror* (Redhill) had their wayzgoose on Saturday last, when they journeyed to Brighton.' Two years later we find the last literary reference to this ancient custom, in F.T. Bullen's *Cruise of 'Cachalot'*: 'Carriages were chartered, an enormous quantity of eatables and drinkables provided, and away we went, a regular wayzgoose or bean-feast party.'

By then the wayzgoose had been insidiously supplanted by the *beanfeast* mentioned by Bullen. By the early 1800s the principal dish no longer consisted of fat geese. No. The bosses and their accountants thought that beans would be just as acceptable, and a hell of a lot cheaper, to put before the working man.

Some etymologists have suggested that *beanfeast* was possibly derived from the Latin *bene*, solicitation, as a collection used to be taken up at these shindigs, but the evidence is against this notion.

Not all bosses were parsimonious, as this piece from the 1805 *Sporting Magazine* shows: 'At a late bean feast, a Gentleman Taylor, celebrated for his liberality, gave a rich treat to his men, at his occasional country residence. It was called a Bean Feast; but, exclusive of the beans, the table literally groaned with bacon etc.'

But we learn from innumerable references to these feasts that beans were an indispensable part of the menu, which were enjoyed by masters and workers alike. They engendered quite a good deal of mutual respect, apparently. And a good deal of wind, I suspect.

✦ WEED

No, I don't mean those garden pests (from Old English *wéod*, by the way), but the word now remembered only in the compound noun *widow's weeds*, the black coats and dresses once worn by grieving widows for a time after the death of their husbands, a fashion now gone in most places, I believe. A weed was also used of a band or crêpe for a man's hat in time of mourning.

Weed once meant any item of clothes. 'Clad in woman's weeds, and carrying on my head a woman's burden', wailed the Scottish writer Lang in *The Monk of Fife* in 1876. Robert Burns was certainly not talking of widow's weeds when he wrote in *Scottish Drink* in 1786: 'Aft clad in massy, sillar [silver] weed, / Wi' gentles thou erects thy head.'

The word was also used of a winding sheet or a shroud; indeed, of whatever a person was dressed in when placed in the coffin. Another Scots poet, Murdoch, in his *Doric Lyre* (1876), often quoted in the dictionaries for his exuberant language, has 'The laird, ye'll mind had twice been deid, / An' twice had waaulkened oot o' the weed.'

Weed is very old, in fact as old as Ælfred's *Boethius* of *c*. 888. It was used by many notable writers south of the Scottish border as well as by Scots penmen. In 1614 Camden wrote, 'They . . . began to wanton it in a new round curtall weede which they called a Cloake.' In 1621 John Fletcher the dramatist in *The Pilgrim* has 'To my house now, and suite you to your worths; Off with these weeds, and appeare glorious.' Pope's translation of Homer's *Odyssey* of 1725 has 'An aged mendicant in tatter'd weeds'. Horace Walpole in *Otranto* has 'One in a long, woolen weed'. Wordsworth's *The Prelude* (1805) has 'Spare diet, patient labour, and plain weeds'. And in 1850 Tennyson in his great *In Memoriam* wrote, 'In words, like weeds, I'll wrap me o'er, / Like coarsest clothes against the cold.'

Oxford says that it is from Middle English *wéde*, representing two formations: (1) Old English *wǽd* feminine = Old Saxon *wâd*; and (2) Old English *wǽde* strong neuter = Old Saxon *wâdi*.

✦ WHAUP

In a few remote areas of Donegal, in the Sperrins of Tyrone, and in the Glens of Antrim you may still hear the word *whaup* when old-timers speak of the curlew, *Numenius arquata*. The word undoubtedly came here from Scotland, although it is also found in England in the remoter parts of Northumberland, Cumbria, Yorkshire and Lincolnshire.

I myself heard the word from a farmer at the back of Muckish mountain in Donegal many years ago; I enquired recently about the word from a young couple from that district who were on their honeymoon in Waterford's Ardmore; it didn't surprise me that they had never heard of the word. Davy Hammond told me of recording a song from an old man in the Sperrins who was more interested in playing a flute for him: 'I whaups a bit on the flute as well, ye know.'

Sir Walter Scott had the word in *Rob Roy* (1817): 'The lapwing and curlew, which my companions denominated the peasweep and whaup.' The *Shetland News* once complained that 'the curlew (whaup) might surely have been scheduled for protection'. That engaging book *Lincolnshire and the Danes* by Streatfield, in which I found many good words which had survived from the time of the Vikings, also had *whaup* for a curlew, but that book was written in 1884 and I am told that the word is now on its last legs there.

There were interesting compounds, recorded by the EDD. *Auld waup-neb* was a name for the Devil. *Neb* means a beak, and the Scots also had the term to describe people, for example, 'Davie Blain's waup-nebbed dochters', which meant long-nosed. The phrase *A whaup in the nest* meant something wrong; 'a thorn in the side'. Rab Burns had this phrase in a poem *To J. Rankine*: 'Now a rumour's like ro rise / A whaup's i' the nest.'

There was a verb *to whaup*, meaning to cry as a curlew. 'What's thou waap-whaupin aboot?' said to a child or anyone making a tiresome or disagreeable complaint, was recorded in Northumberland.

As to origin, the EDD doesn't even attempt a guess. The DSL has Old Scots *quhaip*, *quhap* from 1538, an unexplained variant of Old English *hwilpe*, a kind of sea-bird, of uncertain origin but possibly an imitation of its cry, and cognate with whelp, a puppy, so, 'the yelper, whiner'. The Scots form suggests the existence of an older variant **whelp > whalp > whaup*.

✦ WHIG

I remember discussing the food people ate in the bad old days with a fisherman from Burtonport, Co. Donegal, who was over eighty. He mentioned the dreadful boxty and then his face contorted as he told me about having to drink *whig*, which he pronounced *fwig*. Dreadful stuff, he said, but good for you.

I found this as *whig* in various spellings in the dialect dictionaries. It has been recorded in Ireland, Scotland, and in Northumberland, Cumberland, Lancashire and Yorkshire, Cheshire, Lincolnshire, Northamptonshire and Shropshire. It is glossed by them as whey; sour milk or cream; buttermilk.

Capt. Grose recorded the word in Co. Antrim back in 1790. He defined it as 'a thin, subacid liquor resembling whey which collects on the surface of butter milk when long kept'. John Jamieson, in his Scottish etymological dictionary published in 1808, defined the word as 'the sour part of cream, which spontaneously separates from the rest; the thin part of a liquid mixture'. 'Whig and whey, *serum lactis*', Peter Levins explained in his *Manipulus Vocabulorum*, a dictionary of English and Latin words, published in 1570. In *Gordon's Mill Farming Club*, published in Aberdeen in 1759, and reprinted in 1962, there is this:

> Many of the Country People keep their Cream fourteen, or twenty days, and as they cannot help observing that it acquires a most disagreeable taste, in order to carry off this, they pour into it a quantity of boiled whey; which after it has stood some time, they draw off, and frequently repeat the dose. This liquor they call Whig. The Whig, tho' it carries off much of the ill taste of the Cream, at the same time carries off the Yellow oily part of it; makes it yield less Butter, and what it does yield, is of an ugly whitish greasy colour.

A more palatable beverage made of whey flavoured with herbs was also called *whig*. A correspondent from Northumberland told the EDD that 'the whey was infused with mint and sage, soured a little with buttermilk. It was boiled first, then boiled a little more, cooled and clarified, and when cold, was ready.' Marshall praised the beverage in his *Rural Economy* from Yorkshire in 1788. I asked my man in Burtonport if he ever tasted the like. He replied that he did, and would just as soon drink cat's piss, but that some people put brandy or rum in it to take some of the taste away.

Hence the past participial adjective *whigged*, curdled as milk; broken in whey. William Carleton knew the word. In *Traits and Stories of the Irish Peasantry* he has 'In the beginning we were all as thick as whigged milk.'

Origin? The DSL suggests early Middle English *whig*, of uncertain origin, but possibly connected with *whey* as a northern form.

✦ WHIGMALEERIE

This good old Scots word is, it appears, in danger of extinction. First of all it means a decorative or fanciful object, a piece of ornamentation, in dress, stonework, etc., used generally with depreciatory force, a knick-knack, gew-gaw, bauble, a fantastic contrivance or contraption; also of food: fancy dishes or confectionery.

Robert Burns in a letter of 1773 has 'I, with great formality, produced my whigmeleerie cup.'

Scott, in *Rob Roy*, has 'Nane o' yere whigmaleeries and curlie-wurlies and opensteek [a style of stitching] hems about it.' In *Nigel* the same author has 'In the whigmaleery man's back-shop'. In 1884 R.F. Hardy in *Glenairlie* has a character who wasn't going to change kirks: 'They wiled me there at times, but I couldna bide their wheegmaleeries an' gennyflexions!'

In 1964 a statistical account from Peeblesshire complained of 'the bogus Tudor and Banker's Georgian and the whigmaleeries of the Chambers Institute'.

The word also means a whim, fanciful notion, a fad. In 1786 Burns, in *The Brigs of Ayr*, has 'There'll be, if that day come, I'll wad a boddle [wager a copper coin], Some fewer whigmaleeries in your noddle.' In 1903 S. Macplowter (could that really be his name?) in a Stage-Scottish book called *Mrs McCraw* wrote, 'Am an evenforrit wumman wi' nae whigmaleeries aboot me.'

Both the EDD and the DSL describe a drinking game called *whigmaleerie*. Here's the DSL: 'The name of a ridiculous game which was occasionally used, in Angus, at a drinking club. A pin was stuck in the centre of a circle, from which there were as many radii as there were persons in the company, with the name of each person at the radius opposite to him. On the pin an index was placed, and moved round by every one in his turn; and at whatsoever person's radius it stopped, he was obliged to drink off his glass.'

The earliest occurrence of the word is in the form *figmaleerie*, a fanciful formation possibly based on *fyke*, to move about restlessly, to fidget, from discomfort, itch, excitement, etc. + *ma* + *leerie*, according to the DSL 'originally a meaningless word or element used for rhythmic purposes in children's rhymes and as a suffix in such words as *bummeleerie*, *whigmaleerie* and the like, to denote sprightly, bustling motion, fanciful appearance or the like'.

I don't know why the Scots have taken a dislike to this word, but according to a friend who worked for many years at the DSL, they have, and with a vengeance. I think it a pity to have this fate befall one of Scotland's national poet's expressive words.

✦ WIME

Wime is a good old word meaning to move in a circuitous or erratic fashion, to wander or to twist. It was sent to me a few years ago by Peter Foote, that great scholar of Scandinavian and Icelandic literature who died recently at eighty-five. He dominated his field from his chair at University College London. A shy man with a great sense of fun, he was nevertheless the bane of many pretentious academics: I heard him take a pretentious Irish ass to pieces in London once over your man's dismissal of the Irish-language base of Southern Irish English as unimportant.

He was especially interested in words of Scandinavian origin, of which *wime* is one. He wanted to know if the word *wime* is known in Ireland. It isn't, as far as I know; across the water it seems to be confined to Lincolnshire and Yorkshire, where a bird is said to go *wiming* through the air, and a river to *wime* through a valley. Rock climbers *wime* up a cliff-face, going zig-zag; and many's the Yorkshire toper may be seen late at night *wiming* home from the pub. There are subsidiary meanings as well. 'He *wimed* out the back door when he saw me coming,' means 'He sneaked out.' Hence *wimy*, noun, a sneak, a sleeveen. And in Lincolnshire, *to wime* means to coax, 'get around', wheedle, deceive, especially by flattery.

A lovely word, sadly in danger of dying out, it seems. Oxford has not included it in its latest edition.

The word is probably Scandinavian in origin. The great Norwegian linguist Ivar Aasen mentioned the Norwegian dialectal word *vima*, to tumble, to stagger about.

✦ WINCHESTER GOOSE

I don't suppose the examiners in the Royal College of Surgeons would be amused if a candidate referred to the above in an examination on venereal disease. And yet for centuries the cant expression survived in London and beyond, and was used even by the nobility of the land, both male and female, as an acceptable euphemism for the pox. The term was also used of a prostitute.

It is said to have originated in the public stews of Southwark which were under the jurisdiction of the Bishop of Southwark, who was taunted by Shakespeare in *Henry VI, Part 1*, Act III, Scene I, with his licentious life: 'Thou art a most pernicious usurer: / Froward by nature, enemy to peace: / Lascivious, wanton, more than well beseems / A man of thy profession and degree.' In the same play Shakespeare has 'Winter goose, I cry, a rope! a rope!' In *Troilus and Cressida* he was at it again: 'My fear is this: Some galled Goose of Winchester would hiss.'

In 1611 the lexicographer Cotgrave has '*Clapoir*, a botch in the Groyne, or yard; a winchester goose'. In 1630 Taylor, the Water Poet, has 'Then ther's a Goose that breeds at Winchester, And of all Geese, my mind is least to her.' In 1661 John Webster and William Rowley have in *A Cure for A Cuckold* 'This Informer . . . had belike some private dealings with her, and there got a Goose. This fellow in revenge for this, informs against the Bawd that kept the house.'

The term got the sanction of lexicography again in 1727, in Boyer's *English and French Dictionary*: 'A Winchester Goose (or swelling in the Groin) *un Poulain*'. And in 1778 *The English Gazetteer* (ed. 2) has under Southwark 'In the times of popery there were no less than 18 houses on the Bankside, licensed by the Bishops of Winchester . . . to keep whores, who were, therefore, commonly called Winchester Geese.'

No more needs to be said on this distasteful subject.

✦ WISE

This verb, which means to direct, guide, lead; also to let go; to bring, was once common in Scotland and, across the border in England, in Northumberland and Yorkshire. It was also sent to me once by a woman from Co. Down, but she mentioned that it was a word of her mother's, who came from Dumfries. I have a feeling that it never took root in Ireland; the *Concise Ulster Dictionary* doesn't have it.

John Jamieson's Scottish dictionary of 1808 has the word in the forms *wiss* and *weise*: 'Can ye wiss me to the way?'; 'To weise a ball—to aim a bullet with such caution as to hit the mark.' Walter Scott has the word, as *weize*, in *Rob Roy* (1817): 'Weize a brace of balls through his harn pan [brain pan].'

'Every miller would weise the water to his own mill,' is one of the Scottish sayings in Ramsay's *Proverbs* of 1737. From Northumberland a correspondent sent the EDD this: 'He wis howkin a seugh ti wise the watter away.'

Jamieson also gave us this from Roxburghshire: 'To weise in, or out, to allow to go in or out, by removing any impediment, as by opening a door. To weise the sheep into the fauld [fold, inclosure] or bught [a small pen, usually put up in the corner of the fold, into which it was customary to drive ewes, when they were to be milked], is still a phrase used by our shepherds.' Hence *wising-crag*, a stone guide-post over the Yorkshire Moors.

This word, in all its guises, also means to guide, counsel. 'I wise ye to gang home and redd your ain house first,' is a piece of advice given by a character in *Secretar*, a novel by Alexander Beatty published in 1897. Over two centuries before that, John Ray in his Herefordshire glossary has 'Wise me: tell me, direct me.'

To wise, etc., also meant to use caution or policy to attain any object; to get by skill or cunning; to plan, contrive; to work one's way. From Northumberland the EDD has 'To wise into company or into favour, that is to wriggle into company or into favour.'

And lastly *to wise* meant to entice, lure, persuade; beguile. The *Edinburgh Magazine* for June 1819 had 'The fairies sent him to Craignethan's ha', To wize his daughter him frae.' The EDD also gives us 'The hawthorn blooming, the green spreading meadow, wad wyse me to wander.'

According to the EDD wise is from Old English *wísian*, to guide, point out, show.

✦ WISHT

This is a word associated with the south-west of England and southern Wales; it has also been found in America. A recent survey shows that the word has all but died out in Devon, Cornwall, Somerset and Pembrokeshire. A good word it is, meaning unlucky; uncanny, eerie, awe-inspiring; horrible. A correspondent of the EDD from west Somerset probably got it right when she wrote, 'No doubt the real meaning is bewitched or *evil wisht*, i.e. suffering from the evil eye.' The Devonshire writer Baring-Gould in *Spider* (1887) asked, 'Do y' know what the ash said to the axe? Whether coupled or counter is wisht (unlucky) for me, My wood makes the haft for to fell my tree.' In the *Folk-Lore Record* of 1881 there is this from America: 'Block Island is rather a wisht kind of a place anyway, being haunted by the ghastly wreck of a burning ship, the "Palatine".'

Hence *wish-hounds* or *wisht-hounds*, feared for centuries in Devon. Baring-Gould again, this time from *Idylls* (1896): 'Wild tales of the wish-hounds that hunted across it, fire-breathing black dogs, said to course the wild wastes of a night, driven on by a mysterious hunter, whose horn may be heard, as well as his call to the dogs, but who himself is rarely if ever seen.'

That good Devon writer Madox-Brown added to the mystery in *Dwale Bluth* (1876): 'In the late midsummer twilights came the fearful chase of the yeth or wish-hounds—a beautiful lady in front, her long hair flying behind her, a pack of black fiery-nostrilled hounds and horsemen in the rear.'

In Cornwall, too, similar stories were told. The *Cornhill Magazine* reported in 1887 that 'In the loneliest recesses of these hills the cry of the "whished" hounds is heard, whilst neither dogs nor huntsmen are anywhere visible. At other times (generally on Sundays it is) they show themselves jet black, and breathing flames.'

Wishtness is a noun meaning witchcraft; anything appertaining to the supernatural; a ghost, a supernatural being. From west Somerset a correspondent wrote to the EDD, 'Some result of evil eye; anything mysteriously unfortunate is a wishtness. "I calls it a proper wishtness, vor to zee a poor little crater like her is, wastin away to nothin, and all the doctors can do her no good."'

Wisht also meant affrighted; mad, wild. In a trial for witchcraft held in Taunton, Devon, as late as 1823, this was reported: 'Whilst the fit was upon her, she would look wished, and point at something, crying, "There she stands!"'

A Cornish doctor I know told me that *wisht* meant dismal, lonely, melancholy, sad, in the hamlets that grew around Bodmin Moor. Spectres are still seen there to this day. Old pishogues die hard in that beautiful part of England.

Oxford says that these words are of unknown origin. It is probably wise to leave it at that, though the Somerset explanation given above, bewitched or evil-wisht, appeals to me.

✦ WISP OF STRAW

This was a term applied in days of yore to a strumpet or a *báirseach* or scold.

Bishop John Earle in *Micro-cosmographie or A Peece of the World Discovered*, written about 1628, has 'There's nothing mads or moves her to outrage, than but the very naming of a *wispe*, or if you sing or whistle when she is scolding.' It seems that poor old John had to whistle and sing a lot, and we don't know if he ever resorted to giving her the wisp.

Shakespeare's editor Malone quotes *The Pleasures of Poetry* to show that scolds were made to wear a wisp of straw as a badge of disgrace. More humane than the ducking stool, I suppose, and by all accounts it seems to have worked just as well: 'Good gentle Joan withold thy hands, / This once let me entreat thee, / And make me promise never more / That thou shalt mind to beat me; / For fear thou wear the wisp, good wife, / And make our neighbours ride.' [I don't know what he means by *ride* here.]

Many of the old-timers mentioned the wisp. Listen to the *Knight de la Tour* (ante 1450): 'He writhed a litell wipse of strawe, and sette it afore her, and saide, ladi, yef that ye will chide more, chide with that straw.' Thomas Drant in *Horace, his Arte of Poetrie, Pistles and Satyrs Englished* (1566) mentions 'Women . . . Whose tatling tongues had won a wispe'. In 1626 H. Parrot's *Cures for the Itch* has 'Theres nothing mads . . . her [a scold] more . . . then but the very naming of a wispe.'

And I musn't forget Shakespeare, who in *Henry VI, Part 3*, Act II, Scene II, says, 'A wisp of straw were worth a thousand crowns / To make this shameless callat know herself.'

Oh they were tough times, girls, and no mistake. You behaved yourselves, or else . . .

| Y ~

✦ **YARE**

Once and once only I have heard this word. It was used by a Norfolk friend and it meant brisk, active, lively. He pronounced it *yar*. While the rest of the English-speaking world forgot the word, it still survives in little pockets in Northern England and southern Scotland, and it has been recorded lately in deepest Kent. It is a very old word and it is sad to see it die.

My Norfolk friend's meaning was recorded as early as 1300 in *Richard Coer de Lion*, a metrical romance. Shakespeare, in *Antony and Cleopatra*, Act III, Scene XIII, has 'A halter'd neck, which do's the Hangman thank, For being yare about him'.

In *Twelfth Night*, Act III, Scene IV, he has 'Dismount thy tuck, be yare in thy preparation, for thy assailant is quick.'

In this sense it was often used of a ship, to mean managable, easily handled. John Gower in *Confessio Amantis* in 1390 has 'The wynd was good, the Schip was yare.' I could find no trace of the word in literature in this sense after 1660.

In the sense ready, prepared, it is found in *Beowulf* and before that back in 888 in Ælfred's translation of Boethius, *De Consolatione Philosophiae*. In *Measure for Measure*, Act IV, Scene II, Shakespeare wrote, 'I hope, if you have occasion to use me for your own turn, you shall find me yare.'

Yare is used of implements in the meaning ready for use, in later literature. In 1631 Gervase Markham's *Country Contentment* has 'You shall observe that all your Tooles, Lines, or Implements be (as the Seaman sayth) yare, fit, and ready.' And in 1799 Scott's *Covenanter's Fate* has 'At each pommel there, for battle yare, / A Jedwood axe was slung.' He used the word again in 1808 in *Marmion*: 'The gunner held his linstock yare.'

As an exclamation meaning 'Quick!' you'll find it in *The Tempest*, Act I, Scene I: 'Heigh, my hearts! cheerly, cheerly, my hearts! / Yare, yare! take in the topsail.' North of the border James Hogg, the Etterick Shepherd, had in his 1822 *Perils of Man* 'Yare, yare! Lord sauff us! Here they come! What's to be our fate? Keep close for a wee while.' And I am reliably informed that the exclamation is still heard in Kent's hops country in the rural school yards. Good news.

We have to thank the Anglo-Saxons. Our word came from their *gearo*, ready.

ENVOI ∿

Per Egil Hesla came to the Royal College of Surgeons in Ireland straight from the Norwegian military where he was a young commando and a tank commander, occupations which, according to the RCSI Yearbook of 1971, were merely a preparation for his role in the college rugby First XV and the basketball team which under his command won the Intervarsity Cup three years running. The yearbook included among his other interests, elk shooting, trout fishing, and Molly.

He married his fellow student Molly Brown immediately after graduating in 1971, and they lived near Oslo until she died of a massive stroke while finishing a paper for the World Health Organization which was later accepted by the United Nations to be used in future work in promoting healthcare in the Third World. An Irish diplomat with UN connections, knowing of her indefatigable work in the WHO and other international health organisations, described Molly Hesla to me as 'paediatrician to the world's poorest and most vulnerable people'. She was also a distinguished academic, and was consulted by the Crown of her adopted country.

They had four children: two sons, Asla and Eirik, and two daughters, Margit and Sebjorg, all of whom became medical specialists. Per Egil had resumed his career as an officer in the Norwegian military but now in their medical corps, serving the UN and NATO in Bosnia, Croatia, Nigeria and Somalia, alleviating the suffering caused by wars. He also made time to specialise in neurology and sleep disorders.

I remember Molly with great affection from my own academic year at the RCSI; I had to leave before the Pre-Med exams due to unforeseen circumstances. I remember her especially for the lessons she gave me over innumerable cups of coffee on the Periodic Table of the Elements, a table which, can you believe it, was never once mentioned in the six years I was taught Chemistry in secondary school and later in a Teacher Training College. I remember, too, her placing in Caribbean folklore that reference to the old fisherman dreaming of lions at the end of Hemingway's *The Old Man and the Sea*. Did she ever dream of lions in her youth, those potent symbols of strength and hope, as she fulfilled her dreams of studying medicine? Thanks to the selfless vision of a great mother who moved from Cayman Brac to Jamaica so that she could fulfil her potential, her dreams came true in the RCSI and in Norway.

Here are a few words from her Caribbean childhood, *in memoriam*. I thank Dr Ross Graham of the University of Coventry for them. He found them in *A Glossary of Caymanian Old / Unfamiliar Dialect Words*, compiled by Mitzi Panton, and produced by the Cayman Islands National Archive.

Backing: Carrying a load of sand, wood etc. on one's back, usually in a straw basket.

Brogans: Coarse, stout work shoes.

Colimawbus: Used to describe any kind of unexplained stomach upset; colic.

Cotto: A type of shrub which grew in Cayman Brac on the side of the Bluff, and which produced a sponge-like bloom which was used to scrub floors, etc.

Furdie: Rice porridge with turtle egg-yolks, chiefly made in Cayman Brac.

Heavy cakes: Cakes made from root vegetables such as yams, cassava, or sweet potatoes, with no leavening agent, traditionally cooked buried under hot coals in a heavy iron pot.

Horn Button: A name given in Cayman Brac to Jamaican water biscuits. Also known as *Hard Tacks* and *Hard Crackers*.

Laying Rope: The process of intertwining strands of thatch twine to form a three-strand rope. String from the indigenous Caymanian silver thatch palm was highly prized as it was resistant to salt water.

Muntle: A heavy hand-carved wooden club for killing or stunning sharks and other large fish.

Nash: Vulnerable, sensitive.

Old Wife Skin: The tough skin of the ocean turbot, commonly used for scrubbing the unpainted floors of Cayman homes.

Tie-tie: Home-made sweet and spicy dumplings made from sweet potato.

Unnah: The plural of the pronoun *you*.

Waterset: Any unsuccessful expedition. A term used to indicate an empty net when turtle fishing.

The third College of Surgeons alumnus in the book's dedication, Barry Ó Muirithe, is my second son. He is a Member of the Royal College of Psychiatrists and he has published many articles in learned journals about the mysteries of his chosen sphere of medical science. While in the RCSI he proved himself to be an outstanding debater, and won the Seton Pringle Inter-Year Debating Medal of the RCSI Biological Society in 1983. Pride in his dedication to those on whom God has laid a hand, to translate the Irish phrase, makes me add his name to those of my friends. He was also a brave and accomplished horseman, and as I, like the poet Yeats, find hearteners among such men, é seo do, fara Per Egil agus Molly, le gean is dúthracht.

INDEX